P9-AES-097

Communication and Change

THE EAST-WEST CENTER, established in Hawaii by the United States Congress in 1960, is a national educational institution with multinational programs. Its purpose is to promote better relations and understanding among the nations and peoples of Asia, the Pacific area, and the United States through their cooperative participation in research, study, and training activities.

Fundamental to the achievement of the Center's purpose are the cooperative discovery and application of knowledge and the interchange of knowledge, information, ideas, and beliefs in an intercultural atmosphere of academic freedom. In Center programs, theory and practice are combined to help current and future leaders generate, test, and share knowledge about important world problems of mutual concern to people in both East and West.

Each year about 1,500 scholars, leaders, public officials, mid-level and upper-level managers, and graduate students come to the Center to work and study together in programs concerned with seeking alternative approaches and solutions to common problems. For each participant from the United States, two come from the Asian/Pacific area. An international, interdisciplinary professional staff provides the framework, content, and continuity for programs and for cooperative relationships with universities and other institutions in the Center's area of operations.

Center programs are conducted by the East-West Communication Institute, the East-West Culture Learning Institute, the East-West Food Institute, the East-West Population Institute, and the East-West Technology and Development Institute. Each year the Center also awards a limited number of "Open Grants" for graduate degree education and research by scholars and authorities in areas not encompassed by the problem-oriented institutes.

The East-West Center is governed by the autonomous board of a public, nonprofit educational corporation—the Center for Cultural and Technical Interchange Between East and West, Inc.—established by special act of the Hawaii State Legislature. The Board of Governors is composed of distinguished individuals from the United States and countries of Asia and the Pacific area. The United States Congress provides basic funding for Center programs and for a variety of scholarships, fellowships, internships, and other awards. Because of the cooperative nature of Center programs, financial support and cost-sharing arrangements also are provided by Asian and Pacific governments, regional agencies, private enterprise, and foundations.

The Center is located in Honolulu, Hawaii, on twenty-one acres of land adjacent to the University of Hawaii's Manoa campus. Through cooperative arrangements with the University of Hawaii, the Center has access to University degree programs, libraries, computer center, and the like.

East-West Center Books are published by The University Press of Hawaii to further the Center's aims and programs.

Communication and Change

The Last Ten Years — and the Next

edited by
WILBUR SCHRAMM
DANIEL LERNER

AN EAST-WEST CENTER BOOK
Published for the East-West Center
by The University Press of Hawaii
Honolulu

First edition 1976
Paperback 1978

Manufactured in the United States of America
Composition by Asco Trade Typesetting Limited, Hong Kong
Book design by Roger J. Eggers
Cover design by A.O.K. Hammond

Library of Congress Cataloging in Publication Data
Main entry under title:

Communication and change, the last ten years—and the next.

Papers presented at a conference held at the East-West Center, Honolulu, in Jan. 1975.
"An East-West Center book."
Bibliography: p.
Includes index.
1. Underdeveloped area—Communication. I. Schramm, Wilbur Lang, 1907– II. Lerner, Daniel.
P92.2.C6 301.14 76–18893
ISBN 0–8248–0446–5

Contents

Foreword

All countries are developing countries. Development is the process through which a society moves to acquire the capability of enhancing the quality of life of its people, primarily through the solution of its problems. In this sense, although they have been slow to recognize it, the United States and other affluent countries are still underdeveloped in such areas as urban life, environmental protection, race relations, crime, and other social problems.

The task of developing a country must ultimately be undertaken by the citizens or natives of that country. The idea that more affluent countries have a responsibility to assist less affluent ones has come to be accepted in recent decades. As a new concept, it had many pitfalls as well as certain advantages. We have now learned that any nation that wants to develop—that is, that wants to improve the quality of life of its people—must do so itself, although not necessarily without assistance. Science and certain technology can be borrowed, imported, and adapted from abroad, but ultimately creativity from within is the only answer, for development, essentially, is not a matter of technology or gross national product but the growth of a new consciousness, the movement of the human mind, the uplifting of the human spirit, the infusion of human confidence.

We have come to recognize also that the development of one country does not merely have impact upon that country alone, but actually upon all countries.

Everett Kleinjans
President, East-West Center
(From his Introduction
to the Conference)

1. An Overview of the Past Decade

WILBUR SCHRAMM

In the summer of 1964, a group of scholars, representing the psychological and social sciences, met at the East-West Center to discuss the use of communication in economic and social development. The revised papers of that conference became the book *Communication and Change in the Developing Countries*, edited by Lerner and Schramm, published in 1967 by the East-West Center Press, and circulated widely in several editions.

The discussion that began in Honolulu in 1964 has continued ever since, by mail and in person. To many of the participants in that conference it began to seem in the 1970s that new information on the topic was so substantial, and changes in the situation so marked, that the conclusions of the 1964 meeting should be reviewed after ten years. Thus it came about that in early January of 1975, a few months more than a decade since the earlier meeting, a second conference was convened in the same room at the East-West Center, under the same chairmen and with a number of the 1964 participants, who were joined by other scholars. The purpose was to assess what has been learned in ten years concerning the use of communication in development, the changing needs of developing countries for communication support, and new priorities for communication expertise, communication research, and modern communication technology.

Out of that 1975 meeting has come this volume.

The two conferences met in dramatically different political and economic settings. In 1964, no resident of Earth had yet walked on the Moon. Vietnam had hardly begun to happen. China had not yet emerged from its cocoon. The Third World was not operating as a voting bloc, and no one was thinking about the possibility of what was to happen at the Organization of Petroleum Exporting Countries' (OPEC) meeting of October 13, 1973, or the shattering effect that the manipulation of oil prices and availability would have on the world economy. Watergate and its associated events were not even dreamed of.

Ten years of development since 1964 have had mixed results. A background paper by Eugene Sathre on this topic is not reproduced here in its entirety, but the chief tables have been appended to this chapter. He pointed out that during the last ten-year period for which world figures are available:

- The gross national product (GNP) increased over 50 percent in all of the major developing regions.
- Exports from the developing countries are up 124 percent.
- Nonagricultural employment in the developing countries has risen 52 percent, agricultural employment 27 percent.
- Food production is up some 30 percent.
- The number of physicians per 10,000 population (a measure of ability to deliver health care) has increased overall about 7 percent.
- The annual outlay of aid for developing countries has increased an average of about 9.5 percent a year, and in the last ten years well over 100 billion dollars in assistance funds have been made available.

Looked at more closely, however, these growth figures are less impressive than they seem. An increase of 2.2 percent per year in population has wiped out a considerable share of the economic gains. And while the developing regions have not been growing poorer in absolute terms, they have been falling farther and farther behind the industrialized world. Per capita food production rose 20 percent in the more developed countries (as against 3 percent in the developing areas). The number of physicians per 10,000 also grew faster in the more developed countries, and is now three times as high as in the less developed countries (LDC). The gross national product of the industrialized countries rose rapidly during the decade, and at its end was almost five times greater than that of the developing regions. The exports of the developed countries grew five times faster than that of the LDC during the ten years and made up about 81 percent of the world total at the end of the decade. A rush to the cities (55 percent growth in urban population) in developing regions created special stresses on their economies and the quality of their urban life. And although figures are hard to come by, there is good reason to think that such net gains as there were in the developing regions were unevenly distributed between the already privileged and the underprivileged, so that while the developing countries were becoming poorer relative to the developed ones, within each developing country the gap between the poor and the rich was widening as well. Thus the economic and social development in the ten years was less than had been hoped for.

On the other hand, the decade produced some spectacular gains in communication in these countries. A second background paper, by Schramm—the tables from which are also appended to this chapter—summed up the changes in communication technology. The growth of radio has been dramatic. About 100 million of the approximately 144 million radios in the three great developing regions were added between 1963 and 1973. It has been the Decade of the Transistor! In Latin America, the number of radios more than doubled in those ten years; in Africa, more than tripled; in Asia, it more than quadrupled. An unknown but large percentage of these radios are now in the villages. A conservative estimate is that one-third to one-fourth of all the people in the developing regions now have direct access to radio broadcasts.

The 144 million radios in the three developing regions compare to about 45 million copies of daily newspapers (without figures from China), 28 million television receivers, 14 million cinema seats. Television is increasing sharply in relation to population, although it started in 1963 near zero; daily newspaper circulation is growing at a moderate rate, but more slowly than either of the broadcast media; and the number of cinema seats is actually decreasing in relation to population. There are about 7 million telephones in the three regions, representing an average annual increase of about 6 percent. And about 300 million children and young people of the developing regions are in school.

Along with these gross figures must be mentioned noteworthy developments in the number of universities that are training professionals to work in development support communication and that are doing research on communication; and in the growing number of development programs—agriculture, health, family planning, and so forth—that have established professional departments to carry the program to the people.

Thus the developing countries are expanding their communication systems at a pace significantly faster than their rate of population growth and are taking steps to leapfrog some of the stages in communication technology. Korea is putting up a balloon to serve as a two-mile-high transmission facility for instructional television. Before this is published, India will be using an experimental satellite to bring television programs to 2,500 of its villages. Indonesia, Iran, and Brazil, among other nations, are planning to launch communication satellites. There is no doubt that conditions are far more favorable than they were in 1964 for the use of development communication.

But let us not forget how far behind the rich countries these poorer countries are. Even the rather spectacular growth in radios must be interpreted in light of the fact that two-thirds of the world's people still have no more than one-fifth of all the world's radios, less than one-fifth of the newspaper circulation, less than one-tenth of the world's television receivers, one-sixteenth of the world's telephones. And although the growth in proportion of adult literacy was solid and consistent throughout the ten years, so great was the gain in population that overall there were actually *more* illiterate adults at the end of the decade than at its beginning.

The mood was sober—not depressed, but thoughtful—as the meeting, in its first morning, reviewed figures like these. More than one participant who had been at the first conference remarked how different the tone was. In 1964 the outlook was optimistic. We had a model for development that had proved itself in the Western countries and Japan, and was expected to do the same in the rest of Asia, and in Africa and Latin America. Few people were disposed in 1964 to challenge this model seriously, although the obstacles in its way were recognized and variations were suggested. In 1975, it was recognized that the model had accomplished somewhat less than had been expected of it. Although GNP had reached or exceeded the growth rates of numerous Western countries during their modernizing years, very few countries had reached the point that Rostow described as "takeoff." Efforts to save capital and invest in industry had turned attention away from the problems of the villagers, and stimulated runaway urbanization with its resulting social problems. The condition of a large proportion of the people of the developing world was, at best, not much better in 1975 than in 1964.

Therefore it was not surprising that the early papers and much of the first day's discussion were directed at the patterns of development themselves. The president of the East-West Center, in his opening remarks, spoke of the Quality of Life, rather than economic goals, as a measure of development. Dr. Harry Oshima, who discussed the economics of development at the 1964 conference also, said that "vast changes" had occurred in development economics during the past decade—indeed changes so extensive as really to comprise "a new system of development economics with a different pattern of strategy." These changes, which he describes in his paper in this volume, and which follow some of Kuznets' thinking, emphasized labor-intensive rather than capital-intensive strategy and the agricultural more than the industrial sector. Dr. S. N. Eisenstadt said that the "old paradigm" of development that has dominated the psychological and social sciences for two decades has broken down, and a new one is needed. He did not contend, any more than did Oshima, that the basic economic assumptions underlying development have broken down, but he pointed out that the new model must emphasize the mobilization of human and social, as well as economic, resources, and it must take into greater account the cultural base of change and changes in the cultural base.

Thus one of the legacies of the previous ten years to the 1975 conference was a set of challenging questions about the nature and requirements of development itself. Another of the legacies, as it soon became clear, was that the store of experience and research concerning the effective use of communication in developing countries was incomparably richer than in 1964. Hundreds of experiments had been done, and projects in many countries had been observed and analyzed. The importance of this new fund of expertise and knowledge was underscored by Oshima, in his opening paper, when he described the requirements of the new development strategy he saw coming into existence. He said:

> In sum, the role of mass communication is greatly enhanced in a labor-intensive strategy because more people with less education in remote regions must be reached than in a capital-intensive strategy.... Labor must be re-educated and manpower training re-oriented. Technology of the intermediate type (the up-graded traditional technology, the down-graded modern technology, and the new intermediate technology) must be discovered. Diffused saving in small bits must be collected from the masses of producers throughout the nation instead of in a lump sum from top income groups. New institutions and organizations in the rural areas must be established, while old values must be modified and new values promoted.... The key problem of the new strategy is implementation, so that its success may depend very much on the ability of mass media to inform, persuade, and educate. Mass communication may turn out to be the most important medium of education, whether formal or nonformal, although this was not the case in the capital-intensive growth of Western nations.

These optimistic words inevitably recalled the optimism of the 1964 conference with respect to what communication might contribute to development. The conferees recognized, of course, that it had contributed to many changes in the developing countries—extended opportunities for learning, expanded horizons, changed expectations, set new agendas for national effort, and the like. But the questions asked about what communication had not done that might have been expected of it in 1964 pointed up how thinking about communication in development has changed in ten years. The idea of mass communication as part of a larger system of communication and organizational activities has become so well accepted that it was taken for granted in 1975. The questions, however, kept recalling it: Was communication in 1964 expected to accomplish too much *by itself*? Has there been too much reliance on the idea that knowledge and ideas will "trickle down" from leaders to followers, center to periphery, mass media to broad audience? What is there to learn from development models like those of China and Tanzania where changes in social structure come first, communication is directed toward activating local resources, and the most important development communication is local and lateral? Perhaps the central challenge of the conference to communication scholars and planners was to define in terms of modern knowledge the task of communication as a part of the broader system of change and growth.

With that challenge the conferees went to work. The fruits of their labor are in the following pages.

1a. *Indicators of Growth in the Past Decade*

EUGENE SATHRE

Table 1. Population Growth

	Total Population (000,000)		*Total Increase (%)*	*Average Annual Increase (%)*
	1963	*1973*	*1963–1973*	*1963–1973*
World	3162.0	3792.0	19.9	1.8
Developed Regions	980.5	1076.1	9.7	.9
Developing Regions	2181.3	2716.2	24.5	2.2
Africa	289.0	378.0	30.8	2.8
Asia	1657.0	2030.0	22.5	2.0
Latin America	232.0	304.0	31.0	2.7
Oceania	3.3	4.2	27.2	2.5

SOURCES: United Nations, *Monthly Bulletin of Statistics*, October 1974, pp. 1–5. United Nations, *Statistical Yearbook 1973*.

NOTE: Both Sathre and Schramm said to the conference that the data they were reporting left much to be desired, both in reliability and completeness. These are, however, believed to be the best estimates currently available.

Table 2. Per Capita Food Production

	Index Numbers of Per Capita Food Production		
	1963	*1970*	*1973*
World	100	106	108
Developed Regions[a]	100[b]	112	120
Developing Regions[a]	100[b]	105	103
Africa	102	102	95
Asian Centrally Planned Economies	99	107	107
Far Eastern Market Economies	101	104	103
Latin America	100	103	100
Near East	100	102	99

SOURCES: Food and Agriculture Organization, *Monthly Bulletin of Agricultural Economics and Statistics*, March 1974, p. 2. Food and Agriculture Organization, *Production Yearbook 1972.*

[a] Israel and South Africa are included under Developed rather than Developing Regions.
[b] Index number represents the 1961–1965 average.

Table 3. Nutritional Levels

	Percentage of Per Capita Daily Food Requirements (1970 Consumption)	
	Calories	*Proteins*
World	101	173
Developed Regions[a]	121	229
Developed Market Economies	119	228
Eastern Europe and USSR	124	232
Developing Regions[a]	96	147
Africa	93	141
Asian Centrally Planned Economies	88	153
Far Eastern/Asian Market Economies	93	141
Latin America	106	172
Near East	97	147

SOURCE: Food and Agriculture Organization, *Agricultural Commodity Projections, 1970–1980*, vol. 1, p. 31.

[a] Israel and South Africa are included under Developed rather than Developing Regions.

Table 4. Health Care

	Number of Physicians per 10,000 Population	
	1960	*1970*
World	6.87	7.91
Developed Regions		
Europe	12.07	14.85
USSR	17.99	23.78
United States	13.39	15.78
Developing Regions		
Africa	1.09	1.36
Asia[a]	2.60	2.80
Latin America	5.43	6.54

SOURCES: Bui-Dang-Ha Doan, "World Trends in Medical Manpower, 1950–1970," *World Health Statistics Report,* 27(2):88–98. World Health Organization, *World Health Statistics Annual 1970,* vol. 3.

[a] Does not include the Chinese People's Republic.

Table 5. Urbanization

	Urban Population (000)		*Rural Population (000)*		*% Urban*	
	1960	*1970*	*1960*	*1970*	*1960*	*1970*
World	982,023	1,354,344	1,999,598	2,280,840	32.9	37.2
Developed Regions	538,877	666,028	405,484	386,263	57.0	63.2
Developing Regions	443,146	688,316	1,594,114	1,894,577	21.7	26.6
Africa	48,336	76,487	221,090	267,836	17.9	22.2
Asia	291,321	452,301	1,259,974	1,498,963	18.7	23.1
Latin America	103,306	159,218	110,165	124,092	48.3	56.1
Oceania	183	310	2,885	3,686	5.9	7.7

SOURCE: United Nations, *Statistical Yearbook 1972.*

Table 6. Employment

	Economically Active Population outside Agriculture (000,000)		*Economically Active Population in Agriculture (000,000)*		*% Non-agricul-tural*	*% Non-agricul-tural*
	1960	*1970*	*1960*	*1970*	*1960*	*1970*
World	539.2	729.9	737.8	771.1	42.2	48.6
Developed Regions[a]	310.3	381.6	123.7	100.4	71.5	79.2
Developing Regions[a]	228.9[b]	348.3[b]	614.1[b]	670.7[b]	27.0	34.2
Africa	17.4	27.2	73.6	83.8	19.5	24.5
Far East	162.1	248.1	474.9	514.9	25.4	32.5
Latin America	36.4	51.4	33.6	36.6	52.1	58.5
Near East	13.2	20.9	30.8	34.1	30.7	37.8

SOURCE: Food and Agriculture Organization, *The Statistics of Food and Agriculture 1973*, pp. 131, 137, 138.

[a] Israel and South Africa are included under Developed rather than Developing Regions.

[b] Totals are higher than the sums for the regions listed thereunder due to the inclusion of developing units outside those regions.

Table 7. Economic Capacity

	Gross National Product (US $ at 1971 Market Prices) (000,000)	*Gross National Product per Capita (US $ at 1971 Market Prices)*	*% of World Gross Product*	*% of World Population*
World	3,346,864	908	100.0	100.0
Developed Regions	2,775,150	2,620	82.90	28.70
Developing Regions	571,714	221	17.10	71.30
Africa	79,594	223	2.40	9.70
Asia	316,140	160	9.40	53.70
Latin America	173,820	603	5.20	7.80
Oceania	2,160	462	.06	.10

SOURCE: International Bank for Reconstruction and Development, *World Bank Atlas: Population, Per Capita Product and Growth Rates* (1973).

Table 8. Trade

	Exports (US $) (000,000)		*% of World Export Total*	
	1963	*1972*	*1963*	*1972*
World	153,560[a]	410,760[a]	100.0	100.0
Developed Regions	119,170	333,730	77.6	81.2
Developing Regions	34,400	77,020	22.4	18.8
Africa	7,400	16,890	4.8	4.1
Asia	15,490	39,720	10.1	9.7
Latin America	11,320	19,760	7.4	4.8
Oceania	190	650	.1	.1

SOURCE: United Nations, *Yearbook of International Trade Statistics 1972–1973.*

[a]Totals are not consistent due to roundings and some missing data.

Table 9. Aid

	Aid in US $ (000,000)		*Average Annual Growth Rate (%)*
	1962	*1972*	*1962–1972*
New outflow of long-term capital from developed market economies[a] to developing countries and multilateral institutions	7,444	17,711	9.0
Bilateral commitments of capital to developing countries by centrally planned economies[b]	316	1,492	35.9
Total Aid	7,760	19,203	9.5

SOURCES: United Nations *Statistical Yearbooks* 1966, 1971, 1973.

[a]Totals include outflow from Israel and South Africa.

[b]Totals include commitments to developing countries by Chinese People's Republic.

1b. *Data on Communication Systems in Three Developing Regions*

WILBUR SCHRAMM

Table 1. Total Communication Units and Units per Thousand Persons

	Radio Receivers	*TV Receivers*	*Daily Newspaper Copies*	*Cinema Seats*
Number of Units (000)				
Africa	18,483	1,503	4,775	1,351
Asia	75,987	7,110	21,867	6,163
Latin America	49,850	19,692	18,073	6,284
Units per Thousand Persons				
Africa	54	4	14	4
Asia	41	4	20	6
Latin America	171	68	62	22

SOURCE: UNESCO survey figures, from *World Communication, 1975.*

NOTE: The developing countries included are limited to those for which 1973 UNESCO figures are available. Therefore, Taiwan is not included in any of the figures for Asia, and China is not represented in the figures for daily press or cinema seats. Because they are not developing countries, Japan is not listed with the Asian countries, nor South Africa with the African countries.

Table 2. Comparisons of Media Development

	Radio Receivers	*TV Receivers*	*Daily Newspaper Copies*	*Cinema Seats*
Number of Units (000)				
Africa				
1963	6,020	329	3,319	1,105
1973	18,843	1,503	4,775	1,351
RATIO				
1963:1973	1:3.12	1:4.57	1:1.44	1:1.22
Asia				
1963	17,059	868	14,028	5,193
1973	75,987	7,110	21,867	6,163
RATIO				
1963:1973	1:4.45	1:8.19	1:1.56	1:1.19
Latin America				
1963	22,482	4,756	15,730	7,101
1973	49,850	19,692	18,073	6,284
RATIO				
1963:1973	1:2.22	1:4.14	1:1.15	1:0.88

SOURCES: 1963 figures from UNESCO *Statistical Yearbook*. 1973 figures from *World Communication*, 1975.

Table 3. Number of Telephones in Use

	1962	*1972*	*Ratio 1962/1972*
Number of Telephones (000)			
Africa	2,155	3,733	1:1.73
Asia	5,619	8,460	1:1.51
Latin America	3,733	6,776	1:1.82

SOURCE: U. N. *Statistical Yearbooks*, 1973, 1967.

Table 4. Comparisons of Media Development

	Radio Receivers	*TV Receivers*	*Daily Newspaper Copies*	*Cinema Seats*
Units per Thousand Persons				
Africa				
1963	32	1—	10	6
1973	54	4	14	4
RATIO				
1963:1973	1:1.69	1:5.0	1:1.4	1:0.67
Asia				
1963	12	1—	17	8
1973	41	4	20	6
RATIO				
1963:1973	1:3.42	1:5.0	1:1.18	1:0.75
Latin America				
1963	104	22	73	34
1973	171	68	62	22
RATIO				
1963:1973	1:1.64	1:3.09	1:0.85	1:0.65

SOURCE: 1963 figures from UNESCO *Statistical Yearbook*. 1973 figures from *World Communication*, 1975.

Table 5. Proportion of Adults Literate and Number of Adults Illiterate

Region	*Adults Literate (percent)*	*Adults Illiterate (000,000)*
Africa		
1960	19.0	124
1970	26.3	153
Asia		
1960	44.8	542
1970	53.2	579
Latin America		
1960	67.5	40
1970	76.4	38.6

SOURCE: U.N. *Statistical Yearbooks*, 1966, 1973.

Table 6. Total Educational Enrollment and Percentage of Population in School

	Total	*Primary*	*Secondary*	*Tertiary*
Enrollment (000,000)				
Africa				
1950	9	8	1	—
1960	21	19	2	—
1970	37	32	5	0.4
Asia				
1950	53	44	9	1.0
1960	99	76	18	2.0
1970	181	139	36	5.0
Latin America				
1950	17	15	2	—
1960	31	27	4	1.0
1970	56	43	11	2.0
Percentage of Population in School				
Africa				
1960	8			
1970	11			
Asia				
1960	6			
1970	9			
Latin America				
1960	14			
1970	20			

SOURCE: U.N. *Statistical Yearbooks*. 1966, 1973.

A. RETHINKING DEVELOPMENT THEORY AND STRATEGY

Our conferees were troubled that the past decade did not produce the enhanced "quality of life" that we had hoped for ten years ago. Even the impressive gains of GNP in many countries evaporated when restated in per capita terms, for these economic gains were largely swallowed by the greater increases of population. In several poor countries around the world, the quality of life today is, if anything different, down.

Dr. Harry Oshima, noting that growth must be stunted when it takes an input of 2,000 calories of human energy to yield an output of 2,000 calories of food per day, explains why this simple fact has occasioned such "vast changes" in thinking over the past decade as to "comprise a new system of development economics with a different pattern of strategy." Dr. S. N. Eisenstadt cogently enlarges this "changing vision of modernization" to call for a full rethinking of theory and strategy in the social sciences concerned with development.

These initial papers, in which eminent scholars summoned us to rise above the conventional wisdom and our own current thinking, stimulated much valuable discussion and animated deliberations throughout the conference. To convey the value, if not fully the vigor, of these discussions, we persuaded several of the conferees to write down the gist of their remarks. Thus we are able to include in Part A the condensed comments prepared by Schramm, Rogers, Oshima, Inayatullah, Eisenstadt, and Lerner.

2. Development and Mass Communication—A Re-Examination

HARRY T. OSHIMA

Introduction

Vast changes have occurred in development economics during the past decade. It is not an exaggeration to say that these changes comprise a new system of development economics with a different pattern of strategy. This paper will describe these changes, and then focus on details of those aspects of the new strategy that pose challenges for mass communication. The key problem of the new strategy is implementation, so that its success may depend very much on the ability of mass media to inform, persuade, and educate. Mass communication may turn out to be the most important medium of education, whether formal or nonformal, although this was not the case in the capital-intensive growth of Western nations.[1]

Problems Generated by the Old Strategy

About the time of our first conference, dissatisfaction with the outcome of economic development in the 1950s and early 1960s had surfaced. Despite satisfactory growth rates of overall GNP in real terms (of about 5 percent, or 2 to 3 percent per capita), problems seemed to be emerging everywhere. By the end of the 1960s, there was excess industrial capacity even in the new plants, as well as unemployment and underemployment, urban congestion, rural stagnation, food shortages, income inequalities, widespread poverty, and other anomalies.

Apparently something had gone wrong with the assumption of the old development strategy, which was that if growth of per capita GNP was sustained at rates of about 2 or 3 percent, the benefits would spread throughout the economy and eventually reach all groups. Industrialization with modern technology—based in the big cities, where physical infrastructure and an adequate pool of educated labor existed—could do the trick. This may be designated as a predominantly urban-based capital-intensive strategy, which depended on the growth of large-scale industries using a lot of machines and capital and little labor. The more traditional labor-intensive industries were given low priorities.

Accordingly, most underdeveloped countries focused on rapid industrialization by means of high tariffs and/or import restrictions in order to protect their new industries. They overvalued their currencies so that the new industries could buy machinery and raw materials cheaply, made available large amounts of credit to these industries at low interest rates, gave tax exemptions and subsidies generously, concentrated the construction of roads, utilities, buildings, and the like, in the large cities, and established schools and training centers that turned out workers with skills needed for the new industries. Economists spoke optimistically of "big push," "take-off," "leap forward," and so forth. But, as it turned out, the growth began to slow down (and in some cases bog down) in the second half of the 1960s. The potentials of a capital-intensive strategy seemed to be exhausted within a decade, and all the maladjustments noted above began to crop up.

In was understandable that the old strategy emphasized growth through modern industrialization. Compared to a more labor-intensive strategy, which had to contend with a large mass of small, traditional units of production (workshops, stores, farms), it appeared easy to deal with a small group of large modernized units located in one or two centers. But this strategy failed to realize that sustained growth cannot take place by transplanting modern technology in central areas while neglecting the mass of traditional producers. The basic reason for the failure lies in the problem of effective demand.

Aggregate Demand and Sustained Growth of GNP

For sustained growth to take place, aggregate demand must grow in a sustained fashion, keeping pace with aggregate supply, over a period of two or three decades. The difficulty of a capital-intensive strategy is the inability of aggregate demand to absorb the growing aggregate supply of goods, especially of goods produced by capital-intensive factories. The sluggishness of demand may appear within a decade or two, as suggested by the slowdown in GNP growth of several underdeveloped countries, with widespread excess production capacity and underemployment. The underlying factors responsible for insufficient growth of demand are different from those that Keynes discussed in his short-run theory of fluctuations.[2] Whatever the appropriateness of this explanation for cycles in developed countries, it has little plausibility for underdeveloped countries, where most consumers have such low incomes that they spend it all, and even fall into chronic indebtedness.

In a capital-intensive strategy, for GNP to be rising in a sustained fashion over the long run, entrepreneurs of capital-intensive industries must expect demand for their products to be continuously rising, if they are to plan to expand capacity. But as they expand, their output displaces the more traditional labor-intensive production, resulting in unemployment, underemployment, and low incomes. This dislocation is even greater when the machines, materials, fuel, and so forth, used by the more capital-intensive industries are imported. Since the incomes paid in the capital-intensive industries are considerably higher than in the labor-intensive industries, and since the workers displaced are usually from lower-income groups, there is a tendency for their incomes to fall. Moreover, the greater the emphasis of public policy on capital-intensive industrialization, the less the assistance extended to the labor-intensive sectors—resulting in a slower growth of the labor-intensive sectors, whether these be in agriculture, industry, or the tertiary sector. If, in addition to these policies, there are extensive import-substitution policies (exchange rate overvaluation, high tariff rates and other import restrictions, discriminatory credit allocations and rates), then the resulting distortions accentuate the foregoing dislocations, leaving low rates of capital and labor utilization.

The impact of maladjustments on aggregate demand may be seen in the stylized diagram below. It is termed stylized because the curves of frequency distribution of family incomes have been slightly smoothed and greatly compressed from those in the original diagram, which was too large to be shown in this paper. In the larger diagram, the family income distribution curves for the United States in 1969 (a developed economy with a per capita income of $4,500), Japan in 1971 (a semideveloped economy with a per capita income of $2,500), and the Philippines in 1971 (an underdeveloped economy with a per capita income of $300) were plotted, using data from the official sample surveys of the respective census bureaus. The horizontal axis represents income in U.S. dollars, with incomes in pesos and yen converted into dollars at the respective exchange rates, with adjustments.[3] The vertical axis represents the absolute number of households, but the total number of households for the Philippines and the United States have been standardized (or made equal) to that of Japan. This is to eliminate differences in the size of countries, in order to better focus on the shape and position of each curve.

Although in the original diagram only three countries were plotted, later the curves of family income distribution for Ceylon (1953, 1963, 1970), Thailand (1962, 1968), India (1964), West Malaysia (1970), Mexico (1968), and the Philippines (1956, 1961, 1965) were plotted and all of them turned out to be very similar to the Philippines' 1971 curve in the stylized diagram. More countries in the semideveloped and developed categories are presently

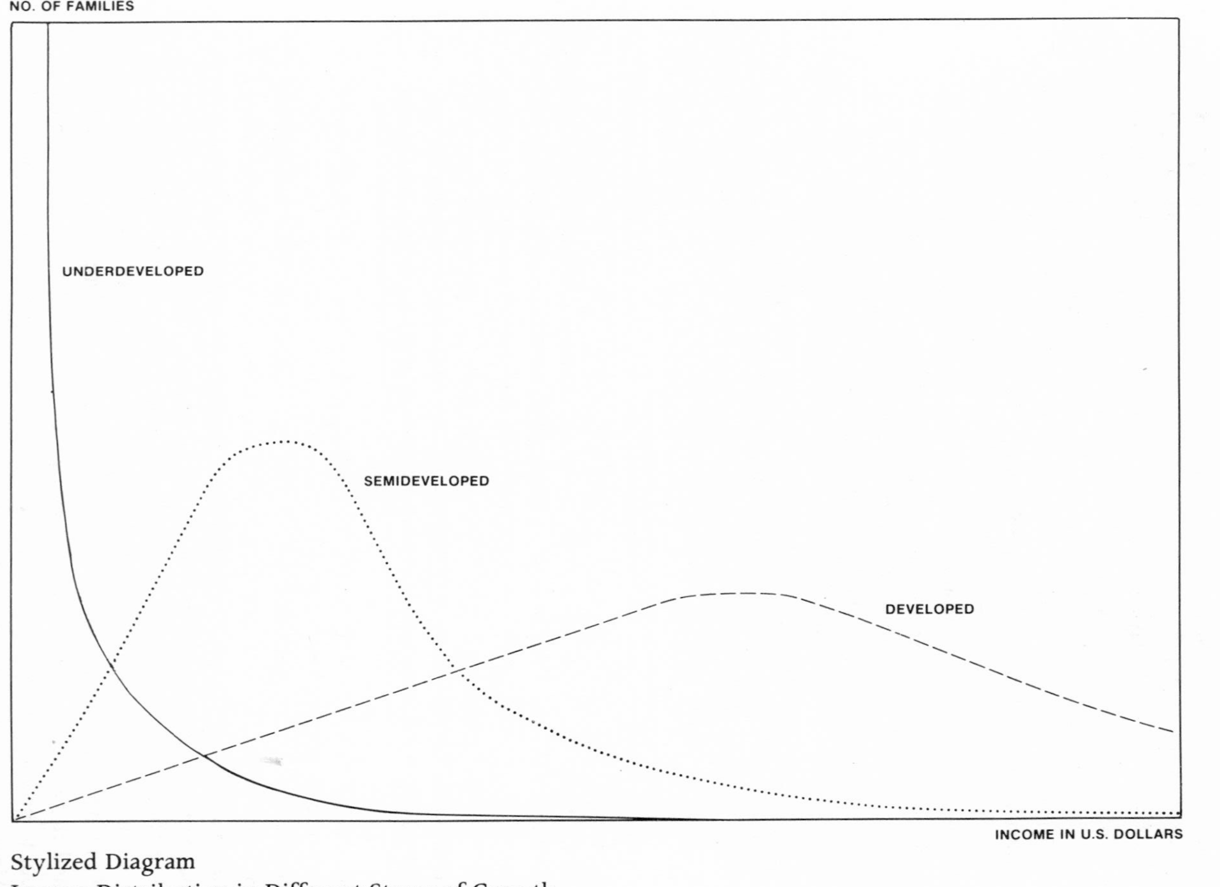

Stylized Diagram
Income Distribution in Different Stages of Growth
(Based on a larger chart computed as described in the text)

being plotted in the diagram. Taiwan, with a per capita income of $650 in 1971, has a curve that lies intermediate between those of Japan and the Philippines on both the horizontal and the vertical axes.[4]

The stylized diagram shows that in the underdeveloped countries the traditional sector, represented by the highly peaked mode to the left near the vertical axis, represents about 80 percent of the population, while only 20 percent represent the modern and modernizing sectors, that is, the flat portion of the curve including a part of the lower slope between the mode and the horizontal portion. Incomes of the families in the modal group are so low that most of the products of capital-intensive technology are beyond the range of purchasing power of 80 percent (or more) of the families, most of whom are peasants in the rural areas or engaged in small industries and services. Their incomes are low because of the low productivity of the traditional techniques and the associated institutions and values.

In contrast, the incomes of most families in the semideveloped and developed countries are within the purchasing-power range of goods made in capital-intensive industries. Those out of the range have incomes high enough to obtain consumer credit. The vast divide between the mode and the low tail of the distribution for the underdeveloped economies (a sharp consumer dualism) does not exist for more developed economies.

Most important is the finding that even with fairly respectable rises in per capita incomes of underdeveloped countries (say, 2 or 3 percent per capita, about a doubling within two decades), there is hardly any dent in the shape of the curves. In the type of curve characterizing family income distributions in underdeveloped countries, the mass market is very thin. Even rapid growth will not enlarge sufficiently the demand for most capital-intensive goods. In these countries, further capital-intensive growth may add mainly to incomes in the horizontal portions. The reason for all this is that the highly peaked mode is caused by the subsistence or semi-subsistence nature of peasant production and handicraft, which are largely for the family, village, or nearby town. The shape and position of the underdeveloped curve is largely associated with traditional agriculture, that of the semideveloped curve with the modernizing industrial sector, and that of the developed curve with the modern service sector. Thus, the inadequate purchasing power is based on inefficient production methods with their associated institutions and values. Besides the problem of effective demand, there is also one problem on the supply side.

In contrast to the demand side, capital-intensive production is able to increase supplies rapidly. (This is one reason for the tendency of entrepreneurs to adopt capital-intensive technology, that is, the speed with which orders for goods can be met.) The establishment of capital-intensive units of production is relatively quick: the corporation as an organization is readily imported; capital can be quickly mobilized through financial institutions such as banks; methods for training manpower are easily learned; physical infrastructure can be built in a short time. To hasten the process, substantial government assistance can be extended (through tariffs, exchange rates, interest rates, subsidies, and training programs) and foreign assistance can be obtained. While the sustained growth of demand depends on the traditional sector, the growth of capital-intensive supplies is not constrained.

Although output can be readily increased, the efficiency with which goods can be produced is not high. Despite many years of government support, and despite low wages and rent, the prices and quality of capital-intensive products are in most cases far from being competitive in the world market. If they were, part of the output could be exported and output would not need to depend on the growth of domestic demand. The reasons for the inefficiencies are many: overprotection and lack of competition; lack of experience by managers, technicians, and skilled workers; inadequacies of physical and institutional infrastructures; absence of a wide range of auxiliary industries; inadequate adaptation of imported processes and product designs to meet requirements of local conditions, which are always different from those of developed countries.[5] To be able to sell abroad, firms in the underdeveloped countries must meet the competition not only of developed countries in the West but also of such Asian countries as Japan, which have about a century of experience in modern economic growth.

In sum, on both the aggregate demand and the supply side there are forces that inhibit sustained growth. While the supply of capital-intensive goods can grow rapidly, the demand for it is limited by the low incomes generated in the traditional sector. After the needs of upper-income groups for these goods are satisfied, the market becomes saturated and the growth of production becomes sluggish. For reasons we have specified above, these goods are both too expensive and too low in quality to be exportable abroad. When this point is reached (as it apparently has been in several countries), the potentials for growth by capital-intensive industries become distinctly limited. A shift to a more labor-intensive strategy becomes inevitable, if the economy is to create sufficient jobs for new workers coming into the labor market and is to continue to grow. Capital-intensive technology cannot raise levels of productivity and income of the low-income groups, as it is far too expensive and sophisticated for these groups. Labor-intensive technology will be needed that is more efficient than traditional technology, and intermediate technology as well.[6]

The Emerging Development Economics

The difficulties discussed above have been compounded by the population explosion of the postwar decades, which in turn has caused a labor surplus and a food shortage in the 1970s.[7] In the coming decades, population is likely to grow at historically unprecedented rates of 2.5 to 3.0 percent per annum, so that the problems of job creation and food production will be with us for some time to come. There is a growing consensus among development economists in favor of a shift to a rural-based, labor-intensive strategy of development—to create more jobs and produce more food. Economists have come out strongly in support of this change in strategy in the United Nations, World Bank, International Labor Organization, Asian Development Bank, and other international bodies; in the Ford, Rockefeller, Asia, and other foundations; in the international aid agencies of the United States, Canada, the United Kingdom, Sweden, Germany, and other countries. Among university economists we no longer hear talk of big push, take-off, leap forward, unbalanced growth, import-substitution, disguised unemployment, et cetera. Instead the talk is now about integrated rural development, agricultural intensification, appropriate technology, labor absorption, small industry promotion, health development, income distribution, and so forth.

The emerging new development economics began with Simon Kuznets' *Modern Economic Growth*, which showed that the economic growth of nations can take place only with incessant changes in economic and social structure, and that therefore it is the intricate interplay of technological and institutional changes that provides the key to the understanding of growth. Other evidence is found in the works of John Kendrick, Moses Abramovitz, E. F. Dennison, and a large body of econometric studies that indicate that the growth of nations could not be understood adequately if only the quantity of inputs of labor and capital in the process of production was considered. A large residue of unexplained growth was left. Nor could the latter be attributed only to technological change. So, economists were forced to take into account noneconomic factors and their interactions with labor, capital, and technology. As we studied underdeveloped economies, we began to realize even more strongly that capital and technology were not enough to produce growth of per capita income (Kuznets 1966; Abramovitz and David 1973).[8]

With the recognition that appropriate institutions and values are necessary for efficient production, these become inputs in the process of production equivalent to labor, capital, and technology. One way of conceptualizing the role of these indirect inputs is to regard them as catalytic agents, that is, substances that accelerate change without themselves being affected by the interaction. (Perhaps technology should be included with institutions and values as catalytic inputs.) They are inputs since they carry a cost tag, and sometimes an extremely high one, such as the effort to establish cooperatives and farmers' associations. Like other inputs, they add to efficiency and productivity, as when radio is used to disseminate information about new agricultural technology instead of sending an extension agent to each farm household. Finally, if catalytic inputs can produce efficiency, then labor-intensive technology can be efficient.

We have pointed out that the capacity of underdeveloped countries to absorb highly capital-intensive, technology-intensive projects is severely limited—limited by insufficiencies of demand (both foreign and domestic), of infrastructure (both physical and social), of experienced managers and technicians, of supporting auxiliary trades and servicing industries. Underdeveloped countries can go only a short way with capital-intensive projects. In contrast, labor is plentiful; thus labor-intensive projects must play a prominent part in an overall development strategy. The mix of capital- and labor-intensive projects in the "package" may vary with the degree of underdevelopment, the extent of labor surplus, the availability of natural resources and other endowments. But it is clear that with a surplus of labor and of capital-intensive capacities, the mix must rely more heavily on labor-intensive projects for the 1970s and thereafter, until such time as full employment is approached.[9]

With population pressing on food supplies and urban space, the predominantly labor-intensive package must be rural-oriented. Food consumption levels of 2,000 to 2,200 calories per day per capita are too low for efficient work throughout the year. The migration from rural areas in the 1960s has left the cities of Asia with a large number of unemployed, underemployed, marginally employed youngsters—as well as squatter families—adding to urban congestion, pollution, and lawlessness. The exodus from the rural areas should be slowed down if urban poverty is to be lessened and food supplies increased.

Finally, income disparities are far too large for income differentials to serve as incentives for hard work. These disparities probably can be lessened by one-quarter to one-third without affecting work incentives. But this will depend on redistribution policies. A predominantly welfare policy, as in Ceylon, may not succeed in redistributing family incomes and expanding national production. But a good labor-intensive strategy can accelerate growth, redistribute family incomes, and promote full employment, as the experience of Taiwan demonstrates.[10]

A Predominantly Labor-Intensive Strategy

The new strategy, because it is rural-based, must be implemented in the regions and the hinterland, not in a few large cities. It must involve large masses of people at the grass roots, not just the urban elites. Away from the cities, people generally are poor, traditional, and with little education. Therefore, the emphasis must be not only on changing technology but also on changing institutions and values. It is certain that the role of mass communication will be more important and complex than in the old strategy.

In this section, the major aspects of a labor-intensive strategy that may be relevant for mass communication will be listed. This task is made easier by various reports of International Labor Organization Employment Missions, the most recent of which are in Kenya, Ceylon, Iran, and the Philippines. The Philippines report, just issued, is entitled *Sharing in Development, A Programme of Employment, Equity, and Growth for the Philippines* (Geneva, 1974). The chief planner of the Philippines, Dr. Gerardo P. Sicat, director-general of the National Economic and Development Authority, has written a book entitled *New Directions in the Philippines*, 1974. The projects selected for discussion here are taken from these volumes.

(*A*) *Revolutionizing Agriculture*: This is the key policy in a rural-based, labor-intensive strategy for Asia. It calls for land reform and for establishing institutions such as cooperatives and farmers' associations to dispense credit, fertilizer, water, extension services, and so forth. The goals are: an increase in agricultural productivity, employment, incomes, food production; wider participation in decision-making; and more equal distribution of income and opportunities. To accomplish these goals, the productivity of the large majority of small peasants throughout the country must be increased.

This is probably the most difficult part of a labor-intensive strategy, but it is overwhelmingly the most important. Information on new technologies must be disseminated, as well as instructions on how best to grow new seeds and crops by using new methods, machines, and equipment, and other inputs such as fertilizer, water, and insecticide. The peasant must be persuaded to join cooperatives and associations in order to minimize the costs of purchasing new inputs and learning new methods. It is necessary for him to change his attitudes toward work, innovation, consumption, saving, and repayment of debts. These are difficult tasks because not only is the peasant illiterate, but he has good reasons for not changing his old ways.[11] For example, the new rice seed may be subject to diseases resulting in the loss of a crop, which may be disastrous for him; multiple-cropping may permanently lower the fertility of his soil; the problems of storing and marketing the new crop may be difficult; or he may have had some bad experience in the past with cooperatives and government agents.

The difficulties are increased by the fact that the best form of promoting agricultural productivity is not adequately known. Some experts advocate corporate, plantation farming; others communal farming, cooperative farming, compact farming, and peasant family farming centered around cooperatives and associations. Probably a mix of these different types is best suited for Asian countries, depending on varying regional characteristics, but with the overwhelming portions to be farmed by peasant families. A basic prerequisite for the success of small peasant agriculture is the establishment of effective cooperatives and other associations, and this is not easy to accomplish.

(*B*) *Promoting Small Industries*: The goal is to raise their efficiency, improve the quality of their product, to export—in sum, to improve entrepreneurship and skills. Similar problems as in (*A*) are faced here. The small proprietor and his workers must be reached through mass media and extension agents and persuaded to adopt better product designs and production methods, to organize more efficiently, and to improve marketing methods. Institutional innovations are needed to achieve economies in the use of equipment, to purchase inputs cheaply, and to market more efficiently. Here, too, the difficulty is that our knowledge of better methods and institutions is limited. For example, to improve traditional technology in small and cottage industries, we do not have adequate intermediate technology (intermediate between traditional and modern, between high labor intensity and high capital intensity).

Similar problems exist for the large numbers of small service units—retail shops, restaurants, and other personal services, transporters, building firms, and the like.

(*C*) *Social and Political Development*: In a rural-based strategy, decision-making and implementation cannot be effectively carried out from the capital city. Local governments and other organizations need to participate fully in planning, decision-making, and execution. Due to poor transportation and inadequate mobility, mass communication must be relied on to transmit information and education in a two-way flow from the center to the hinterland and vice versa.

Long neglected because of the emphasis on large urban areas in a capital-intensive strategy, the delivery of health services to rural areas can be improved by the mass media. Proper nutrition in the lower income groups is necessary in a labor-intensive strategy that calls for more efficient work efforts. Since formal schooling in the past has failed to educate the present generation of adults to the occupational needs of labor-intensive projects, it falls on the mass media to rectify this situation as well as to raise literacy levels. Young people and women comprise groups that can be mobilized for rural development—the former for infrastructure construction and the latter for institution building.

(*D*) *Overcoming Opposition*: Finally, there is a small but influential group strongly opposing a labor-intensive strategy. Because they occupy positions of power, they can cause confusion and raise obstructions. Their views must be brought out in discussions conducted through the mass media and efforts must be made to persuade them of the necessity of labor-intensive policies—keeping in mind Keynes' advice that the "gradual encroachment of ideas" over vested interests takes time to occur.

In sum, the role of mass communication is greatly enhanced in a labor-intensive strategy because more people with less education in remote regions must be reached than in a capital-intensive strategy. Its role in promoting economic growth is much more complex for several reasons. Labor must be reeducated and manpower training reoriented. Technology of the intermediate type (the up-graded traditional technology, the down-graded modern technology, and the new intermediate technology) must be discovered. Diffused savings in small bits must be collected from the masses of producers throughout the nation instead of in a lump sum from top income groups. New institutions and organizations in the rural areas must be established, while old values must be modified and new values promoted.

Conclusion

The foregoing suggests that the role to be played by mass communication is different both quantitatively and qualitatively in the new strategy. It may be out of ignorance on my part concerning the present status of mass communication in Asia that I raise the question: Are the mass media prepared to meet the challenge posed by the new strategy? Are they organized, equipped, and staffed to do the complex job? A changeover from a capital-intensive to a labor-intensive strategy is a revolution, in which there is a shift of public policies—from those catering to the productivity and well-being of upper-income groups to those centered on the masses of lower-income groups. A labor-intensive strategy requires many new institutions, and one of them certainly must be an effective network of mass media.

With apologies again for my ignorance of matters relating to mass communication—although having lived in Japan in the early 1960s I have seen the benefits derived from Japanese media programs—I will be bold enough to raise some issues and questions. The wide-ranging examination of national development policies and institutions in recent years has turned up some serious limitations not only in development economics and strategies but also in other spheres. Medicine, engineering, administration, management, and so forth, in developing countries have all been found to be influenced too heavily by theories, concepts, techniques, and procedures suited to Western conditions. Western growth took place under conditions of relative labor shortage, so that Western material and social technologies tended to be highly capital-intensive and labor-saving. I have attempted to show elsewhere that the great population density of Asia, especially in the fertile river valleys, is the historical product of the large labor requirements of monsoon paddy-rice agriculture. This agriculture requires many times the labor necessary for growing wheat and maize in the West because of the need for transplanting seedlings during the planting season instead of broadcasting seeds and also because of the use of knives and sickles for harvesting instead of the larger scythes found in the wheat culture of the West. It is this great population density that distinguishes Asia not only from the West but from the rest of the world. The destruction of handicrafts by the emergence of Western industrialization transformed this density into a labor surplus. Monsoon Asia's material and social technologies thus are founded on labor intensity.[12]

Since formal education in Asia, together with other institutions, has been found to be too Western, the question arises: Are the hardware and software of mass communication also unduly influenced by the West and unsuitable for a labor-intensive strategy? In the West, growth and structural changes took place slowly, over several centuries. There was ample time for institutions and values to adjust to technological and economic changes. This is by no means the case in underdeveloped countries today. Moreover, it takes too much time for formal education to do the job. Should, then, communication emphasize more the task of changing values and institutions, without which labor-intensive methods may not be efficient? If so, how is this to be done? Shouldn't there be some coordination of various of the mass media, and shouldn't experts in mass communication work closely with planners, administrators, extension agents, and local officials? Is there a need for mass media efforts on the Japanese scale, or perhaps one even larger, more pervasive and intensive, and more innovative in design and conception?

Although the tasks of mass communication in a labor-intensive strategy are greater, the base of information and data is much smaller. This base must be considerably enlarged, both with respect to conventional kinds of information and also others pertinent to the needs of a labor-intensive strategy. If new institutions are to be established and made effective, data on their activities should be collected and the reasons for successes and failures evaluated and propagated. If social values are to be modified, more information on what they are and what their roots are needs to be collected. More broadly, an intimate knowledge of all major aspects of the social and cultural conditions—recreation, leisure, and living patterns—of people in all walks of life must be obtained if mass communication is to be informative and persuasive.[13] There is a close correlation between good economic data and good development economics; this may be true also in the case of communication and information.

These suggestions will be expensive to implement. But communication is an important input in labor-intensive policies, and the failure to provide it may be even more costly. Moreover, the cost of this input must be borne for a long time to come, if the example of Japan is relevant, for, in Asia, even after full employment is reached, labor-intensive development cannot be suddenly switched to a capital-intensive one. The mix of labor- and capital-intensive projects in the policy package can only be changed slowly because of the high ratio of population to rice lands. Too rapid shifts to capital intensification of industries will throw out too many workers for agriculture to absorb and, conversely, too rapid capital intensification of agriculture will throw out too many workers for industry to absorb. But this does not mean that high levels of income growth and low levels of income inequalities cannot be attained by technology that is relatively labor-intensive. For this, mass communication must play its part in a labor-intensive strategy of national development.

NOTES

1. The basis of this speculation is the casual observation that the average adult Japanese worker appears to have learned more from newspapers, books, magazines, radio, and television than from his earlier formal education. But having said this, it becomes immediately apparent that there is a complex interaction between formal and nonformal education and, within the latter, between in-service learning and mass communication.

2. In Keynes' theory, aggregate supply tends to outrun aggregate demand because as real incomes rise, absolute volume of consumption will not increase as much as the income increases. Keynes attributed this tendency to some "fundamental psychological rule." While such a tendency may hold for a small group of high-income modernizing families (perhaps no more than 10 to 20 percent), it probably does not hold for the large majority of lower-income consumers.

3. The exchange rates used are 3 Philippines pesos and 250 Japanese yen to the U.S. dollar. These rates were used because the market exchange rates understate the value of currencies in less-developed economies, where a wide range of goods do not enter into international trading. In any case, the exchange rates used do not matter much in the stylized diagram.

4. More detailed discussion on the stylized diagram is found in my paper, "Perspectives in Income Distribution Research," presented at the Seminar on Income Distribution, Employment, and Economic Development in Southeast and East Asia, December 16–20, 1974, Tokyo. By the end of summer 1975, this will be published jointly by the Japan Economic Research Center and the Council for Asian Manpower Studies, Manila.

5. In Japan in the late 1950s, in order to sell refrigerators, washing machines, electric fans, and so forth, it was necessary to design basic models as small as one-fourth the size of Western ones—not only to sell to low-income families but also in order to make possible their installation in tiny Japanese homes, stores, shops, offices, farms, and to fit them into the living patterns of the Japanese.

6. The growth of Western and Japanese economies in the eighteenth and nineteenth centuries was a mix of labor- and capital-intensive technology, with the mix slowly shifting from a predominance of the former to the latter. This took place gradually over many generations as technology advanced, as capital accumulated, as skill and experience were acquired and institutions were devised. Moreover, the range (measured by capital intensity and skill intensity) from the most labor-intensive to the most capital-intensive technology was much narrower before than today.

7. This section summarizes the first portions of my previously published papers (Oshima 1973 and 1971).

8. One striking piece of evidence from underdeveloped countries is the difficulty the Green Revolution is encountering in raising yields to anywhere near levels that technologically the new seeds are capable of making possible. Another is the low level of productivity and efficiency in even the most modern factories in the developing countries.

9. The policy package refers to government expenditures and investment. Private investment, without the subsidies and assistance noted previously, need not be labor-intensive. A predominantly labor-intensive package of government investment, therefore, does not preclude the growth of capital-intensive investments by the private sector.

10. Central to the new economics of growth is the distribution of income. As structural changes occur in the course of growth, their impact on the incomes of

families and individuals will differ in varying degrees. In the stylized diagram above, growth is measured on the horizontal axis and distribution on the vertical axis. As a nation grows, the shape and position of the distribution change.

11. Some economists think that because peasants are rational, market signals are all that is necessary to get them to change. But this rationality is conditioned by the new environment, and this is very different from the West. Mass communication and other means must be used, in addition to market signals, to persuade peasants to change.

12. Data on density, et cetera, are given in my "Seasonality and Unemployment in Monsoon Asia," *Philippine Economic Journal* (First Semester 1971): 63–97. Even as early as 1800, labor requirements per acre in U.S. wheat farming were no more than five or six days, as compared to about twenty-five days in Southeast Asia and fifty days in India and East Asia today. In Java, the recent introduction of the sickle to harvest the short-stalked high-yielding rice varieties in place of the knife has resulted in unemployment of harvesting workers.

13. The Japanese government and mass media have recently gone into hundreds of surveys dealing with opinions, satisfaction, desires, need, and so forth, of various groups of people.

3. The Changing Vision of Modernization and Development

S. N. EISENSTADT

The Earlier Model of Modernization

We witness today very far-reaching changes in the vision of modernization and development in the social sciences. In this paper I would like to trace some of these changes and see where they bring us today.

The initial model of modernization was based on a dichotomous conception of tradition versus modernity. The roots of this conception can be found in Tönnies' distinction between *Gemeinschaft* and *Gesellschaft,* in Sir Henri Maine's distinction between status and contract, or even in Durkheim's early distinction between mechanical and organic solidarity.

These conceptions were more fully elaborated in this century with the great upsurge of interest in underdeveloped societies, the "Third World," and the emergence of "New States." The major focus of these concerns was how to "develop" these underdeveloped societies. This interest gave rise to a spate of studies in all the social sciences, starting with economics. These studies developed the initial paradigm of "modernization," linking together the study of change with the earlier systemic and behavioral approaches, ultimately articulating some of the basic issues of sociological theory.

The crucial theoretical nexus of this paradigm was the redefinition of differences between various societies, particularly between traditional and modern ones, in terms of their "systemic autonomy"—the range of societal issues both internal (social, cultural) and external (technological or economic) with which they could "cope." In this framework, traditional societies were perceived as basically very limited in their capacity to cope with problems or master their environment, while modern societies were seen as coping with a continuously wider range of their internal and external problems and environments.

The qualitative characteristics of modern life, such as rationality, liberty, or progress, were usually subsumed under these "systemic" qualities of societies. Special emphasis was given to the ability to cope with social change in general, with economic development and industrialism in particular. This theoretical framework produced a variety of concepts that emphasized the expansion of systematic qualities or capacities. The most important concepts were those of economic growth, which became central in studies of modernization. (Deutsch 1961, pp. 17–24; Almond and Verba 1963, p. 9; Apter 1968; Lerner 1964, pp. 53–85; Lerner 1968, pp. 386–395.)

The Concept of Stages in Modernization

These studies contained some broader theoretical implications by conceiving of societies as systems coping with various internal and external problems. These problems were defined in rather general terms, as in the four phases or needs of Parsonian analysis, or in the somewhat more concrete specification of the major crises of modern political systems as proposed by Almond, Pye, and other members of the Social Science Research Council's Committee on Comparative Politics. They indentified these crises in terms of: (1) identity; (2) legitimacy; (3) penetration; (4) participation; (5) integration; (6) distribution.

These crises—and especially the internal ones—arise, according to this model, through the process of social mobilization. They vary at its different stages, as do the organizational structures that seek to cope with these problems. A relatively close relationship between the problems arising at each stage of social mobilization and the specialized structures designed to cope with them was often assumed. Since it was assumed (as implied in the theories of "convergence") that basically there exists only one "good" or "true" way of coping with these problems, it followed that there existed only one—or at most a few—"natural" ways in which such organizations could or should function. Each organization—whether party, bureaucracy, or factory—was assumed to have such an "ideal" structure, and its proper functioning was contingent on the development of certain specific prerequisites, for example, universalism or specialization.

Thus, these studies depicted a close, almost unvarying, connection between development in different parts of a society; the similarity of "stages" of development in various societies; the explanation of differences between modernizing societies in terms of their passing through such respective "stages" as well as their "convergence" as the ultimate "end-result" of modernization.

Evolutionary Concept of Modernization

This emphasis on systemic differences between modern and traditional societies had several important theoretical implications. First, it reintroduced evolutionary perspectives in social science and especially the concept of stages—but here with special emphasis on the mechanisms and conditions of transition from traditional to modern society, and on the variable capacities of different traditional societies to effect such transition. Second, it became connected (through its evolutionary perspective) with a new evaluation of modern society.

The concrete analyses of bourgeois civil society, of the passing of the Ancien Régime, or of the capitalist order, which predominated in many classic works of sociology, gave way to emphasis on such abstract features as social mobilization, structural differentiation, or the general character of industrial societies. These features were seen as providing the most pervasive force of change in the modernizing world. A crucial connecting point between such general categories and the evolutionary perspective, in which the unity of mankind was upheld, was the "convergence" theory—the theory that ultimately all modern, industrial systems will develop similar major institutional features. Behind this theory loomed a conviction of the inevitability of progress toward modernity whether by political or industrial development.

These paradigms chiefly attempted to explain the processes, with their variations, in the possible transition from traditional to modern society. The basic model that emerged out of all these researches assumed that the conditions for development of a viable, growth-sustaining, modern society were tantamount to continuous extension of modern components and to destruction of all traditional elements. According to this view, the greater its characteristics of structural specialization, the higher a society ranked on various indices of social mobilization. Concomitantly, the more thorough the disintegration of traditional elements, the more able a society would be to "develop" continuously—to deal with perennially new problems and to develop a continuously expanding institutional structure; to increase its capacity to absorb change; and, implicitly, to develop other qualitative characteristics of modern societies such as rationality, efficiency, and a predilection to liberty.[1]

Scholars working within this paradigm developed a series of assumptions that guided the first group of researches dealing with modernization. The first assumption posited almost total covariance of rates of change, and very close interrelations of almost all major aspects of "development," in all major institutional spheres of society (Hoselitz 1961; Levy 1965, pp. 29–40). This assumption predicated that modernization processes of the different institutional spheres tended to go together and to coalesce in relatively similar patterns. This covariance was very often formulated in terms of the systemic "needs" of a "modern" societal system, in which the basic outputs of one subsystem provide the prerequisites for the functioning of other subsystems.

A second assumption held that once the institutional kernels of such systems were established, they necessarily would lead to the development of similar irreversible outcomes in other spheres and to the general process of sustained development, all presumably moving in a common evolutionary direction (Rostow 1961; Blackmer and Milliken 1961). This assumption, which could be found with different degrees of explicitness in many early studies (e.g., in Rostow's "stages of economic growth" or in the first analyses of the so-called New Nations), tended to merge with another assumption: namely, that the continuity of modernization, of "sustained growth" in any institutional sphere, was usually assured after the initial "take-off" (Rostow 1961).

These assumptions guided many of the early researchers on modernization, and in particular those attempting to explain the variability of transitional paths to modernity, by influencing their choice of major problems for research. Some researches concentrated on identifying the "solvent" (or pushing force) that could propel the "take-off" into modernity. Initially there was a strong tendency to assume the primacy of the economic sphere; stress was placed, therefore, on the economic solvent for development. However, the assumption of economic primacy was discarded relatively early in the game, when it was realized that the development and effective functioning of a modern economic system could not be understood in economic terms alone. When, consequently, the analysis of the noneconomic preconditions of development came to the fore, it became usual to identify the process of "social mobilization" and the extension of "empathy" as such a solvent.

Other studies attempted to establish the best sequence of institutional development that facilitated the transition to a modern society. Here, the pioneering work was Daniel Lerner's *The Passing of Traditional Society*, which proposed the sequence of urbanization, literacy, extension of the mass media, wider economic participation (i.e., per capita income), and political participation (voting) as the natural order of political modernization. Lerner's work stimulated a long series of comparative studies in the same vein.[2]

It is significant that the very attempt to explain the variability of transitional societies gradually undermined the paradigmatic model of modernization. Typologically, transitional societies, standing between traditional and modern societies on different indices of "modernization," constituted some special "stage" in the development of human societies in general. This concept also had a historical connotation, which stressed the tendencies inherent in these societies that pushed them in the direction of modernity.

As a result, the early studies subordinated the "systemic" qualities and possibly homeostatic tendencies of transitional societies to their presumed "dynamic" tendencies. Transitional societies were seen as transitory, even though it was recognized that some transitional societies might "halt" at a certain, even early, stage.[3] Different nonmodern societies were compared in terms of the "weight" of tradition in resisting the impingement of modernizing forces from inside or outside.

While there was growing recognition of the diversity of transitional societies, it was still assumed that such diversity would disappear at the end-stage of modernity. This assumption can be best seen perhaps in the theory of the convergence of industrial societies already alluded to. To quote Goldthorpe:

> The diversity within the industrializing process which he [Kerr] emphasizes turns out to be that evident in the *relatively early stages*—in Rostovian language, those of the "break with traditionalism," "take-off," and the "drive to maturity." And when the question arises of the "road ahead"—for already advanced, as well as developing societies—Kerr's view of the logic of industrialism is in fact such as to force him, willy-nilly, away from a multilinear and toward a unilinear perspective: or, to be rather more precise, to force him to see hitherto clearly different processes of industrialization as becoming progressively similar in their socio-cultural correlates. As industrialism advances and becomes increasingly a world-wide phenomenon, then, Kerr argues, the range of viable institutional structures and of a viable system of value and belief is necessarily reduced. All societies, whatever the path by which they entered the industrial world, will tend to approximate, even if asymptomatically, the pure industrial form. (Goldthorpe 1971, pp. 263–288)

The tenacity of the initial paradigmatic assumptions can also be discerned in the analysis of the possibilities that some societies will halt at a certain transitory stage. The recognition of these possibilities gave rise to the concepts of "breakdowns" of modernization and of "political decay," (Eisenstadt 1964, pp. 345–367; Huntington 1965, pp. 386–430) and to the analysis of the conditions under which they might occur. But these analyses were still largely bound by some of the premises of the earlier models. What might happen after such "breakdowns," or what type of sociopolitical orders could develop after such periods of decay, remained obscure. Rather, these analyses somehow assumed that after such a breakdown there would be either a new resurgence toward modernity or a general regression toward some (unspecified) chaotic instability.

Breakdown of Some Assumptions

Above all, the assumption implicit in many studies, and the one most closely related to the dichotomous conception of traditional versus modern societies—that the less "traditional" a society is, the more capable it is of sustained growth—was proven incorrect.

It became clear that the mere destruction of traditional forms did not necessarily assure the development of a new, viable, modern society. Often the disruption of traditional settings—the family, the community, or even the political order—led to disorganization, delinquency, and chaos rather than to a viable modern order. In addition, it was realized that in such countries as Japan or England, modernization had been successfully undertaken under the aegis of traditional symbols (such as the Crown) and even under traditional elites. Even where the initial impetus to modernization was made under the aegis of antitraditional elites, these groups often tried to revive some of the more traditional symbols of their society (Eisenstadt 1966; Ward and Rustow 1963). Finally, there grew a renewed awareness of the possible contradictions between different qualitative aspects of modern life—especially between "rationality" on the one hand, and liberty, justice, or "solidarity" on the other. It was perceived that traditional societies, by virtue of their traditionalism, might be better able to nurture these latter qualities than are modern societies.

Beyond such general qualifications of the initial approach, several more specific findings indicated that the concrete empirical relations postulated by the initial paradigm of modernization were incorrect. Although some minimal development of various sociodemographic indices seems necessary for the development of any modern structure, further extension of these indices does not necessarily assure the continued processes of modernization and the creation of viable political or social structures. Thus, several countries in Central and Eastern Europe, Latin America, and Asia seem to have reached at certain levels a negative correlation between such sociodemographic indices as literacy, spread of mass media, formal education, or urbanization on the one hand and the institutional ability to sustain growth or to develop libertarian or "rational" institutions on the other.

Even more paradoxical were the somewhat later findings that in some cases, India for example, a relatively low level of social mobilization and a different sequence of mobilization—especially the greater development of education and mass media as against urbanization and industrialization—not only were compatible with the evolution of a relatively viable, modern political entity, but might even have contributed to it. Additional evidence has accumulated that the prerequisites for development of a relatively high degree of urbanization and industrialization could vary in different contexts; the process need not always follow the European pattern, which served as the basis of many of the first formulations about such prerequisites (Eisenstadt 1966). All of these considerations have contributed to the undermining of the assumption about an assured continuity of growth after "take-off." In both the economic and political spheres it became quite obvious that no assurance of such continuity was warranted.

The undermining of these assumptions led to the recognition of ambiguities in the concepts of transitional societies and "breakdowns" of modernization. It became clear that such breakdowns did not necessarily mean a total collapse of these new regimes or their retreat to some traditional form. True enough, such societies certainly differed in many ways from the modern Western ones; but they were by no means simply "traditional societies." They evinced some capability of adaptation and continuity and they developed policies aimed at assuring the conditions of such continuity—even if these policies were not necessarily connected with far-reaching institution-building or with a very active, positive attitude to change.

The Concept of "Dichotomy" Challenged

The initial model of modernization began to break down in the 1950s. The central focus around which criticisms converged was, as we have seen, its inability to explain the variable patterns of traditional societies, their internal dynamics, as well as their independent development of different political and economic complexes. Such criticisms touched not only on the problems of modernization, but also on some very central problems of sociological analysis. Behind much of the debate there also loomed clear political and ideological differences, sometimes forcefully expressed.

Some critics challenged the basic validity of the tradition-modernity dichotomy, and the supposed ahistoricity and Eurocentricity of the initial model. Others attacked some of the basic assumptions of the model, especially its "developmental," evolutionary, and "functional-structural" systemic-assumptions.

The dichotomy of "traditional" versus modern society was undermined by the recognition of the fact that even if traditional societies were typologically different from modern ones, they might greatly vary in the degree to which their traditions impeded or facilitated the transition to modernity, thus necessitating a more analytical distinction between different types of "traditions." From this, two crucial aspects emerged. First, partial "modernization"—that is, development of some institutional frameworks sharing many characteristics of modern organization (such as a modern factory)—might take place in segregated parts of a still "traditional" social structure without necessarily giving rise to an overall change in the direction of modernity. It might even reinforce traditional systems by the infusion of new forms of organization. This possibility has, as we shall see, far-reaching implications for the working of social systems.

The second aspect was what may be called the systemic viability of the so-called transitional systems. Recognition of this aspect is first and most clearly made by Fred Riggs, especially in his work on the Sala model based on his studies of the Philippines and Thailand (Riggs 1964; Riggs in Gallaher 1968, p. 143; Riggs in Montgomery and Siffin 1966, p. 225; Riggs 1966). Riggs attempted to show that, under the impact of forces of modernization coming from the West, a previously traditional system tended to develop into a new type of social or political system; and that such a new system, often described as "transitional," develops systemic characteristics of its own, creating its own mechanisms of stability and self-perpetuation.

These reconsiderations of the tradition-modernity dichotomy were connected with a reappraisal of the importance of historical continuities in shaping the directions of societal development. Even in the first stages of research on modernization it was realized that some of the differences between the structural and symbolic contours of various modern societies might be related to different historical traditions.

Initially, such continuity was perceived as persistence of some broad cultural orientations—an approach very often related to the "culture and personality" school—with little attention being paid to the more structural aspects of modern societies (Spiro 1968, pp. 558–563; Pye 1962). The development of such concepts as "political culture" provided a very important link between such cultural orientations and more specifically structural aspects of behavior (Almond and Verba 1963, p. 9). Later, recognition grew that such differences may also persist in crucial structural areas—such as the rules of the political game, the various aspects of social hierarchy, and the like—and that these variations might evince a very large degree of continuity with historical traditions in different societies.

An important development in this context was the concept of "patrimonialism" to describe the political regimes of several of the new states (Weber 1947; Eisenstadt 1971, p. 146; Eisenstadt 1974; Roth 1968; Zolberg 1966). The use of the term "patrimonial" to depict these various regimes emphasized the inadequacy of the older assumptions. First, it showed that many of these societies and states did not develop in the direction of certain modern nation-states. Second, it demonstrated that these regimes did not necessarily constitute a "transitional" phase along an inevitable path to modernity. Third, it indicated that there was nevertheless some internal "logic" in their development. Fourth, it emphasized that at least part of this logic derived from some aspects of the traditions of these societies.

Recognition of the importance of such historical forces and their analytical implications tended to stress the relative autonomy of the symbolic sphere in relation to structural aspects of social life, a recognition that came to be of crucial importance in the reappraisal of the place of tradition in social life.

The Model Challenged on Historical Grounds

The allegation of the ahistoricity of the modernization model was developed along two distinct directions. One stressed evaluation of contemporary development in terms of the "unfolding" of traditional forces rather than their alleged "transition" toward a seemingly fixed end-stage of modernity. The other—and, in a sense, opposite—direction of criticism stressed the specific, unique, historical experience, discounting any general process of modernization. This approach emphasized that modernization is not a universal process in which all societies participate or which is inherent in the development of every society; but, rather, that it represents the unique historical situation connected with European expansion. This criticism appeared in two different yet closely related guises. One—perhaps best exemplified in the work of Bendix and Riggs—argued that modernization does not have any definite, universal, systemic, symbolic and/or structural characteristics; it is basically a specific one-time historical process that spread Western culture throughout the world and induced late-comers to emulate these Western models of industrialization, political unification, and the like (Bendix 1967, pp. 292–346; Riggs, in Gallaher 1968, p. 143).

The second trend is probably best repesented in recent Marxist writings. These claim that the abstract analytical categories used in the modernization studies, and the general distinctions between traditional and modern societies, tend to lose sight of the historically specific setting of the processes they study. Specifically, these processes are part of the expansion of capitalism and of the consequent establishment of an international system (imperialism) composed of hegemonous and dependent societies.[4] According to these writers, the differences between modern and "traditional" societies lie in their relations of imperialism and colonialism, of exploitation and "dependency." The patterns cannot therefore be measured according to some seemingly universal characteristics derived from the features of the "dominant," "hegemonic" societies (Bodenheimer 1968, pp. 130–159; Furtado 1970).

Thus Gunder Frank argues that indifference to the historical context of the world-wide system within which the underdeveloped countries have lived, and consequent inattention to the international structure of development, completely distorts the reality of present transformations and the future prospects of underdeveloped societies. So-called traditional societies, it is asserted, are no more lacking in entrepreneurship, specialization, and differentiation than advanced ones. Many once prosperous societies are now underdeveloped as a result of the intervention of imperial interests in their economies. Current trade and "aid" policies are widening the material gap between rich and poor nations. The myopia of developmental theorists, if not ideological, results from their tendency to view societies in static isolation without an adequate context in the international pattern of relationships. According to this view, the proper object of research and theorizing is the explanation of both development and underdevelopment in terms of the structure and operation of the international economy (Walton 1972).

Inconsistencies among the Criticisms Themselves

Thus criticisms from many different vantage points have been leveled at the original paradigm of development, attacking most of its premises, undermining many of its basic assumptions, questioning the validity of most of its conclusions and even of the problems posed by it. Yet, the picture is made even more complicated by the fact that many of the criticisms are mutually inconsistent.

Thus denial of the distinction between "traditional" and "modern" societies and emphasis on the vitality of traditions could be coupled, as in Benda, with an antirevolutionary or antidevelopmental view of the impact of "modern" social forces on Indian or Indonesian societies. In such a view, these "modernizing" forces were themselves a passing stage, a sequel of colonial rule, to be followed by the reemergence of basically traditional patterns of society and culture (Benda 1960, pp. 205–208; Benda, in Hunsberger 1957; Eisenstadt, in Rivkin 1968, pp. 35–62).

But this denial could also be connected, as by Omvedt, with a somewhat different view that claims that the "modern" European colonial regimes stifled the development of forces inherent in the traditional setting—forces that might have facilitated an autonomous transition to some form of modernity, which might or might not have been similar to the "Western" nation-state or "revolutionary" class-society (Omvedt, in Desai 1971, pp. 119–138). Similarly, the negation of the old dichotomy could be connected with a somewhat "conservative" ideological political stance; with a strong emphasis on a nongradualistic or "revolutionary" conception of breakthrough to modernity; or with the acceptance of some characteristics of the Western model—such as political participation or industrialization—as valid goals for modernization.

At the same time, those who stress the importance of revolutionary breakthroughs may differ with respect to their evaluation of traditional forces as potentially creating revolutionary conditions. They may also differ with respect to the relation of such revolutionary breakthroughs to the more routine aspects of modern institution-building.

One view, represented by Omvedt among others, points out that traditions conventionally seen as dysfunctional for development may, in fact, be incompatible only with one type of development (e.g., liberal, industrial capitalism), while making possible another road to modernization (e.g., socialist industrialism). According to this thesis, the "usual" view of traditional forces as an impediment to development constitutes an ideological guise for the imperialist type of development (Omvedt, in Desai 1971, pp. 119–138; Bodenheimer 1968, pp. 130–159). Authors with revolutionary orientations—as, for example, Sinai or Wertheim—seem to be less beneficently disposed toward "tradition" and see in it an impediment to modernization (Sinai, in Desai 1971, pp. 53–76; Wertheim, in Desai 1971, pp. 149–159), just as do some of their "Eurocentric" and "evolutionary" opponents.

Even more mixed are the different analytical connections that may be made from the emphasis on the importance of leadership, modernizing elites, and their choices in the process of modernization. Such an emphasis can be connected with a conservative approach that lays stress on the unfolding of tradition, or with a revolutionary one emphasizing the necessity to break through the limitations of tradition. It could also be connected either with a strong denial of the systemic qualities of societies or with an emphasis on the constriction of choice given to leadership by the basic systemic problems of industrialization (Kerr et al. 1964; Shils 1962). Likewise, it connects with the assumption of the ultimate convergence of all industrial societies or, conversely, with the emphasis on different possible outcomes of the process of change (Sinai, in Desai 1971, pp. 53–76; Wertheim, in Desai 1971, pp. 149–159; Omvedt, in Desai 1971, pp. 119–138).

Similarly, while some of those who stress the historical uniqueness of the process of modernization also deny the systemic qualities of social order, others tend to combine emphasis on historical uniqueness with a stress on specific structural and systemic characteristics—such as the spread of capitalism and the "dependency" that develops out of it (Wertheim, in Desai 1971, pp. 149–159; Furtado 1970; Bodenheimer 1968, pp. 130–159). It is beyond the scope of the present paper to go into all the detailed technical implications for sociological analysis that these imply.[5]

An Emerging View of Modernization

We might, however, ask ourselves where research on modernization goes from here. However great the differences among these studies, one thing is agreed upon: most traditional societies have been caught up in the challenge of "modernity" that has spread from seventeenth-century Europe throughout the world.

Modern societies, as contrasted with more traditional ones, have continuously faced the crucial tendency of their central framework to "expand." This tendency to expansion, which distinguishes modern from traditional societies, manifests itself in growing social mobilization and structural differentiation on the one hand and in demands for growing participation in societal centers on the other (Eisenstadt 1973).

These differences between "traditional" and "modern" social and cultural orders have, of course, been stressed in the early literature. Yet, unlike the "classical" paradigm, the more recent picture of this process indicates that "modernization" does not constitute a "unilinear" demographic, social, economic, or political process that leads—even if haltingly or intermittently—to some plateau whose basic contours, whatever the differences in detail, will be everywhere the same. Rather, modernization has to be seen as a process or a series of processes with a common core that generates common or similar problems.

These processes of growing differentiation, social mobilization, and breakdown of traditionality—unparalleled in the history of human societies—create within the societies in which they occur certain basic problems of regulating the necessarily increasing conflicts that develop among newly emerging groups; of integrating these groups within some common institutional framework; of developing some new foci of collective national identity in which tradition, modernity, and change are to some extent combined. The most general problem is the ability to sustain an institutional structure capable of absorbing changes beyond its own initial premises. Such a structure must deal continuously with new and changing problems; it must also produce qualities of participation and liberty as well as a degree of rationality.

But although these processes of development, and the problems to which they give rise, have some things in common, yet the structural and cultural conditions under which they may arise—and the responses to them—may vary greatly among different societies. The differences are evident not only, as was so often stressed in the early literature, in the degree of social mobilization and structural differentiation that develops within each of them. It is now clear that, in the structural organizational field itself, they may vary greatly in the degree of coalescence of "modern" institutional complexes—that is, of industry, of political parties, of family structures and kinship organizations. Such differences appear also in their conception of themselves and of their past, in their relation of the parameter of these traditions to the extension of participation, liberty, or justice. All these differences shape the constitution of the new, posttraditional orders—of their organizational, institutional, and symbolic aspects alike.

It is thus clear that some modernizing societies tend to "develop" in directions that do not necessarily lead into any single "end-state" envisaged by the various "evolutionary" models of modernization.

Here, of crucial importance has been the growing recognition that what was earlier considered as "breakdowns" of modernization does not necessarily mean a total collapse of new regimes or their retreat to some traditional form. While they certainly differ in many ways from the Western models, the new societies are by no means simply "traditional societies." None of these posttraditional social orders has a perfected institution-building capacity. Within each of them there could develop different types of crises, breakdowns, and regressions. These tend often to coalesce into some broader sociopolitical models, such as those designated as "absolutist," "estate," "nation-state" models, as well as the patrimonial and neopatrimonial models. Each model may comprise different degrees of social mobilization and economic development, different types of coalescence, different institutional patterns. Similarly, each model may comprise different degrees of ability to institutionalize, in some viable way, new types of center-periphery relations, and variant capacities to cope with continuously emerging conflicts.

The differences between such models may be very closely connected with the development of different patterns of political ideology; different conceptions of the relations between the political, cultural, and the cosmic orders; different relations between the technical, administrative, and symbolic aspects of political life. Thus they may give rise to regimes in which there is a much smaller identity between political and cultural centers, that is, centers in which the nation-state no longer constitutes the "natural" unit of a modern political order; and to different patterns of collective identity and of political participation than those that developed in the European or other postimperial centers.

Finally, the various models of posttraditional regimes may evince conceptions of sociopolitical order and modes of coping with political problems that show great similarities to the conceptions and modes that were prevalent in their traditional settings, thus exhibiting a crucial continuity of traditions.

A Pluralism of Models

But it need not be assumed that any specific society must always remain within the same "model"—that it cannot, as it were, change the model according to which its structure is crystallized.

The crystallization of the symbolic and organizational patterns of different modernizing societies is, of course, influenced by many different conditions. Among those of special importance seem to be the level of resources available for "mobilization" and institution-building; the pattern of impingement of "modern" forces on the respective societies; the structure of the change situation in which they were caught; the different traditions of their "premodern" socioeconomic structures; the perception of choice by different elites and groups in given historical situations; and their ability to implement such choices. The interaction between these different sets of conditions produces different responses to the challenge of modernization. Exploration of all these processes is still very much before us as an important part of the agenda for comparative sociological research.

Nevertheless, these inquiries indicate that the crystallization of posttraditional orders does not occur simply by a "natural" unfolding of their traditions. Choice is a very strong element and raises a series of deep problems for each society. Whereas the range of choices is not unlimited, their crystallization in any specific situation is not entirely predetermined, either by new structural developments or by "tradition." In structurally similar situations, there is always some range of possible alternatives. Choices are manifest on different levels, being perhaps most visible with respect to the types of political regimes that may develop. On a level somewhat less fully institutionalized, but not necessarily less pervasive, choices also emerge in the patterns available for reconstructing traditions, especially the ways in which symbols of collective identity are shaped. The situation can be perceived in terms of cultural continuity or discontinuity; various symbols of collective identity can be discarded or incorporated into the new frameworks. Such elements of choice are especially prominent in the reconstruction of the symbolic frameworks that constitute a society's self-conception.

A Broader View of Modernization

The preceding analysis provides us with some indications of an emerging view of modernity broader than that envisaged in the early model of modernization. It stresses the historical dimension of the process, emphasizing that it is not universal, something "given" by the very nature of humanity or by the natural development of human societies. Instead, the modernization process is bound to a certain period in history, even though it was continuously developing and changing throughout this period.

These challenges of modernization are basic for most contemporary societies. Though the process certainly is pervasive in the contemporary setting, it is not necessarily irreversible in the future. It would be wrong to assume that once these forces have impinged on any society, they naturally push toward a relatively fixed end-result. Rather, as we have seen, they evoke a variety of responses that depend on the broad sets of internal conditions of the developing societies, on the situation in which they are caught, and on the degree to which the international system fosters "dependency" or "competition."

NOTES

1. For two of the fullest expositions of this model, see: Lerner 1968: 386–395; Cyril Black, *The Dynamics of Modernization* (New York: Harper and Row, 1966). For some misgivings, see: Wilbert E. Moore, "Social Framework of Economic Development," in *Tradition, Values and Socio-Economic Development*, edited by R. J. Braibanti and J. Spengler (Durham, N.C.: Duke University Press, 1961), pp. 3–57.

2. See for example: Wilbur Schramm and W. Lee Ruggels, "How Mass Media Systems Grow," in *Communication and Change in the Developing Countries*, edited by Daniel Lerner and Wilbur Schramm (Honolulu: The University Press of Hawaii, 1972), p. 75; Chong-Do-Hah and Jeanne Schneider, "A Critique of Current Studies on Political Development and Modernization," *Social Research* 1968 (35): 10–159.

3. Of special value is a series of Studies in Political Development made under the sponsorship of the Committee on Comparative Politics of the Social Science Research Council and published by Princeton University Press, Princeton, N.J., between 1963 and 1971. The studies, each containing a number of pertinent essays are: *Communications and Political Development*, edited by Lucian W. Pye; *Bureaucracy and Political Development*, edited by Joseph LaPalombara; *Political Modernization in Japan and Turkey*, edited by Robert E. Ward and Dankwart A. Rustow; *Education and Political Development*, edited by James S. Coleman; *Political Culture and Political Development*, edited by Lucian W. Pye and Sidney Verba; *Political Parties and Political Development*, edited by Joseph LaPalombara and Myron Weiner; and *Crises and Sequences in Political Development*, edited by Leonard Binder, James S. Coleman, Joseph LaPalombara, Lucian W. Pye, Sidney Verba, and Myron Weiner.

4. Some of the most important papers representing this point of view have been collected in James D. Cockcraft, Andrew Gunder Frank, and Dale L. Johnson, *Dependence and Underdevelopment—Latin America's Political Economy* (New York: Anchor Books, 1972); Andrew Gunder Frank, *Capitalism and Underdevelopment in Latin America* (New York: Monthly Review Press, 1967); Pablo Gonzales Casanova, "Les Classiques Latino-Americains et la Sociologie du Development," *Current Sociology* 18(1): 5–29; Gail Omvedt, "Modernization Theories: The Ideology of Empire," in *Essays on Modernization of Underdeveloped Societies*, edited by A.R. Desai (Bombay: Thacker and Co., 1971), pp. 119–138; Suzanne Bodenheimer, "The Ideology of Developmentalism: American Political Science Paradigm–Surrogate for Latin American Studies," *Berkeley Journal of Sociology* 35 (1968): 130–159; Fernando Henrique Cardozo and Enzo Faletto, eds., *Dependencia y Desarollo en America Latina* (Mexico City: Siglo Veintiuno, 1969).

5. A further exposition of these problems is given in Eisenstadt 1973.

3a. *End of an Old Paradigm?*

WILBUR SCHRAMM

Eisenstadt's point is simple and straightforward: he says that the "old paradigm" of development that has dominated psychological and social science for two decades has broken down, and a new one is needed.[1] By *paradigm* he means in this case a model or set of relationships that will explain and predict the social changes that precede and accompany development. He feels that the nature of a new model of this kind is becoming evident, but the model itself has not emerged in any detail.

He is *not* saying that the basic *economic* assumptions underlying development have necessarily broken down. Any social model of development includes efficient management of resources. He *is* saying, however, that development requires mobilization of human and social, as well as economic, resources, and that this process is no longer satisfactorily explained by the old paradigm.

What is the "old paradigm"?

It is essentially a model of growth. Some of its best-known early statements were in Lerner's *Passing of Traditional Society* and Rostow's *Stages of Economic Growth*. Rostow described modernization as a movement from traditional society through a point of "take-off" into a situation of self-sustaining growth. A basic index was GNP. Basic social indices were urbanization, development of the communication system, and amount of political participation. Lerner suggested a sequence of institutional developments leading to take-off: urbanization, literacy, extension of mass media, higher per capita income, political participation (voting). The essential point was that growth in one of these spheres stimulates growth in others, and all spheres of society move forward together toward modernization. Lerner suggested also a psychological prerequisite of modernization: the development of *empathy,* meaning the ability of a person to imagine significant change in his own status—a Turkish peasant becoming able to imagine himself president of the republic, or an Indian tenant farmer becoming able to imagine that he might be a landowner or storekeeper.

Perhaps the best overall summary of this social approach was Karl Deutsch's concept of "Social Mobilization," defined as "the process in which old social, economic, and psychological commitments are eroded and broken, and people become available for new patterns of socialization and behavior." Indices of this kind of social mobilization were considered to include higher differentiation of roles within society, the freeing for development of resources previously ascribed to fixed groups (kinship, religious, etc.) and the development of specialized types of social organizations (market mechanisms, voting and party activities, bureaucratic mechanisms related to development, etc.) Deutsch saw urbanization as perhaps the most important single external sign of such change.

Eisenstadt notes an evolutionary quality about this paradigm, an extension of Darwinian thinking to social change. Not only was change in one social sphere able to stimulate change in others, but social modernization was able to generate continuing change, and also to absorb the stress of change and adapt itself to changing demands. In other words, the process seemed relatively irreversible. Once the necessary conditions were established for take-off, a country took off, became modern, stayed modern.

The model is familiar to all of us, and we have seen the indices of its occurrence. What, then, does Eisenstadt think is wrong with the "old paradigm?"

Chiefly that it works better as a description of what has happened in Western countries than as a predictor of change in non-Western countries. Even in countries where the process had apparently already taken place, there was less then a perfect fit to the model. England, for example, had retained many traditional patterns and mechanisms despite being the home of the Industrial Revolution. Japan had kept many of its own societal ways of dealing with problems despite a miraculous growth in industry and commerce. In new states whose politics had largely been shaped by "modern" (Western) models, he says, there "emerged a new phase in which older, traditional modes or models" tended to reassert themselves. He finds less inevitability, or irreversibility, about the paradigm in non-Western societies than might have been expected. For example, partial "modernization" in traditional society need not "necessarily give rise to an overall change in the direction of modernity, but might even reinforce traditional systems."

Two important insights have helped to explain these findings, says Eisenstadt. One came chiefly from anthropologists and historians, who argued the importance of culture and tradition. He makes much of the significance of "cultural codes," which he defines as the way a culture has learned to cope with certain kinds of problems. These ways of coping, he says, are much different in different cultures, and tend to persist even when a culture goes through some of the changes we call modernization. He suggests that communication scholars might contribute in an important way to the understanding of cultural codes through studying popular culture.

The second insight came from Marxist scholars, who emphasize the history-specific setting of present-day modernization. One chief element in this is the relation to the new developing states of "imperialism and colonialism, exploitation and dependency." Thus, according to proponents of this point of view, the "old paradigm" lacks generality because it always exists not only in a local cultural setting, but also in a particular international setting that has been characterized most often by Western capitalistic expansion and domination.

Eisenstadt concludes that the "old paradigm" lacks the necessary generality, and we are ready for a new overview. The new paradigm of modernity will take for granted that:

(1) The process is not something universal, something "given" in the very nature of humanity or in the cultural development of human societies, but, rather, fully bound to a certain period in human history, pervasive but not necessarily irreversible.

(2) The process is not "purely temporal or chronological," but rather due to the development of certain cultural or social characteristics, the very ones stressed in the recent literature. However, when these forces have made themselves felt in any society they do not necessarily push toward a given, relatively fixed "end-plateau." Rather they evoke from different societies different responses depending on the internal conditions, the cultural codes, and the international relationships of the society.

(3) The process requires a more complex picture of the nature of societies and cultures than has usually been included in the "old paradigm." It need not be assumed "that different cultural forces and structural processes always tend to vary in a one-to-one relation" or to "unfold together in some preordained direction." The nature of the cultural codes, and the variety and degree of development of different subsystems within the society, may lead to a quite different result.

Therefore, some of the problems and hypotheses of modernization, in Eisenstadt's words,

> . . . have to be reformulated in a direction of greater specificity. Instead of asking for a general universal precondition of a universally valid model of modernization, more specific questions [should be asked] about the development or impediments to the development of different patterns of symbolic modernity and rates of organizational development and modernization in different institutional spheres. . . . Similarly, instead of assuming the existence

> of general sequences of patterns of social mobilization which are "good" for modernization, we must investigate the possibility of different variations in such patterns and their influence. (Eisenstadt 1973: 362)

In other words, to put it simply, things are not as simple as had been assumed, and the generality sought by the old paradigm may not now be possible. Back to the old drawing board!

NOTE

1. Where direct quotes of Eisenstadt's words are cited, they derive from his chapter in this volume or from his book, *Tradition, Change, and Modernity* (1973).

3b. The Passing of the Dominant Paradigm—Reflections on Diffusion Research

EVERETT M. ROGERS

There is no single place in the literature of development where the dominant paradigm of development has been concisely and clearly described (in fact, in the 1950s and 1960s it probably was not fully realized that there *was* a dominant paradigm). After reviewing a sample of this literature, I have distilled the following four main elements in this conception of development:

1. *Economic growth* through industrialization and accompanying urbanization, approximately equivalent to passing through the Industrial Revolution. It was assumed that development performance could be quantified in economic terms: GNP, per capita income.
2. Capital-intensive, labor-extensive *technology* mainly imported from more developed nations.
3. *Centralized planning,* mainly by economists and bankers, in order to guide and speed up the process of development.
4. The *causes of underdevelopment* lay mainly within the developing nation, rather than in their external relationships with other countries.

The classical diffusion model fit this dominant paradigm quite well, as we claimed previously. The paradigm of development implied that the role of communication was (1) to transfer technological innovations from development agencies to their clients, and (2) to create an appetite for change through raising a "climate for modernization" among members of the public.

But as a paradigm shift occurred in the conceptualization of development in the early 1970s (table 1), the appropriate role for communication also began

Table 1. Emerging Alternatives to the Dominant Paradigm of Development

Main Elements in the Dominant Paradigm of Development	*Emerging Alternatives to the Dominant Paradigm*	*Possible Factors Leading to the Emerging Alternatives*
1. Economic growth	1. Equality of distribution	1. "Development weariness" with the rate of economic development during the 1950s and 1960s 2. Publication of the Pearson Report 3. Growing loss of faith in the "trickle-down" theory of distributing development benefits
	2. Quality of life	4. Environmental pollution problems in Euro-America and Japan 5. *Limits to Growth*
2. Capital-intensive technology	1. Integration of "traditional" and "modern" systems in a country 2. Greater emphasis on labor-intensive technology	1. Pollution problems 2. The energy crisis following the 1973 Yom Kippur War
3. Centralized planning	1. Self-reliance in development 2. Popular participation in decentralized development planning and execution (e.g., to the village level)	1. The People's Republic of China's experience with decentralized, participatory development (that became widely known elsewhere after 1971) 2. "Development weariness"

Table 1. (continued)

Main Elements in the Dominant Paradigm of Development	*Emerging Alternatives to the Dominant Paradigm*	*Possible Factors Leading to the Emerging Alternatives*
4. Mainly internal causes of under-development	1. Internal and external causes of under-development (amounting to a redefinition of the problem by developing nations)	1. The rise of "Oil Power" in the years following the energy crisis of 1973–1974. 2. Shifts in world power illustrated by voting behavior in the U.N. General Assembly and in the U.N. World Conferences at Stockholm, Bucharest, and Rome in the early 1970s

to undergo questioning. Actually, the "new development" paradigm (or paradigms) is only emerging, and its exact nature is not yet evident in any detail. Nevertheless, the "new development" (and certain of the world events leading to the paradigm shift that produced it) contains some obvious implications for communication's role in development.

For instance, the main target audience for development efforts, world-wide, should become villagers in the "Fourth World." The rising power of the oil nations since 1973, and their suddenly increased wealth, has given a sudden boost to their development efforts. Previously, almost all of the "Third World" countries were poor. Now about 250 million people in oil-exporting countries (including such populous nations as Indonesia, Nigeria, Iran, Algeria, and Venezuela) have the economic requisites for rapid development. Some observers divided the old Third World countries into two (rich/poor) categories by splitting off a "Fourth World" of forty countries with about 900 million people (about one-fourth of the world's population) averaging a per capita income of less than $150 per year. The Fourth World is concentrated in the Indian subcontinent, Sub-Saharan Africa, and in pockets within Latin America (such as North East Brazil). Oil power has set back the pace of development in those resource-poor nations, who are now faced with rapidly rising energy and food prices, and a scarcity of foreign exchange.

The growing concern with equality as a main dimension of the "new development" points toward priority for the Fourth World countries, and the main target audience for development in those developing nations are the relatively least-developed segment of the total population: villagers and, to a lesser extent, urban poor. In most of Latin America, Africa, and Asia, this target audience represents a majority of the nation's population. Thus development policies must become less elite-oriented, and more concerned with equalizing the socioeconomic benefits of development.

Diffusion research has always been oriented toward villagers in developing nations, and has probably been one of the least urban/elite types of communication research in these national settings. So diffusion research fits well into a study of the village audience in Fourth World countries.

However, the diffusion model has not been utilized in the past in ways that the "new development" paradigm(s) implies for the future: two-way, participatory, and bottom-up. Whether the diffusion model can be fruitfully applied in these new ways and in alternative directions remains to be seen.

3c. *Old and New Strategies—An Economist's View*

HARRY T. OSHIMA

Some conference participants said that economists regard increase of GNP and national income as the *goal* of development. This is not fair to economists. Most of us think of GNP as a good *measure,* and a starting point for analysis, of *economic* growth—not as a development goal. (See the various works of Simon Kuznets.) Economists regard the growth of GNP as the major *economic means* to a better quality of life. Consumption as the goal of economic activity is a view found in any economic textbook.

What precisely constitutes the desired quality of life is, of course, not clear. But few will dispute that reducing the *arduousness* of manual labor—whether in agriculture, industry, construction, or mining—is a prime element of a higher quality of life in the poor countries. For example, in monsoon Asia, rice cultivation is one of the most strenuous forms of human labor. It is said, in the Philippines, that even the tough *carabao* will refuse to do more than a normal amount of plowing in a given season. No matter how good the health delivery system, the school system, the cultural system, and the political system, one can never achieve a high quality of life without reducing the arduousness of human labor. The lives of human beings in the developing countries are not far removed from the lives of beasts of burden. If the calorie consumption of food is no more than 2,000 per capita per day (as it is in most of Asia)—and if it takes 2,000 calories of human energy to produce the 2,000 calories of food —then there is a limit to what the "barefoot" doctor can do to improve health and what the dedicated teacher can do to educate children (who cannot learn on an empty stomach).

In all fairness to the leading advocates of capital-intensive strategy, they hoped to reduce the role of human beings as beasts of burden by using more machines and high technology. The view I expound in my paper implies that it is too simplistic to say that the way to development in labor-surplus countries is to replace men with machines.[1] The most naïve rationale I have heard of capital-intensive strategy was made by India's chief planner, who brought out charts showing that per capita income was correlated with per capita steel production (in private conversation, 1962, New Delhi). By contrast, other advocates have more sophisticated versions of capital-intensive strategies. Let me just cite two of the most influential books: Albert O. Hirschman's *Strategy of Economic Development* (1957), and Ragnar Nurkse's *Problems of Capital Formation in Underdeveloped Countries* (1953). Both argued for "big pushes," the former on a selective basis and the latter on all fronts. (It is said that Mao's "great leap forward" movement was heavily influenced by these books, especially Nurkse's.)

But none of these advocates displays any trace of obsession for maximizing only the growth of GNP. It was only after Khrushchev's famous challenge to the West, to compete with socialist countries in accelerating the growth of GNP, that it became so prominent a concern. Then, too, the emphasis of Hirschman and his colleagues upon a predominantly capital-intensive strategy was due to the extreme difficulties of dealing with numerous small peasants and other small producers, and the limited knowledge and experience we possessed about developing poor countries. In this kind of situation, the suggestion (by Kuznets and others) that the Industrial Revolution was preceded by an Agricultural Revolution in the West was brushed aside by leaders such as Nehru and Mao in the 1950s.

The pessimism expressed in this conference reminds me of meetings I have attended where development planning in the 1960s was evaluated. This pessimism seems to me healthy and worthwhile if it leads to a dose of humility, but not if it leads to skepticism for the future. Nothing worked quite as well in the 1960s as we thought it should have because we were moving in the wrong directions. Since economic development strategy, which is the heart and core of planning, was wrong, it was inevitable that development planning was not as successful as we wanted it to be. Nevertheless, even with the right strategy, a healthy dose of humility is needed in order to avoid major mistakes in its implementation.

Highly optimistic statements were made by some of our conferees about Marxist strategies, particularly the Chinese model. This is understandable in the light of the historically unprecedented achievements made by China since it switched to a labor-intensive strategy—in equalitarianism and full employment, in widening opportunities for education, health, and other social services. But admiration should not blind us to certain problems that China must solve in the coming decade. One such problem is economic growth. This problem can be placed in the context of our conference discussions.

There was a very interesting discussion on group work in China and the use of group pressure to push slow and lazy workers to produce up to the norm of hard-working members in the team or group. What is the mechanism that insures that the Chinese system raises the norm of the group or the total team production? Group pressures may succeed in pushing the output (and presumably the quality) of the laggards, but how adequate are they in raising the output (and quality) of the hard-working members, particularly in the long run? In Japanese economic growth, group work and pressures are important, but these have been coupled with large year-end bonuses (as large as three to six months' regular pay)—a form of profit-sharing in a substantial part of the added output. These large bonuses are then saved by the receivers, and directly or indirectly become the source of capital formation (or accumulation of machines). This, in turn, enables the Japanese to reduce the strenuousness of manual work in agriculture, industry, and the service sector, as well as in the homes (washing, cooking, cleaning, etc.).

In capitalist societies, workers and entrepreneurs have the incentive to save in order to improve the efficiency of their production, whose means are privately owned. Accordingly, most of the savings are made by individuals. But in socialist societies the means of production are state-owned and there is little incentive to save, to buy stocks or machines, to accumulate for old age, for contingencies, or for one's children. My guess is that the individual savings rate is low and the state must do nearly all of the capital accumulation. In order for socialist societies to grow rapidly, the state (or some public group) must do all the accumulating, and this in turn means that most of the increment must be taken over by the state (or the commune or other collective). But if this is done, where is the material incentive of the hard worker to raise the norms of his group in the long run? There is a close connection between the incentives to work harder and more efficiently, to save, and public ownership of the means of production in developing countries, where output is produced directly by human hands.

It should be said that I am not a specialist in this field and it may be my limited knowledge of the economics of communism that leads me to raise these queries. It may also be that I am not aware of ways to overcome these difficulties. The problem may become less acute as these countries begin to reduce the arduousness of human labor with mechanization and succeed slowly in changing human values. But this may be a slow process.[2]

It is interesting to note in the foregoing speculation that in the socialist countries mass communication (which, as Schramm has pointed out, is the medium through which social processes and relations are carried out) must concentrate on persuading people to work hard and to exceed previous norms; whereas in capitalist countries there is little need for such emphasis by the mass media. Instead, because of the individualistic nature of society —"the strong becoming stronger" and "the weak weaker"—the mass media are preoccupied with ways of improving the lot of the lower-income group. So, the problem of equity in the distribution of income and in the opportunities for social services becomes (or should become) the basic problem.

If this is so, underdeveloped countries in Asia that choose to keep the means of production in private hands must find ways of promoting production (via teams, groups, cooperatives) and equity in the distribution of public services—learning and adapting from the experience of China and Japan. Profit sharing must also be explored, for the problem of poor countries is not only equity but also growth; and—for Asian countries, with their unique monsoon paddy agriculture and high population densities—collective, cooperative production is the only way to get efficiency in a predominantly labor-intensive strategy of development.

For me, the conference discussion regarding the integration of "big" technology (space satellites and giant balloons) and "small" technology in the villages (radio, TV, newspapers, etc.), soon to be operative in India, Indonesia, and the Republic of Korea, is most exciting. The potentialities seem enormous. If the "software" of this integration is worked out closely and skillfully with the planners and implementers of the new strategy, the prospects are good for its success in achieving both growth and equity.[3]

NOTES

1. Too simplistic because the sustained growth of the ability to produce goods efficiently involves more than machines and technology; there are many noneconomic factors involved, and complex interactions among these variables—much of which we do not yet understand.

2. In the original commune, the attempt was to collectivize consumption in order to force the reduction of consumption and increase savings. But apparently collectivization of consumption, which must go hand in hand with collectivized production, was not successful.

3. As I write the above, a report comes from Peking that there will be a shift in emphasis in 1975 from heavy industries to light industries, in order that more consumer goods can be produced as incentives to peasants to work harder and produce more. Apparently there is a limit to the amount that the state can take away from peasants (as forced savings) to finance the production of capital goods that are collectively owned. And that limit may be in the propensity to work. If this is so, this announcement is consistent with the speculations made above.

3d. *Reconsideration of the Western Model*

INAYATULLAH

The question of what models of development would be effective in helping the less-developed countries break through the vicious circle of poverty has become more urgent during the last decade as the strategies employed for this purpose have not produced the desired results. The issue was raised in our 1964 conference and produced an interesting debate that is represented by two papers published in the volume resulting from that conference (Lerner and Schramm 1972, chaps. 7 and 8).

The controversy was provoked by Professor Lerner's remarks about the relevance of the Western model to the developing countries and the ethnocentric predicament of an Asian intellectual in rejecting it. He made several points:

1. He argued that American interest in development of the less-developed countries has been increasingly depoliticized, implying that American professional social scientists and intellectuals were guided not by political but by professional considerations when they argued the universal relevance of the Western model. This he contrasted with the politicization of development policy in Asian countries, where public leaders harped on anti-Western feelings to win popular support and create artificial unity, and where intellectuals lacking freedom shared the ethnocentric predicament of the public leaders.

2. This ethnocentrism, he argued, was "not merely a self-indulgent nuisance but actually a major obstacle to development progress." The Western model, which non-Western leaders apparently rejected, incorporated certain values such as material welfare, power, rationality, and skill

that were universally desired. It exhibited "certain components and sequences whose relevance is global." As demonstrated by Western experience, modernization occurs when industralization, urbanization, and literacy reach a certain level. Exposure to the mass media occurs in a particular sequence, raising popular participation in economic and political life. When this sequential process is disturbed by policy choice, modernization is affected, usually adversely.

3. This also suggests that modernization requires transformation of social institutions, which occurs when sufficient changes occur in individual behavior.

These observations, as I then understood them, seemed to imply that the range of choice, with regard to ultimate ends and means of modernization, was narrow. The sequential process of modernity was historically determined and could be altered or tampered with only at one's peril. There was room for marginal adaptation and for invention of "functional equivalents," but not for radical departures. In sharp contrast with Professor Lerner's position, I argued the following:

1. That Western social scientists involved in technical assistance programs tend to adjust their perspectives to the political context of these programs. They prescribe solutions compatible with the global interest of their countries, and reflect ethnocentrism about the superiority of their culture and institutions. They exaggerate the relevance of the Western model of development to non-Western countries.

2. That the intellectual perspective of Western scholars on the development of societies is conditioned by a narrow and shaky unilinear view of the history of man, which implies that societies at lower levels of development are inexorably bound to travel the same historical path through which the advanced industrial Western societies achieved their development.

3. That the relevance of the Western model to the condition of non-Western models should be critically examined rather than presumed, that non-Western societies should make a conscious autonomous choice about models of development they want to follow and that they should be inventive in developing new models of development.[1]

Developments of the last ten years have revealed several errors in my arguments, errors that are more methodological and conceptual than substantive. These errors included, first, suggesting a normative model of development that should be followed by the non-Western countries, rather than specifying the extent of freedom available to them for choosing a model and assessing the probability of emergence of such a non-Western model. I also exaggerated the extent of freedom available to the non-Western countries, ignoring the constraints imposed by the historical evolution of these societies and their contemporary internal and external environments. Further, I used a blanket concept of the Western model, bundling together cultural and institutional aspects. This created a wrong impression—as if everything Western was or should be suspect and there was no room for selective adaptation.

Second, my failure to explore further the implications of the proposed non-Western model exposed it to the charge of being a superficial replica of the Western model. It could be legitimately argued that the Western model was as much concerned as mine with increasing control over nature, with increasing national self-determination, and increasing self-control in individuals. What I failed to elaborate was the notion of establishing a balance among the three proposed goals of development, that is, control over nature, over national destiny, and over one's self. I did not elaborate the idea that excessive concern with control over nature could lead to destruction of nature, subjugation of weak nations by strong nations to control their resources, and regimentation of the individual. An exaggerated concern with national determination could hide aggressive designs against the independent existence of other nations, make international cooperation difficult, and make repression of the cultural and political minorities unavoidable. Excessive preoccupation with increasing individual self-control, in terms of personal salvation, could diminish the energy required for achieving social goals. A conscious direction of the development process should attempt to maximize gains in all three aspects simultaneously. The evolution of such a model, I thought, could be possible in the East, if enough inventiveness was deployed for this purpose and if full advantage of Western experience was taken into consideration.

NOTE

1. It is now apparent that the two papers meant different things by the term "Western model." While I understood by it a cultural and institutional complex, Professor Lerner meant by it increasing industrialization, urbanization, literacy, mass media, and popular participation (Lerner and Schramm 1972: 114). Thus, by defining exposure to the Western model in this way, Professor Lerner could rightly claim universality for it. But apparently the 1964 conference was, on this issue, the victim of a serious gap of communication.

3e. *Toward a New Paradigm*

DANIEL LERNER

Just ten years ago, during the first conference on Communication and Change, I wrote a new preface for the paperback edition of *The Passing of Traditional Society*. This preface concluded: "The best service a model can render is to hasten its own obsolescence by leading to a better one. I look forward to this outcome in due course" (Lerner 1964, p. x). That the paradigm proposed by that book has proved useful to scholars over the past two decades makes me happy. That it has "hastened its own obsolescence" by leading to more comprehensive data-mapping and more specified inferences makes me happier still.

My disagreement with Dr. Eisenstadt, therefore, involves no defense of the "old paradigm," of which I am alleged to be one of the perpetrators, but rather a conception of how to move toward the "new paradigm." Our differences may be merely terminological. If so, it is important to set the terms of discourse straight, for they refer to two fundamental questions: (1) How does social science work? (2) What is the proper work of social science?

How Social Science Works: "Continuities"

The concept of "continuities" as the generic mode of work for all sciences was proposed by R. K. Merton.[1] Its key terms are replication, cumulation, continuity. Its lesson is that any useful paradigm does not come to an *ending;* it goes through a continuous *passing*—by retesting, revalidating, reformulating.

A good example of scientific continuity was given to this conference, ten years ago, by Dr. Schramm. In his paper (with W. L. Ruggels) entitled "How

Mass Media Systems Grow," Dr. Schramm retested the paradigm I had proposed in *The Passing*. Here are his words:

> One of the fascinating findings is that urbanization seems, on the basis of 1961 data, no longer to be so basic to the growth of literacy and the mass media as Lerner had found it to be on the basis of data approximately ten years older. The question is raised whether the spread of transistor radios, roads, and rapid transportation into the villages, overleaping illiteracy barriers and effectively reducing distance, have not made urbanization less essential to the general growth pattern.
>
> The more basic import of this chapter, however, is that our concept of the growth pattern of mass media in relation to other elements of society may have been too simple. There is serious doubt that any single pattern will explain the differences that appear to exist by regions and cultures. (Lerner and Schramm 1972, p. 57)

These words are both scientific and sage. They are scientific in that they report a replication with newer and fuller data; a cumulation by comparing the old and new findings; a reformulation of differences between the old and new in terms of a hypothesis capable of explaining these differences. They are sage because they counsel us to be wary of monolithic theorizing and to respect the "scientific pluralism" that promotes replication, cumulation, continuity.[2] This leads to the second fundamental question on which I beg to differ with Dr. Eisenstadt.

The Proper Work of Social Science: "Regularities"

It is my view that the proper work of social science is the finding of *regularities* in the human condition—those common characteristics that unify human beings everywhere despite the endless diversity of the characteristics that differentiate them. This is the view put forward most eloquently by the late, great anthropologist Clyde Kluckhohn in his essay "Common Humanity and Diverse Cultures" (Lerner 1959, chap. 9). I fear that Dr. Eisenstadt's injunction that we seek "culture-specific" findings may be interpreted in ways that will divert social science from its proper work.

A great, though nameless, sage taught us that in *every* man there are some things he has in common with *all* other men, with *some* other men, with *no* other man. The first is mainly the province of physiology, which deals with such universal human functions as breathing and sleeping, digestion and excretion. The third is mainly the province of clinical psychology, which deals with individual "deviants" from collective "norms" in specified contexts. Between the everyman of physiologists and the only man of clinicians lies the vast range of beliefs and behaviors that every living person shares with *some* other living persons. These are the stuff from which we must fashion the "regularities" that are the proper work of social science.

I fear that Dr. Eisenstadt's advocacy of the "culture-specific" will divert the quest for a new paradigm onto an abandoned sidetrack. This danger to social theory and research, while important to all of us as scholars, is magnified by its potential impedance of development policy and strategy. Recall the reaction of an intelligent and irate Samoan to a Western anthropologist lamenting the passing of old ways: "What do you want us to do, pickle our culture in formaldehyde for you?"

The point is that our critical need for development theory and research, development policy and strategy, is not "culture-specific" but "culture-interactive." While the world is not yet, or soon to become, a "global village," it is true that nowadays there is "no place to hide." The era of the "first world communication network" is upon us. It involves not only the high communication technology of satellites, but the traditional communication technology of talking together (aided by jet aircraft) that enables us, for example, to reassemble here ten years later.

Again, our present conference illustrates the point. Ten years ago, Inayatullah presented the conference with a ringing demand that we concert our efforts "Toward A Non-Western Model of Development" (Lerner and Schramm 1972, chap. 7). This strong demand by our Pakistani conferee was explained—only an apparent paradox, given the friendship among international conferees—by our Indian conferee, S. C. Dube, who quite properly pointed out:

> Many of these countries have acquired national independence through struggles that were intensely anti-Western. Hatred for Western domination was accompanied invariably by antipathy for things Western. Revival of native traditions —historical or mythical—was an important objective of their struggle for the achievement of national independence.

While sympathetic to Inayatullah's depiction of the past and present—although the phrase "cultural imperialism" applied to development aid raised my hackles then and does so now—I went to great length in my own chapter to exorcise the nativistic spirit that underlay many of these hatreds. I pointed out that ethnocentrism and xenophobia are no more admirable in the underdeveloped East than in the overdeveloped West. I rejected the spurious dichotomy between "spiritual East" and "material West" because what much of the developing East wants is precisely those material goods that became available first, by historical happenstance, in the West. What we needed, then as now, is neither a Western nor a non-Western but a global "development model"—with all the variations that people work upon theoretical paradigms as they go about their business of living. (Lerner and Schramm 1972, chap. 8).

This time Inayatullah comes to us not with a hot demand, but with a cool question: "Is there an Asian pattern of development?" His answer does not follow the path of Eisenstadt's priority to the "culture-specific" but rather of Kluckhohn's concern for "common humanity and diverse cultures." Readers of Inayatullah's preceding comment and later paper on "Western, Asian, or Global Models of Development" will perceive that both of us have learned much in the past ten years—and largely by interaction with each other. From strident emphasis on our "culture-specific" differences we have moved toward acceptance of "regularities" in the human condition. This is the way any new paradigm, worthy of general acceptance, will go.

NOTES

1. See our joint paper "Social Scientists and Research Policy" in Lerner and Lasswell 1951; also the series of books under the title Continuities in Social Science, which Robert K. Merton initiated for The Free Press.

2. It is relevant to note that a volume of the most important replications of *The Passing of Traditional Society* over the years is being prepared for the "Continuities" series of The Free Press.

B. FOUR PATHS TO DEVELOPMENT

First among the "four paths to development" discussed in our conference was the Comilla experience in Bangladesh, surely one of our world's most hurt and troubled areas. It was led, appropriately, by Akhter Hameed Khan, founder of the Comilla Academy and its revered leader for thirteen years. With the humility of Gandhi, in whose pantheon he belongs—partly *because* of his Muslim heritage—Dr. Khan gave us an excessively modest account of Comilla's achievements. Fortunately, the best of his "disciples" were trained by him to become independent and articulate "spokesmen." Two of these—Rahim of Bangladesh, Inayatullah of Pakistan—were among our conferees. Their comments stimulated Dr. Khan to respond in terms of "The Models We Studied," which dealt as well with their comments as with the overall "rethinking" in Part A.

A "second path to development" is laid out in the heartening account of what a "Mothers' Club" has been able to accomplish in a Republic of Korea village. As told by D.L. Kincaid and June Ock Yum, this path presages fruitful activity—other than childbearing—for women throughout Asia. We have seen that the "population explosion" that plagues poor and populous countries can be brought under control by public policy, as in Taiwan. This paper, which reports what may be the most important women's movement since the ancient Greek drama of *Lysistrata,* has already found "resonance" among women in many parts of Asia and the Pacific.

Dr. Dube's review of the past ten years in India is sobering and analytical, but does present a "third path to development." In the conference, he was questioned sharply by Kusum Nair, many of whose questions remain to be answered.

So do the many questions raised by the "fourth path to development" represented by Mao's China. Godwin Chu's paper raised pointed queries among the conferees. Tillman Durdin, after forty years of observing China, asked: "How Durable Is Mao's Policy?" Harry Oshima, contrasting China's with Japan's economic experience in managing team work, asked: "How Workable Is Mao's Strategy?" Part B concludes with a reconsideration of China's experience with development communication by Schramm, Chu, and Yu. Within the global framework of development effort, they ask: "How Transferable Is It?"

4. The Comilla Experience in Bangladesh—My Lessons in Communication

AKHTER HAMEED KHAN

Experience of Pilot Projects

For thirteen years I worked in a rural development academy in Comilla, and now I am working in Peshawar. I have, therefore, more than a decade of experience to review, but first I must admit its limitations. Primarily we were concerned with pilot projects. Our projects obviously were hothouse plants—or, to change the metaphor, little islands in a stormy sea. Much was achieved with great effort in small areas. However, when our models were duplicated elsewhere, we helplessly watched their distortion—or waited patiently while others of our models, auspicious and promising in our eyes, were indifferently ignored. As experimenters, we found both fulfillment and frustration in ample measure.

Our Low Status

In our country's hierarchy, our Comilla Academy did not rank high. As its director I was picturesquely designated as the head of a subordinate office. Now and then I escaped from the straitjacket because I had the peculiar good fortune of having resigned long ago from the prestigious Imperial Civil Service. Surprisingly its halo still clung to my head. My old colleagues, sitting in superior positions, treated me as an equal, not as a subordinate. One of them, then the chief secretary, acceded to my requests for cooperation—remarking succinctly, "You are a fool, but a good fool. So I will let you go ahead." For my part, I had enough discretion to ask for a little at a time, never too much. When I implored him to give us one thana, a small administrative unit, as a laboratory, we got a thana. Later, when we desired to experiment with a big unit, the district, we were put off. The director of the academy was tolerated by the poor thana officers, but he was sent home by the mighty district officers.

Our Many-Sided View

Notwithstanding his low status, the director, from the academy's vantage point, had a many-sided view of rural development. It was indeed a complex process. It did not begin and end, as some experts imply, with the villagers. Our rural development, like the Holy Ganges, originated in the heights and wound its tedious way through many political and bureaucratic jungles. In our pilot projects I dealt with five partners, as I called them. First and foremost were the high officials, those who made or unmade policies, the ministers and secretaries. The academy, more or less, was their handmaiden, or call girl. They were our taskmasters. They defined the problems and fixed the framework of solutions. We could, at best, slightly modify or refine and polish. The second partners were the rulers' mentors, the foreign advisers and experts. As paymasters they usually dictated the timing. The third partners were lower officers, whose low morale mattered more than the good intentions at the top. The fourth partners were the academy's instructors, the researchers and trainers, a bright and conceited group. And last, but of course not least, were the villagers—with their schisms and factions, their passionate prejudices, their exaggerated hopes and fears. Perforce the director had to be a juggler of words.

Communicating with the Instructors

My lesson in communication began with the instructors. Before arriving in Comilla, we had spent one whole year at Michigan State University, supposedly learning our future job. Although that proved rather elusive, we learned a good deal about each other. Our group was composed mostly of sharp-witted youths, proud and ambitious. Apart from prospects of promotion, we talked much about academic freedom, which meant our supremacy. Decked with foreign diplomas, we thought we were peacocks of paradise. In reality we were doubly alienated. While we regarded the bureaucrats with contempt tinged with jealousy, we regarded the villagers with contempt tinged with pity. Our doctors of philosophy had grandiose notions of research: programming computers and marshaling armies of investigators. My humble suggestions of personal visits, walking tours, and camps were viewed as an affront, as though I proposed turning doctors into nurses. If I had been a simple bureaucrat I would have been overwhelmed. Luckily my own experience as a college teacher saved me. They could not pin me down. Having been both a magistrate and a professor, I was a nimble bat, a beast as well as a bird. Moreover, I knew the villagers better than the youngsters did. I tried my best to bridge the gulf between the instructors, the officers, and the villagers. Thanks to the enthusiasm of some of my colleagues, I succeeded to a limited extent. The tensions, however, did not disappear. Keeping together the academy and the projects, my plight was like that of a polygamous patriarch whose peace is much disturbed by *zenana* bickerings.

COMMUNICATING WITH THE OFFICERS

The disdain of the academics was reciprocated by the bureaucrats. Our trainees asserted that they knew more about rural problems than the instructors, and denied that quotations from foreign books were relevant. We swallowed this bitter pill, and in the course of time improved our qualifications by survey and action research. Our pilot projects served as valid examples. It was well known that farmers are not convinced without lifelike demonstrations. We discovered that officers were equally wary of verbal theorems. Gradually we earned their attention, but we could do little about their low morale. They had too many grievances. They feared but did not respect their superiors, the directors. Familiarity with the villagers had bred more contempt than affection. Their view was generally dark and despairing. After observing our best efforts, they shook their heads and said: "This is good, but our department, our directors, think differently. They will not let us work. You should convince them first." And they spoke the truth. In the rare case when the secretary of a department, the policy-maker, sincerely embraced our model, and exerted himself to cooperate, the morale of the field staff rose rapidly. Only in such a case did the academy serve as a bridge between the making and the implementation of policy. That exceptional secretary, alas, did not last long.

COMMUNICATING WITH THE SECRETARIES

At that time the departmental secretaries were pivots of government. If ministers were gods, the secretaries were prophets. Recently they have suffered a fall, but ten years ago they were riding on high horses. They usually belonged to the elite civil service. There was little doubt about their intelligence or competence, or about their hubristic insolence. However, as pullers of all the strings, they themselves were woefully overstretched. The system seized them like a boa constrictor. They rushed from one time-consuming meeting to another, and, in between, read heaps of files and received numberless visitors and telephone calls. Always busy counting the trees, they never saw the woods.

Evening after evening, in the company of elaborately dressed wives, they attended long dinner parties. Their minds were whirls of platitudes and trite opinions; their careers were games of musical chairs. Flitting from job to job, they acquired a lack of commitment, a butterfly mentality. Spiritually identical to their inferiors, they at heart too were skeptical of, and indifferent to, rural progress. However, that did not prevent them from sponsoring short-term, flamboyant plans. As a matter of fact, the ministers, the secretaries, and many foreign mentors loved to promote quick miracles. Their favorite slogan was: "Nothing was done before us; everything will be done by us." Perhaps they knew too well that before long they would be safely gone. The academy, after years of experiments, offered improved models for agriculture, education, and health. Although we solicited many secretaries, none took us seriously. We could not communicate with butterflies.

Communicating with the Villagers

For me it was easiest to communicate with the villagers. Although I spoke their language with an accent, I never felt or was viewed as an alien. I loved the great outdoors. Reading and walking were my two passions. To march fifteen miles on short rations was for me an agreeable task. As an amateur ascetic, I admired the patience and puritanism of the peasants. As an amateur Islamist, I admired their living faith. At the same time I had no romantic illusions about them. I realized clearly the need for reform, for new attitudes and institutions. Yet I was not a blind Westernizer. I had excluded from my own life those Western mannerisms by which our privileged elite isolated themselves from the common people. I had escaped from the golden ghetto when I abandoned imperial service. Therefore I was at home everywhere.

I have mentioned how my boss, the chief secretary, agreed to my requests because he thought I was a good fool. On another occasion, an eighty-year-old villager told me: "Sahib, we have been cheated many times. Now again you are asking us to put our money in the cooperatives. It is a risk. But you seem to be a good man. We will run the risk for your sake." After him, everyone in that village joined the cooperative. I often visited the patriarch, and when he died I missed him. There were many others like him who valued my human worth, not my office or patronage. Trust, not cleverness, was the medium of communication.

Refining and Reconstructing

The academy's instructors were social scientists, not technicians. We applied ourselves first to a thorough examination of our area. Then we undertook, as handmaidens, to refine and polish departmental programs. Through protracted observation we found that, broadly speaking, there were two major weaknesses in them. In the first place, although the objectives were unexceptionable, many assumptions were unreal. Secondly, the mechanism of persuasion and execution was defective.

We refined the assumptions and reconstructed the mechanism. For us, the participation of our clientele was a *sine qua non*, an indispensable condition. We discovered that this was dependent on the formation of groups and institutions, which in turn depended on the regular and continuous training of group representatives and institutional leaders. To find true representatives was imperative, for, in our villages, wolves quickly volunteered to herd the sheep. It was their traditional privilege. For the peasants and laborers, the emergence of leaders from their own ranks was the fulcrum of uplift.

These generalizations may appear vague and disjointed. Nonetheless they are drawn from real experience. Perhaps a discussion of specific programs may elucidate. I will, therefore, describe how we hobbled along a tortuous path.

"Basic Democracy"

The first program we dabbled in was local government. It was then supremely important because it happened to be our president's favorite concubine. He had inherited the outlook of British proconsuls, who, in the imperial era, praised the simple rural folk and derided the upstart urbanites. Like the proconsuls, he wanted to put down the "townies" and lift up the "rustics." He aspired to find a political base in the countryside, but, cast in the mold of an old viceroy, he was not a master builder like Chairman Mao. Our rural champion antagonized the urban classes, but could not attract or organize the rural masses. His basic democracy made the local councillors electors of president and parliament. Local government could hardly survive such inflation. It was an attempt to cover the sheep of local government with the bull of national politics. As a result, the poor sheep died an unnatural death.

A Local Government Model

Difficult as it was to separate the president's Siamese twins, we endeavored to evolve a good local government model. We made it realistic by reducing the second tier from a subdivision to a thana, from five hundred to one hundred square miles. We made it effective by constituting a Thana Training and Development Center (TTDC), where departmental officers joined hands with elected representatives. We made it significant by entrusting it, as the foremost task, with the construction of the infrastructure works of drainage, link roads, and irrigation.

The combination of local government, departmental services, and infrastructure works made the model active and popular. It no longer remained a bombastic figment. Participation was secured and sustained by means of innumerable training classes, reinforced by simplified instructional material. The impact of the TTDC and the infrastructure works was felt quickly and widely. For a short while, before the political explosion, development assumed the shape of a movement.

Of course the council leadership was firmly in the hands of the dominant class. Impatient intellectuals blamed us for conspiring with Kulaks. Our learned professors did not realize that traditional leaders cannot be displaced until the underdogs learn to fend for themselves. As for the much-denounced corruption, that also descended, like the Holy Ganges, from the Himalayan summits. Being no more than low-caste clerks, we could not teach the high-caste rajahs.

Increased Agricultural Production

Undoubtedly our government's most pressing need was increased agricultural production. Two programs had strived to achieve it: community development and agricultural extension. The first relied upon multipurpose workers and village councils; the second relied upon agricultural assistants and supply of inputs. There was much rivalry between the two. Now, after ten years, the community developers were slinking off, while the agriculturists were preening themselves to solve the food problem in two years.

Their proposals were precise: more assistants, more demonstration plots, more teaching of improved methods, more supplies. Thus in two or at most three years, most farmers would use better seeds, more credit, more fertilizers, more water, and better cultural practices. They would easily produce two or three extra million tons of grain. Unfortunately the goal that seemed seductively near at the beginning was tantalizingly distant at the end of the stipulated period.

Reconditioning of Agricultural Programs

We reconditioned agricultural programs by adding three new links: the TTDC, the works program, and the small farmers' cooperatives. The TTDC not only brought services and supplies closer to the villages; it also coordinated them better. The works program removed hurdles and started the sequence of progression. Believers in agricultural extension ignored these hurdles, or assumed that someone else should remove them. Our research proved that, in most villages without substantial infrastructure works, preaching of improved agronomy was putting the cart before the horse. Finally, the cooperatives obtained zealous involvement of the small farmers, which could not be obtained either by community development multipurpose workers or by the agricultural assistants.

Promoted comprehensively in the above three ways, production increased in our project—at first slowly, and later rapidly. It was perceptible and well documented. But our demonstration did not convince the Department of Agriculture. They smiled at our obsession with groups and institutions and stuck firmly to their five "firsts." All the time they continued to predict a solution in two years. I understand they are doing it to this day.

Reconditioning the Cooperative System

Cooperatives in our country were as old as agricultural extension and as ineffective. Although introduced originally to save peasants from moneylenders, the societies had been captured by the big farmers, the new moneylenders, and the traders. On the whole these societies were not of much interest or benefit to peasant proprietors. We reconditioned the old system for their sake, and made the cooperative into the small producers' trade union, the forum for their managerial and technical training, and the vehicle for accumulating and investing capital. Thus defined, the objectives became understandable to the peasants.

The institutional framework for ensuring these objectives comprised weekly meetings of each group, weekly thrift deposits, selection of a manager and a model farmer from the group, weekly training of managers and model farmers at the thana centers, and finally a federation of the village societies in the thana. We proceeded cautiously in the beginning because the task of organizing peasant farmers was both novel and difficult. The first societies, the nuclei, formed very slowly, but afterwards the clusters grew and spread all around. We found our peasants as ready for group discipline as our factory workers. Generally our cooperatives, unlike the local councils, were not dominated by the big farmers.

These cooperatives created a new awareness and new leaders. Naturally the moneylenders, traders, and contractors became hostile. They were firmly linked with the urban political leaders. I often feared that they would one day undo our work.

Training New Leaders

The nerve center of our movement was the weekly village meeting and the weekly TTDC training class. The former created group cohesion, the latter gave constant impetus. With the formation of groups, the scope for managerial and technical skill expanded. The managers and model farmers were carriers of a new activism. They were emergent leaders. Their orientation was different from that of the traditional leaders. The new leaders were not self-advancing touts; they were well-controlled emissaries. They were organizers, not petitioners. Their connection with the TTDC, renewed every week, was the fruitful contact of students with teachers. The gathering at the center fastened the new leaders in a fraternal and professional bond.

We replaced the government village-level worker, who in reality supervised five villages, with a manager and a model farmer for each village, chosen by the group itself. Each manager and model farmer was trained directly by the TTDC experts. In a manner of speaking, an inefficient middle man in the delivery of advice and supplies was eliminated. Thus a major step was taken toward the peasants' self-management and self-reliance. However, the prospect of fewer government "workers" did not at all please the departments. Instinctively they hated decentralization, delegation, and autonomy. And they ardently desired their own battalions of assistants.

Application to Family Planning

In the family-planning program, we made a threefold application of our technique of finding, training, and utilizing rural talent. For commercial distribution of contraceptives, shopkeepers and others were appointed as commission agents. We easily found more than 400 agents for our 300 villages. Within a year they were selling 50,000 condoms monthly. For educative publicity we enlisted village poets and singers to go reciting from market to market. A comparison of their rhetoric and logic with that of government publicists was highly instructive. For access to the segregated Muslim wives, we selected village midwives.

These midwives were generally illiterate and destitute women who supervised the birth of children. Their profession was considered mainly as a menial job of cleaning filth. About 150 enrolled, gladly came every week, and patiently learned the principles of hygiene and the alphabet. Just by teaching them to pare their nails and use dettol, I am sure we saved many lives. After a year of weekly coaching they began to look and behave like midwives, not like scavengers. Furthermore, they persuaded hundreds of women to use an intrauterine device and sold thousands of contraceptives every month. In our area the gross birth rate showed a documented decline between 1964 and 1968. After that came the deluge!

Training the Imams as Teachers

We trained the imams (prayer leaders) as teachers of adults and children. Every Muslim village had a mosque and an imam. In olden days he was both a spiritual and secular teacher. A hundred years of British rule deprived him of his secular role. He was gradually cribbed and confined to religious rituals, and the confinement made him an obscurantist. He opposed all innovations as foreign evils. As the villagers remained deeply religious, the obscurantism of the imams caused national schizophrenia. It was essential to involve the imams in the process of development.

As soon as an integral teaching function was assigned to them, their response was as positive as that of the midwives. The imams willingly came to the training classes at the TTDC and learned teaching methods, Islamic and world history, general science, agriculture, animal husbandry, et cetera. They became scrupulous teachers of cooperative members and their children. It seemed to us that we had found the key for solving the intractable problem of rural illiteracy. But the department of education thought otherwise. Our educational brahmins regarded the imams as untouchables. They insisted that unless the imams tied the sacred thread of matriculation, they could not be admitted as teachers.

Up and Down the Spiral

Our programs for women, youths, and artisans were organized on similar lines. It is wearisome to repeat the story. I learned much by practice in Comilla. Now, like an old tart, I am selling in Peshawar the wrinkled charms of thana centers, works programs, village cooperatives, weekly meetings, thrift deposits, training classes, and so forth. I am meeting the same response and resistance as if I were living again in the 1960s.

I have heard of a spiral of progress. If there is such a spiral then we are, like toy monkeys, going up and down, up and down it. In the India of my youth, compassionate Hindus maintained decrepit cows in *go-shalas* (cow homes). To my jaundiced eyes some national governments and world organizations look like *go-shalas* for the venerable cows of rural uplift, community development, agricultural extension, and adult education. The fact that I am on display here in Honolulu this week reminds me that I am an ancient cow myself—thin, mangy, and feeble.

4a. *Factors Related to the Success of Comilla*

INAYATULLAH

Apparently the conclusions of my principal chapter in this volume, that Western technical assistance stifles creativity in Asian countries, are contradicted by the success of Comilla. All the conditions unfavorable to creativity appeared to be present there. Michigan State University (MSU) was associated with the development of the academy and its program from its very inception; a team including several MSU professors devised the original program. The Ford Foundation and International Cooperation Administration (ICA, predecessor of AID) provided financial assistance. Most of the faculty of the academy stayed at MSU for about a year; later, several staff members went there for graduate studies. The director of the academy generally welcomed foreign assistance, and several American advisers worked at the academy for different periods of time. At its initial formative stage, there were two American advisers working closely with its faculty.

If, then, all the circumstances that stifle local creativity, according to my hypothesis, were present, how could one explain the success of Comilla? How did this innovation emerge under such unfavorable circumstances? I suggest that deeper analysis of the Comilla program will support my hypothesis, as I hope to show in the following pages. Four basic factors explain the success of Comilla; all are directly or indirectly related to my hypothesis.

Personality of the Innovator

Probably the most crucial factor was the personality of Dr. Akhter Hameed Khan, the acknowledged source of all of Comilla's significant innovations.

Certain characteristics of his personality were conducive to an innovative leadership role.

It may be recalled that Dr. Khan resigned from Indian civil service in order to live a virtuous life as well as to serve the common man. This early resignation from the most prestigious service in India on the basis of personal idealism reflected his decision to opt for a creative life rather than the routinized life of a bureaucrat. It shows a high level of what Max Weber called "this-worldly asceticism."

Khan gave up the life of material comfort and glory and opted for a life of material deprivation and discomfort in response to an inner calling to serve an ideal. Had Khan adjusted to the demands and pressures of bureaucratic life, as several of his contemporaries did, his idealism would have been compromised and, like his other colleagues in the service, he would have lost the innovative capacity and creativity that he put to work in Comilla seventeen years later.

In his religious beliefs, Khan has shown a critical orientation. He was born into a traditional Muslim family and at one time worked with a very activist Islamic movement, the Khaksars. But devotion to traditional Islam could not survive his considerable study of other religions—especially Buddhism, which, sometimes jokingly and sometimes seriously, he announces to be his religion. Simultaneously, he admires Tolstoy, Lenin, Mao, mystics, and revolutionaries, reflecting impatience with dogmas and doctrines. Dr. Khan is an erudite scholar, well read in the literary classics of East and West, and the history of India, the Islamic world, and Europe. He has studied Islamic jurisprudence from its original sources.

The above description of some aspects of Khan's life shows an openness to cultural influences emanating from many modern and traditional sources, a capacity to establish direct contact with rural people, and a strong inner urge to live for an ideal. These characteristics proved an asset in the initiation of the Comilla experiment, which required originality of thinking, hard work, devotion to a cause, contact with rural masses, and a disposition to learn from them. A personality confined by the bureaucratic role, purely fed on Western or traditional knowledge, and alienated from the masses by comfortable living conditions, could not have become the source of such an innovation.

Autonomy of The Academy

A second factor that explains Comilla's success is the high degree of autonomy that the academy enjoyed within the existing bureaucratic system of Pakistan, which was more oriented to the maintenance of the status quo than to change. If the academy could not break through the shackles of this system, it would not have produced the innovative program it did. True, the academy was formally a subordinate organization within the governmental machinery. But Dr. Khan's status as a former civil service officer and his reputation as a devoted social worker and visionary won him the high regard of civil servants in both the provincial and the central governments. He had access to all senior servants and exercised great influence with them. This is evident from the fact that, when the academy program was subjected to serious criticism by its board of governors for deviating from its prescribed role, Dr. Khan could, through his former colleagues, persuade the governor of East Pakistan to support and save the program.

This type of trust was needed only at the initial stage of the work. Once the usefulness of the Comilla experiment had been demonstrated, then autonomy was conceded as a right. The then president of Pakistan, Ayub Khan, publicly praised Comilla Academy's work and assured Dr. Khan of all support. From this stage onward, nobody could interfere with the academy's plans and innovations. The academy had also established mutually supportive links with the Planning Commission, which sought its help and advice to experiment with new programs. This linkage enhanced the academy's professional autonomy rather than curtailed it.

The academy also enjoyed a high degree of autonomy in its relationship with Michigan State University, the Ford Foundation, and other agencies for technical assistance. The assistance flowed in to support the programs evolved by the academy, and usually it was the academy that determined what aid to accept and on what terms. As high a degree of autonomy as the academy enjoyed, however, autonomy itself would not have led to innovation if innovative capacity had not preexisted in the leader.

"Localization" of Scholars

A third factor was the demonstrated capacity of the academy to "localize" American advisers and American-trained instructors by forcing them out of their ivory towers. In the first half-year of its establishment, the academy required instructors to visit villages frequently, to invite farmers in groups to the academy, and to thus learn *from them* about their problems. There was a certain degree of resistance by some faculty members whom Khan calls "peacocks of paradise decked with foreign diplomas." But Khan, with his unusual persuasive powers, could overcome this resistance and convince both American advisers and the faculty to accept a more innovative and challenging role. Gradually the faculty broke out of its academic shell and established direct contact with rural reality. The proficiency of American advisers and local instructors in social science techniques was put to the best use for identifying problems, for generating empirical data on rural communities, and for evaluating the effectiveness of the academy's program. The social research was tightly geared to the innovative role Dr. Khan's vision gave to the academy.

Openness to Different Models

Without adopting a single model, the leadership of the academy studied and absorbed the spirit of several models of development. This was very unusual under the circumstances prevailing in the 1950s, given the political climate of Pakistan and the dominant influence of the American technical assistance program. This openness to several models—without uncritical commitment to relate their different elements to the solution of local problems—proved to be a crucial factor in ensuring the success of the Comilla program.

I think all four conditions were both sufficient and necessary. Without the presence of critical analytical orientation, devotion to a cause, and urge to help the rural people in the innovator, the presence of other conditions would not have led to the desired results. Without the necessary autonomy, the innovator would not have been free to test his ideas, and the innovations would have been nipped in the bud; at least one attempt was made in this direction. Without localization of the scholars, necessary research for developing and testing the usefulness of the program would not have emerged. Finally, an uncritical commitment to a single model would not have permitted the synthesis that emerged.

4b. *"Top-Down" Communication in the Comilla Project*

SYED A. RAHIM

While he directed the Comilla Academy, Dr. Khan was fond of using the phrase "priming the pump." He was the man who took the responsibility for priming the "local pumps of rural development" in Comilla, which, once started, would generate local action and participation. Dr. Khan had clearly set out a number of interrelated ideas and principles on rural development. Whenever he went out to the villages, he talked about these ideas in very simple terms, using many rural analogies. Initially, the communication in Comilla was from the top down. It was essential to prime the pumps, so that self-sustaining local action could be generated.

The importance of top-down communication should not be underestimated. It is necessary to start the engine of local initiative and action. Once local participation is initiated, open communication in all directions is necessary to strengthen and maintain it. Experiences in Tanzania and China clearly show that ideological communication from the party cadres to the people is essential both for generating and for sustaining local action.

To bring the story up to date, I will report that the Comilla model has been accepted by the government of Bangladesh as the basis of a national program known as the Integrated Rural Development Program and is included in the first five-year plan of Bangladesh. The objective is to introduce the Comilla type of cooperative in large numbers of thanas in Bangladesh. The pilot project in Comilla is still running under the guidance of the Bangladesh Academy for Rural Development. But I think that the dynamism of the pilot project, the innovative experimentation in Comilla, has diminished due to the absence of Dr. Khan.

4c. *The Models We Studied*

AKHTER HAMEED KHAN

1. Pakistan inherited the following fundamental rural problems:

   A. Chronic or acute food shortage, previously called "famine"

   B. The twin issues of privilege and poverty: unequal distribution of income disparities

   C. Growing distress leading to dangerous unrest: rural revolt, agrarian revolution

2. Closely related to the above problems as causes and effects were the following:

   D. Inadequate administrative infrastructure

   E. Inadequate physical infrastructure: isolation; inadequate irrigation, drainage, and roads

   F. Miserable educational, medical, and social conditions

   G. Alarming population growth since 1950

3. Rural development basically was an attempt to solve these problems. Generally it comprised the following:

   A. Higher agricultural productivity

   B. Land reforms

   C. Institution building (especially local government)

   D. Improved rural administration

   E. Building of physical infrastructure

   F. Educational, medical, and welfare programs

   G. Population control

4. In the contemporary world, many other countries had similar programs. The successful models of rural development that we studied carefully were:

A. Japan
B. Taiwan
C. Israel
D. Some East European countries, e.g., Yugoslavia
E. The People's Republic of China

5. More recently, the Chinese model has appeared to be most effective in most respects.

5. The Needle and the Ax—Communication and Development in a Korean Village

D. LAWRENCE KINCAID AND JUNE OCK YUM

> In the past, it took over a week to plant the rice in our stony field, but this year in cooperation with one another we finished in one day. . . . At the meetings I can hear something useful for our life and I am encouraged and hopeful when someone says that we can lead a better life in the future by working hard today.
>
> Park Kyung Ai

> [They learned] . . . to be dutiful to their parents-in-law, to take better care of their husbands, and knowledge of their children's education. . . . The Mothers' Club enlightens the people to save money: this is the basic spirit of the club.
>
> Chung In Chul

The woman and the man who made the above statements both live in the small Korean village of Oryu Li. They are married to one another, and they are describing the same thing: how the organization and struggle of the Mothers' Club contributed to the development and quality of life in their village. Yet they seem to be talking about two entirely different things. In a sense this is true, as we shall see below.

This paper makes four points relevant to the process of socioeconomic development and modernization:

1. that the process of development and modernization means different things to different people and contains a mixture of both modern and traditional human values;
2. that women can make a difference in this process if they are well organized and given support;

3. that development does not occur immediately in response to the external input of resources, but occurs over time from the struggle to find better solutions to critical life problems; and
4. that the development of the capacity to use communication for development—to gather, transform, and create new information to solve social and economic problems—is more important than economic growth per se since it is a prerequisite for viable, self-sustaining economic growth over time.

Support for these four basic themes of communication and development come not from a generalizable sample of nations, nor individuals within one nation, but rather from one small village in Korea. Hence, the lessons to be learned rely heavily upon the intrinsic theoretical relevance of this case, and not upon the usual criteria of regularity or reproducibility of the development pattern to be described. We will compare the village of Oryu Li only to itself at different points in time. The purpose of this paper, then, is to present a concrete, illustrative case of socioeconomic development on the village level in order to shed light upon the most general processes of communication and development.

Background

To understand the case of Oryu Li requires some knowledge of its specific historical and socioeconomic context. In many respects Korean culture was traditionally more Confucian than that of China. Before contact with Western cultures in the late nineteenth century, woman's place in society was accurately described by the Korean word for housewife, "inside person." It was strictly improper for women to take the initiative in activities outside their own homes. They existed without status until they produced sons for their husbands. Family life was guided by the five Confucian virtues of proper relationships: between lord and subject, father and son, husband and wife, elders and juniors, and friends. Woman's role was always subordinate, first to her father, then to her husband, and finally to her eldest son.

Change began slowly after contact with Western culture in the late nineteenth century, increasing greatly in scope during the Japanese annexation from 1910 to 1945, the disruption caused by the Korean War from 1950 to 1953, and the American influence during the reconstruction era. "When the whales fight, the shrimp suffers," is an old Korean proverb that rather concisely describes that nation's traditional relationship with the large superpowers in Asia that surround it. This pattern worked to the Koreans' advantage in the 1960s, however, when the dramatic economic growth of Japan and the stability in the relationships of China, Russia, and the United States created a good environment for their own economic growth.

From 1960 to 1970, the average rate of growth of Korea's Gross Domestic Product was 8.9 percent. The birthrate declined during this same period from 43 to 29 per 1,000 population. Per capita income reached $261 by 1971, and the net rate of population growth today is around 1.9 percent. The rapid rate of industrialization during the 1960s was accompanied by such rapid urban immigration that almost 50 percent of the Republic of Korea's 35 million people were living in urban areas by 1974. The changes were so great that one of the world's most densely populated countries actually suffered from a labor shortage in the rural sector in the first few years of the 1970s.

To restore their country's rural-urban equilibrium and improve the rural standard of living, the government launched the national SaeMaul Undong, or New Village Movement, in 1970, to mobilize the human and material resources of the villages for their own development.

The Story of Oryu Li

Oryu Li used to be known as the poorest village from the poorest township in ImSil County, Jeon Ra Bug Province.[1] Five hundred twenty people live there in 103 households snuggled tightly between the community rice paddy and the slopes at the base of the mountains. In 1968, each household had barely one-half hectare of land, whereas the average for the rest of the province was almost twice that. Because of their lack of resources and level of poverty, most villagers could not afford to send their children to middle school or high school. Over the last decade most of the young men and women from Oryu Li were forced to leave for the city to find jobs as factory workers or housekeepers.

Eighty households are members of the dominant Kang family clan. The next largest family clan, the Yoo clan, consists of only eleven households. In 1968, the village clan structure was one of the major obstacles to development. According to Chang Young, husband of the Mothers' Club leader:

> This village was once well known for its lack of cooperation, because of the tight family clan system and its location next to the train station. But now, because of the Mothers' Club activities, there is much better cooperation today. Their leader accomplished this by enlightening the other village women who did not understand the advantages of cooperation, and by minimizing the importance of clan membership for village improvement.

The development of Oryu Li did not occur overnight; it began with the organization of the village Mothers' Club in 1968 and reached its present level of cohesion and activity only after considerable struggle and personal sacrifice by its members. By looking at the events and problems that have occurred since 1968, we can identify the patterns of actions and reactions that eventually strengthened the Mothers' Club as a force for village solidarity and socioeconomic development.

Organization

Formal organization of the Oryu Li Mothers' Club was accomplished with one meeting during the visit of the township secretary and the provincial field agent of the Planned Parenthood Federation of Korea (PPFK). The PPFK organized over 12,000 Mothers' Clubs in rural villages throughout Korea in 1968, and the number has grown steadily to over 24,000 in 1974 (or over one-half of Korea's natural villages). The four initial objectives of the Mothers' Club Program were: (1) to create a local and voluntary movement of mothers to encourage family planning practice, (2) to aid fieldworkers in finding new acceptors of this practice, (3) to serve as an interpersonal channel for family planning information and supplies, and (4) to encourage participation in community development activities.

The club's original ten members had to overcome many obstacles. In the beginning, the members' husbands had very traditional attitudes about women, and most of them disapproved of the use of contraceptives in family planning. Because of the village's problems with the Communists during the war, many village elders were still wary of any public meetings that took place. The village men criticized the Mothers' Club activities. Their parents-in-law did not understand the purpose of the club, so that many members experienced very difficult situations in their homes. Ashamed of attending public meetings, they began meeting secretly because of fear that their families would openly object to their participation.

These early meetings were not easy. Mrs. Kang, one of the present work group leaders, recalled how ". . . difficult it was to unify so many different opinions about how to collect funds and establish a cooperative store for the village . . . and about the amount of grain each member should save in their mutual credit union."

To overcome these problems, Mrs. Choi, the first leader of the club, encouraged the members to show *extra respect* to their elders, their in-laws, and their husbands. They even agreed to prepare special meals for their husbands once every month to exemplify their traditional role as wives and improve the relationship with their husbands.

While they discussed and learned about family planning among themselves, they began concentrating on the immediate goal of creating a small emergency credit and savings fund, on the intermediate goal of establishing their own cooperative store for small household goods, and on the ultimate goal of providing a better education for their children. Soon the village elders realized that their daughters-in-law were behaving better than before, and they gradually began encouraging them to become more active in Mothers' Club projects. Eventually, meetings were held openly under the traditional village meeting tree once every month, and under a full moon until the village obtained electricity.

The Gift of the Family Planning Pig

Early in 1971, the provincial PPFK branch office gave a small baby piglet as a prize to one Mothers' Club in each of the thirteen counties of the province. The purpose was to stimulate the most promising clubs to undertake joint livestock projects to increase their income. When Oryu Li was given the piglet for that county, the Mothers' Club was faced with an immediate problem: Where would they keep it? Who would feed and take care of it? After it matured, then what? Who would benefit from it? They held meetings every day to discuss the problem until they finally worked out a plan to care for the piglet, and then to breed it later to increase the club's savings fund. They note with considerable pride today that of the thirteen piglets given as prizes only theirs and one other survived (or was not sold for an immediate profit).

This project was a success from the standpoint of cooperation and mobilization of the club's members, but the pig itself did miserably in the beginning: her first litter had only two female piglets, followed by just two male piglets in the second litter. Since most pigs produce much larger litters (from four to seven piglets), their pig soon became renowed throughout the area as the "family planning pig of Oryu Li." Since the pig belonged to the Mothers' Club, it was accused of taking PPFK's national slogan too seriously: "Girl or boy, stop at two and raise them well." They kept the pig in spite of her early difficulties, and she eventually produced a normal litter for them. Although we have no direct evidence of this, it is likely that the joke about the "Mothers' Club pig" made it easier for village members to talk further about family planning and how it works.

The Club's New Leader

While the Mothers' Club was being organized in Oryu Li, Mrs. Chung Moon Ja and her husband, Chang Young, were in the mountains two kilometers above the village, trying to establish a small livestock operation by themselves. With fifty cows, they soon found themselves overextended. When some of them began dying of an uncontrollable disease, they were forced into bankruptcy and had to leave the mountain. Their original plan, to save enough money to move to Seoul and educate their three children, had to be abandoned. Instead, they decided to move into the village of Oryu Li. Since the train station was in Oryu Li, they had often stopped there on their trips to Jeon Ju City, the provincial capital. Mrs. Chung had become good friends with Mrs. Choi, the Mothers' Club leader. They frequently discussed the problems of the club, and since Mrs. Chung had graduated from high school, her advice and suggestions were often used by the first leader.

When Mrs. Chung and her husband moved into Oryu Li in April 1971, Mrs. Choi asked her to become the formal leader of their club, finally persuading her to accept by agreeing to continue herself as the club's vice-leader. As an outsider, Mrs. Chung was met initially with mistrust, resistance, criticism, and some open hostility from members of the dominant family clan. They blamed her for an unfavorable newspaper article about their village's earlier involvement with the Communists. She finally convinced them that the reporter did not interview her for the story. Then she was accused of reporting some of the villagers' illegal connections to a nearby electric power line. She denied it, and when they finally learned that she had been falsely accused, they became sympathetic and began to cooperate. The first leader's support was crucial, since her husband was the village chief and a member of the dominant Kang clan.

Under Mrs. Chung's competent leadership, the rate of Oryu Li's development increased greatly. She completely reoriented the club after becoming leader. At her first meeting she proposed five basic goals: (1) family planning, (2) village improvement, (3) love for Korea, (4) love for our neighbors, and (5) love for god. After a general consensus was reached, they decided to begin by building a Mothers' Club bank, a general fund (separate from their individual savings and credit union) that could be used for mutual development projects, and ultimately for their children's education.

Mrs. Chung first heard about this idea on a weekly KBS radio program, "Let There Be No Despair" (Chulmang eun Opda), a half-hour documentary "drama." The program that influenced her was about a village like Oryu Li that learned to overcome its despair and prospered by starting a cooperative village bank (fund). She told the other members about this story in order to convince them to start their own mutual fund for the future. Meanwhile, she visited the five most stubborn elders in the village, and persuaded them to become consultants for their club projects. Once they accepted, they became very helpful to the club.

In the summer of 1971, the club members pooled their savings to buy cloth from which they made uniforms to sell nearby middle-school children for their school's annual sports competition. The combined profit of this first project was 6,000 *won* (U.S. $15), half of which the club donated to the school for the sports event. The rest was used to start the club's own mutual fund. Although this was a small start, through it the club members earned considerable respect from the school officials, from surrounding villages, and from resistant members of their own village. More importantly, it convinced the Mothers' Club members that they were capable of creating ways to earn money for their mutual fund.

Just before the annual harvest, Mrs. Chung proposed that they formally open an account with the Agricultural Cooperative Bank, and learn the correct procedures for deposits, withdrawals, and bookkeeping. After everyone agreed to join, she proposed a substantial increase in the scale of their club's operation. She recommended that they each begin saving

100 *won* (U.S. $.25) and increase their rice savings to one full *twe* (about one liter) every month. Then she proposed that they expand the membership of the club so that they could accumulate a larger base to invest in money-making projects and increase their fund more rapidly.

The original ten members of the club balked at this idea, claiming that the 9,900 *won* they had already saved belonged to them only, and should not be shared by new members. Finally, Mrs. Chung just said, "Okay, you take all of your money out of the fund, and I'll lend the fund 10,000 *won* of my own money to get it started again." This remark made quite an impression on the other members. According to Mrs. Kang Sang-Ryae, ". . . all the members were greatly moved by her unselfish act, and they contributed their money voluntarily." The club soon grew to forty-one members, and they began working together in their free time harvesting rice on neighboring farms for 4,000 *won* per day.[2] They often had to leave their homes before dawn to get the extra time. Many of their regular household duties had to be sacrificed to do this, but they accumulated almost 120,000 *won* by the end of the harvest, just enough to take over control of one of the two village wine houses and make their dream of a cooperative store a reality.

The Family Planning Crisis

Before the Mothers' Club was organized in 1968, a few women used contraceptives secretly out of fear that their husbands might beat them. The first family planning fieldworker who visited Oryu Li was severely criticized by some of the village men. In a nearby village, the first field-worker was beaten and forced to leave. Nurses who visited Oryu Li had to work secretly, and there were often many unexplained side effects from the contraceptives. The Mothers' Club members gave some of the reluctant village women enough confidence to try contraceptives, but in the beginning it was often difficult to distinguish those who accepted from those who opposed family planning, because everyone was afraid to talk about it.

Between 1968 and 1970, however, several women in Oryu Li began using the oral contraceptive. Then one of the first women to use the "pill" became seriously ill and almost died. When everyone heard about this, thirteen other women who were taking the pill decided to stop at the same time. By the time Mrs. Chung became the leader in 1971 there were twelve new unwanted babies in Oryu Li. To restore their faith in "scientific" family planning, she invited two university health lecturers whom she had met during a training program in Jeon Ju City to visit their village and explain why the pill has bad side effects for only certain kinds of women. Then the lecturers taught the women about the "loop" (IUD or intrauterine device). After these lectures, Mrs. Chung told the club that anyone who felt uneasy about the pill should come with her to the clinic to have a loop inserted. Eighteen women volunteered to go with her to get loops.

Twelve members finally had loops inserted, but one of them was never completely convinced that loops were really safe. She soon suffered severe side effects and her fear increased. Mrs. Chung wrote her a letter every day from Seoul where she was attending a training program for new leaders, but when she returned she realized that the only solution was to take the member back to the clinic to have the loop removed. Later she apologized to the whole club for trying to persuade someone to accept a loop against her will. Fortunately, there were no serious problems with the other mothers who volunteered.

Oryu Li's experience with family planning is unique for several reasons. The Mothers' Club program legitimized their club, providing them for the first time with an open forum in which family planning and other mutual problems could be freely discussed. Secondly, their example suggests that the visit to a clinic and the adoption of family planning may be more readily accomplished by a collective, group decision, rather than a private, individual decision. And finally, although the original objective was to establish a channel for family planning information and supplies, their example has revealed what may be more important contributions to the family planning program: the capacity to obtain the help of outside health resources when they are needed, and the capacity for personal follow-up and support by experienced members for those who are risking the use of contraceptives for the first time. It is impossible for doctors, nurses, or fieldworkers to provide the close, personal support that Mrs. Chung gave to her neighbor in Oryu Li. The Mothers' Club made this the specific responsibility of the leader and other members, and their meetings gave them the place and time to do it together.

Development Projects

From the winter of 1971/72 to 1974, the Oryu Li Mothers' Club initiated an extraordinary series of mutual development and income-earning projects. This period coincided with the Ministry of Home Affairs' new rural development program, the SaeMaul Undong (New Village Movement). The Mothers' Club readily accepted its expanded role as Oryu Li's SaeMaul Undong Women's Club, and the members were well prepared for its three basic means to village improvement: cooperation, self-reliance, and diligence.

To clean up their food storage places and get their food off the ground, they built concrete stands for their *kim chee* (pickled vegetables) jars; then they decided to modernize their kitchens by rebuilding their cooking stands and stoves with concrete bricks. Since they needed $250 to do the kitchens of all forty-one members, Mrs. Chung suggested that everyone lend the club her gold wedding ring. These would be pawned and when they had enough money from other projects they would buy the rings back. Some members were afraid of what their husbands would say if they found out, so she asked them, "What good does it do to wear gold rings when our village is so dirty and needs to be improved?" Moved once again by their leader's logic, the younger women donated their gold rings, from the pawnage of which the club obtained $200 to buy materials. Nevertheless, they decided to keep this a secret until they were able to redeem their rings.

They used the money to buy cement for brick-making. Once they had the cement they divided themselves into eight work teams of five members each. The first set of bricks froze and broke apart. Either it was too cold or the material was poorly mixed. So, they invited men in the village who were more skilled at brick-making to work with each team, under an agreement that the men would be exempt from other New Village Movement duties. Since the women had given some *kim chee* to the soldiers at the train station the year before, they were able to persuade the soldiers to haul two truckloads of sand from the river. They also used the concrete to build a public bathhouse for the village.

Early in 1972, Mrs. Chung heard that the government was promoting its reforestation campaigns by providing chestnut seedlings to village development councils. She told the county chief that Oryu Li had very little land for rice cultivation, but that the villagers could use the surrounding hills to grow chestnut trees. He was skeptical at first because the ground was still hard from the freezing winter, and he doubted whether *women* could dig holes 60 centimeters deep, which the seedlings required. But Mrs. Chung was persistent, and he finally promised them 2,000 chestnut trees.

The other members of the club were overjoyed to hear the good news. In their enthusiasm they dug each hole 100 centimeters deep in the still-frozen hillside, even though 60 centimeters would have been enough. They expected that the planting of 2,000 trees would require "at least two days, but they were so eager that they finished in one day."[3] People in the surrounding villages could not believe such a feat was possible. They charged that the soldiers from the nearby station had helped dig the holes the previous night. The women were unperturbed, aware that this rumor stemmed from the soldiers' previous help with the sand.

After the seedlings were planted, the women decided to build a chestnut tree nursery. To do this more efficiently, they organized the village men under thirty years old into a Young Men's Club. Together they planted 16,000 seeds, and now they have over 10,000 new seedlings. They planned to donate $500 from this project to the village fund, and divide the rest among the members of the Young Men's Club and the Mothers' Club.[4] According to one of their members, "These chestnut trees have become our greatest hope for the future . . . and for better education for our children. We take care of our chestnut trees as if they were our own children."

This kind of statement offers a glimpse of the real meaning of these chestnut trees to members of the Mothers' Club. Their long-term economic investment and increase in income cannot be slighted, but they represent much more than an agricultural commodity to Oryu Li. Once they were securely planted they became a symbol of the new consciousness of the Mothers' Club members: they represented the "we" quality of belonging to the club, and the growing belief that "we can do it ourselves." This message could not go unheeded by the men of Oryu Li. The sign of the Mothers' Club was placed directly in front of the chestnut tree nursery by the main road into the village. Its presence served as a constant reminder to everyone of what the club was trying to achieve. And finally, the chestnut tree itself is a traditional symbol of endurance and prosperity, especially during the cold winter days when chestnuts are roasted at home, or sold in the streets of the cities. The chestnut trees represented a permanent long-term commitment to the struggle for a better life.

After the trees were planted, the club members turned to their spring planting of rice and barley. Since they had no extra land for their club, they persuaded their husbands and other villagers to help them clear the rocks and heavy stones from the vacant land next to the river. Then they convinced the soldiers to transport ten truckloads of extra topsoil to improve their new plot. They planted the barley crop too late in the year, however, so only half of it was good. Another part was lost during the heavy rainy season in July and August. Then the remaining crop was rejected by the government purchasing agency for not being dry enough to measure and store properly. After requesting more time to dry it again, the women returned to the village and divided themselves into three special teams: (1) to enlighten the other villagers about the fixed price system offered by the government to support prices, (2) to dry the barley crop more thoroughly, and (3) to take the barley back the second time and check the government's official regulations and standards for purchasing grain. Although they eventually had to sell their remaining crop at a loss, they were satisfied with their club's effort, and felt better prepared for the 1973 crop.

The Governor's Surprise Visit

Late that year the provincial governor made an unexpected visit to Oryu Li while visiting New Village Movement projects nearby. The governor's advance man arrived early and told Mrs. Chung to gather all the women for a meeting because the governor wanted to talk to them. She objected, "The women are working in the field, not dressed for a meeting. . . . Why don't we get the fertilizer and have them putting it on the chestnut trees when the governor arrives?" The governor was very impressed to see the women working so hard together. He went to Mrs. Chung's house and for over two hours she told him of all of the problems and activities of the club.

Her exposition was so intense and emotional that the governor was actually moved to tears at one point. As he explained later, it was the first time he had wept in forty years, but it was from a feeling of gladness (*kam kyuk*) for what the club members had been able to accomplish with so little. This visit confirmed his belief that the New Village Movement was being led by the women in his province rather than by the men. Before leaving, he donated 300 sacks of cement to the Oryu Li Mothers' Club, and he agreed to get electricity and improve the road to their village ahead of schedule. Later, he commented that ". . . even in heavy men's work, women can be effective. . . . I think that I am one of the few government officials who recognizes that woman power is so strong."

Several days later, Mrs. Chung was asked by several village men to come to one of their houses. Inside were many of the husbands of the women who were not members of the Mothers' Club. They claimed that the governor's gift of cement was for the whole village, *not* just the members of the Mothers' Club. According to Mrs. Chung the whole future of the club was at stake:

> I didn't know what to do. The members were really counting on the cement to finish their kitchens. I had to refuse them. . . . Finally, I just told them that even President Park would say that the cement should go to those who work, *not* the ones who do nothing. Then I had a good idea. I offered to share the cement with all members of the Mothers' Club, even those who joined *after* the cement was donated. They had no choice but to accept this generous offer. Only their stubbornness would prevent their wives from joining the club and sharing the cement.

Outsmarted by Mrs. Chung's generous offer, the men left the meeting deadlocked by her compromise offer.

The husbands of the nonclub members made Mrs. Chung realize that not all the women in the village were able to participate in the club even if they wanted to. Some had to stay home to care for their households and younger children, rather than participate in the New Village Movement projects of the Mothers' Club. With the other members, she immediately began preparations for a special feast for the whole village: (1) to honor their own husbands' sacrifice for them, and (2) to dramatize the benefit that their club's activities were having for the whole village. Afterwards, the club membership grew from forty-one to fifty-three mothers.

There are several possible explanations for Mrs. Chung's successful confrontation with the rest of the village over the distribution of the cement. She knew that she had enough support; the club membership had grown to forty-one by then, and included the village chief's wife as vice-leader. Mrs. Chung's own husband was already with the nonmembers' husbands when she arrived at the meeting, and his support before and during her response was a critical factor. Considerable change had already occurred prior to this crisis. The achievements of the Mothers' Club were obvious to everyone, including many outside government officials, a fact that her opponents could not have overlooked when she invoked the president's name in her reply.

And finally, to have acceded to the men's demands would have seriously undermined the future efforts of the other Mothers' Club members. She had no choice but to resist. But the way she resisted was most important of all: with compromise, deescalation of the conflict, and an offer to join and share the rewards.

There is another explanation that comes not from the description of the event itself, but from another traditional Korean proverb: "A fellow with an ax is no match for the one with a needle."[5] Unless the axman dares to use his mighty ax, he must surrender to the needlewoman. The prick of her needle may cause a small pain, but the fall of the ax means instant death. Therefore, at the crucial point in a fight between a man and a woman, the man must yield or risk losing her. This makes the female of the species actually more deadly than the male. It would have been more harmful to Oryu Li if Mrs. Chung had "lost face" before her club members than if these men as a group yielded and let their wives join to obtain a share of the cement.

A Factory for Oryu Li

In the fall of 1973, Mrs. Chung began looking in nearby cities for some way that the young girls in their village could work during the winter months to earn extra money for their future marriages. She finally found a factory that produced traditional silk belts for export to Japan. After returning to the factory four times, she at last succeeded in obtaining some materials to try weaving the belts in the village. At first most villagers objected, saying that the wages would be too low, but a few volunteered to try it. Mrs. Chung returned to the factory with examples of their work and pleaded with the company president to build a factory for the young people in her village. When he asked if they had a hall for his looms, she was forced to lie that they already had one.

They were finally given ten new *obizime* hand-operated looms from Japan in October 1973, which Mrs. Chung had to install in her own house. Ten of Oryu Li's most skillful girls were selected and an expert from Japan came to teach them the techniques of weaving. The first few belts were not woven very well, but they improved rapidly after Mrs. Chung reminded the girls that their work would symbolize the quality of Korean craftsmanship when they were eventually sold in Japan.

Similar machines were installed experimentally in four other villages, but the work done in Oryu Li was superior. The company agreed to build a hall to house the factory in their village. There the machines from Mrs. Chung's house and the other villages were installed. On January 15, 1974, an official ceremony was held to honor its completion. Forty-eight young girls who had been forced to leave the village to work in the city returned to learn how to weave and earn a living in Oryu Li. Since Mrs. Chung's most difficult problem with the Mothers' Club was the members' lack of basic education, she immediately began special courses for the girls to compensate for the schooling that their families were unable to afford for them. Since they were too tired to study at night, they used the time from 8:00 to 9:00 A.M. for a middle school correspondence course, and worked from 9:00 A.M. until 7:00 P.M., with one hour for lunch and another hour for recreation in the afternoon. With skill, each girl can earn about U.S. $1 per day, which is more than twice as much as their mothers were making harvesting rice on neighboring farms. Mrs. Chung has never forgotten the remarks that a university professor made to her in Seoul the year before: "Any country that attaches importance to women's education is on the road to development."

New Land for the Village

In the winter of 1973/74, the villagers of Oryu Li heard a rumor that the government planned to sell to private individuals the land the Mothers' Club had reclaimed by the river—the same land that they had cleared with their own hands to grow barley. They had obtained permission to use this land, and they had been paying taxes on it each year. Mrs. Chung informed the New Village Movement leader, and he and her husband spent over two months going through the necessary procedures to purchase the land from the county government. They were nearly finished when the provincial government intervened and prevented the county office from handling the matter, claiming that the land near the river belonged to the province.

Desperate to save the land they had struggled so hard to obtain, the people found that they had no one to turn to except their Mothers' Club.

By the time this problem had occurred, however, the power of the club had grown considerably. Most of the county and provincial officials had grown accustomed to dealing directly with Mrs. Chung rather than with the village chief when they wanted the village to do something. It was much easier for the club to gather the villagers for meetings, and to get their cooperation. Furthermore, word of the success of the Oryu Li Mothers' Club had spread throughout Korea, and by the time their land was threatened Mrs. Chung was making regular appearances as a guest lecturer at the New Village Movement training institute in SuWon (near Seoul). She had recognized long ago that villages in Korea where high government officials were born, or had relatives, could easily get support for their projects, whereas villages like Oryu Li had no one to rely on for support except themselves and so had to make themselves and their efforts known.

Mrs. Chung finally went to the provincial government herself, and argued with the head of the Planning Department for a whole day. The Mothers' Club of Oryu Li had become "famous enough that they had to hear our claims." The government finally yielded to the club's demands for the land.

Purchasing the land used up all of the extra money that the village had available. The family clan fund of over one hundred sacks of rice was quickly depleted, and if it had not been for the Mothers' Club general fund, which had grown to over one million *won* ($2,500), they would not have been able to obtain the land.

Ironically, it was land, the oldest and most traditional value in Korea, which led to the final integration of the Mothers' Club with the traditional family clan system in Oryu Li.

By the summer of 1974 almost all of the women in Oryu Li belonged to the club. There were 50 regular members with equal shares in the general fund, and another 112 associate members who could not afford the high initial deposit to join the general fund, but who had personal savings and credit accounts and attended all of the meetings. Through Mrs. Chung's contacts at the SaeMaul Undong training center, their village was able to acquire 120 new piglets, which are now divided among nineteen households and managed by the Young Men's Club. Their newest project is to grow ten different kinds of Oriental herbs for sale in the cities as traditional herbal medicine.

The Lessons of Oryu Li's Development Center

Is development merely the investment of capital, or the acquisition of modern technology as a means to higher income? If so, then Oryu Li's example suggests that all that surrounding villages have to do is plant chestnut trees on their mountains and acquire pigs and a silk belt factory. The outcome would be obvious: the market value of chestnuts and pigs would drop, and there might be a shortage of fodder for the pigs. A shortage of feed for Oryu Li's pigs actually did occur in 1974, partly due to the number of villages that were also trying to raise them. Oryu Li's response to this new threat is more indicative of the key element of development than the acquisition of livestock.

When they heard about the feed shortage in their area, the club held an emergency meeting and decided upon the best course of action to take. They found out which government official had control over the available supply, and they persuaded him to maintain an adequate supply of fodder for their pigs since they were ". . . a Mothers' Club project for the SaeMaul Undong." In more general terms, (a) they acquired the critical information at the right time, (b) they processed that information well enough to understand what to do, and (c) they created new information leading to an appropriate action to solve the problem. This is a statement about the capacity of the Oryu Li mothers to use communication for their own development.

Creative problem-solving and effective communication are necessary (though not sufficient) prerequisites for socioeconomic development. The input of material resources, energy, and information is necessary for development, and an increase in output per unit of input (efficiency) is an important criterion for defining socioeconomic development. But the case of Oryu Li underscores the critical role of the transformational processes that take place to create a set of output resources from a set of input resources. The specific inputs and outputs of Oryu Li are not so important, and other villages may have to find entirely different kinds of projects for their own development. How material resources and energy are transformed is only one kind of transformational capacity of a system. Mrs. Chung and Oryu Li have taught us the importance of communication as a transformational process for socio-economic development. The key lesson from our historical description of Oryu Li's success is that what is said (or not said) by one person to another at critical points in time is crucial to the direction and rate of change that takes place. From this point of view, the Mothers' Club and the emergence of Mrs. Chung's leadership were basically a reorganization, or restructuring, of the patterns of communication and decision-making within the social system of a traditional Korean village.

The final lesson from Oryu Li is that growth in the transformational capacity of a social system does not necessarily take place at a continuous rate of change. In terms of an economist like Kenneth Boulding, ". . . in economic development, a society sometimes seems to operate according to a step-function, and quite suddenly adopts new rates of production and consumption, or savings and investments. There is, perhaps, something inherently unpredictable about these step-changes." (Boulding, in Klausner 1967, p. 106). Elsewhere, he describes step-changes as a "systems break," where a system operates at a continuous and predictable level until a key variable or process goes beyond a critical "threshold" and irreversible processes set in that result in profound system changes. In social systems like Oryu Li, such a system break may result from revolution, adoption of a radically new ideology, legitimization of a new organization, emergence of a charismatic leader like Mrs. Chung, or perhaps a combination of several of these factors with a realization of what women, with the help of men, can do for their family and community once they have caught the vision of their own power.

NOTES

1. This material has been adapted from Kincaid et al. 1974.

2. At 200 *won* (U.S. $.50) per day's labor, it would require at least twenty members to make this amount. Women are generally paid about one-half the daily wage that men receive.

3. This statement reflects the enthusiasm of the club members. The club leader corrected these figures later: actually, digging the holes and transplanting the trees took five days, fertilizing another three. Eight days for the whole job is still a remarkable achievement.

4. Thirty to fifty percent of this nursery was later destroyed by flooding in 1974.

5. Cited in Tae-Hung Ha, *Guide to Korean Culture* (Tokyo: Yonsei University Press, 1968), p. 363.

6. Development Change and Communication in India

S. C. DUBE

On August 15, 1947, when India entered the dream world of freedom, her euphoria was tempered with an acute awareness of several gigantic problems. The thin upper crust of the society had attained for itself a reasonably high standard of living, but the masses lived at a level that could be described, at best, as subhuman. The magnitude of poverty manifested in mass hunger, disease, and illiteracy was truly horrifying. The basic task before the country was to alleviate the condition of the common man and relieve him of his misery and suffering. The leadership realized that it had many promises to keep. Some of these promises had been made somewhat rashly, without sufficient understanding of the immensity and the complexity of the tasks involved in their fulfillment. But the country could not go back on them; the cherished goals had to be achieved.

Planning was very much in the air even before India attained independence. These pioneer efforts lacked rigor and sophistication, but they did, nevertheless, initiate a useful dialogue, collect valuable basic data, and turn up a series of hypotheses that were helpful to planners in coming to grips with the economic and social realities of postindependence India.

Assumptions behind Indian Planning

India launched her first Five Year Plan in 1951. This plan consolidated a large number of development projects that were already on the ground, but it also generated considerable fresh thinking toward integrated and comprehensive development planning. Some of its assumptions continue to be operative even today, when the country is reshaping its Fifth Plan. Over two decades of experience have imparted a sense of greater realism to the planning endeavor and have brought about a flexibility of approach involving situational choices and pragmatic adjustments. Indian planning techniques also have acquired greater refinement and sophistication. However, one finds a degree of continuity in regard to the assumptions about how development takes place and how it can be achieved in a country like India.

One major task before the planners was to identify the causes of India's retarded economic growth. They recognized that, preceding independence, the country had registered only limited and partial development. Per capita income and the standard of well-being had remained more or less stagnant. Industrialization made only a limited impact. In the late nineteenth century, India started receiving machine-made goods from abroad. These imports adversely affected traditional crafts and cottage industries, without creating a strong impulse for development through industrialization. In consequence, there was a general decline in productivity both in agriculture and in traditional industry. Gradually underemployment increased. Part of it was absorbed by traditional institutions like joint family and caste, but their shock-absorbing capacity was not limitless. Further increases in underemployment led to the rise of pathetic contentment, fatalism, and apathy. The environment was not propitious for economic and social progress. Available surpluses were used up mainly in buying imported goods. At the end of the nineteenth century, the only industries that had firmly established themselves in the country were cotton textiles and jute. Agriculture continued to suffer neglect.

During the two world wars, other industries were set up in the country. This was due to: (1) a more positive government policy dictated by war needs; (2) a change in the terms of trade in favor of the producers of manufactured goods as against the primary producers. This enabled some capital formation in the industrial sector. The limited gains in the industrial sector were offset by rapid deterioration in the agricultural sector. This condition did not augur well for the substantial and overall economic development of India.

The occupational structure in the early years of India's independence was disturbing: 68 percent of the country's working population was absorbed by the agricultural sector, 14 percent by large- and small-scale industries, 8 percent by trade and transport, and 10 percent by professions and services, including domestic service. Productivity in the agricultural sector was visibly low; in organized industry, commerce, and transport it was approximately three times more than in agriculture. The growth of organized industry, as well as commerce and transport, was not rapid enough to absorb the underemployed population on land. This underemployment, which was slowly emerging as undisguised unemployment, especially in the rural areas, was a pressing economic problem with major social and psychological consequences.

Planning, therefore, had to address itself mainly to mass poverty and unemployment, particularly in rural areas. It was assumed that economic development could be promoted only if the country had the readiness to develop and apply modern technology to the processes of production both in agriculture and industry. Underdevelopment thus was viewed essentially as a consequence of insufficient technological progress. In positive terms, to ensure development the country had to adopt, and, where necessary, to adapt, modern technology and learn to utilize its resources toward attainment of accepted and predefined ends.

While a constant effort had to be made to utilize known resources as well as to search ceaselessly for new resources, it was essential to keep in mind that transformation of resources requires application of new skills and know-how. In fact these are as important, or nearly as important, as capital formation. A country cannot hope to develop if it does not give sufficient attention to the creation of such skills and to the enlargement of its know-how.

Rate of population growth, inputs in planned development, and national output are closely interrelated. Given the shortage of land and capital equipment in India, it was considered essential that the population growth not outpace economic growth (resulting in nonavailability of capital for further economic development). Efforts to stabilize population growth had to take into account the effects of public health programs and disease control, both of which contribute to increasing survival rates. Indian planners assumed, therefore, that they would have a situation involving severe population pressure: for 1951–1960 the assumption was a growth rate of 12.5 percent; for 1961–1970 it was 13.3 percent; and for 1971–1980 it was 14 percent. These estimates put the population in 1960/61 at 408 million and in 1974/75 at 434 million. Even at the time of publication, there was some reason to suspect that these estimates were generally on the low side. The alarming growth rate meant that fertility control, in all its aspects, had to become a national policy.

The economic arithmetic of planning indicated the need for massive inputs of capital. The proportion of investment to national income, in the first Five Year Plan, was assumed to be about 5 percent in 1950/51; this was expected to rise to about 20 percent by 1968/69, and to remain stationary at that level thereafter. During the First Plan, the incremental capital output ratio (ICOR) was 1.8:1. This fruitful output was attributed partly to good monsoons and to the utilization of unused capacity. For the Second Plan, ICOR was estimated to be 2.3:1. For the next three plans, ICORs were assumed to be 2.6, 3.4, and 3.7 respectively. These ratios were described as "a shorthand description of the productivity of capital in various sectors." It was assumed that productivity depended also on other factors such as the degree of technological improvement associated with capital investment, efficient handling of new types of equipment, and the quality of organizational and managerial skills. Effective 1956/57, the First Plan assumed a marginal rate of savings of 5 percent and postulated that the rate of investment would go to 20 percent of national income by 1968/69. The framers of the Second Plan soberly realized that these expectations were unrealistic and projected a slower growth for the investment coefficient; from 7 percent in 1955/56 to 11 percent in 1960/61, to 14 percent by 1965/66, and to 16 percent 1970/71. At this point it was likely to remain stable for a few years, going up to 17 percent by 1975/76. The planners were cautiously optimistic: "A new investment rate of 16 percent or 17 percent of national income is decidedly high, though not unattainable."

The planners realized that population control, capital formation, and capital inputs require careful determination of priorities, as well as a propitious social framework and an adequate structure of motivation. Considerable sacrifices are needed for the attainment of long-term planning goals, but planning cannot address itself only to a remote future. It has to take into account current situational pressures and attend to changing social needs. The First Plan (1951–1956) generally attempted to raise the standard of living through increased production, but it also had to curb inflation and rectify food shortages. The Second Plan (1956–1961) addressed itself to accelerating industrialization, with particular emphasis on basic and heavy industries, but it had to take cognizance also of mounting unemployment and the need to expand employment opportunities. It had, at the same time, to respond as well to the growing demand for social justice by building into its strategy policies that would contribute to the reduction of inequalities in income and wealth and result in a more even distribution of economic power.

The Third Plan aimed at increasing national income 5 percent or more per year by designing investment patterns to sustain this growth rate during subsequent plan periods. It continued to give attention to basic industries, but it also had to formulate projects aimed at achieving self-sufficiency in foodgrains. It was responsive as well to mounting pressures for social justice and for creation of new employment opportunities. The Fourth Plan stressed self-reliance and was aimed at achieving equitable distribution of income. Once again, it accorded high priority to agriculture. The Fifth Plan accents social justice. Besides restoring health to the Indian economy, its major emphasis is on fulfilling the minimum needs of the underprivileged sections of the society.

Planning is an instrument of social policy; to be meaningful, all plans should be oriented to a set of broad social objectives. In this respect the Indian planners adopted the social goals enshrined in the Indian constitution. The country was committed to democratic socialism. Its planning effort, therefore, had to function within the framework of a democratic polity and it had to move toward the realization of a just and egalitarian social order without deviating from its democratic ideals. The conflicting demands of freedom and social justice had to be reconciled with tact and firmness. Without ruthlessly curbing the liberties enshrined in the constitution, the country had to move expeditiously toward establishing such an order. The underprivileged, the deprived, and the degraded were to be given special attention; separate provisions were made for the development of the scheduled tribes, the scheduled castes, and generally the backward classes.

The need for fundamental alterations in the structure of the society was recognized, although a clear blueprint of the new social framework was never offered. The demand for reform of agrarian structure was most persistent. Several legislative measures were promoted to bring about changes in this sphere. The planners were also sensitive to the growing demand for reducing economic and social inequalities. They assumed that certain changes in social structure were "preconditions" for accelerating development. The exact nature of these structural modifications, however, remained undefined.

It was assumed that the private and public sectors could coexist, the former requiring social control, the latter gradually moving toward the commanding heights of the economy. Even a "joint sector" was visualized, in which private and public sectors could collaborate, and a significant role was assigned to the "cooperative sector."

Finally, it was understood that development gathers momentum and becomes self-sustaining with active participation by the people. Measures were devised to associate them with the process of plan formation and implementation. New institutional structures, calculated to ensure such participation, were also visualized and created.

Achievements and Failures

The assessment of India's efforts at planned development, both at home and abroad, is generally negative. Such a verdict is one-sided and unfair. In judging India's performance, we must keep in mind the hurdles encountered. Continuing confrontation with Pakistan, the Chinese military adventure in 1962, the Indo-Pak war in 1965, recurrent years of drought, the influx of millions of refugees from East Pakistan, another war with Pakistan on the Bangladesh issues, failure of the monsoons shortly after this war, mounting inflation, and the unprecedented rise in the price of petroleum—all these were formidable obstacles in the way of the smooth implementation of India's development plans. Against these odds the level of performance in several sectors is certainly creditable.

Take, for example, the growth of infrastructure for industrialization and of industrial production. With 1960 as base, one finds that in two decades the general index of industrial production has moved from 54.8 in 1951 to 180.8 in 1970. Progress in the manufacture of machinery (including electrical machinery), metal products (especially steel), transport equipment, fertilizers, and so forth, has provided conditions for the growth of a self-reliant economy.

The gains in the field of education, at least quantitatively, are breathtaking.

In 1950, 22.3 million children were enrolled in elementary schools; in 1973 their number was 78.8 million. There was a corresponding rise also in secondary and higher education. In 1950, only 1.21 million students attended secondary schools, in 1973 their number was 8.50 million. In 1950, only 0.33 million were in institutions of higher learning; in 1973, 3.4 million. In this period, expenditure on education increased over tenfold (a statistical "order of magnitude"): from Rs. 1,140 million to 13,000 million. The quality of the educational system leaves much to be desired, but it cannot be denied that its phenomenal quantitative expansion has contributed to the equalization of educational opportunity.

Similarly, impressive gains have been registered in the expansion of health services over the past two decades: the death rate dropped from 27.4 to 15.1 per thousand; life expectancy at birth rose from thirty-two to fifty years. Medical education institutions rose from 30 to 100, some having the highest international standards, and their annual intake capacity rose from 2,500 to 12,500 a year. Great killers like malaria, smallpox, and cholera have been contained.

Science and technology have not lagged behind. Significant achievements have put the country on the road to self-reliance. The experimental explosion of a nuclear device for peaceful and developmental purposes in 1974 is but one landmark. Research by Indian agronomists has evolved several high-yielding varieties that contributed dramatically to the Green Revolution. The full import of scientific and technological advancement will become evident a decade or two from now.

On the negative side, one finds a series of heartbreaking failures. The country has not been able to make any dent in the abject poverty of its masses: over 40 percent of its people continue to live below the poverty line. Their number is not declining; in fact there are reasons to suspect that it is increasing. Despite the much-publicized Green Revolution, India cannot produce enough food for its needs. While total production of foodgrains doubled over the last two decades (from 55 to 110 million tons), these gains have largely been offset by the rate of population increase (from 2 percent to 2.2 percent). The public distribution system has failed to ensure equitable distribution. The weak and vulnerable cannot afford food at current prices. They have neither enough calories nor enough protein; the supply of milk and baby foods is even worse. An unusually high proportion of children suffer from physical and mental deficiencies due to chronic malnutrition. Rural and urban housing is equally dismal. The country cannot find the resources to support even a modest slum improvement program to provide only the minimum civilized amenities for the increasing slum dwellers.

Most of the gains of two decades have been appropriated by the 20 percent to 30 percent upper stratum of society. They have a disproportionate share of consumer goods and the best of education and health services. The masses appear to be relegated to a perpetual culture of poverty. Social inequalities have increased and a parasitical class indulging in unabashed conspicuous consumption has emerged. Despite the creation of 20 million jobs in the organized sector (13 million public sector, 7 million private sector), unemployment is mounting; over 14 million are without jobs and 8,000 new names are added to the unemployed rosters daily. The situation is grim: injustice has provoked anger, frustration, and erosion of faith in social institutions as well as deterioration of social, economic, and political discipline.[1]

Why does the country find itself in this sorry predicament?

In two decades of planning, India has achieved many of its output goals: it began faltering during the Fourth Plan, which was, in a sense, a nonstarter. Its basic weakness appears to lie in the failure to formulate, articulate, and implement its distributive goals. The planning apparatus finds itself in disarray mainly because of distributive failures. Evidently Indian planning overemphasized output goals; social goals receive only passing mention in plan documents and their actual implementation is low-key. We now have the sobering realization that even substantial increases in GNP do not necessarily bring about the improved welfare and development of the society at large. No serious effort has been made to evolve clear and precise indicators of social development. The entire notion, it now appears, requires fresh thinking. A modest beginning in this direction has been made in the Fifth Plan, with its "minimum needs" program that is designed to improve the quality of life of the common man.

Economic arithmetic plays a major role in planning, but it can be only an exercise in futility if it is not enmeshed with realistic political choices. Even the most carefully formulated plans go awry if there is no political will to work resolutely toward their realization. In India one notices a glaring absence of fit between the arithmetic of economics and the calculus of politics. Political exigencies have made a series of demands on the planning process, but the latter has rarely responded adequately. Many of the needed structural changes have not occurred in Indian society because of the lack of political will.

Sustained development also presupposes a high level of organizational capability in handling interrelated tasks: maintenance of law and order; smooth functioning of supportive mechanisms; timely and accurate anticipation of needs, problems, and crises; and adequate response to new challenges. Efforts to streamline, to reorient, and where necessary to restructure the bureaucratic apparatus in India for efficient performance of development functions have so far not been very successful. Indian bureaucracy has continued to grow in size, but its operating culture has not shown much social sensitivity. Its ethos continues to be generally negative, restrictive, and oppressive; its thinking is stereotyped; and its performance is invariably wooden and precedent-bound.

The quality of planning depends greatly on the presence of an adequate information system. Indian planning had to start with a poor statistical base. The situation has improved greatly, but in several sectors planning still has to proceed without a reliable data base. Vertical as well as horizontal movement of information is slow; it often follows a meandering and tortuous path. Feedback leaves a great deal to be desired. In consequence, there are self-defeating delays, irrelevant planning, and sloppy implementation.

Thus, the Indian development effort needs a new orientation. It must be focused on the needs of the underprivileged and the downtrodden who constitute the overwhelming majority in India. Output goals should be directed to enriching the quality of life of the poor. To this end politics and economics must move together. Hard political options must be taken, the organizational structure strengthened, problem-solving capability sharpened, and an adequate information system devised. Development that caters only to the privileged classes and ignores the masses hardly deserves the name by which it goes.

Lessons of the Last Ten Years

Looking back, Indians will recall the last decade as years of tragedy and triumph, of humiliation and glory, of traumatic experiences and renewed faith. These years have taught several valuable lessons that contribute to a reorientation of Indian thinking on national priorities and development planning.

The brief frontier confrontation with China gave India a serious jolt. While it contributed immeasurably to promoting national unity and solidarity, it threw the country's economy out of gear. Before India could recover from this shock, the ferocious but inconclusive war with Pakistan erupted in 1965. The Third Plan, consequently, was in disarray. Drought and near-famine in several areas contributed to further deterioration. Then came the crushing burden of East Pakistan refugees and the high cost of yet another war with Pakistan. The short-lived euphoria of a decisive victory boosted the country's morale, but it did nothing to improve the grim economic situation. International monetary crises, runaway inflation at home, and the mounting prices of oil added new uncertainties to the course of development. India had to rethink its national objectives, planning priorities, and development strategies.

It is now evident that Indian planning cannot ignore the changing international situation. Reordering India's external relations is an imperative imposed by the fickle and even cynical conduct of interstate relations during the last decade. India has to refashion its policies to serve the cause of international amity without detriment to her national interest.

India recognizes that in the contemporary world an organized pattern of interdependence between nations is a necessity, but it has learned not to take continued international cooperation for granted. Today India has a more realistic understanding of international aid and the strings attached to it, and has adopted a more cautious policy toward it. The country has resolved to restrict international assistance as much as possible and is evolving a new strategy that, in the foreseeable future, would do away with it altogether. The new policy of self-reliance has two major expressions: export promotion and import substitution. This entails new domestic economic policies that, based upon a more relevant science and technology, will make India self-reliant in both agricultural and industrial production.

Today India understands better than ever before the paramount importance of national cohesion and solidarity. This has led to integration of the output, the cultural, and the order goals in its development planning. National integration is vital for sustained economic development. Increased production, though essential, is not enough; equal attention must go to distribution. Higher GNP and per capita income mean nothing if a country's masses subsist below the poverty line and are uncertain even of their daily bread.

Last, but perhaps most important, is the new thinking that has been generated toward framing an appropriate model of development. It is all too clear that India will be chasing a mirage if it makes a bid to attain Western standards of affluence in the near future. It has initiated, therefore, a search for alternative designs for living that would emphasize quality of life rather than material acquisition. There is growing disenchantment with the high consumption model; India is slowly but unmistakably moving toward a pattern that would discourage consumerism and would replace it by a system of adequate and efficient social services. In this context it is curious that India has rediscovered Gandhi via Chairman Mao. The new objectives have not yet been clearly articulated, but there is a ferment of thought and the country is looking for viable alternatives. The directions are clear.[2]

Communication in Development

Indian official documents do not explicitly state the role of communication in planned change, but there is a general awareness that it can play a significant part. Indian development strategy emphasizes attitudinal change, motivation, and participation. Communication is regarded as a mobilization mechanism and government is making increasing inputs to media growth. It is difficult to offer a reliable guesstimate of total Plan allocations for communication, as they are distributed among several ministries and their various departments. The allocations made to All India Radio (AIR)—the most important among the media—indicate the increasing importance that government attaches to communication: First Plan, Rs. 21.9 million; Second Plan Rs. 56.7 million; Third Plan, Rs. 76.4 million; Fourth Plan, Rs. 400 million; and Fifth Plan, Rs. 1.3 billion. From 1972 to 1974 (the last year of the Fourth Plan), the expenditure of All India Radio was Rs. 466 million. Table 1 presents the budgetary allocations for different divisions of the Ministry of Information and Broadcasting, which reflect the increasing government inputs over nearly a decade.

Table 1. Budgeted Allocations of the Indian Ministry of Information and Broadcasting

	Budgeted Allocations	
Ministry Division	*1965/66 (Rs. Million)*	*1973/74 (Rs. Million)*
All India Radio	67.40	305.50
Advertising and Visual Publicity	19.60	38.36
Field Publicity	5.92	11.41
Films Division	11.60	24.51
Photo Division	1.00	2.27
Press Information Bureau	5.30	8.74*
Publications Division	3.74	7.69
Songs and Drama Division	1.37	8.08

*Includes provision for Family Planning publicity also

In the first twenty-five years of India's independence, communication played an important part. The mass media have broadened the cognitive maps and mental horizons significantly, especially among the educated and urban population. This generated an expectation of change and prepared the society —or, at any rate, several segments of it—for acceptance of change. Thanks to the mass media, today there is a greater awareness of national issues and problems. They have also promoted nation-ness by putting across the message of national integration. The newspapers have exposed inefficiency and injustice and have championed popular causes.

In its early and experimental use to support development programs, communication played a direct and useful role in two areas. The community development movement experimented with several communication strategies, using traditional channels and idioms as well as mass media. Its use of interpersonal communication and of method-and-result demonstrations succeeded in changing attitudes and teaching some new techniques. The family planning program also initiated some bold and imaginative strategies along similar lines. The use of mass media in education, public health programs, and citizenship training was limited.

The intention of the national leadership all along was to gear the mass media to the processes of planned development. The Indian press was exhorted time and again to be responsive to the new aspirations of the people and to help in creating a climate propitious for rapid development. State-controlled All India Radio was required to devise special programs for the rural sector and for the working class. The accent in these programs was to be on developmental change. It was repeatedly asserted that television in India was not to become a status symbol or an object of elite consumption;

it was to develop as an instrument of socialization for a progressive and dynamic society. It was expected that the Indian film industry, one of the largest in the world, would take up broad social themes and make its contribution to the emergence of an ethos of modernization. A Film Finance Corporation was set up to encourage production of socially relevant movies.

In the last ten years the mass media have tried to respond positively to leadership expectations. Almost all major newspapers are privately owned; the most important either are owned by influential industrial and commercial houses or have strong financial links with them. The government has been contemplating measures for the diffusion of newspaper ownership, but it has so far not taken any concrete steps in this direction. A number of newspapers are owned by political parties or by other organized interests. Despite the interests of their owners, some newspapers do follow an independent line. Because of the diversity of their ownership, interest, and readership, the newspapers do not reflect a uniform approach; there is considerable variety in their coverage and treatment of the news.

The primary function of newspapers is to provide information on events at home and abroad; Indian journalism is heavily oriented toward political news and comment. The second major function that Indian newspapers appear to perform adequately is to focus attention on issues and problems and to initiate debates on alternative approaches. The questions they take up may relate to global issues like nuclear disarmament, environmental pollution, population explosion, or energy crisis; or they may relate to specific national and regional issues like inflation, unemployment, slums, public disorder, juvenile delinquency, atrocities on the Harijans (untouchable castes), endemic poverty, and so forth. Yet a third role in which Indian newspapers have distinguished themselves is surveillance of the political environment. They have functioned as effective watchdogs and have exposed corruption, nepotism, inefficiency, and assorted failures or misdeeds with courage and conviction.

India has a free press that has been unsparing in its criticism of the inadequacies, imperfections, and failures of government policy. On occasions the government has been peeved by the scathing and relentless criticism of the newspapers, but so far there have been very few glaring instances of attempts to curb their freedom. Newspapers have their own self-regulating mechanism and, in certain areas such as intercommunal harmony, they abide by their professional code of ethics. But development journalism is yet to find roots in India: the village rarely gets into the news or views. Perhaps the only notable exception is provided by the national daily *The Hindustan Times*, which carries a weekly feature on a village it has "adopted." This newspaper's interest has brought many development projects to the village. Its columns have given systematic coverage to the trends of change they have brought about.

Nation-building departments and agencies of government publish a large number of periodicals in such diverse fields as agriculture, rural development, cooperation, family planning, power and irrigation, and nuclear energy. Besides reporting progress of projects in hand and initiation of new programs, they carry some useful articles in their respective areas of interest. A recent innovation in this field is the publication of a wall newspaper, *Hamara Desh* (our country), which is produced in six languages, including English. It aims at highlighting the people's efforts to bring about national achievements. It has a fairly wide distribution to educational institutions, factories, and offices.

Development departments of the states also bring out their own periodicals. Their pages are often adorned by the pictures and exhortations of politically important personages. It is difficult to say how far they succeed in diffusing the development message or the techniques and skills involved. Mention may be made here of the excellent work being done by the extension service divisions of some agricultural universities established in the last two decades. Their bulletins carry timely information packages useful to agriculturists, horticulturists, poultry farmers, and dairymen in organizing their day-to-day operations.

All India Radio is a government monopoly and has a large network of broadcasting and relaying stations. State ownership imposes a consistent uniformity in its policy. It devotes a substantial part of its time to news, comment, entertainment, and culture; but it also gives strong support to development plans and projects of the government. AIR has been broadcasting rural programs for over three decades, but in recent years their time has been extended and their content and style have been modified. Most stations broadcast these programs daily from thirty to ninety minutes. Their main ingredients are news of interest to villagers, weather reports, and a bulletin of market rates of agricultural commodities. Talks by experts on agriculture, health, sanitation, family planning, and education are sometimes followed by discussions. Plays, skits, features, and folk music are interspersed with items of special interest to rural women, youth, and children. The language used is simple and the style is direct. Despite high illiteracy, the spoken word has been used very effectively in these programs. Some stations have created special characters, "radio personalities" whose appeal extends even to urban areas. A Radio Rural Forum is broadcast for thirty minutes two days a week as part of the general rural schedule. These special broadcasts, aimed at approximately 27,200 forums, deal exclusively with problems of agriculture and farm management. The feedback is reported to be excellent. Analysis of a random sample of these programs, broadcast from four stations located in the Hindi-speaking area, indicates that they are largely built around questions asked by the listeners.

Eight years ago, specialized cells were set up by AIR at a few selected stations to extend information to agriculturists on a package of improved practices to enable them to adopt high-yielding varieties. Today such units are located at thirty-four stations in different parts of the country. Since 1971 the farm and home programs organized by special cells have been combined and are now broadcast together. Every morning there is a five-minute bulletin giving topical hints to the farmers for the next twenty-four hours. This bulletin also includes special instructions to the Village Level Workers, which some stations repeat in the afternoon. The main one-hour program is broadcast at a convenient evening hour and includes entertainment, education, and hard-core agricultural subjects. This program is a collaborative venture of three ministries—Agriculture, Education, and Information and Broadcasting—with help from FAO, UNESCO, and UNDP. Agricultural universities cooperate by preparing materials for the five-minute morning bulletin.

An effort has been made to link the farm and home programs with a village-level organization called the Charcha Mandal (discussion group). There are 300 such groups, 100 of them composed exclusively of women. Each group receives a transistor set at half the normal cost if it agrees to listen to the program two days a week and hold a brief discussion on it. Questions raised in discussion are communicated to a farmers' training center. The extension service responds by resolving the difficulties of listeners and by providing necessary service. To enhance the efficiency of Village Level Workers in IADP (Intensive Agriculture Development Program) areas, 5,000 transistorized sets have been distributed among them. They are expected to listen to the programs intended for them and, at least once a week, invite the farmers to a listening session.

Most radio stations regularly broadcast special programs for rural women who have been organized into Mahila Mandals (women's clubs) to hear and discuss the program. In six states, where an intensive nutrition program was undertaken, UNICEF provided 5,000 transistor radios to enable women's clubs to listen regularly to these nutrition broadcasts, which also focus on women's roles as farm workers and homemakers. A recent innovation is the "School in the Air" broadcast from four stations, which offers comprehensive educational courses on selected agricultural topics at fixed hours. Evaluation of its performance speaks so well of its success that five stations are experimenting with a variant of its program.

Ten years ago one would have spoken with restraint of the impact of broadcasting on agriculture and allied subjects. The spirit behind the experiment could be commended but the results were unpredictable. Through trial and error, experiment and innovation, AIR has increased its credibility and some agriculturists are learning to depend upon it for information and guidance. Its entertainment programs still are popular, but there is little doubt that in years ahead its development-oriented programs will draw larger audiences.

Television is still in its infancy in India. It was intended principally for education and development, but the five operating stations appear to be catering more to the affluent urban population. Individual television sets in rural India are relatively rare; few villagers can afford their high cost. Of 163,446 sets owned on March 1, 1974, only 77 belonged to rural Tele-Clubs. The number of urban Tele-Clubs is larger; 162 of them were located in educational institutions, community centers, and other comparable organizations. Opinion is divided about their utility and effectiveness. Affluent peasants, especially in the prosperous states of Punjab and Haryana, own sets, but their primary interest appears to be in entertainment programs telecast from stations in India and Pakistan. Urban television owners are all rich or upwardly mobile, and prefer weekly feature films based on colorful scenes and songs. Despite claims to the contrary, entertainment and news take more broadcast time than education and development. The Satellite Instructional Television Experiment (SITE), scheduled to begin on June 3, 1975, is oriented to development and education almost exclusively. It is planned to reach 2,400 villages in the six states and could become a powerful instrument of education and citizenship training. But its real effects will have to be studied.

Indian films have responded only nominally to the appeals to emerge as a powerful medium working for social transformation. Some notable exceptions apart, Indian movies continue to remain aloof and remote from contemporary social realities. Year after year the industry produces films aimed at the box office. These films are a curious blend of romance, sex, glamor, violence, mystery, and showmanship. Occasionally they glorify the Indian tradition; national integration and some pressing social problems are touched upon in passing. Films of the latter category fail to make an impact because they have to make too many concessions to the requirements of box office success. A few progressive slogans and pious sermons thrown in with a lot of irrelevant absurdities do not leave any in-depth message. Support of the Film Finance Corporation has certainly brought out some excellent art and experimental films, but the medium needs a more positive social reorientation. The government's Films Division produces newsreels and documentaries. Many of these are trite and trivial, but some of them have both artistic merit and a high impact message. The successful short films demonstrate the strength of the medium, but its full potential remains to be realized.

Some Difficulties and Problems

There are several difficulties and problems in the way of effective media utilization. First, the reach of the mass media is still limited. Some English-language newspapers enjoy national reputation and have sizable circulation (see Table 2), but they do not reach down to the villages, and their readership is restricted to the small English-reading minority. Indian-language news-

Table 2. Circulation of Important English-Language Newspapers in India

Name of Paper	Circulation	
	1965	*1971*
Indian Express (Ahmedabad, Bangalore, Bombay, Delhi, Madras, Madurai, and Vijayawada editions)	352,106[a]	462,009
Times of India (Ahmedabad, Bombay, and Delhi editions)	195,354[a]	262,302
The Hindu (Bangalore, Coimbatore, and Madras editions)	141,327[b]	201,357
Statesman (Calcutta and Delhi editions)	151,341	193,522
Hindustan Times (Delhi)	115,632	149,566
Amrita Bazar Patrika (Calcutta)	111,738	114,118
Tribune (Chandigarh)	62,655	105,153

[a]Ahmedabad edition was not published in 1965.
[b]Only Madras edition was published in 1965.

papers have registered both quantitative and qualitative growth (see Table 3) and they have a respectable rural circulation in Kerala, Maharashtra, Tamil Nadu, and West Bengal. But their focus is mainly on politics and literature; development issues are discussed less frequently. Since 1973 the newspaper industry has been in crisis. Because of scarcity of newsprint, papers have had to limit their size, increase their price, and restrict their circulation.

Thanks to the "transistor revolution," the reach of the radio has been extended considerably. It is no longer a novelty in the countryside. According to the latest figures available, the total number of licensed radio receivers increased from 3,736,688 in 1963 to 14,033,919 in 1973. While statistics are lacking on this point, one can safely hazard a guess that over two-thirds of the added radios are in urban areas. The number of AIR broadcasting stations has gone up in the last ten years: from thirty-four principal and seventeen auxiliary stations to forty-five full-fledged radio stations, twenty-five auxiliary stations, and five auxiliary studio centers. In addition, two centers are broadcasting commercial programs. These stations have 109 medium-wave and 32 short-wave transmitters with transmission power of 4,138.90 KW and 1,620.50 KW respectively. The present installed capacity can cover 67.5 percent of India's territory and 80.3 percent of its population. The

Table 3. Language and Periodicity of Indian Newspapers and Periodicals

Language	*Dailies*		*Tri-, Bi-Weeklies, Weeklies, and Fort-nightlies*		*Monthlies*		*Quarterlies, Semiannuals, and Annuals*		*Total*	
	1964	*1971*	*1964*	*1971*	*1964*	*1971*	*1964*	*1971*	*1964*	*1971*
English	56	78	355	518	749	990	549	804	1,708	2,390
Hindi	149	222	911	3,800	604	907	90	177	1,754	3,116
Assamese	1	2	13	19	10	14	5	6	29	41
Bengali	7	15	236	288	221	295	95	162	559	760
Gujarati	34	43	169	219	235	281	44	51	482	594
Kannada	36	39	121	139	92	109	12	18	261	285
Malayalam	35	60	59	152	149	246	9	23	252	481
Marathi	41	77	179	331	162	245	55	88	437	741
Oriya	4	7	19	33	38	59	9	18	70	117
Punjabi	17	18	78	118	93	99	5	24	193	259
Sanskrit	1	1	5	4	10	11	6	12	22	28
Tamil	28	97	197	219	200	278	10	21	435	615
Telugu	13	17	120	168	145	190	7	11	285	386
Urdu	68	102	431	596	261	278	12	29	772	1,005
Bilingual	12	24	208	355	253	399	105	177	578	955
Multilingual	0	4	43	67	74	91	45	55	162	217
Others	12	15	61	80	69	91	20	42	162	228
TOTAL	514	821	3,204	3,676	3,365	4,583	1,078	1,718	8,161	12,218

population covered by medium-wave rose from 55 to 78 percent. Many areas still cannot be satisfactorily served because of the low power of the medium-wave transmitters.

There are competing pressures on the limited broadcasting time available to the stations. An analysis of program content of AIR's home service in 1973 shows this distribution of time: music 42 percent, news 22 percent, talks and discussions 8 percent, dramas 4 percent. Together these programs took 76 percent of the broadcasting time. The remaining 24 percent was devoted to what are known as "special programs": 6 percent rural, 2 percent tribal areas, 1 percent women's programs, 1 percent children, 2 percent educational, 1 percent industrial, and the rest (9 percent) miscellaneous.

Total broadcasting time in 1973 was 270,347 hours and 17 minutes (see Table 4). Within these time constraints, AIR cannot give enough attention to all the different regions and groups, in all the languages and dialects, it serves. For example, the lone radio station in the state of Himachal Pradesh is required to serve a large mountainous territory in which as many as 38

Table 4. Percentage of Time Devoted to Programs by All India Radio

	Percentage of Time	
Programs	*1961*	*1973*
Music (Indian and Western)	46.9	42.2
News	21.4	22.0
Talks and Discussions	5.3	8.0
Dramas	4.8	4.0
Special Broadcasts	21.6	23.7
Rural programs	2.0	6.2
Women's programs	8.0	1.4
Educational programs	3.0	2.4
Others	8.6	13.3[a]

[a] Of this time, 1.9 percent was devoted to programs for tribal areas, 1.3 percent to children's programs, 1.5 percent to industrial programs, and the rest (8.6 percent) to programs of miscellaneous categories.

dialects are spoken. It can barely find the time to have short programs in 12 of these dialects. Most of its broadcasting time goes to programs in Hindi, English, Urdu, and now even Sanskrit—languages confined largely to urban areas. The difficulties of AIR are multiplied: its home service has to cater to 19 principal languages, 135 regional and tribal dialects. To increase the frequency and duration of development programs, it is obviously necessary to have more transmitters of greater power.

Television is still in the experimental stage, with only four program-originating and -transmitting centers and one relay center. Its five transmitters have a nominal power of 35.6 KW, with effective radiated power of 232.20 KW. Today television can cover only 2.7 percent of the area and 4.7 percent of the population of India. The number of licensed sets was only 163,446 on December 31, 1973.

It is difficult to visualize any substantial expansion of the mass media in the near future. First, the indications are that for a decade or so newsprint is likely to be in short supply. This is bound to inhibit the growth of newspapers. Powerful radio transmitters are expensive and require scarce foreign exchange. Despite these difficulties, substantial expansion of the radio network is planned, but the time available for development broadcasts may still be inadequate. Television, but for the areas served by SITE, will gradually cover all the metropolitan centers. There is little likelihood of its reaching even 10 percent of the villages in the next twenty years. Thus, we are left with only one choice: we must make the most effective use of what we have.

Second, effective utilization of mass media requires a large number of specialists who can handle their hardware and software components. Such experts are in short supply. Only about a dozen newspapers have a positive policy of developing creative talent. The prevailing operative culture of AIR and Indian television inhibits innovation. They often encounter annoying and thoughtless political interference. An important factor responsible for the slow growth of expertise in development communication is the second-class status accorded to rural broadcasts and broadcasters. The government, it appears, is beginning to recognize the merit of professionalism in broadcasting. The top position of director general of AIR has recently been given to a competent professional; several of his predecessors were drawn from the general administrative service. Its reorganized divisions, including those dealing with development, are being headed by persons with trained competence. Concerted efforts are being made to update the capabilities of the 15,887 regular employees, 3,067 staff artists and production staff of AIR. In 1973, twenty program courses and seven technical courses were organized by AIR's Staff Training School. These are steps in the right direction. But such courses must be evaluated carefully—and something must be done to raise the economic and social status of the staff and artists dealing with development programs. Tangled red tape in AIR's bureaucratic organization should be cut to permit imaginative innovations.

Third, our understanding of how the mass media function, what impact they make, and how we can use them to produce desired effects is still meager. New research insights in this field are necessary. There are no reliable studies on the impact of newspapers, posters, and other publicity materials and movies. AIR has a growing organization for audience research. Its different units have produced some useful profiles of radio and television audiences and their leisure utilization, studies on perception and comprehension, and evaluations of different categories of programs. In the last ten years the quality of studies done by this organization has improved greatly, but they need more theoretical sophistication and methodological rigor. Being a subordinate organization, the Audience Research Center and its units have to be careful about the sensitivities of the bosses. Useful as their work is, there is a real need for greater involvement of independent agencies in communication research.

A large part of communication research in India, as in many other developing countries, is based so much on foreign models and tools and is so imitative that its validity is open to doubt. New conceptual frameworks and methodological approaches, relevant to Indian conditions, are needed for meaningful results. Such research alone can provide valuable guidelines to action. Effective communication links between those who investigate the problems of communication and those who operate the media should be forged to ensure full utilization of research results. Substantial research should be focused on the operational needs of the communication program, involving continuous interaction between researchers, programmers, and policymakers.

Finally, there is the paramount need for a well-thought-out communication policy. The situation today is somewhat chaotic: a multiplicity of agencies appear to be pulling in different directions. Priorities are set in an ad hoc manner, mostly with short-run objectives in view. There is little connection between priorities for different sectors: agriculture, public health, and family planning. The total effort lacks coordination. In the last ten years, some measures have been taken to improve the situation and bring about greater coordination. For example, AIR is cooperating with relevant agencies in updating knowledge among Village Level Workers about intensive nutrition, "School in the Air," farm, and home programs. What is now needed is a comprehensive policy that will harmonize and integrate the long-run and short-range objectives of development communication, bring about meaningful linkages between communication strategies for different sectors, and coordinate effectively the formulation of communication policy as well as its implementation.

Lessons of the Last Ten Years

Let us briefly recapitulate some lessons learned by India about development communication in the last ten years.

The case for development communication is often overstated and oversold. This causes disenchantment and frustration. We now see in clearer perspective what communication can do and what it cannot do for development. It is essential not to repeat the mistake of overemphasizing its role.

The indirect contribution of communication to the development process is important. It can be a powerful instrument in building durable and cohesive national bonds in a multireligious, multiethnic, and multilingual society. It can contribute also toward the creation of an ethos of change and progress. These functions should be reflected adequately in the communication strategy for development. Creation of an attitudinal and motivational infrastructure must be viewed as one of the paramount objectives of a development communication policy.

By itself communication does not produce development. The strategy of planning must evolve a clear set of priorities as to timing and balance in its diverse development projects. It should also visualize adequate support in the form of guidance, supplies, and services to these projects. Communication should be tailored to fit the requirements of each facet and phase of contemplated streams of development.

There is an unfortunate tendency in developing countries to be attracted toward new technology and to neglect more traditional methods of interpersonal communication. Western models of media use often are not relevant to the situation of countries like India. A constant effort has to be made, therefore, to find the right "mix" of traditional and modern models to produce the desired effect.

There is unmistakable evidence to suggest that, in developing countries, mass media acquire a stereotyped image of their function. They are viewed more as instruments for dissemination of information and entertainment than as vehicles for carrying development messages and imparting knowledge and skills. A constant effort has to be made, therefore, to change the stereotyped image of the media and to project them in relation to their envisioned development functions.

We now know that even the most imaginative communication cannot produce instant or even rapid change. The early results of successful communication do not go beyond creation of awareness and generation of interest. When the credibility of a program is established, people learn to rely and even depend on it. At this stage, it is time to reorganize the transmission pattern on the basis of feedback. Communicators in India were disappointed when their initial efforts did not produce development miracles. Today they have the satisfaction of seeing that many farmers are guided in their seasonal and day-to-day routine by the information transmitted to them by AIR agricultural programs.[3]

Another lesson we have learned is that multimedia and multichannel communication produces results much faster. Coordination between different agencies operating different categories of development programs is also essential. The warm reception given to some of the composite and well-integrated development programs of AIR, and the evidence of their general effectiveness, demonstrates the value of coordinated effort.

Finally, we realize that only by cautious experiment and innovation can effective strategies of communication be developed. It is essential to keep our approach pragmatic and flexible. A constant effort should be made to build up expertise in the field of development communication.

THE TASK AHEAD

If the mass media are to perform their development role satisfactorily in the next decades, they will have to address the challenges that Indian society faces. They will also have to equip themselves adequately to discharge this mission creatively.

The mass media have done well in arousing awareness and interest, but this function will have to be performed now in such a manner that only realistic and attainable expectations are aroused. They must continue to focus attention on national problems and to initiate debates on alternative strategies of solving them. The watchdog function of the mass media is well known. They will have to continue a close surveillance of the economic, social, and political environments and bring to light mistakes and failures, but in doing so they must take care that they do not demoralize and destroy those who make mistakes in good faith or those who are innocent. Restoration of faith in national institutions and inculcation of economic, social, and political discipline are the prime needs of the day. Communication, by itself, cannot hope to undertake such herculean tasks. Such endeavors must have wider policy support. But there is a great deal that the mass media can do. Toward this end they will have to reorient themselves and to put in concerted and disciplined effort.

The new communication strategy must project the vision of society as it is likely to develop under the relentless pressure of recurrent crises, and also of the society man can shape for himself if he decides to step into the future with forethought and careful planning. It is becoming increasingly evident that a high consumption model of society is irrelevant for India. The society of the future will have to underplay personal consumption and concentrate on a variety of social services uniformly available to all sections of society. Human groups learn to adjust to realities. In helping them adapt to the emerging situation, the mass media can play a significant role. The media can confer prestige. Let this prestige go to new values and ideals, to their protagonists and supporters. They can also involve themselves more centrally in citizenship training, health education, noninstitutional and informal education to make the concept of life-long education a reality.

In conclusion, communication is a necessary but not sufficient condition of development. It can project the image of society as we wish it to be, help in reshaping attitudes and values, lend a helping hand in imparting knowledge, and even teach some necessary techniques and skills. It must be seen as a useful tool of the policy processes that restructure society. Communication can be good or bad, functional or dysfunctional, depending on those who control it. To prepare for the shocks of uncertain tomorrows, the communication media must sharpen their capability to produce desired results.

NOTES

1. See Lerner's discussion of "rising frustrations" in chapter 16.
2. See the discussions of "new models" in chapter 3.
3. See chapters 8, 9, and 11.

7. Group Communication and Development in Mainland China—The Functions of Social Pressure

GODWIN C. CHU

What is unique about the use of communication for development in the People's Republic of China?

The Chinese Communists have used communication rather intensively for ideological indoctrination. But so have the Nazi Germans and the Soviets, to mention two recent examples. The Chinese Communists have not hesitated to apply coercion when it served a purpose.[1] Neither have the Russians and the Eastern European Communists. While the Chinese Communists have been influenced by the Leninist theory of "agitprop," they have applied it in a much different, much broader way than the Russians.[2]

What is uniquely Chinese is the way communication has been used to form new groups; it is not merely an instrument of political surveillance and control as it is in Russia. Rather, the Chinese have used the groups to generate social pressure and apply it to the restructuring of economic, cultural, and family relations—indeed, to every process of a changing social system.

Virtually every Chinese today belongs to one or more of these groups. The groups are given a considerable amount of local responsibility and initiative, within the general directives of the party and the guidance of the cadres. Once the patterns of group processes are institutionalized, the party can steer development with a minimum of direction and force. Whatever the issue—whether to participate in a production campaign, to practice economy in consumption, to criticize Lin Piao and Confucius, or to assign birth quotas—the group takes the directives from above and works out a way to carry them out. To use an analogy suggested by Wilbur Schramm, the groups in China have become local engines that run on their own fuel, as it were, through the social pressure the members themselves generate by interpersonal communication within the group setting. Through the new groups, the party has largely succeeded in overhauling the Chinese social system into one capable of implementing development according to Mao Tse-tung's approach.

In this paper, we shall discuss (1) the process by which the new groups have been formed in China to replace the old, (2) the application of social pressure in groups, (3) the functions of the group in the broad task of development, and (4) the addictive effects of social pressure. We shall focus our discussion primarily on groups in rural China, although urban groups share many similarities.

Processes of Group Formation

The traditional Chinese village prior to 1949 was built upon the kinship system (Yang 1945). The village's economic resources, primarily land and production tools, were concentrated in the hands of those kinsmen who were landlords. They wielded social influence, held the power of local decision-making, and controlled a major portion of productive activities in the village. Because the landlords and the tenants often belonged to the same extended family, their relationship was not one between a master and his servants, but was modified by their kinship ties. It was primarily the sustaining kinship structure that provided stability in the Chinese villages through the ages.

Breaking Up the Old

The objective of the Chinese Communist party was to break up the kinship-related agricultural production system and replace it with one based on collective ownership and collective labor. The first step, taken immediately after the party seized power in 1949, was the Land Reform.[3] The decision was made by the party's top hierarchy as part of its long-term commitment to the Communist ideology. But the reform was implemented by involving the peasants at every stage of the program. It was through their participation that new groups were formed to replace the old landlord-tenant structure.

What the party first did was to arouse dissatisfaction among the peasants with the traditional system. Following much publicity on the Land Reform campaign in the mass media, the party sent work teams to the villages. When a team arrived in a village, its cadre members immediately made a public announcement of the objectives of the Land Reform, with a warning to the landlords that they must cooperate fully. The cadres then visited the poor peasants and tenants to make their acquaintance and to learn about their sufferings. The peasants were called together and encouraged to share with one another their past experiences. A number of meetings were held at which the peasants were asked "to spit bitter water," that is, to tell their own stories in order to convince one another that the old system must be changed. By this time, not only had a feeling of dissatisfaction been aroused, but also a sense of common identity had begun to emerge. The party called this common identity "class consciousness." It was only after this stage had been reached that the peasants were considered ready to take action against the landlords.

At this time, an alternative to the traditional system was suggested to the peasants: Take away the land from the landlords and redistribute it among themselves so that they would become independent farmers. Even with the promise of material incentive—the acquisition of land that the peasants treasured dearly—this step was often difficult for the peasants to contemplate. Largely because many of the landlords were their relatives, the peasants often hesitated to confront them. The party sought to ease the pain of confrontation by focusing the initial purge on a few landlords who had mistreated and exploited their tenants. These individuals, officially referred to as *eh pa* (villains), were brought forward for mass trials in the village.

Acting upon the cues given by the work team cadres, a few peasants would speak up at the mass rally to expose the wrongdoings of the landlords, and other peasants would support the charges. This was the peasants' first behavioral commitment to the process of socialist transformation. An intense atmosphere of mass involvement was gradually built up to create a sense of urgency and legitimacy for whatever actions might be taken against the landlords. In most cases, the landlords surrendered their land and properties. In more serious cases, the death penalty was imposed. The confiscated land, properties, cattle, and farm tools were redistributed to the poor peasants and tenants. Before the Land Reform, the agricultural population in China was estimated to break down into less than 10 percent landlords and rich peasants who owned about 70 to 80 percent of the arable land, some 70 percent tenants and poor peasants, and about 20 percent middle peasants. After the Land Reform, the composition was officially estimated at about 80 percent middle peasants and 20 percent poor peasants. (See note 3, Liao, "The Dazzling Achievements. . . .")

By expropriating the landlords and condemning them to be a class of social outcasts, the Land Reform was the first step in changing the village structure and organizing the Chinese peasants into new, party-controlled groups.

Interim Confusion

The old institution of agricultural production was destroyed. Former tenants now worked as independent small farmers. However, the removal of the landlords also suspended some of the functions they once served, particularly in providing rural credit, marketing, and coordinated use of labor and farm tools. There was a temporary institutional vacuum in the villages. In the confusion, some of the party rural cadres took advantage of the situation to buy up land and operate high-interest loans.[4]

This development was not surprising. The Land Reform eliminated the landlords as a stabilizing force in the villages, but did little to change the behavioral patterns of the peasants. For ages they had been dependent upon their superiors for help. They had never learned how to organize themselves for group action other than in the kinship framework. Now that their kinship superiors were gone, they had to turn to somebody having authority. The rural cadres simply filled that need.

The party's response was a two-pronged Rural Rectification campaign that began in 1952/53 and was designed to curtail the power of the party's rural cadres and give the peasants a role that eventually changed their traditional norm of noninvolvement into active participation in local decision-making.[5] This campaign paved the way for organizing the peasants into new functioning groups that were suitable for collective labor and capable of managing their own affairs.

The Land Reform had been carried out in the years immediately following the party's overwhelming military victory in the civil war. The spirit of revolution had been strong. The many actions—organizing the peasants, purging the landlords, seizing and redistributing the land—had kept the rural cadres busy and in a state of high morale. With the conclusion of the Land Reform, things began to fall back to a routine. Many symptoms of the old Chinese bureaucracy began to reappear. One common ill was known as "commandism"—relying on mass obedience of administrative orders for the carrying out of new programs.[6] Compliance was expected even though many of the orders were unrealistic. Nepotism and corruption were not uncommon.[7] At the same time, a tendency known as "rich peasant thinking" became widespread, as many rural cadres placed family prosperity ahead of revolution. Some cadres who had bought up land hired others to work for them, thus establishing themselves as new landlords (Berstein, in Lewis 1970, pp. 239–267). There was general ignorance of the Communist ideology. Some lower-level cadres filed false reports for their superiors and made no attempt to communicate with the peasants.[8]

In the winter of 1952, the early days of the Rural Rectification campaign, the party sent teams of specially trained cadres to the villages to correct this situation. Meeting with the cadres, the work team members began by criticizing themselves for inadequate supervision. It was emphasized that the only way to develop an efficient party organization in the village was for every member to engage in voluntary self-criticism and mutual criticism. This was followed by a series of criticism sessions attended by party cadres in the village, in which each member examined his political consciousness and job performance, and criticized his own errors and those of others. Disciplinary action was taken against serious offenders.

The village cadres were forced to abandon their positions of superiority, from which they had issued orders to the peasants without giving explanations. Instead, they were required to communicate with the peasants, to explain to them the objectives of new programs and to seek out their opinions and suggestions. In this way the peasants were encouraged to keep a watchful eye on the cadre members. Gradually, the peasants began to learn their new roles as participants, and to voice their opinions regarding the practical aspects of production and other collective affairs in their village—but always within the limits set by the party's policies.

Establishing the New

At the same time, the peasants were organized into collective production groups. It is important to note that the party did not attempt to build its new rural institution from scratch. To ease the process of transition, it took as a basis an old institution that had existed in rural China for centuries, the institution of informal mutual help among peasants. Chinese peasants have always extended help to each other in the form of labor, cattle, tools, and occasionally credit. In the past such exchanges were made generally among relatives within the kinship network. The exchange was informal and regulated by reciprocity rather than contractual stipulations. The recipient of help knew from age-old norms when and how much to repay.

The party expanded this old institution by organizing the peasants into mutual aid teams.[9] A small village of fifteen or twenty families would operate as one or two teams. Larger villages were divided into more teams. In most areas, beginning in the spring of 1953 following the Rural Rectification campaign, the peasants were first organized into temporary mutual aid teams for simple, seasonal exchange of labor, following the patterns of earlier experiments tried by the Chinese Communists in North China back in 1943. The purposes were to share the use of draft animals and farm tools and to pool labor resources, generally among relatives and neighbors, during the busy sowing time, summer cultivation, and autumn harvesting. During the slack season, when there were only odd jobs to be done, the peasants would do them separately and individually. Seasonal mutual aid did not change the basic characteristics of individual farming, but it prepared the peasants for the eventual collective farming that was to follow.

When the peasants had become more or less accustomed to this new form of labor relations, the mutual aid teams were converted from a seasonal to a regular, year-round basis. Membership in a regular mutual aid team was meant to be permanent. Peasants in the same team helped one another at all times. They worked according to simple production plans and began learning to manage their productive activities. Some teams used their increased income to buy farm implements and drafts animals as common property.

In December 1953, the government of the People's Republic announced its Agricultural Cooperative Movement. This was one step further toward collectivization. The mutual aid teams were combined into larger units known as agricultural producers' cooperatives, with an average size of about 160 families. Altogether more than 740,000 cooperatives were eventually organized.[10] While the Mutual Aid program was built upon the traditional norm of reciprocity among Chinese peasants, the agricultural cooperatives called for collective planning of production and collective use of cattle, farm tools, land, and manpower. The cooperatives were characterized by the peasants' contribution of land as shares and by centralized management in the hands of the cadres.

In the elementary cooperatives, which began to replace the mutual aid teams in 1954, the land titles, cattle, and farm implements remained with the peasant members. The distribution of crop income among the members was based partly on the number of shares each member had acquired by transferring his land to the cooperatives, and partly on the amount of labor he and his family had performed. In the advanced cooperatives, which replaced the elementary cooperatives in late 1956, the number of shares no longer made any difference. The distribution of crop income was based solely on labor performance. Except for private plots around the house and small livestock, all land, cattle, and major implements were collectively owned. In August 1958, the party took another step and began reorganizing the advanced cooperatives into people's communes.

Communication and Social Pressure

In the process of change from independent small farming, in the wake of the Land Reform, to agricultural cooperatives, the Chinese peasants went along with the party's decisions dutifully, although perhaps reluctantly. The situations surrounding these changes, however, were different from those present before the Land Reform. While the landlord-tenant relations contained seeds of grievances capable of stimulating widespread dissatisfaction, the Chinese peasants were mostly satisfied with the independent small farming after they had acquired land, and did not want to have any further change. A typical example was the much publicized case of Li Ssu-hsi, a peasant of Hunan. Li was quoted by the *People's Daily* as saying:

> . . . all my life I have suffered hardship. Now that I have been given land, I am completely satisfied, so why continue to make revolution.[11]

Thus the party was not able to arouse dissatisfaction as a motivation for the next step of change. Instead, it sought to emphasize the importance of commitment to communism and to build up ideological value-attachment as a substitute motivation in place of dissatisfaction. Revolution was proposed as an end in itself, not just a means.

During the Land Reform, a basis of identity for the peasants was built upon their common sufferings at the hands of the landlords, but this basis had been somewhat weakened with the landlords' removal. The party had to use continued class struggle as a rallying point, citing the presence of ex-landlords and ex-rich peasants as a potential threat, so as to strengthen the peasants' conviction.

While the Land Reform was in progress, the peasants had been induced to make their first behavioral commitment in the mass trials of villains. Such inducement was no longer essential. Having taken their first step in the Land Reform and having accepted the redistributed land, the peasants had in effect tied their future with the party. Breaking away would be difficult.

Social Pressure for Change

The party authorities probably realized that the strength of ideological commitment and revolutionary fervor at that time was insufficient to motivate the peasants to give up their land and join the cooperatives. Some pressure would be necessary. This was achieved through the skillful use of communication, along with coercion.

The mass media, particularly the newspapers, played the role of announcing the general directives, providing specific instructions, and serving as a mechanism of feedback from the grass-roots level. Throughout these movements, problems and difficulties of transition experienced by peasants in various localities were rather openly reported and discussed in news and feature stories. In addition to carrying useful information, the importance of which was fully recognized, the media also sought to create a semblance of nationwide enthusiasm by publicizing the actions of model villages that were eager to implement the collective movements. Meanwhile, cases of erroneous thinking and behavior, like those of Li Ssu-hsi, were brought to public attention and criticized.

More important than the mass media was the network of interpersonal communication that had begun to take shape in the villages after the Rural Rectification campaign, in the context of the small study groups. In a peculiar way, the communication network in the village's new group structure both made it easier for the cadres to apply pressure on the peasants and, at the same time, gave the peasants some sense of participation so that the constraints of collectivization seemed somewhat muffled. At every stage of change, the rural cadres were required to call the peasants together to explain the objectives and ask for their support. Usually, some of the progressive peasants would respond enthusiastically. Yes, they were eager to get the cooperatives organized and to carry the revolution forward. Once the stage was set, other peasants found it difficult not to follow. Meanwhile, a nationwide campaign was launched to criticize the "rich peasant thinking" as exemplified by Hunan peasant Li Ssu-hsi. Every peasant was required to participate in the campaign by denouncing the "rich peasant thinking" and by examining himself for a possible leaning toward this erroneous thinking. A peasant who showed signs of reluctance would become a local target for criticism by others, a process which would then be followed by his own self-criticism and promise of reform.

In this way a perception of new group norms governing the do's and don'ts gradually emerged through the process of communication within the group. These new norms became the guidelines supporting the party's programs of change. This step was tantamount to the group's acceptance of the agricultural cooperative programs. Once this was achieved, the peasants were asked to discuss the practical ways of implementing the party's instructions according to their local conditions. Such discussion gave the peasants a feeling of having a voice in the movement. Using these tactics, the party was able to transform China's vast rural population from small independent farming to agricultural cooperatives in less than six years.

The same communication and pressure tactics were used in the Commune Movement of 1958, and again the Chinese peasants complied. Within a matter of a few months, the 740,000 agricultural cooperatives were reorganized into some 24,000 people's communes.[12] However, because of the drastic restrictions placed upon family life—dismantling the family kitchen and eating in commune mess halls—and abolition of the small private plots around the farmhouse—passive resistance was widespread. The situation was so serious that a year later the party had to retreat from the original concept of communes and move in the direction of the advanced agricultural cooperatives. Family life is now allowed and the small private plots have been restored.

Social Pressure for Labor Performance

Because of its severe denunciation and sparing use of material incentives, the party has had to rely on other means for maintaining a sufficiently high level of labor performance by peasants and workers. Symbolic rewards are employed rather extensively. Individual workers and units that distinguish themselves in production competition campaigns are singled out for recognition. Outstanding units are given red flags. Individuals who work hard are awarded buttons to wear. Those who have achieved superb performance are voted labor heroes.[13]

Intense pressure to work was often felt by individual workers during a campaign in the form of fear that their unit would otherwise fall behind. This can be illustrated by the experience of a female medical student who was sent to help in construction work during the Great Leap Forward:

> Well, we were supposed to work eight hours a day but there were so many "challenges" and "counter-challenges" between the various units that we were frequently told to work extra hours. There were three eight-hour shifts but those with "high political consciousness" refused to stop work when their time was up—and their display of enthusiasm spurred on the less active students,

> because no one wanted to be criticized as ideologically backward. How I remember those cold wet early spring days when we slipped and fell under our heavy loads, covering our faces and clothes with mud. But we all worked like mad because we wanted to prove our political soundness. (Harper 1964, p. 63)

The fear of being left behind was alleviated by mutual assurances to boost others' spirits. After returning from work, according to this student, they did not go to bed immediately. They attended group discussion meetings to review their work and morale:

> When we discussed the work amongst ourselves we were always careful to say something like "It's tough, but nothing is insurmountable in the socialist society, and nothing is difficult for one with noble ambitions. . . ." (Harper 1964, p. 65)

Social pressure is exerted also in informal talks or criticism sessions within the group. How informal social pressure works to prevent slack performance is illustrated by Chen Yung-kuei, the leader of the model Tachai Production Brigade:

> In our Tachai we had a member who could join our labor, but he did not work hard. Since the liberation he had been depending on relief. During the autumn harvest of 1960, he owed our collectivity 60 JMP, and did not have money to pay for his grain. His woman said: "Hey, it's getting cold. How come they haven't given out relief cotton jackets?" It just happened that the few relief cotton jackets from the state had been given to the old bachelors. So none was left for him. So he talked to me: "How come I didn't get any relief?" I said: "You can work, so from now on I am not going to give you any relief. Relief won't do you any good."
>
> In 1960, he worked only some 260 days, and his woman worked 14 days. The two of them got about 270 days. Because we didn't give him relief, we overcame his dependent thinking. In 1961, he worked even during the winter, and his woman went to the field whenever she had time. He got 361 days and his woman got 140 days. He not only did not lack food, but got some surplus and saved more than 200 JMP. He had 500 catties of grains stored in his home.[14]

It may be noted that the informal social pressure in this case was backed by economic sanctions. The experience of a Chinese worker who went from Macao to China in 1958 to join the Great Leap Forward illustrates how group criticism is employed to correct poor production performance:

> [A worker with a poor record] was officially warned that he must catch up with the more progressive workers. If the case was serious enough and he didn't improve, he was criticized at a public meeting. Everyone had to attend and a ranking cadre announced the culprit's name and offense. The workers were obliged to criticize the offender and suggest ways in which he might be punished. . . .(Harper 1964, p. 149)

The combined use of limited material incentives, symbolic rewards for distinction in competition campaigns, and social pressure by peers has apparently been effective in keeping the labor performance at an economically viable level.

Functions of Group in Development

By instituting the new Chinese groups, the party has created an effective agent for the state that can (1) carry out the development programs, (2) exercise social control over the group members, and (3) provide a mechanism for conflict resolution and group integration at the grass-roots level. We shall discuss each function briefly.

A major difficulty experienced by many developing countries is not merely the dissemination of information about new programs. With adequate use of the mass media, aided by traditional word-of-mouth channels, the government usually can get the message around. The real hurdle comes at the acceptance and action level. How can a change agency get the villagers to accept the program and take the recommended action? With the Chinese groups, for example, the communes and production brigades, this is not a serious problem. The party has only to send the directives and instructions to the communes. From there on, the commune's cadres and the peasant members take care of the rest through a continuous flow of communication within the group.

Two important features have made it possible for the Chinese groups to function effectively in this manner. One concerns the role of cadres. As agents of the party and the state, the cadres see to it that the directives from above are carried out. They have a responsibility to make sure that the party's basic policies, that is, denial of individual interests and prevention of revisionism, are strictly followed. They play an important part in the group's activities by suggesting general courses of action. But they do not have the authority to tell the peasants exactly how to implement the programs. This limitation leaves room for the peasants to express their views and sometimes to criticize the conduct of the cadres.

The second feature concerns the group ownership of production means and material resources. In general, a commune is required to manage the use of its own resources and, except in situations of emergency, receives no help from the state. In this way, the party has made it both necessary and feasible for the commune members to rely on themselves. They either swim or sink. Besides, since the collective ownership system makes it unlikely for individuals to realize appreciable personal gains, the group can plan the use of the resources at its disposal primarily for achieving the objectives of the development programs, instead of being overly concerned with protecting vested interests.

The group also serves as an effective mechanism for social control. Erroneous ideology and undesirable behavior by the party's standards are brought to public attention in the study group sessions. There, through self-criticism and mutual criticism, pressure is brought to bear on the deviant individual until he pleads guilty and promises to rectify his error. The frequent interactions among the people while working and meeting as a group make it unlikely for anyone to maintain a deviant position for any length of time without being detected and criticized. The group influence is so overwhelming that there is practically no private life.

The group provides a well-regulated setting for its members to air some of their petty grievances and minor conflicts over the use of resources and allocation of status within the group. No one is allowed to challenge the basic party policy, or to suggest a course of action along the line of Liu Shao-chi's revisionism. Within these rigid lines, however, the peasants are allowed to criticize the erroneous behavior of the cadres, to complain about the loss of manpower because of too many meetings, or to gripe about minor inconveniences.[15] These complaints are actively solicited by the party once in a while to prevent the accumulation of tension or friction that may have resulted from the heavy demand of labor performance. To the extent that the group members can periodically bring their contentions into the open for public discussion, the severity of conflict within the group is likely to be reduced and group cohesion maintained. The presence of ex-landlords and ex-rich peasants as a deprived negative reference group, ready to be criticized and blamed for production failures, further contributes to integration among the poor and lower-middle peasants. The peasants' life, hard as it may be, appears to be much less deprived in comparison to that of the ex-landlords and ex-rich peasants.

Problems of Efficacy

Why do the Chinese groups function so effectively as a mechanism for applying social pressure on their members?

At least two aspects of the Chinese groups may be noted from the individual's perspective. One is a high degree of permanence. Whether one works for a commune or a factory, one has no choice of occupational mobility. Only the party can move an individual from one post to another, and this is apparently not done frequently. Thus when a person joins a commune or a factory, he expects to stay with it until he is told otherwise. Because of the total absence of individual choice of group membership, the individual has no way of avoiding the social pressure.

The other feature of the group in China is its comprehensiveness and dominance over one's life. An individual belongs to essentially one formal group. Almost every aspect of one's interactions—economic, political, social, and cultural—takes place within the same group context. Everything is done within the group, whether it is to work, to discuss political ideology, to criticize one another, or to enjoy revolutionary opera. The group dominates the individual's total life. Because of the heavy dependence of an individual on his group, both economically and otherwise, he has to submit to the group pressure.

Social pressure can be examined from the group's perspective. We sometimes speak of a group as if it were an entity having a life of its own, whereas we are actually using the term "group" as a shorthand expression for the rather complex processes of interactions that bind a number of individuals together. The sustaining forces that keep a group intact are partly affective and partly instrumental through mutual interdependence. A nuclear family as a group is an example in which the affective component is relatively strong. A work crew, on the other hand, stays together more out of instrumental than affective considerations. The Chinese groups are not devoid of their affective components. But a Chinese production brigade, for instance, functions as a group largely because of instrumental reasons. For the peasants, the production brigade is the unit in which they seek survival together.

The necessity to seek survival collectively is a result of the group reward system the party has imposed on the Chinese peasants. During the past, the distribution and withdrawal of reward were largely centered on the extended family. Thus the extended family was a powerful basis for exerting social pressure. Now the extended family is no longer the source of material reward for the Chinese. Although the nuclear family is still functioning, it has practically no basis of productive resources that it can claim as its own. Members of a nuclear family work only as labor hands for the production team. It is therefore the production team that has assumed primary responsibility to provide for the material needs of its members, through either production or exchange. The production yields are more or less equally shared among the peasant members.[16] Because of this group basis of economic life, the members cannot afford to permit slack performance by any individuals, particularly when they are not obligated to one another by strong affective ties like those of an extended family. Strictly speaking, it is not the group as an entity that exerts social pressure. Rather, it is the members in the group who bring pressure to bear on their peers because their poor labor performance may adversely affect the group's welfare.

For very much the same reasons, we can see why the members of a Chinese group would have to apply social sanctions on individuals who manifest erroneous thinking or undesirable behavior. The Chinese group, whether a production team or a work team, does not exist in a social vacuum. It is a small unit depending on a broader social system for economic supplies, symbolic reward, and political recognition. In short, it depends on the larger system for its own survival. For this reason, it simply cannot ignore among its members the existence of any ideology and behavior that are taboo to the larger system.

The reactions of the Chinese group in this regard seem to follow a pattern. When no criticism campaign is decreed by the party, the group usually shows some degrees of tolerance as long as the tendencies of deviance do not attain serious proportions, because constant criticisms among its members would tend to create too much friction within the group. We may call it a communication of silence, transmitting a message not by what one says but by what one does not say. However, once a criticism campaign is ordered, then the group, under the direction of its cadres, has to demonstrate its own ideological soundness by starting self-criticism and mutual criticism. Failure to do so would jeopardize the standing and even survival of the group.

Effective as it may seem, social pressure in the Chinese groups does have its limits. The case of the People's Commune movement in 1958 indicates what some of the limits are. While exerting social pressure, the group cannot totally ignore the affiliative needs of human beings as they are fulfilled in family life. And it cannot deprive the peasants of the last remnants of individual family production—the small private plots.

The dependence on social pressure instead of material incentives for maintaining labor performance seems to have a price. There is some evidence to suggest that, when individuals are prompted to work largely by group pressure, they tend not to perform well once that pressure is withdrawn, as if they had become addicted to pressuring. Even the promise of material reward does not seem to be a motivation strong enough to make up for the lack of social pressure. This can be illustrated by two contrasting cases. The general impression about Chinese refugees who have escaped to Hong Kong is that, at least during the initial period of adjustment, many are not energetic workers when they are not closely supervised. Wages alone do not appear to be sufficient to make them work as diligently as the Hong Kong workers do. Perhaps these refugees have become so accustomed to heavy group prodding that once they are placed in a social environment where no such prodding is exerted upon them, they simply do not work as hard.[17] It is entirely possible that the refugees may be highly atypical and not representative of the people in mainland China as a whole. But the phenomenon noted among the refugees has also been observed among ordinary peasants within China. A case reported in April 1974 in a Liaoning provincial radio broadcast suggests that when no social pressure was applied the Chinese peasants did very poor work, even when given extra material reward.[18] This phenomenon may explain why the party has found it necessary to launch one production campaign after another in order to keep up group pressure and prevent labor performance from slipping.

NOTES

1. For an analysis of Chinese Communist techniques of persuasion and indoctrination, see Frederick T. C. Yu, *Mass Persuasion in Communist China* (New York: Praeger, 1964); also Franklin W. Houn, *To Change a Nation: Propaganda and Indoctrination in Communist China* (Glencoe, Ill: Free Press, 1961). One example of the use

of coercion has been analyzed in Edgar H. Schein, *Coercive Persuasion: A Socio-Psychological Analysis of the "Brainwashing" of American Civilian Prisoners by the Chinese Communists* (New York: W.W. Norton, 1961).

2. "Agitprop" refers to agitation and propaganda, in Lenin's terms. See Alex Inkeles, *Public Opinion in Soviet Russia* (Cambridge, Mass.: Harvard University Press, 1962). While both refer to interpersonal communication, in Soviet Russia, propaganda applies to the elites while agitation is directed to the mass of people. The Chinese Communists used both terms interchangeably shortly after they gained power. For instance, a pamphlet published in 1950 on how to stimulate labor performance among industrial workers contained fourteen articles, all of which used the two terms synonymously. See *How to Manage Well the Propaganda and Agitation Work for Industries* (Peking: Hsin Hua Book Store, 1950). In a policy statement contained in a *People's Daily* editorial on January 3, 1951, the Communist party dropped the term "agitation" (*ku tung*) because it sounded odd in Chinese and recommended only the term "propaganda" (*hsuan chuan*).

3. See Liao Lu-yen, "The Dazzling Achievements on the Agricultural Battle Front in Ten Years," in *The Glorious Ten Years* (Hong Kong: San Lien Book Store, 1959), pp. 120–126. Eyewitness accounts are available in C. K. Yang, *A Chinese Communist Society: The Family and the Village* (Cambridge, Mass.: M.I.T. Press, 1965), pp. 131–145; also in Han Yi-wei, *Three Years of Revolution* (Hong Kong: South Wind Publishing Co., 1955), pp. 47–58.

4. "A Report on How Party Secretaries in Various Regions are Correctly Carrying out the Rectification Policy of the Party," *People's Daily*, April 2, 1953. Also, "How to Handle Rural Party Members Who Hired Workers, Operated Loans, Set Up Business, or Leased Land," *Tientsin Daily News*, February 27, 1953.

5. "Some Experiences from the Rural Rectification Campaign," *People's Daily*, April 2, 1953.

6. An Tze-wen, "We Must Carry out a Resolute Struggle of New Three-Anti Movement in Various Organizations in the Entire Country," official report presented at the First National Committee of the People's Political Consultative Conference on February 7, 1953. Released by New China News Agency on February 9, 1953.

7. Ibid.

8. *Shansi Daily*, August 22, 1951.

9. Wang Chien, "The Mutual Aid and Cooperative Movement in North China," *People's China* 8 (April 16, 1953): 8–11.

10. See Chou En-lai, "The Great Ten Years," in *The Glorious Ten Years* (Hong Kong: San Lien Book Store, 1959), p. 38.

11. "*New Hunan Daily* Discusses Li Ssu-hsi Thinking," *People's Daily*, September 26, 1951.

12. See Chou En-lai, "The Great Ten Years," in *The Glorious Ten Years* (Hong Kong: San Lien Book Store, 1959), p. 38.

13. Liu Chien-kuo, "Contest between Red Banner Sections and 'Six Good' Workers," *Workers Daily*, May 27, 1961.

14. Chen Yung-kuei, "The Revolutionary Spirit of Tachai People," in *Irrigation and Electricity*, 1964, no. 4, reprinted in *People's Handbook 1964*, p. 86, compiled by Takung Pao and published by Hsinhua Book Store (Peking).

15. Such complaints have been published in letters to the editor of the *People's Daily*. For example: A Reader, "Prohibit Waste in Pursuit of Formality," *People's Daily*, July 17, 1967; A Reader, "In Harvest Time, Do Not Forget Austerity," *People's Daily*, June 23, 1968; Tsui Cheng-yao and Heh Kwang-shan, "Fewer Meetings and Shorter Meetings in Busy Time," *People's Daily*, April 26, 1968; A Poor Peasant,

"Co-op Stores Should Provide the Masses with Convenience and Help with Production," *People's Daily*, May 12, 1968.

16. It should be noted that those individuals who are offspring of ex-landlords and ex-rich peasants are not treated as commune members and are assigned fewer work points. See "Rural Class Policy in Yang Chiang County," *China Monthly* 10 (October 1966): 972.

17. It is also possible that after years of submission to group pressure, the people of mainland China have become so conditioned to depending on their groups that they do not know how to function adequately when placed in a social environment where such pressure is generally not so heavy. This possibility was suggested by Sally Reston when she discussed the Chinese refugees in Hong Kong: "They (the people in Hong Kong) are finding a very curious thing about these 25-year-olds who come in there, both men and women, young men and women, that they don't know how to maintain themselves independently. Everything has been done for them in China, their housing, their medical care, their education, their transportation. They don't have to queue up for anything. So that when they get into independent society they really don't know quite how to operate." See Appendix, "Eric Sevareid's Interview with James Reston," in Tillman Durdin, James Reston, and Seymour Topping, *The New York Times Report from Red China* (New York: Quadrangle Books, 1971), p. 357. The interview was broadcast by CBS on August 31, 1971.

18. "Liaoning Commune Big-Character Poster Criticizes Work Point System," Shengyang, Liaoning Provincial Broadcast, April 20, 1974, Foreign Broadcast Information Service, FBIS–CHI–74–80, pp. 13–14.

7a. How Durable Is Mao's Policy?

F. TILLMAN DURDIN

Dr. Chu has given a clear and succinct overview of how mutual surveillance by group members operates in the development of collectivized agriculture in China; also of the importance of interpersonal and other types of communication in the working of the system.

Questions naturally arise, such as the significance of the Chinese communist system, its usefulness for other societies, and the transferability of Chinese communication techniques for use elsewhere. There is also the question of the effectiveness of the system for the Chinese themselves.

Dr. Chu has described the basic characteristics of the system. By way of comment on these questions, perhaps I can add a little further illumination based on knowledge gained from my observance of the system over a period of seven years in Hong Kong and a 1971 visit to several communes in China, where I talked with commune members. As Dr. Chu has indicated, the system is a unique combination of Marxist-Maoist ideology and traditional Chinese social values and methods of social action. Its uniqueness is evident from the fact that it operates quite differently from methods used in agricultural development in other Communist countries, despite its claim to be based on Marxism-Leninism.

The traditional element in the China system is in the strong emphasis on group action; this follows old patterns of large-family cooperation, village solidarity, and mutual responsibility in these groups. However, in China today, the authoritarian and Marxist component, in my view, is more important than the traditional elements in the system. The system in China could not operate without the overall centralized direction of a strong, disciplined Communist leadership with a clearly perceived ideology and a determination to establish and develop a Marxist socialist society and economy. This leadership is in control of all media, all channels of information and opinion from both inside and outside the country. It guides, if not directly controls, all forms of activity—education, culture, individual relationships, travel—indeed, all aspects of life. At small group levels, as Dr. Chu has said, there is wide scope for group members, by discussions, complaints, and criticism of themselves and each other, to influence implementation of programs within the system, but members are not permitted to change, or to advocate change, in its basic character.

In imposing its will, the leadership, through the medium of the cadres in charge at the lower levels of society, makes sophisticated use of the dialectical factor in Marxist ideology. It is this factor that prevails in the handling of groups. The Chinese Communists make a simple application to everyday life of the thesis, antithesis, synthesis of Hegelian philosophy, calling it the "theory of contradictions." Another way they have of putting it is "one divides into two." In everything, Mao Tse-tung argues, there are "contradictions." In other words, there are individuals and forces in society that will oppose the policy or the objective of the moment—for example, in rural areas, the work program or work methods (one divides into two, the forces for and against). The procedure for dealing with this phenomenon is to struggle and criticize until the "contradiction" is overcome, until synthesis is achieved—that is, until opposition is overcome, at least temporarily.

If the contradiction or opposition is not fundamentally against the system, it is a "contradiction" among the people and is dealt with through the normal use of criticism, self-criticism, and social pressures within the group. If it is fundamental, the opponent is branded a class enemy and is subject to very severe "struggle" and possibly grave penalties—purging from the group, sentencing to forced labor at a state farm, or some such punishment.

It is amazing how the operation of this dialectical approach has become virtually automatic through practice over the last twenty-five years within the Communist society of China. It is used over and over again to enforce conformity. It operates against a background of fear that deviation can bring harrassment from within the group, guided by a cadre schooled in procedures and ideology; and fear that, if persisted in, deviation can result in one's being designated as a class enemy, with all the dire consequences that follow. In big so-called rectification campaigns in China, allowance is made for finding 5 percent of the population "dangerous class enemies" who must be dealt with severely. This is by way of saying that roughly this percentage of the population has manifested serious opposition to the policies and methods of the regime.

Deviation can take many forms. The one against which the regime constantly inveighs, and against which struggle is regularly waged in the groups, is showing "capitalist tendencies." This can mean a family spending too much time cultivating its tiny private plot or making handicrafts for sale in the markets, while neglecting labor in the collective. Or it can mean hoarding food or trading on the black market. Sometimes whole production teams of several hundred people are denounced for capitalist tendencies.

In the great game of "contradictions," the regime never lacks for scapegoats, someone or some group to struggle against. At one time it is those who show capitalist tendencies. At another it is the proclaimed or potential "class enemies," alleged intriguers against the whole system. At still another it is a class called the "middle and upper-middle peasants." The rural group called "lower and lower-middle peasants" is regularly favored; members have priority in getting on revolutionary committees, becoming party members, getting children into middle school or university, running the school system, and so forth. They are the rural base of the Communists, the idea being that since their previous bad lot is improved by the new system they stay staunch supporters of the regime. There are nationwide groupings of lower and lower-middle peasants, and periodically they are called on to struggle against and curb capitalist or other deviationist tendencies in the group called middle and upper-middle peasants. Seemingly these are hold-over designations from the social relationships that existed when the Communists came to power; the status rankings of that time persist. Apparently the Communists feel that the more well-to-do peasants of twenty-five years ago (well-to-do probably because they were more able and industrious) most easily lean to opposition, deviation, and capitalist tendencies, and therefore need to be kept in line by the lower and lower-middle group.

But there are other ways the regime gets the rural work force to perform, ways in which communication of many kinds has a part. Dr. Chu has cited some, particularly interpersonal surveillance. Others include constant exhortation by the media, especially the ubiquitous wired communication networks. A recent report by the Peking Hsinhua news agency said the wired communication network, constantly extended over the last two decades, now connects more than 90 percent of all the households in China, from the snowbound plateau of Tibet, through the mountains of Kweichow and the plains of Manchuria, to the lowlands of the Yangtze Valley. This means a wire leading to a loudspeaker that is regularly emitting hortatory propaganda, reports of production achievements, model peasants, successful dam building, birth control injunctions, seasonal rural work programs, new victories in road construction, and so forth—not only in all public places but in almost every household in the country. Then there is television, with its package of similar agitprop, as well as the use of big-character posters. Peking opera troupes tour the countryside giving the standard dramas of triumph over landlords and foreign imperialists, plus skits depicting the virtues of hard work, service to the state, and the achievements of classes in Maoism and other pundits of communism. One standard propaganda method is gathering aged peasants around and having them recount the bitter experiences of pre-Communist days. Another is sending out traveling exhibits illustrating the hardships and oppression of those days.

So, it is a system mixing clash-and-struggle with massive exhortation and some lighter inspirational fare. As Dr. Chu has said, it works; it has brought about impressive rural development, not only economical but improved health care, education, sports, and the like. It summons a mass participation and has generated widespread mass support for the Communist regime. The communication component is predominantly interpersonal and verbal, as Dr. Chu has said, and is an integral part of the whole process of establishing and consolidating a Communist society.

As a development technique, the system has not achieved the rate of growth displayed by other, freer, less-controlled societies in underdeveloped countries. Most non-Communist countries of Asia have gone forward at a faster rate than China. But with the Peking regime, politics is in command. Indoctrinating the people and founding the system are more important than economic growth; to them these are the most essential parts of the development process. So, in Peking's eyes, the system has been a success. Parts of it may be transferable elsewhere, but the system as a whole belongs uniquely to a Marxist China and may not readily be adaptable to other societies.

7b. *How Workable Is Mao's Strategy?*

HARRY T. OSHIMA

As I read Dr. Chu's paper, the system of group work in China reminds me of Japan's system of team work, which may lie at the core of Japanese efficiency and growth during the past one-half century. The Japanese system is too complex to be described here, but one difference is worth noting, as it may have relevance to Durdin's speculation that the Chinese system may be losing its steam and its potential for rapid growth. (There are a number of English-language books on Japan's system by economists, e.g., Abegglen [1973] and one by sociologist Chie Nakane [1970].)

Group pressure is one of many ways to assure hard work by each member within a team or group in Japan. More important may be the complex system of material incentives, one of which is the large annual bonus (equivalent to one to six months' annual pay). This is in effect a system of profit-sharing that propels the Japanese to work hard and efficiently. The question that emerges is: What is the mechanism that ensures that the Chinese system raises the total output of the various groups or teams as a whole? Group pressures can succeed in pushing laggards and slow workers in a given group to produce as much as the more efficient within the team, but how adequate are they in raising the output of the more efficient? This is of major importance if the output norms of a given team are to rise to assure that overall national growth is sustained. There must be some method of raising the norms of each team in China in contrast to raising the output of the slow worker within a team (since all societies must strive to increase group norms). The question is: What are these methods and how effective are they or will they be over a long period?

7c. *China's Experience with Development Communication—How Transferable Is It?*

WILBUR SCHRAMM, GODWIN C. CHU, AND FREDERICK T. C. YU

The Chinese have hesitated to recommend their methods to other countries; rather, they have insisted that each country must find its own way. Deputy Foreign Minister Chang Han-fu refused to say that other nations should adopt China's way; that is "a matter entirely for decision by the people of the countries concerned," he said.[1] The overwhelming preoccupation of Chinese political leadership has been with making their own approach work. In so doing they have never hesitated to borrow or absorb anything from other countries that seemed promising and was consistent with their basic approach. Other countries can look in the same way at the Chinese experience.

It is well to remember that the Chinese experience took the direction it did not only because of Mao and his approach, or because of the Marxist-Leninist ideology behind it, but because these ideological elements were modified by the long-held Chinese cultural codes and values, and because they were being implanted in the Chinese people with their extraordinarily industrious nature.

Maoist emphasis on ideology rather than on technical expertise reminds one of the Confucian elevation of the ethical generalist over the professional specialist. Even the Maoist brand of populism is not totally unrelated to the kind of populism in old imperial China when emperors ruled as sons of heaven. Maoists have replaced the authority from heaven with the power of the people. But both imperial rulers and Maoist revolutionaries share the belief in the potency of human will and place enormous faith in the capacity of the masses, once aroused, to perform superhuman tasks. After all, the popular story of "How *Yu Kung* (meaning Foolish Old Man) Removed the

Mountains" was not a Maoist invention. Furthermore, all this was happening in the excitement of a revolutionary movement, under the guidance of a leader who believed in constant "revolutionary renewal."

These and other circumstances—for instance, the overwhelming military victory that brought the Communist party into power—must be kept in mind when another developing country looks over the border at China and asks whether some bit of the Chinese experience and method might be transferred elsewhere. Are the conditions suitable? Are they comparable to those in which the method has worked impressively in China? What prerequisites are there? For example, some aspects of Chinese development seem to require a considerable degree of control, a single party, pervasive and powerful cadres, state monopoly of the communication media, submergence of individual goals and aspirations. To what extent is a borrowing country prepared to accept those preconditions? To appreciate what China has accomplished is therefore not necessarily to decide that China's method of doing it is transferable.

But given these caveats, what is most interesting to us about China's use of communication for development?

1. *Interpersonal communication*. For one thing, unlike many countries who have put their hopes (and budgets) into new communication technology, the Chinese have depended basically on interpersonal communication—face-to-face talk, the discussing and deciding group, and the meeting.

2. *The cadres*. The chief channel to inform and guide this interpersonal communication has been the politicized, obedient, and usually resourceful cadres—twenty-some million among them. They carry communication both up and down, to and from top leadership, and horizontally into the village, neighborhood, commune, or factory. The cadre members are generalists, politically educated to see the "big picture" as the party sees it, skilled at group interaction, responsible for guiding the truly remarkable amount of communication and decision-making that goes on locally.

3. *Localization*. Indeed, one of the most striking features of the Chinese experience has been the amount of decentralization of responsibility for development, delegating it to the local community. No community, of course, challenges with impunity the principles of the basic approach—socialism, collective equality, self-reliance, the guidance of the party, and so forth. No one challenges, at least now, the words of Mao. The policy decisions are made at the top. But within these boundaries, a very great deal of the problem-solving and innovating necessary to development is expected to occur in the local community.

How can farm or factory productivity be increased? Should crop rotations be changed? What is wrong with the morale in the tool shop? How many children should the community limit itself to having this year? What young people within the designated social classes should be permitted to go away to school? What kinds of curriculum should the local school teach according to Mao's instructions in order to be useful to the community? What criticism should be directed at the factory management committee? These and other practical questions are usually assigned to the local community, and the answers are not in many cases sent down from the top. They are most commonly solved in meetings, large or small, in committees or study groups, work groups or official gatherings of the commune or village, or serious talks between cadre members and peasants.

4. *The engine of the system.* So far as one can tell, the engine that makes Chinese development run is the social pressure and morale generated by this local communication and cooperation. It is a phenomenon familiar to social psychology, but perhaps never so broadly demonstrated. For the cadre member lives in meetings, and, outside work, so do the Chinese peasant, worker, and soldier. Every Chinese belongs to something, and it meets frequently. He goes to meetings and learns to participate.

Considerable coercion was applied in the early years to break the old traditional norms of noninvolvement and establish the new norms of participation. Once the new norms are accepted, the group process itself provides the necessary social pressure to keep the engine running. The Chinese therefore becomes involved in the local plans and problems he helps to consider. He commits himself. He knows what his neighbors or co-workers are doing; they know what he is doing. The cadres know what everyone is doing. Therefore, if one should not live up to responsibility or commitment, there is no place to hide. So development goes forward in the strong light of community surveillance, with a very high percentage of participation, and a very strong pressure to live up to what is expected.

This is not to imply that these local development engines can run without fuel. Without the necessary resources, much of the social pressure would go to waste. Without seeds and fertilizers, the farms could not do what they are expected to do; without contraceptive materials, the birthrate would have been less well controlled. Without the leadership of the cadres, local initiative might have gone in any number of directions. But in the absence of widespread material incentives, it is undoubtedly these social relationships and the psychic income derived from them and from social recognition that provide rewards and incentives for the considerable effort being asked of the Chinese people.

5. *The mass media.* Although the most important development communication in China is interpersonal, much of it in groups, the mass media are not neglected. To an outsider they seem to be managed rather skillfully in a sort of contrapuntal relation to the local groups and the cadres: that is, they provide a way for the cadres to hear policy, for the 800 million to hear or read the words of their top leaders, for information to travel both to and from the center. They announce and support the endless stream of campaigns.

They pick up innovations from local communities and recommend them for trial elsewhere. They announce local successes and awards. They help apply social pressure and condemn ideological failures. And they report on the surrounding world, as the Hsinhua news agency sees that world.

Although Western media are used to a much higher degree for entertainment, Chinese media are not long-faced; but they are deadly serious about development and the socialist revolution. They are not full of "media personalities." And, of course, there is a similarity about them, which grows from the political control and the lack of an adversary press. But the difference between Western and Chinese media may not lie so much even in the single viewpoint as in what surrounds the media, for in the West the mass media have a personality of their own and find their own place in the living pattern of their users. In China, they feed directly into the enormous structure of meeting time and community discussion, and into the information being carried by the cadres, the loudspeakers, and the posters. The whole communication picture blends together. But there is no question as to what is the principal element within it. That is the local, interpersonal communication, in which the people are trying to master the "correct" way of thinking about society and to solve the problems of their own community.

6. *Unity of communication.* Perhaps one of the chief reasons why a development campaign has a better chance in China than in a less fully controlled and directed country is this lack of separation of one part of the communication experience from another. There is little separation between entertainment and the socialist revolution, between technocracy and politics. Everything is politics, everything is the socialist revolution, and everything is development. Popular songs, dance performances, cartoons, even the Peking opera, are supposed to carry a political message. The cadre members in a commune or a factory are responsible not only for special problems, but for the whole development problem in their locality. There is not (as in most developing countries) a specialist who comes from the center or the district headquarters to help the farmers, a family planning worker who comes to convince the families to use contraceptives, a health expert who comes to teach people to dig wells or boil water. There are technical specialists on occasion. But the cadre members are seldom merely technical specialists.

Some difference between this kind of cadre and the typical development field service may be noted. As George Verghese pointed out, the field services in a country like India, no matter how skillful, are departmentalized and loyal to their own units of government. In the spirit of civil services everywhere, they are more comfortable with stability than change. They are concerned with developing their own program—agriculture, family planning, health, or whatever—and only incidentally with the remainder of the development program.

This problem of departmentalization also exists in China to some extent, in a phenomenon known as the *Peng Wei Chu I* (departmentalism) principle. In general, however, the Chinese cadres seem to be more concerned than their counterparts elsewhere with the entire problem of reconstituting society, with building a new China and a new Chinese man or woman. The technical details are seen as part of the ongoing revolution and development, and fall into focus with the larger picture.

7. *The educational system.* Another very important aspect of Chinese development communication is a completely revised educational system. The educational problem the Chinese were trying to solve is widespread among developing countries. Many countries, like China, have realized that their schools are serving the elite rather than the masses, and are related to the old social system (often to a colonial system) rather than to the new system being built. Many countries, like China, have realized that they could not afford to extend the elite schools to all the people. But after the Cultural Revolution, China moved with typical energy to do something about it.

In some respects their solution was like what they did about health care—lowering the average quality in order to make care more widely available. Similarly, the Chinese opted to discard some of the elite schooling, and move the center of the school system precisely where the center of development activity was—to the local community. The local communities were charged with developing a reduced curriculum that would be most useful to their own development program.

The manner in which these new curricula were adopted seems to be one of the best illustrations of how the mass media are being used in relation to local communication. The different communities made and tried different curricula, combining essential subjects with work and with ideological instruction. The national press picked up one of these curricula (which had apparently been tried out successfully and which met the requirements of party leadership), and Mao praised it as a model for other communities. It was described in some detail. How many other schools put in this same curriculum thereafter we do not know, but at least the example combined in a very interesting way local initiative and central guidance. And it probably provided a central tendency for future curriculum-making.

Education of the people in "correct" thinking is still the essence of creating the New Chinese Man. But education is defined rather more widely by the Chinese leadership. What goes on in the meetings, with the cadres, at work, is considered education. So are the sessions of self-criticism and criticism of others. The older people are contributing when they tell the younger ones what China used to be like. And certainly the admission of worker-peasant-soldier students to universities, according to Chairman Mao's "July 21" instruction, is an educational policy of considerable importance. In other words, a very extensive system of nonformal and formal education, geared to the needs of the ongoing social revolution, according to the party's policies, has been and continues to be a key element of the development program.

8. *Some distinctive features of media use.* Other characteristics of media use are perhaps less distinctive to China than those we have mentioned, except for a few, of which we can give examples here:

(a) The Chinese have reestablished some important links of social communication by rather unusual methods. They have made it necessary for bureaucrats, scholars, university students, and other city people and "white-collar" workers to spend some months at a time working and living with peasants and workers. This is part of the nonformal education mentioned above; it also establishes communication links between persons and groups who otherwise would have only generalized knowledge of each other, but whose assignments within the development effort are clearly related.

(b) As might be expected, there is a high incidence of patriotic and revolutionary appeals, and references to Chairman Mao, in the development communication of China. After twenty-five years, rather special efforts are still made to retain the atmosphere of revolution and nation-building, and the consensus that it creates.

(c) "Rectification" and "renewal" are important principles of Chinese development that are reflected in the communication arrangements. The movement must renew itself periodically. A worker, cadre member, leader must stand back every so often and review his performance, being ready to criticize himself and join in other criticism, so that the whole performance can be purified of errors. This is the reason for the sessions of self-criticism, the criticism of others, the invitations to criticize through *tatzepao* (invitations that are sometimes abruptly withdrawn). It is also the reason for the "remembering" meetings, when older people recall the hard and oppressed past, so that the present can be seen in perspective.

(d) To Mao, the major obstacle to development is the stubborn persistence of petty individualism that includes, among other sins, various forms of selfishness. The recent campaign "to destroy selfishness and establish collectivism" (*po szu li kung*) is simply another variation of a continuous thought reform and class struggle in an effort to eradicate the disease of individualism and to inculcate revolutionary values and attitudes through an instrumental triad of "struggle-criticism-reform" (*tou, pi, kai*). That one should be selfless and learn to serve the people is by no means a new notion. This is taught in every country and religion. But to try to exorcise a nation of egoism and selfishness through massive, penetrating, and shrewd use of communication, with the conviction that this can, in fact, happen, is something distinctively Maoist. How it will turn out we do not know, but this uncompromising stress on personal change as an integral part of the process of development is far from common in development communication.

POINTING TO THE FUTURE

This, of course, is an inadequate picture of what China is doing with communication. But enough is known to indicate that an extraordinary amount of activity with development communication is under way in China, that some rather effective methods have been found to transform this energy into social change, and that the methods used are somewhat unlike those in use elsewhere.

China's experience in development is both a success story and a tale of woes. Over the years there have been severe setbacks and tragic mistakes. There was considerable, indeed excessive, violence in early movements. There was the period of woodenly imitating or swallowing raw the Soviet model of industrialization. There were drastic moves such as the Great Leap Forward movement that was launched in 1958 and was abandoned two years later after the nation plunged into a deep economic quagmire. The Commune movement was by no means smooth.

In spite of Mao's teaching on egalitarianism, Chinese society is not yet egalitarian. It remains stratified, and many visitors to China have returned with tales of differences in income and styles of life. And there is plenty in the Chinese press to suggest that bureaucracy, though greatly reduced perhaps in offices and personnel, is still a common malady among government workers; that there is the recurring tendency of cadres wanting to live a life better than that of the masses; that not all urban youths go to the countryside with enthusiasm; and that the party still has a long way to go to eradicate bourgeois ideology, to dig out the roots of revision, to stamp out individualism, to change people's outlooks and to cultivate and create the new Chinese Socialist man. Maoists are determined to turn the proletariat, as the Marxists have taught, from "a class in itself" into "a class for itself." They have scored some spectacular victories, they have suffered some crushing defeats, and they still face staggering problems.

Finally we come back to the question with which this paper began: how much is transferable? Especially the "local engine" and the cadre system that seem to be the essence of the Chinese pattern—are these transferable elsewhere? Certain related questions suggest themselves at once: Transferable where? To what kind of social system? and how much of the Chinese system must be transferred before one of its elements will work efficiently?

We are going to suggest three propositions. (1) The more similar the social system, the more likely that a specific part of the Chinese experience can be satisfactorily transferred to it. (2) A nonsimilar system can transfer as much of the Chinese experience as it is willing to pay for socially, politically, economically. (3) The lessons most developing countries can transfer from the Chinese experience are more often likely to be general than to be specific.

Let us briefly introduce these starting points for discussion.

(1) The more similar the social system, the more likely that a specific part of the Chinese experience with development communication can be satisfactorily transferred to it.

The Chinese pattern of development is really one piece. The things done with communication fit into it. They fit together with the kinds of control being exerted, the kinds of incentive being offered, the pattern of distribution of power, the ideas that are being advocated. If any essential part of the system is borrowed without the parts related to it, the result is necessarily an improvisation that is unlikely to work as well as it did in China. Efficient borrowing therefore requires either congruent systems surrounding what is borrowed, or changes in the direction of congruence.

For example, it would seem likely that Tanzania, which has a single party and a strong leader, which is committed to socialism and local self-reliance, which (like China) is relying on interpersonal communication rather than new communication technology, could more efficiently borrow from the Chinese experience than could El Salvador, where nothing less than a social revolution could bring its system into even approximate congruence with China's.

Other things being equal, it would seem that a military government might be better able to transfer some of the Chinese patterns than a civilian government, because the military already has the discipline the cadres require and is prepared to exert as much control as may be needed; and furthermore is accustomed to the efficiency of communication within the ranks that the Chinese Communist party also requires. This may seem like an odd idea, because military governments are typically antisocialistic and dedicated toward preventing, rather than stimulating, change. But the new politicized generation of military officers might find this very thing an interesting possibility.

How much of the Chinese experience could be transferred across the Himalayas to India, where there also have been experiments in socialism and where the need for population control and for improved conditions in the villages and the city slums is at least as great as China's was? Could a cadre system be created (in place of the present departmentalized services) to carry development as a whole to 400 million villagers, and start local development "engines" in those villages? We suspect the answer is that it might require more basic economic and political change than India is now prepared to make. If the question had arisen in the first five years after independence, when the Congress party still represented something like a national consensus and when strong leadership and strong impetus toward change still existed, the answer might have been different.

Difference in systems does not necessarily mean that borrowing is impossible. A borrower can revise the Chinese practice to fit his own system, or can change his own system to fit the new practice. Therefore:

(2) A nonsimilar system can borrow as much of the Chinese experience as it is willing to pay for socially and otherwise.

Any change is bought at a price. The swift change asked for in social and economic development may require a very high price indeed. The greater the difference between the borrowing country's system and the Chinese system, the more change that will be required, and the higher the likely price.

For example, almost any developing country can put in "barefoot doctors" (and many countries have done so, under such names as paramedics or medical or nursing aides). This costs something, but not an impossible sum. It will cost some actual money out of the pool for medical services, and it will probably cost the friendship of the medical profession. More important, it will take a courageous decision because it will, as we have suggested, amount to lowering the average quality of medical care in the country in return for extending care to more people. And any country that experiments with a system of "barefoot doctors" may run the risk of simply turning out more "barefoot bureaucrats."

There is almost a worldwide movement to bring nonformal education to rural people, and some of the Chinese experience is clearly relevant here. If a country goes about the task as seriously as China has done, some support will probably have to be taken from existing urban and elite schools; for with 20 or 30 percent of the national budget already in education, it will be almost impossible to add any money for education overall, and there must be a reallocation of resources at the cost of present education.

Costs like these do not seem impossible. Similarly, in some countries it would be relatively easy to introduce a program of self-reliance and cooperative activities at the local level. But such a program requires both guidance and incentives. To provide suitable incentives in some countries would require redistribution of land and a revision of the whole economic structure. In some countries it would require nothing less than a revolution.

One of the most bothersome costs of borrowing parts of the Chinese system would be the amount of control required over the expressions and actions of citizens. The kind of social pressure that seems to work so effectively in China probably cannot be brought about without a commensurate degree of control. In some cultures this would be an acceptable cost, in others an impossible price to pay. This is what each country will have to decide.

(3) The lessons most developing countries can learn from the Chinese experience are more often likely to be general than to be specific ones.

For example, any country that needs to learn the lesson can learn from China's experience the importance of involving the local people in planning and managing their own development, the usefulness of devoting a special part of the development effort to peasants and workers, the importance of relating one part of development to others, the necessity of providing educational opportunities fitted to the needs of a community rather than to a scholastic tradition. These are general things, and any country can work out its own pattern for doing them; China has shown how important they are.

Still more generally, one can learn from China the need to make development an all-out effort if it is to succeed. In China, development is not something for planners or bureaucrats or leaders only; it is for everybody. Everybody has a responsibility for it and takes part in it. As we said earlier, in a sense China's whole program is development, because it is the continuing revolution to restructure society and build the new state. Looking even over the fence at China's effort, one can hardly escape the feeling that what is happening there is a broader and more general effort than development in most countries.

Finally, it is possible to learn the development lesson that China's own leaders have tried to teach in saying that whether a country follows the Chinese example is for the country to decide: a country must find its own way to development. Some specifics can be borrowed from the Chinese experience by some countries where the price is relatively low or where the borrower is willing to pay the social price. But the chief things to be transferred to most developing countries are insights and understandings—general, rather than specific. For the specific programs, including many of the uses of communication, most developing countries, drawing from wherever examples are available, must find their own ways of accomplishing these.

NOTE

1. Quoted by Stephen Uhalley, "China as a Model of Revolutionary Development," *China Notes* 10 (Summer 1972): 25.

C. THE CHALLENGE OF RURAL DEVELOPMENT

As indicated by the papers in the preceding section, rural development was identified by our conferees as a key issue for the decade ahead. Accordingly, Dr. Rahim's paper identifies and evaluates three main "communication approaches" to this objective that have been tried in various developing countries: extension and community development, ideology and mass mobilization, mass media and education. Dr. Kearl then focuses on agricultural development, which is the economic core of rural development efforts, and analyzes the shift from the classical diffusion model to the package programs and induced innovation models. He concludes with a call for "newer models" in terms approved by Dr. Webster, who finds that we are at "a watershed in communication for rural development."

8. Communication Approaches in Rural Development

SYED A. RAHIM

Introduction

This paper is an attempt to examine a number of communication approaches in rural development in less-developed countries. Our aim is to see how certain assumptions and principles of rural development influence communication, and what some of the implications of different approaches of communication are.[1]

In identifying and examining different approaches of communication in rural development we shall use a simple system of classification. We assume that the main flow of communication in rural development is vertical. This upward and downward flow is between a relatively small group of people planning and implementing development programs and a large mass of rural population participating in and benefiting from development. Horizontal communication within the leading group and the rural population is a secondary flow stimulated by and dependent on the vertical communication.

The leading group may consist of professional planners, educators, administrators, specialists, and technicians organized into one or more change agencies in the public or the private sector. Alternatively, the leading group may be trained political cadres belonging to the ruling political party.

The rural population involved in development communication may be individual families, village communities, or new groups organized into associations, cooperatives, communes, etc.

The dominant characteristic of communication messages may be ideological or informational. The ideological messages are exhortative. They emphasize political ideas that motivate and guide action, explain the world in terms of an action-oriented belief system, justify collective action, and create social solidarity (Sigmund 1972, pp. 3–5, 41–44). The informational messages are educational—directed toward increasing awareness, interest, knowledge, and the capacity to make rational decisions at the individual and group levels.

The main channel of communication may be mass media or interpersonal. The mass media are centrally organized and are designed to reach a large number of people. The messages flow through the network of radio, television, and newspaper. The interpersonal channel is decentralized. The messages flow as people talk to each other or exchange written statements. Group meetings, discussions, and informal training and demonstrations are the common setting of interpersonal communication. The village-level extension agents, opinion leaders, and political party cadres are the key elements of the interpersonal communication channels in rural development.

To summarize, the main factors differentiating various approaches of communication are as follows:

1. The leading group promoting development and initiating communication:	(a) Professionals organized into the bureaucratic-technocratic change agency (b) Political party cadres
2. The rural population as beneficiaries of development and participants in communication:	(a) Individual families (b) Existing village communities and groups (c) Newly organized cooperatives, associations, communes, etc.
3. Communication channels:	(a) Mass media (b) Interpersonal
4. Communication messages:	(a) Ideological (b) Informational
5. Communication flow:	(a) Vertical (b) Horizontal

The Extension and Community Development Approach

Perhaps the oldest and the most common approach of rural development communication in less-developed countries is the extension service for the dissemination of useful and practical information on agriculture, home economics, and public health. This approach is based on ideas borrowed from the West, particularly from the United States. The rationale for this approach is that there is a growing body of practical knowledge available from scientific and technical research that can be extended to the individual rural families to help them improve their output and welfare. The assumptions underlying this approach are that the rural families are interested in receiving new information and that they have the necessary supporting resources or can procure them in order to apply the new information in useful activities.[2]

In general, extension services in developing countries are offered by different departments of the government bureaucratic organization. Professional administrators, specialists, and technicians organize the services. Each department extends the services to the rural population by its own single-purpose extension agents. The extension agents visit the villages, arrange demonstrations of improved practices, and contact individual families. They also send regular reports to their departments on the conditions of crops, livestock, public health, sanitation, and so forth. If the conditions become serious on account of flood, drought, or epidemic, the extension agent is engaged in emergency measures and relief operations. The reporting and emergency duties sometimes become his primary function.

The community development approach of rural development is the result of a number of different influences: (1) dissatisfaction with the uncoordinated extension activities of competing government departments, (2) the successful example of planned development in the Soviet Union, (3) sociological theory and principles of community organization and social change, and (4) international development assistance from the United Nations and the United States. The communication approach in community development can best be discussed with reference to the Indian program.

The Indian approach is based on the assumption that the great mass of the illiterate and poor rural population is a highly valuable development resource. The individual rural families and the communities can be guided to the path of development if they are given practical knowledge of the social and natural sciences and technology. The government has the main responsibility for bringing together the forces of the rural mass and the sciences and technologies. This has to be done quickly, but gradually enough so that the pattern of life in the villages is not seriously dislocated. It can best be done by a decentralized interpersonal communication system at the community development block level. Each community development block is served by a team of multipurpose village-level workers supported by the subject-matter specialists at the block level, and supervised and coordinated by the block development officer. The total program is planned, guided, and supported by a national-level community development organization.[3]

In the community development approach, the multipurpose village-level worker is the key communicator. Usually he is a high school graduate trained to work as a communicator-guide-teacher to the rural people. Although he has a rural background, he does not belong to the village community. His socioeconomic status in the society makes him more of a mediator between the rural elite and the development bureaucracy of the government (Dube 1958, pp. 157–221).

A notable variation in the extension and community development approach of communication is practiced in a number of less-developed countries. This variation is based on the assumption that the local leaders and local voluntary organizations in the villages can become effective extension agents if trained and supported by the development agencies. Such a method can make much better use of the interpersonal communication and influence network in the village community than the extension method using government agents. It can work still better if the peasants are organized into cooperatives or associations, and the organization leaders are trained and guided to perform extension services for their members. This method is used in the French African "animation rurale" program of Senegal, Ivory Coast, Dahomey, and Togo (Goussault 1968, pp. 525–550). In Bangladesh and Pakistan, the rural cooperatives under the integrated rural development program make intensive use of this method of communication and extension.[4]

The extension and community development approach of communication has no direct political role or function. But in a number of countries the local government institutions and the local political leaders bring to the notice of the government agencies the development problems and needs in their constituencies. They put pressure on the government agencies for allocation of resources in the development projects of their choice. In India, a few states have achieved notable success in integrating the community development organization with the local government institution.

The Ideological and Mass Mobilization Approach

Rural development in China and Tanzania illustrates a different communication approach that makes intensive use of interpersonal channels activated by the political party cadres. In this approach the message contents are predominantly ideological—the informational messages are always related and subordinated to the ideological contents.

Rural development is conceived as a process of radical change in social relations leading to new social formations in the rural society. Therefore, the main function of development communication is seen as that of promoting and heightening the political consciousness of the peasants and workers in the villages. The primary emphasis is given to the peasants' and workers' collective control over the basic means of production, and to self-reliance by mobilizing internal resources rather than borrowing and importing technology from outside.

In Tanzania the ideological messages in rural development communication originate from the Arusha Declaration of the ruling Tanganyika African National Union (TANU) party, and the essays on African socialism and socialist education written by Julius Nyerere. The theme of the ideological messages is that the African socialist society is based on *ujamaa* or familyhood. The village community is an extended family, with each individual worker contributing labor for the benefit of the community and with the community taking care of each member. The African socialism rejects capitalism, which is based on the exploitation of workers by owners of capital. It also rejects doctrinaire socialism based on the concept of inevitable class struggle.

The rural population in Tanzania is constantly exposed to the ideological communication transmitted by the party cadres and government officials in interpersonal conversations, village meetings, and rural training centers. The people learn about the four kinds of evil exploitation—feudalism, capitalism, imperialism, and parasitism. They are persuaded to adopt the traditionally rooted but newly conceptualized socialist way of life based on the collective control of the major means of production, cooperative management, and self-reliance. The villagers also receive technical information on better practices of agriculture, health, cooperation, and so forth, from the government extension agents, professional teachers, and trainers. Such information is delivered to assist the villagers in implementing the principles of socialist cooperation and self-sufficiency in their daily activities.[5]

The ruling and only political party of Tanzania (TANU) assumes the primary responsibility for rural development communication. The basic unit of the TANU is the cell consisting of a small number of households. The main functions of the cell are: (a) to bring peoples' problems and grievances to the party and the government, (b) to communicate to the people the purposes, plans, and problems of the government and the party, and (c) to mobilize groups for the implementation of development projects. The cell leader is the key communicator. He maintains close personal contacts with the individual members of the cell, mobilizes groups of members for development activities, and provides feedback to the party and the government (Connors 1974).

The Ujamaa village experiment in Tanzania is an attempt to build the basic units of a true African socialist society by organizing voluntary collective villages. Its aim is to build new villages that will own and manage development resources collectively, and will depend on the government for only a minimum amount of assistance. At present there are about 4,500 Ujamaa villages covering about 13 percent of the population. Development communication in these villages is more intense than in the rest of the country. Since these villages are highly organized, the normal cell system is replaced by an elected TANU committee that maintains direct communication links with the top level of the party hierarchy.

In the Peoples' Republic of China, rural development is based on a new social formation that evolved from the traditional mutual aid teams to production cooperatives to communes in a very short period. The commune and its components—the village-level work teams and the production brigades—form a multipurpose political, administrative, and organizational unit. The commune is managed by a peoples' council consisting of 100 to 120 elected representatives. The peoples' council elect a peoples' revolutionary committee (ten to twelve members), which is the chief executive committee of the commune. The peoples' revolutionary council is linked to and guided by the Communist party of China (Aziz 1973).

The structure of communication in rural development is highly organized through two basic processes—the "mass line" and the "criticism and struggle" procedure. The "mass line" is the vertical communication process that regulates the relationship between the top- and lower-level party officials and the members of the commune, work brigade, and work team. "Criticism and struggle" is the horizontal communication that regulates the ideological education, conflict management, and decision-making at different levels (Dittmer 1973).

The mass line communication ensures a circular flow of information—from the masses to the leaders, and back to the masses. The party cadres' interpersonal communication with the people generates a great deal of unorganized information on the problems and needs and the peoples' opinions and ideas about how the problems can be solved and the needs can be met. This information is transmitted to the higher levels of the party and the state organizations where it is processed, evaluated, and utilized in formulating development policies, programs, and activities. Then the party and the state organizations send back messages in the form of instructions, directives, recommendations, and suggestions to the successive lower levels until the communication reaches the communes, production brigades, and work teams (Liu 1971). At each stage of this vertical (up or down) flow of information the process of horizontal communication is activated in the criticism and struggle sessions. These are highly intensive interpersonal small group communication sessions. They are regularly held at different levels to evaluate and share information, criticize individual actions that indicate deviation from the party line, resolve conflicts, ensure discipline, make decisions, and create consensus.

The two basic processes discussed above are closely integrated into a single communication structure. The Chinese leaders are greatly concerned about the possible danger of bureaucratization of the mass line leading to communicative alienation between elites and masses and negligence of ideological education. Chairman Mao and his close associates have made attempts to fuse the two processes by massive campaigns and movements. The great proletarian cultural revolution may be viewed as one such attempt at combining "mass line" and "criticism and struggle" into a single massive communication process.

The Mass Media and Education Approach

In this communication approach to rural development, the mass media play the dominant role in delivering informational messages to the rural population. The messages flow from a centralized, nonpolitical organization managed by professional communicators. Although many developing countries make some use of this approach, it is perhaps most widespread in the Latin American countries. We shall examine this approach with reference to the Accion Cultural Popular (ACPO) program in Colombia. This program has developed from a small experiment started in 1947 to a national program covering the entire rural population of Colombia. It has earned an international reputation and has influenced many similar programs in Latin America (Brumberg 1972).

Accion Cultural Popular is based on the assumption that the main barriers to rural development are: illiteracy; ignorance; traditional attitudes of conformity, passivity, dependence, and fatalism; and lack of spiritual, civic, and community values among the rural peasants and workers. The main task of rural development is to remove these sociopsychological and cultural barriers. It can only be done by a massive "fundamental integral education" of the illiterate and ignorant rural adults. This fundamental integral education strives at imparting basic information and knowledge on (1) literacy, (2) mathematics, (3) health, (4) economy and work, and (5) spirituality. The information and knowledge have to be relevant to the real life situation of the rural people.

The ACPO is Catholic-church sponsored but administered by a centralized autonomous organization in Bogota. The program is managed and implemented by professional administrators, educators, specialists, technicians, and field organizers. The knowledge and information delivery system of ACPO is built around a radio network and a cultural division responsible for the preparation of educational programs and printed materials (weekly newspaper, textbook series, posters, etc.).

The largest radio network in Colombia, Radio Sutatenza, is owned and operated by ACPO. It has a daily nineteen-hour broadcast program. The news and educational or informational programs make up about two-thirds of its radio programming. The remaining one-third of the program is general entertainment. The educational-informational programs are of two types: (1) radio school broadcast and (2) open broadcast. The radio school broadcast is a sequence of instructional courses directed toward small groups of individuals. The radio school groups are often all members of the same family or close neighbors who meet informally at one participant's house to listen to the radio class. These groups are organized and supervised by local volunteers. The open broadcast is directed toward individual farm families. It delivers practical information on agriculture, home development, health, and so forth, and motivates the farm families to adopt improved practices.

The radio schools are provided with textbooks, a weekly newspaper, posters, and other visual materials. Each school receives a set of these materials to supplement radio instruction. Additional support is provided by voluntary organizers, trained local leaders, and the parish priests.

The mass media-and-education approach emphasizes individual learning and education. The protagonists of this approach expect that the media programs will be effective in removing ignorance and negative attitudes and values from a large section of the rural population. As individual learning and education take place, rural people will become concerned about their problems and will acquire the necessary knowledge and skills to solve those problems. They will be motivated to initiate social actions for the family and community development. The motivation will come from within. It will not be necessary to use communication from outside to mobilize social and political action in support of development. This approach is so sensitive about political or governmental "manipulation" of rural development that it tends to remain isolated from other rural development programs operated by government agencies (McAnany 1973).

The Effects of Communication Approaches

How are the different approaches of communication affecting rural development? Any detailed examination of this question will require intensive research. In this paper we shall make some tentative observations and indicate the need for further study and investigation.

The current situation in a number of developing countries suggests that the extension and community development approach has generated much awareness and interest in development among the rural population. As a consequence, the demands for technological innovations, the inputs required to adopt innovations, and institutional reforms for wider distribution of the benefits from innovations have increased sharply. In most countries the governments are now faced with an enormously difficult challenge. How can these demands be met with very limited national resources, grossly inadequate foreign aid, untrained manpower, and scarce managerial and administrative capacities? The flow of scientific and technical information and advice from the West has reached the villages and aroused the expectation of the people. But the corresponding flow of material resources needed to transform information into practice has not taken place.

The general tendency of governments in these countries has been to yield to pressure from the relatively prosperous class of people in the rural society.[6] Thus the so-called green revolution has come to benefit the landlords and rich peasants much more than the poor peasants and landless workers. Some political stability has been achieved on account of a closer interdependence between the urban and rural elites. On the other hand, a large-scale private transfer of wealth and talents from the rural to the urban area and the migration of rural poor to the cities in search of food and employment have created a potentially explosive situation.

The beneficiaries of rural development—the relatively prosperous class of people in the villages—have become a powerful political force. They have established effective communication linkages with the sources of power at the national level. They are now demanding more complex and better technical information, more productive material inputs and consumer goods, and more effective social and administrative services from the government. The ruling elites are under constant pressure to respond to those demands by increasing financial allocation to local development projects, expanding extension and information services, arranging better training facilities, strengthening inputs distribution, increasing the import of new inputs and consumer goods, and coordinating and integrating various services offered by different departments of the government.

In contrast, the poor villagers who do not own adequate means of production to apply the new technologies have become more desperate and alienated. They are unorganized, and have no communication linkages with the sources of power at the national level. They cannot exert sufficient pressure on the government to bring about institutional changes that would create opportunities for them to participate in the processes of development. Many leaders in the government admit the need for institutional change, and the desirability of organizing and mobilizing the rural poor. But they do not take any immediate and significant action. The political forces operating in favor of the poor villagers are not strong enough to compel the leaders to initiate radical reform.

The mass media-and-education approach seems to have been less effective in reaching the rural mass than the extension and community development approach. For instance, a recent estimate shows that the ACPO radio schools could reach only about 5 percent of the potential rural audience in 1968. The landless peasants were not reached to any significant extent. The ACPO has done well in reinforcing the innovative behavior of the land-owning and more progressive elements of rural Colombia. It facilitated the spread of technological innovations. But there is little evidence that the rural population have achieved the level of social consciousness and discipline needed for voluntary mobilization and participation in development. The ACPO program has achieved success in raising the level of literacy and knowledge among the small section of the rural population who participated in its programs. This small section of people has not yet shown any active sign of initiative or leadership in educating and mobilizing others (Brumberg 1972; McAnany 1973).

There is some clear evidence that the mass media educational efforts are more effective when linked to local leadership and organizations interested in development. Strong motivational and inspirational messages from the media are effective in stimulating the local leaders and organizations to mobilize local human resources. However, such efforts to gain the support of the local power structure or to develop new power structures would undoubtedly lead the media to deal with the major social and political issues. It is difficult to see how the assumptions and principles of the mass media-and-education approach would be consistent with such activities.

The ideological and mass mobilization approach has been highly effective in certain rural development programs. In Tanzania, communication and education have been instrumental in evolving a new sociopolitical infrastructure for formulation and implementation of decentralized self-reliant rural development projects. Strong communication linkages between the poor rural communities and the central authority have been established (Connors 1974).

The Chinese leaders have achieved considerable success in mobilizing huge numbers of rural people for labor-intensive rural works programs of flood control, irrigation, road-building, and land development. Although such mobilization imposed rigorous discipline on the participants, the rural people seem to have responded with interest and enthusiasm. Radical measures of land reform no doubt created the conditions for massive participation of rural people in the works program. But no less important was the effect of intensive communication campaigns. Communication was used in heightening the ideological and collective spirit and creating intense emotional commitment (Yu, in Lerner and Schramm 1972; Chu, this volume). It enabled the people to accept hardship and endure the sacrifices needed for the implementation of rural works programs.

The effectiveness of the ideological and mass mobilization approach of communication in China is also demonstrated in the way socialization of the agricultural sector was accomplished. A series of radical programs, from land reform to commune, were implemented in rapid succession throughout the country without disrupting production in any major way. Moreover, substantial adjustments in those programs were made from time to time. This dynamism in rural development seems to have been possible due to a powerful feedback mechanism that kept the leaders alert and sensitive to the reactions of the rural people.

The flow of communication through the elaborate interpersonal network supported by the mass media promoted and diffused local innovations, successful adaptation of new techniques, and ingenious use of local resources. For the rural people of China all those activities involved much hard work, sacrifice, some wastage of resources, and occasional frustration. But they encouraged local initiative and self-reliance. The people learned the hard way of development. At the same time the government's problem of securing foreign aid and importing technology from outside was reduced.

It is difficult to assess the impact of ideological communication on the attitudes and values of rural people in China. One may infer that the ideological communication approach not only exhorts people to adopt a new pattern of behavior but also explains to them why such behavior is essential for the benefit of the communities and the nation. The rewards of conformity and the dangers of deviation are made clear in very practical terms. The people become more conscious of their social responsibilities, and develop a uniform set of practical guidelines for the interpretation of reality and "proper" behavior and action. In this process their freedom to make alternative decisions is no doubt reduced, but at the same time the risks associated with uncertainties are also diminished. Such restrictions on behavior during a period of great social change probably help people to quickly adapt to changing situations (see chap. 7).

Some Research Implications

Before concluding, we shall make a few observations on some research implications of the analysis presented in this paper. First, it appears that certain political and institutional factors greatly influence the design and effectiveness of communication strategy in rural development. Research is needed to better understand how such factors and communication are interrelated and influence each other. Second, better conceptualization and understanding of the development functions of communication message types (e.g., ideological, informational) are essential to gain insight as to how communication affects rural development. The orientation of the source and the theme of the message are important factors that determine who in the rural areas can be reached and with what effects. Third, the developing countries are innovating systems of interpersonal communication and ways of linking the mass media with such channels. A systematic study of such experiences will be very useful. Finally, comparative studies of different communication approaches may provide useful guides for transferring rural development ideas and practices from one country to another country.

NOTES

1. For a lucid discussion on communication and development, see Wilbur Schramm, "Communication and Change," in *Communication and Change in the Developing Countries*, edited by Daniel Lerner and Wilbur Schramm (Honolulu: University Press of Hawaii, 1972).

2. For a brief review of extension approach, see Haile Menkerios, *Agricultural Extension Services* (Essex, Conn.: International Council for Educational Development, 1972). Mimeographed.

3. Descriptions and reviews of community development programs are available in many publications. See: *Community and Agricultural Development in Pakistan—Speeches of Akhter Hameed Khan* (East Lansing, Mich.: Asian Studies Center, Michigan State University, 1969), pp. 1–9; Carl Taylor, Douglas Ensminger, Helen W. Johnson, and Jean Joyce, *India's Roots of Democracy* (Bombay: Orient Longmans, 1965), pp. 169–193; E. H. Valsen, *Community Development Programs and Rural Local Government* (New York: Praeger, 1970); P. R. Dubhashi, *Rural Development Administration in India* (Bombay: Popular Prakashan, 1970), pp. 67–74; Kusum Nair, *Blossoms in the Dust* (New York: Praeger, 1962).

4. The cooperative approach of rural development designed in Comilla is radically different from the community development approach. However, in terms of the

categories used in this paper its communication strategy is closer to the community development communication approach than the other two approaches discussed later in this paper. For a description and analysis of the Comilla approach of rural development, see: Akhter Hameed Khan, *Comilla's Principles of Rural Development*, in *Rural Development in East Pakistan—Speeches of Akhter Hameed Khan* (East Lansing, Mich.: Asian Studies Center, Michigan State University, 1964), pp. 9–10; Arthur Raper, *Rural Development in Action* (Ithaca: Cornell University Press, 1970); Akhter Hameed Khan's paper in this volume.

5. A recent World Bank study reports: "Thorough knowledge of Nyerere's essays makes for neat verbal shorthand in Tanzanian communication." For a brief review of communication and education in Tanzania, see World Bank Group, *Torches in the Night—Educational Experiences in Tanzania and the Ivory Coast* (Washington: IBRD), 1973.

6. Commenting on India's community development program, Myrdal noted: "It can no longer be regarded as a program to supplement the lower strata's efforts at self-help; it has become in fact a device for chanelling governmental assistance to the not-so-poor." See Gunnar Myrdal, *Asian Drama*, vol. 2 (New York: Pantheon, 1968), p. 1343. Also note Dube's comments on communication in India: "Powerful vested interests often tend to monopolize beneficial innovations. . . . Such vested interests often exploit the institutional innovations also to their advantage. For instance, creation of *panchayet raj* institutions under the program of democratic decentralization was utilized by them to reinforce their position in the power hierarchy of the community." S. C. Dube, "Communication, Innovation and Planned Change in India," in Lerner and Schramm 1972: 156–157.

9. Communication for Agricultural Development

BRYANT E. KEARL

The biggest single change in the past decade in thinking about agricultural development is the rising awareness that the subject has two distinct facets for which quite different strategies may be needed.

Governments in the developing countries are understandably concerned about food production and, in most cases, achieving some level of self-sufficiency in food supplies. Thus national programs continue to ask how gross production and marketable surplus can be maximized.

At the same time there is a growing consciousness that most of the people in most developing countries are rural. Their personal needs, which are not always fully satisfied by a national food production policy, are legitimate, and policies must treat rural people as persons to be served by development as well as "resources" for the nation to use. Those who accept this view are asserting that distribution of production gains is as important as increases in gross production, and that social costs and benefits deserve attention whenever economic costs and benefits are discussed.

This paper seeks to describe the resulting shift in communication policies: from a relatively narrow focus on transmission of messages from authoritative central or national sources to a broader view that encompasses communication at and among all levels in a developing agricultural country.

The years since World War II, in which the world has groped toward a definition and strategy of agricultural development, have seen a convergence of several lines of thought with regard to communication.

One line has given priority to the task of conveying technical and scientific information to audiences of widely varying backgrounds, interests, and needs.

Another has viewed rural development more as a matter of changing the way people think: the values they cherish, their aspirations, and their recognition of the place they hold and could hold in the larger community.

A third has recognized the significant organizing task that is involved in bringing together the package of physical and service resources that will make human aspirations achievable.

The fourth, seldom explicitly recognized in any of the other three, challenges the ability (and right) of forces outside a community to determine what is in that community's best interest. It views feedback not simply as a device to make external manipulation more effective, but as a tool to make external forces more responsive to the rural community. For this purpose it calls for steps to make each community better informed, better organized, and more articulate.

It is important to recognize that throughout this period communication has operated within, and to some extent been a prisoner of, whatever was the currently dominant model of change. Strategies for agricultural development have not been entirely within the communicator's control, but they have had profound implications for his own strategies in using communications channels and messages.

The Diffusion Model

The Diffusion Model was the first widely accepted view of how agricultural development occurs and how it can be promoted. Drawing heavily upon Western and especially upon American experience, this model is based on the observation that in any agricultural setting some farms are demonstrably more productive than others. This is true whether production is measured per unit of land area, per unit of labor input, or as a function of all inputs. High productivity has usually correlated closely with willingness to modify technology and utilize innovations.

Some major steps in development and refinement of this theory are reported in the work of Ryan and Gross (1950), Wilkening (1949), and Beal et al. (1957). A comprehensive summary is provided by Rogers and Shoemaker (1971).[1]

Early research on the diffusion process was directed at delineating stages through which individuals are presumed to pass in adopting agricultural innovation: awareness or "first knowledge," interest, evaluation, small-scale trial, and adoption. (It was, of course, recognized that any of the first four stages could terminate in "rejection" rather than "adoption.")

There was evidence that a farming population could be categorized into "innovators," "early adopters," "early majority," "late majority," and "laggards" with respect to any particular widely accepted new technology or practice.

These insights made it possible to ask what personal characteristics were associated with individuals who seemed regularly to fall within each category. Innovators, for example, proved to be a type with special willingness to take risks and learn about unfamiliar ideas. "Early adoption" had a negative correlation with a personal philosophy of dogmatism and fatalism. But early adoption had a positive correlation with mass media exposure and involvement in interpersonal communications. Earlier adopters also tended to have more education, larger farm units, higher social status, and more social participation than other farmers.

Acceptance of the Diffusion Model placed heavy emphasis on communication, both of the information needed to evaluate and apply innovations and of messages calculated to promote a readiness to consider change.

One of the first formal studies that might have suggested major modification of the Diffusion Model was Frey's investigation (1952) of soil erosion control measures followed by farmers in western Iowa. This study examined the gap between the erosion control practices recommended and those actually followed on 144 sample farms. Four-fifths of the farm operators, Frey concluded, adopted far fewer erosion control measures than those responsible for public programs were recommending.

> The disparity between farmer objectives and those of public programs could not be attributed entirely to a lack of information or a failure on the part of the operators to recognize erosion control problems. Many were familiar with the different methods of erosion control and also freely mentioned numerous soil erosion problems on their farms. . . . Although additional education would no doubt modify the objectives of the farmers to some extent, they appeared aware of the erosion control benefits. . . . Farmers did have an appreciation of the recommendations even though they were not willing to follow them. Only 12 percent of the operators said that they did not expect benefits from using more control measures. (Frey 1952:981–982)

Forty percent of the farmers in Frey's sample explained their slowness to adopt by saying they were not prepared, financially and otherwise, to make the shift toward forage production and livestock farming that the soil erosion control measures would have required. One-third mentioned difficulties in their land rental arrangements and in getting their landlord's cooperation. Nearly a third mentioned competing demands on the financial resources available to them. One-fifth felt they might not be operating the farm long enough to make such investments in erosion control measures worthwhile.

The lessons from Frey's study, not fully incorporated into development programs even today, would seem to be that:

1. The way the farmer perceives his situation will govern his response to recommendations received from outside, and both his perceptions and his situation may differ considerably from that assumed by development planners.

2. Individual farm situations differ more widely, as regards land tenure and capital and labor supply, than macrolevel programs and recommendations often recognize.[2]

3. Appropriate programs usually cannot, therefore, be designed with-

out informed local input, an awareness of local variations, and a systematic effort by change agents to monitor the compatibility of their objectives with the personal and economic objectives of the farm family.

Three sets of observations began to cast doubt on the adequacy of the Diffusion Model as a guide to agricultural development strategy.

First was simply an awareness that diffusion programs were failing to bring the desired dramatic gains. Hayami and Ruttan (1971) curtly conclude that technical assistance and community development programs based explicitly or implicitly on the Diffusion Model have failed to generate "either rapid modernization of traditional farming or rapid growth in agricultural output."

Second was the increasing consciousness of situations in which farmers were blocked from accepting innovation because of situational factors beyond their control.[3]

Third was the growing suspicion that, instead of a large body of unused scientific knowledge awaiting the traditional farmer, there was often little new technology that actually suited his situation and was within the limits of his resources.[4] Schultz (1964) argued persuasively that traditional farmers usually were making highly efficient use of the production resources, including technology, realistically within their control. While recognizing that lack of functional information can be a factor in slowing the pace of change, he challenged the idea that economic rationality went hand in hand with material prosperity; it simply had a better chance to express itself, in modern terms, among those farmers who had better access to resources.[5] Heady (1965), without inferring that technical knowledge was always adequate, hypothesized that in some regions of less-developed agriculture "the supply of capital and its price is more important than restraints in the supply of technical knowledge in bringing forth greater productivity." Such arguments called for a more sophisticated prescription for change than simply "more aggressive communication and extension programs." They also began to cast doubt on the explanation so often heard in the preceding two decades that superstition and irrational "cultural factors" were the major obstacles to agricultural modernization.

Uncritical acceptance of the classical Diffusion Model actually was an obstacle to development of the model itself. For a long time its attention to interpersonal communication tended to focus on the "opinion leader" and "early adopter." Felstehausen (1973) notes that this preoccupation "led many extension and assistance agencies to virtually ignore social and institutional structures in promoting development." Barghouti (1974) points out that most rural communities in the developing world have one or more organized local social groups: women's groups, mothers' clubs, self-help committees, adult education and literacy classes, maternity and child health clinics, and community training centers. Yet the classical Diffusion Model accorded such groups only a modest role even in the dissemination of information, and paid almost no attention to their potential in facilitating group decision-making and legitimizing decisions through group consensus.[6]

Another limitation of the classical Diffusion Model was the narrow role it accorded feedback. By implication, a farmer rejected an improved practice either because the message was not sufficiently clear and persuasive or because the farmer was "not progressive." Feedback was aimed at modification of messages, not of programs. Little was done to encourage farmers to test recommended practices with the genuine intention of letting their experience exert an influence on practice recommendations, supporting institutions, or investments in research.

Dandekar has stressed both the urgency and the practical difficulty of overcoming this customary one-way flow of bureaucratic communication:

> Traditional knowledge is authoritarian in the sense that it is handed down from one generation to the next by the authority of tradition. On the other hand, modern science is experimental. Every bit of it is supposed to be verifiable by experiment or observation, and it is the privilege of every man to put it to such a test . . . .
>
> This difference between traditional knowledge and science is likely to be overlooked by official extension agencies, because within the official hierarchy knowledge and all that passes under that name moves from the Secretary to the Deputy Secretary of from the Director to the Deputy Director, until to the last functionary at the village level, all along fully protected and secured with the sanction of authority.
>
> As a consequence, when his turn comes, the last extension man at the village level himself tries to pass on to the farmer the little piece of knowledge or information in an equally authoritarian (and therefore unscientific) manner, changing it from scientific to traditional knowledge as he does so. (1972: 2)

Rao notes that in the Indian setting, because of this deficiency, the matching of the farmer's needs with the technology available became simply a series of trials and errors in the field. "Vertical communications in the extension agencies related to the performance of existing programs, and rarely to data on farmer needs" (1972: A–164).

A final but major source of disillusionment with the Diffusion Model is traceable to its heavy identification with the mass media. This was primarily an accident of ancestry: the Diffusion Model emerged in a Western economy and society where a widespread mass media system existed.[7] Consequently, the role of the mass media was stressed prominently and persistently throughout early studies of the diffusion process. Diaz-Bordenave (1972) describes the Latin American countries in the 1950s as "flooded" with communications technicians, communications hardware, media campaigns, and training courses. He contends that "considerably more faith was put on the means of communication than on their content."[8]

The more that became known about the mass media contributions to agriculture in the developing countries, and particularly those of the printed media, the less their role seemed to resemble that hypothesized by the Diffusion Model. Beltran reports that "agricultural diffusion studies in the Latin American countries . . . revealed at least one major difference [from those in the United States]: among the Latin American farmers, the influence of mass media on adoption of innovations is minimal or nil at practically every stage of the process" (1974*b*: 21).

Beltran (1974*a*: 17–20) notes four essential aspects of a satisfactory mass communications systems, and argues that rural areas in the developing countries are ill-served in all four respects.

1. *Mass media availability.* "Despite dramatic advances in the spread of the media, especially radio, large segments of the rural population are still without real access to the mass media system."

2. *Access to mass media messages.* "In general the distribution of mass communication opportunities follows in Latin America the steep pattern of stratification that characterizes the socioeconomic structure prevailing in the region."

3. *Content of mass media messages.* Because rural peasants are not a profitable market for media that depend heavily on commercial advertising, "the mass media are, eminently and not accidentally, oriented to the urban audiences that constitute the market."

4. *The code of mass media messages.* "Given that mass media are strongly urban-oriented, they codify their messages in styles corresponding to the urban audience. . . . 'That which may be of direct value in improving agriculture is beyond the comprehension of those who could best use the information.'"

How these and other deficiencies have affected agricultural content in the mass media of Latin America is described by Fett (1974*b*) in these terms:

> Media are generally urban-centered. Media control tends to be in the hands of people with little understanding of and sometimes little sympathy for farm people and their problems. Even the media interested in agriculture tend to be more responsive to the concerns of agricultural supply industries, government officials in agriculture, and buyers of farm products than to the producer himself. The abundance of agricultural development agencies in many developing countries, each competing with the others for governmental financial support, leads each to put its agency public relations goals ahead of the agricultural producer's information needs. Meanwhile many mass media have small staffs and a great deal of news to cover, no one to specialize in agriculture, and no reason to include informational articles about farming in preference to 'hard news.' In many regions there is little mass media penetration into rural regions; this is especially true of the print media. What little agricultural news is carried may either be irrelevant to local needs or difficult to understand or both. All in all, it is no wonder that mass media are so seldom mentioned by Latin American farmers as a significant source of useful information on agriculture. (personal communication)

The Package Programs Model

Basically the Diffusion Model can still be viewed as extremely useful; there is ample evidence that many farmers and regions do benefit from vigorous efforts to provide them with new and useful knowledge. But experience has also demonstrated that broad and dramatic changes in agricultural productivity and rural family welfare will not occur through the diffusion route alone. Johnson challenged the notion that "if research results are available a good extension program is about all that is needed to give significant results."

> In the underdeveloped parts of the world, fertilizer, pesticides, better seed, and simple tools cannot be found in local villages. Also, credit is available only at very high rates of interest (if at all) and the producer is not assured of a market for additional output. Consequently, even when the producer becomes convinced that it would pay him to use more fertilizer in combination with other improved methods, he cannot do so because the essential materials and services are not available to him. (1965:213)

Additionally, Johnson described price incentives as a much more powerful stimulant when they can be combined with "a package of improved technology and a companion package of services."

The package approach[9] also found support in the work of Heady (1965) on requirements for more rapid application of research. He recommended that in countries where diets were at or near the subsistence level, a priority should be placed on agriculture and particularly on the basic crops (including those necessary to insure an adequate basic diet) instead of livestock and other products demanded by high-income consumers. At the same time, he suggested providing a "bundle" of critical techniques that might include improved seeds, plant protection, fertilization, and irrigation where readily available.

In the ensuing years the Package Programs Model was adopted widely, in one form or another, in a great many developing countries. We will mention briefly three of these experiments, in India, Mexico, and the Philippines.

India's Intensive Agricultural Districts Program (IADP), implemented at first in fifteen districts and subsequently in more than one hundred others, was the earlist extensive implementation of the package approach.[10] Although it had a communication component, the IADP approach put much more of its reliance on steps to provide adequate producer credit, timely supplies of seed and fertilizer, essential marketing services, and technical and farm management services.

The IADP program involved a commitment at the highest levels of government for a coordinated effort to provide these essential components. "It is apparent that a package field program requires facilitating programs, which must be provided by public and private agencies outside the farming community. . . . It is also apparent from experience in India and elsewhere that the package approach will not work miracles in two or three years" (Johnson 1965:223).

The communications tasks involved in coordinating components of a Package Program were further defined in the Puebla Project (Mexico), designed to offer "an effective strategy for addressing the small farm problem . . . an integrated plan of action aimed at generating and applying relevant technology within a local setting" (Diaz-Cisneros 1974:5). The project differed significantly from other high-yielding input programs in its emphasis on low-income farmers. Although the program in India had in no sense ignored the low-income sector, most package programs (notably, the country programs to promote high-yielding grain varieties) have assumed that, considering the urgencies of food problems and the sum of social benefits involved, total food production must be the primary goal and the distribution of benefits within agriculture can be given only incidental attention. The Puebla Project deliberately chose to work in a low-income region, with corn (maize) farmers who were entirely dependent on rainfall for their agriculture and who had limited access to credit, markets, technical assistance, and inputs. Stimulating agricultural production within the framework of the project was, in other words, viewed as a question of "changing the individual behavior of a large number of persons who play a role in the production process, i.e., *campesinos*, agronomists, bankers, etc." (Diaz-Cisneros 1974: 88–90).

One of the most recent applications of the Package Programs Model is the Philippine "Masagana 99" program, launched in May 1973 to concentrate on a single crop, rice. This interagency effort uses a vigorous mass media communication program, with particular emphasis on radio as the medium with widest coverage. But it also specifically includes (a) a massive credit program through three different kinds of financial institutions, (b) an infrastructure program to facilitate product flow, (c) a price support program, (d) organization of farmers' groups to facilitate the flow of credit and information, (e) an interagency authority to coordinate actions, and (f) involvement of top-level political leadership, nationally and in each province (Drilon 1974).

None of the package program experiments has as yet been adequately evaluated. Although Cano and Winkelmann (1972) describe the Puebla Project as producing results that are "undeniably significant," they note several unresolved issues. A package program necessarily starts with a narrow focus (usually the production needs of a single crop or a limited number of crops). How to extend such a program to additional crops and to factors other than production is seen as a challenge to development strategy.

Evaluations of all of the package programs agree on the severity of the problems faced in coordinating institutional contributions.

> The first concern must be the preparation of all aspects of the bureaucracy. Cooperation among . . . agencies is not automatically to be expected. It may

> touch on pre-existing rivalries, and raise questions of who should initiate action in these other ministries. . . . Therefore a conscious program of communication within the structure of the government in lining up the needed support and enlisting all who need to know and be involved is the essential first step. (Crawford 1974:62)

One virtue of the package approach is that it is, itself, a communication device to attract the attention of bureaucrats, businessmen, opinion leaders, scientists, and others whose cooperation is required. The success of any particular package program is in large measure a reflection of how well it has been able to keep key people in all of the key agencies informed and convinced as to what their contribution must be.

For the communicator, the significance of the package program has been that previous stress on communication to the farmer has been appreciably broadened to include communication among agency representatives, and also upward communication from the rural family to the agencies involved in agricultural development. (Inputs must be available at appropriate times and places, and only the farmer can report whether they were. Market malfunctions are readily seen by the producer and others directly involved, but are not always communicated to those who could make changes. How well the production incentives included in the package actually motivate the producer is another question that requires that policy people listen to the farmer's voice.)

Fett (1974*a*: 192) spells out the communications implications of such thinking:

> What is needed is more dialogue *with* farmers rather than merely communication *to* them. Unfortunately, we not only aren't very much disposed to do this, we also aren't very well equipped to do so. Two-way communication is not easy to bring about. Formal organizations are structured to facilitate top-down communication rather than bottom-up. Change agencies expend great efforts in diffusion of information but little effort in infusion. . . . By infusion we do not mean the same thing as feedback. Feedback, as generally conceptualized, is the response to a message received, while infusion is more of an elicited response of a felt need. It is information-seeking on the part of the diffusion or change agency.

Esman (1974:74) contends that "agencies must expand their capacity and inclination to get information from the ground and to establish and maintain dialogue and information exchange with their clients." Grunig (1974:41) has noted the difficulty that agencies staffed from the middle class have in relating well to lower-income groups: "Communication accuracy with the clients decreases as one moves up the organizational hierarchy." Similar views are expressed by Velazquez (1974:6): "Communication between small landowners, usually illiterate, with technocrats and representatives of government agencies is difficult and requires painful work and innovation."

Sources of New Technology and Institutional Change

Both the Diffusion Model and the Package Programs Model assume as their starting point a "given" body of currently available farm technology and existing rural institutions, within which the program for agriculture must be created. The suitability of that technology and those institutions was seldom questioned so long as agricultural development was defined simply as an effort to increase gross production and marketable surplus (although even for that purpose it deserved closer scrutiny; for example, it is increasingly obvious that technology developed along Western lines is likely to have a labor-saving bias rather than the capacity to use abundant labor intensively and productively[11]).

When the well-being of subsistence farmers, landless laborers, and other low-income rural people began to be accepted as a development goal, the relevance of "given" technology and institutions began to be challenged. McNamara was not the first, but certainly has been one of the most eloquent, in guiding attention in this direction:

> Within the rural areas the poverty problem revolves primarily around the low productivity of the millions of small subsistence farms. . . . Without rapid progress in small holder agriculture throughout the developing world, there is little hope either of achieving longterm stable economic growth or of significantly reducing the levels of absolute poverty. The fact is that very little has been done over the past two decades specifically designed to increase the productivity of subsistance agriculture. (1973:1)

There are more than simply humanitarian reasons for responding to this challenge. A large number of agricultural economists now agree with the position stated by Lester Brown:

> There is evidence that small farmers, when they have effective access to agricultural inputs as well as health and education services, engage in labor-intensive agriculture and generally average considerably higher yields per acre than do farmers on large holdings using hired labor or tractors. (1974:60)

Nevertheless, the senior FAO officer in Asia warns that small farmers continue to be at a disadvantage, compared to their larger neighbors, in exploiting opportunities, technology, services, and resources (Umali 1974:4). He argues that a quarter century of experience with strategies that "by-pass the small farmer must surely convince us that something is grievously and basically wrong with the process of development."

Why have agricultural technology and institutions responded so slowly to the small farmer's needs? The best current explanation can be drawn from the work of Ruttan and Hayami (1972), who fix upon the market mechanism, broadly defined, as the principal factor determining the direction agricultural innovation will take. Thus in countries where labor has traditionally been scarce and expensive (such as the United States), technology and institutions were forced along labor-saving lines. Where land was the initially limiting factor (as in Japan), economy in land use was the goal toward which market forces guided technology and institutional change.

The Ruttan-Hayami Induced Innovation Model hypothesizes that technical change is "guided along an efficient path by price signals in the market, provided that the prices efficiently reflect changes in the supply and demand of products and factors and that there exists effective interaction among farmers, public research institutions, and private agricultural supply firms" (Ruttan and Hayami 1972: 137–139).

This analysis goes far to explain why the low-income or subsistence farmer and the landless laborer are not always well served by market-induced changes in technology and institutions, for every country has some percentage of its rural population only marginally involved in the market economy, and the countries with furthest to go in development are exactly those where this percentage is largest.

Dorner (1973) has particularly questioned reliance on the market mechanism as a way of modifying institutions. Ruttan and Hayami hypothesize that institutional innovations occur because it "appears profitable for individuals or groups in society to undertake the costs" (1972: 60–61). Dorner (1973: 6) believes one must ask: "Profitable for whom? . . . Obviously those individuals and groups who are firmly attached to the growth process will seek changes to strengthen their favored position. But what about the excluded masses who have only meager and insecure opportunities with the present system? Is it reasonable to assume that institutional changes demanded by the former will result in major improvements in the opportunities available to the latter?"

What Dorner says about institutions could be echoed with regard to technology. For example, in a country that exports large quantities of rubber at favorable prices one can see how the market mechanism would guide a large share of research investment into removing constraints on rubber production. What market mechanisms would direct comparable attention to research on home-grown food crops that rubber-tapping families need for subsistence and improved nutrition? When market signals suggest that commercial poultry production is beginning to be profitable, one can recognize the stimulation for research that will help the commercial poultryman solve his production problems. What would it take to generate comparable research to help rural families solve the disease problems, save on feed, and get more eggs and meat from small flocks of fowls kept around the yard for family use? Home-grown fresh fruits and vegetables could mean a great deal to family nutrition in many countries and regions; what market mechanism would promote research on their production unless commercial market prospects were in sight?

Despite these reservations, it is well to recognize the durability and power of the market mechanism and to ask what can be done within its assumptions to generate more relevant technologies and institutional changes. Ruttan and Hayami suggest several specific steps that relate to communications. Because much of the responsiveness of a market system depends on a communications infrastructure, they urge public sector investments in "modernization of the marketing system through the establishment of the information and communication linkages necessary for the efficient functioning of the product and factor markets" (1972: 143). They favor the promotion of organizational communications channels, noting that the desired "dialectic interaction among farmers and research scientists and administrators is likely to be most effective when farmers are organized into politically effective local and regional farm 'bureaus' or farmers' associations" (p. 139). They conclude that one of the limitations of research facilities in many developing countries is "isolation from the main currents of scientific and technical innovation," and they therefore give priority to the improvement of communication within the scientific community.[12]

Toward Newer Models for Communications

It may be useful to recapitulate the communications implications of the successive models of agricultural development, and these have been summarized in Table 1.

The Diffusion of Innovation Model contributed to a stress on mass media, and especially on media of nonlocal origin and control. The task of communication was to bring into the community ideas and information from outside. Feedback had the function of testing the adequacy of the message and guiding its modification to make it more effective. There was little in this model to modify the emphasis on national media, supplemented where possible by regional outlets, which was being promoted in so many countries out of a legitimate concern for the communications needs of nation-building and development of a national consensus.

The Package Programs Model did little to shift attention from national or central media and messages. Where package programs were successful they necessarily paid attention to the particular needs of individual farm operators, for informational inputs as for other inputs. Nevertheless, messages were still viewed mostly as coming into the community from outside. Localization and stress on local media were justified as ways to make externally originated messages more accessible, comprehensive, and persuasive. Autonomous local communications had little or no place in the Package Programs Model.

The Induced Innovation Model rightly accorded great power to the market, and called for improvement in market communication linkages. It also stressed the usefulness of farm organizations as channels of communication and pressure to make the system responsive. Nonetheless, it probably does not represent adequately those on the fringes of or outside the market

Table 1. Communications Considerations Involved in Successive Models of Agricultural Development

	The Diffusion Model	*The Package Programs Model*	*The Induced Innovation Model*
HOW GAINS OCCUR	By wider diffusion of demonstrably improved farming practices	By identification of packages of inputs that dramatically increase output on farms and in regions where they are applicable	By responses within the system that create a steady flow of innovations and needed institutional changes as costs and potential benefits change
PURPOSES OF COMMUNICATION	To motivate farmers to consider the possibility of change; to convey factual data needed in adoption of specific improved practices	To insure that all needed inputs are available at proper times and appropriate locations	To insure that awareness of costs and benefits will generate prompt technological and institutional responses
MAIN DIRECTIONS OF MESSAGE FLOW	Primarily from those charged with identifying better practices, to those expected to adopt them	Inter- and intra-agency communication to coordinate availability of all elements in the package of inputs	Two-way flow of information about product and factor markets, to facilitate prompt responses throughout the system
ROLE OF FEEDBACK	To check adequacy of messages (accuracy, relevance, comprehensibility) as a guide to message revision	To monitor program performance as a basis for modifying its content (but not its goals)	To convey market signals to those allocating scientific and technical resources, those conducting research in agriculture, and those who can take initiative in modifying institutions

Table 1. (Continued)

	The Diffusion Model	*The Package Programs Model*	*The Induced Innovation Model*
CRITICAL COMMUNICATION REQUIREMENTS	Mass media; local extension workers and the informational materials to support them	Channels for liaison among agencies Vertical communication from the field to the levels at which agency decisions are made	Modernization of marketing system by creating informational and communication linkages needed for effective functioning of factor and product markets Information channels for effective organization and management of scientific and technical resources Farm organizations to give effective voice to farmers' needs for new technology and for modification of institutions

NOTE that each successive model encompasses and adds to those that precede it.

economy—landless labor, subsistence farmers who have little to buy or sell, and small farmers whose marketings and input purchases are of least consequence.

All three models have made and continue to make significant contributions to programs of agricultural change. Yet one cannot escape the feeling that a strategy that does not go beyond them will be inadequate to the challenge of the years ahead. What is beginning to arouse attention is a model of agricultural development that is increasingly decentralized and user-oriented, with simultaneous attention to the needs and preferences of rural families as well as to national production goals. Rao (1972) states the argument in this way:

> The developmental effort has been motivated by macro-level objectives and perceptions. This has tended to make the system conceive the problem simplistically in terms of aggregate output and international comparisons on yield. . . . An underlying change that is needed lies in projecting the farmer as end-user and reference point in the entire communication system for technology transfer. (A–169, 170)

In its most rigorous terms, a user-oriented model is described as having five essential points:

> First, that user need is the paramount consideration and the only acceptable value-stance for the change agent; second, that diagnosis of need always has to be an integral part of the total process; third, that the outside change agent should be non-directive, rarely, if ever, violating the integrity of the user by placing himself in a directive or expert status; fourth, that the internal resources, i.e., those resources already existing and easily accessible within the client system itself, should be fully utilized; and fifth, that self-initiated and self-applied innovation will have the strongest user commitment and the best chances for long-term survival. (Havelock and Havelock 1973:8)

This concept is extraordinarily difficult to apply in agricultural development, since decisions about the allocation of human and other resources usually emerge from national goals that, initially at least, are as likely to consider the preferences of the rural family an obstacle to be overcome as an end to be satisfied.

At the very least, however, development is beginning to be seen as a process of successive problem-solving in which the needs of those who face the problem are articulated and communicated to the "experts" who have resources of knowledge or research to contribute.

The challenge that this way of thinking presents is to bring to development a larger share of the rural community's own potential contribution.

There are several reasons why this does not occur spontaneously:

(1) Most rural people have some difficulty in identifying the choices that are or might be open to them in relation to the resources they have or might reasonably expect to obtain. Too often, their option is only to accept or reject what is offered, and they have little direct chance to help create options that reflect their own ideas and values.

(2) Many rural people have difficulty in articulating their needs and preferences. The tools of the cosmopolitan urban world, tools of analysis as well as tools of communication, are often unfamiliar to them.

(3) Few groups in a low-income rural society are in position to make their voices heard or to get their views taken seriously at the higher levels of government policy.

Freire (1969) has argued the importance of attacking these limitations in any program of rural development, and Diaz-Bordenave (1972) has identified eleven communications-related actions he believes would be required:

1. "Conscientization" of leaders
2. Training farmers in communication skills
3. Development of feedback mechanisms
4. Mass education through the mass media
5. Rural organization for group pressure
6. Communication participation in program planning
7. Institutional development and coordination
8. Transfer of technology and popularization of research results
9. Information organization and distribution
10. Technical training of the landless agricultural labor force
11. Family planning information and education

It is to be noted that the majority of these steps fall largely or entirely outside the "transfer of knowledge" mode that initially played so large a role in the view of communication in agricultural/rural development.

The roles hypothesized for farm organizations (as, for example, in the Induced Innovation Model) are appreciably broadened by this thinking. Organization is seen as doing more than simply representing the occupational needs of farm operators. Organizations that may have begun with a few specific purposes are seen as growing both in size and scope, encompassing larger numbers of rural people, and permitting group action and the expression of group views on every matter of concern to them, not just those related to farm production and marketing.[13]

Esman notes the important communication functions that can be performed through organization, and stresses the particular value of small farmer participation.

> Farmers' organizations can articulate the needs of their members to governmental agencies, aid in diffusing information, help integrate activities of agencies, and exert pressure on government. . . . Thus the key to a strategy for rural development—one that incorporates the elements of effective two-way communication—is the creation and strengthening of formal constituency organizations among small farmers. (1974: 74–77)

In trying to visualize what other steps would best respond to the new communications challenges, several options come to mind.

It seems apparent that rural people need better opportunities to get experience with the written and spoken word: opportunities to put in writing messages that will be read, opportunities to speak in public and to gain confidence in doing so. Promotion of functional literacy seems to be part of this prescription. Rural community organizations can contribute greatly to all of these goals.

One should not be too hasty in writing off possible mass media contributions. The undeniable fact that their performance so far has been disappointing is no measure of what their potential might be. Bostian (1966: 20–22) has listed a series of steps that could be taken to make existing media more effective in improving traditional agriculture. He has also noted that the potential for mass media contributions to a two-step flow process has undoubtedly been underestimated for the developing countries.

> When locally relevant, instrumental, persuasive information is available via mass media, the two-step flow operates at a higher level than in developed countries. . . . Leaders (in the rural community) are on the lookout for instrumental information; a local demand exists for such information, thus increasing the two-step flow. (1970: 115)

Finally, strong and autonomous locally based communications media—community newspapers, rural organization newsletters or newspapers, local radio transmitting stations, and the like—seem essential if programs of development are to mobilize maximum contributions from the communities they are intended to serve. Unless one is prepared to believe that the only important messages in development communication are those that flow from the top down (or the center outward), more energy and imagination must be devoted to the wider dispersion of communication skills, resources, and control. This needed dispersion is primarily geographical, but it should also be viewed as broadening the communication opportunities of economic and social strata that up to now have been more communicated to than involved in communication to others.

There are stubborn obstacles to such dispersion.

First are the obvious economies of scale that result when expensive communications media can be concentrated in a few institutions and a limited number of hands. The cost of each message transmission is dramatically reduced by a national media system consisting of a handful of centrally edited newspapers and magazines and a radio-television system that scatters its transmitters but keeps its programming concentrated in a few locations. Independent and autonomous media, no matter what the form of their financing, represent a drain on national resources that frugal planners find hard to justify.

Second is the very real political problem that dispersed and independent media can present. Beyond simply their potentially divisive effect as promoters of regionalism, they present the issue of how to make sure that they represent a variety of local views rather than simply giving the existing local power structure an added source of control.

Third is the argument for excellence in technical performance. The material presented by dispersed and autonomous local media will inevitably be less professional in form and style than that carried by a well-staffed, well-financed national network.

The fact remains that important communications functions, especially in agricultural development, are inadequately performed by national or even regional media.[14]

The agricultural communications strategy of the future will undoubtedly be a mixed strategy. It will continue to include national and regional mass media. It will continue to stress ways to make the messages in these media more understandable and more relevant. But it will certainly also be directed at ways to unlock the energy and creativity that is latent in the rural community. Until an economy has gone rather far in development it will be continuously short of professionals well-trained in such fields as agriculture, marketing, rural health, vocational education, and community leadership who can work effectively in rural districts. These talents, and the initiative to utilize them, will either have to be developed within the rural community or will not be available to it.

Even ten years ago the agenda for applied research on communications in agricultural development could confine itself to a single question: how can messages about improved farming practices be made more persuasive and brought more fully to the attention of the man on the land? Today two important new questions have emerged. Although not yet the focus of much research, they are at least beginning to be asked:

1. What channels of communication, administrative and otherwise, will best integrate the contributions of diverse public and private agencies in meeting agricultural development needs?
2. What communications channels and devices will help rural people clarify their alternatives, organize their resources, and make those outside the community aware of their needs?

One change is slowly but surely making itself felt. The usual stance of economic planners is to view labor and management—and this means the whole working population in rural areas—as "factors" of production, and thus to ask how they can be "utilized efficiently" in the production process. The appropriate role for them is, in other words, defined in terms of broad national goals.

Attention in recent years has shifted to the small farmer and his family as people, not simply as units in an equation for agricultural production. This will inevitably revise our model for agricultural development. Once it is accepted that the well-being of each individual and each unit has validity alongside national goals, some new requirements for communication arise. What will be increasingly added is a judgment that, to the maximum extent possible, the decisions that relate to development need to be decentralized and placed close to the people they affect.

Acceptance of such a position has profound implications for communication. It says that rural people need channels not only to make themselves heard outside their community but to let values and alternatives be formulated, discussed, and crystallized within the group as well. The development of strong and autonomous local organizations and local communications media, both formal and informal, may well be the greatest challenge in the decades ahead.

NOTES

1. Two useful critical analyses of the diffusion model should be mentioned. Bohlen (1967) suggests research needed to refine the model. Rogers, in chap. 11, describes modifications that must be made to fit it into more recent experience with the process of change.

2. Note the warning of Esman (1974, p. 72) that "the needs, capabilities, and eligibilities of small farmers tend to be situationally specific and individualized." Brown and Kearl (1967) had earlier stressed the need for communications channels that respond more adequately to local situational differences.

3. In analyzing this problem, Mosher (1966) concluded that it was a mistake to try to deal with communication questions in isolation from consideration of such essentials of agricultural growth as satisfactory markets, improved technology, locally available supplies and equipment, production incentives, and transportation. Communication must be treated as an "important component" of all of these other agri-support activities, valuable when they are available but in no way able to compensate for their absence.

4. Note for example the statement in the *CIMMYT REVIEW 1974* (annual report of the Centro Internacional de Mejoramiento de Maiz y Trigo, Apdo Postal 6-641, Mexico 6, D.F. Mexico) that in the effort to improve corn (maize) production in the Puebla region of Mexico between 1967 and 1973 "no 'high-yielding varieties' were found superior to local varieties" (p. 60).

5. Empirical evidence that traditional farmers adjust their technology in response to change in resources and incentives began to accumulate quickly; see Hopper (1957), Krishna (1961), and Falcon (1962). The traditional farmer's professional competence is most eloquently described by Hatch (1974:7): "Small farmers are vastly more knowledgeable than most of us can imagine. . . . They learn to make and use their own work implements. They learn to 'read' the soil, the weather, the heavens. They learn to study their crops for disease, insect and rodent damage, and water requirements—often on a plant-by-plant basis. They learn to follow a specialized farm task calendar, meet sequential task deadlines, and keep careful count of the passing days. They learn to build irrigation structures which are adjusted to soil quality, slope of the land, crop requirements, and water availability. They learn to make maximum use of their entire property, allow no part of their harvest to be wasted, and even collect weeds and stalk residue to feed to their animals or use as fuel. They learn to salvage all they can when their crops are destroyed by rain, floods, droughts, wind, insects, and other calamities. They learn resourceful strategies of adjustment to unexpected contingencies arising out of weather, market, labor, and cash constraints. . . . [The small farmer's] knowledge is eminently practical, representing a series of rational, time-tested, and cost-effective practices which have been developed to cope with [his] particular resource and environmental constraints. . . . For these reasons we cannot afford to dismiss or ignore his knowledge if we wish to assist him. . . . In brief, we need to recognize him for what he is—a professional—granting him co-equal participation in the design and implementation of agricultural development programs."

6. A related issue is the overidentification of the Diffusion Model with cultures in which decisions are viewed as primarily an individual matter, in contrast to cultures where group consensus may be a prerequisite to individual action. Barghouti cites rural Kenya communities in which farmers who had attended farmers' training centers were trying recommended new corn varieties with evident success. Yet widespread local adoption was not achieved until the community itself was approached as a social unit. He cites a report by Lang (in Mahar et al. 1971) of similar experiences in northern Tanzania, where recommended livestock practices were adopted by Sukuma herdsmen only after discussion and endorsement by the community.

7. See Kearl (1965) for a brief statement of some of the significant ways in which a "communications-saturated" or "media-saturated" setting differs from most of the settings in which development is being sought.

8. Some evidence that the charge is justified is found, for example, in bibliographies and reading lists of the period. The Katz and McGowan list of U.S. readings in development (1963) cited fifty-eight references in its section on communication. All but nine of these deal explicitly with mass media or with technology for message transmission. Another chapter on "The Development Process and Its Setting" lists twenty-four references relating to the individual and the rural community, but there is no suggestion that these are viewed as relating to communications needs or strategies.

9. Note that this discussion confines itself to package programs aimed solely or entirely at changes in agricultural production. Agricultural package programs no doubt benefited from, but are significantly different from, such integrated rural development programs as the T.V.A. in the United States and the Comilla Academy in what is now Bangladesh.

10. This program was first outlined in a Ford Foundation agricultural production team "Report on India's Food Crisis and Steps to Meet It," published by the government of India in April 1959.

11. Note the paper by Oshima in this volume (see chap. 2), which demonstrates why the institutions and capital-intensive technology of industrial nations are so often unsuitable elsewhere in the world. He describes a growing consensus among development economists for a shift toward a rural-based, labor-intensive strategy that, among other benefits, would help generate consumer demand to absorb the fruits of increased productivity.

12. Awareness of this latter need, and of the limitations of existing channels of scientific communication, will often call for some unconventional approaches. For example, the International Rice Research Institute (IRRI), the International Institute for Corn and Wheat Improvement (CIMMYT), and to a lesser degree other international research institutes have created extraordinarily effective networks of personal communication by bringing together international trainee groups and by the international travel of their own professional staffs. Trainees include research workers, extension workers, and administrative personnel, and they come from most of the grain-producing countries of Asia, Africa, and Latin America for several months' study of rice production at Los Banos (Philippines) or corn or wheat production at El Batan (Mexico). On their return they maintain contact with the institutes, personally and through technical publications and visits by institute staff members. This contact helps young professionals maintain their knowledge and competence, keeps the institutes informed of changing research needs, and lets institute staff members give their advice and support to efforts made in individual countries to put together all of the elements of a high-payoff inputs package.

13. This need for organizations of rural people to become more comprehensive has been noted in the recent evaluation of the Puebla Project (Diaz-Cisneros 1974: 349–

350). ". . . Despite the importance of these campesino organizations in the success of the action program, they are still far from representing an effective means to solve the wide range of village problems affecting their everyday life. Most of these problems require collective action." The author notes among this group of Mexican farmers a "growing campesino awareness of the possible collective movement beyond higher corn production."

14. This is the view that apparently is guiding India's planners in their announced determination to continue to promote decentralization of the private newspaper press and governmental radio and television; see the communications section of the *Second India Series of Studies,* issued in draft form by Tata Economic Consultancy Services, Bombay, 1974. Note also the Oshima paper, chapter 2: "In a rural-based strategy, decision-making and implementation cannot be effectively carried out from the capital. Local governments and other organizations need to participate fully in planning, decision-making, and execution."

9a. *The Present Watershed*

R. LYLE WEBSTER

Although our conference heard some determined dissents among discussants, I would be brash indeed to question the general findings of Kearl's paper, which confirms that we are at a watershed in communication and development, particularly for rural development. I do have a few observations and questions, which have been triggered mainly by his paper but which also apply in differing degrees to much that appears in this volume.

Assuming we are at a watershed, we know how it is on this side of the height of land, but what are we talking about for the future? Over many years in public information work, I have developed a fairly useful way to determine if there is substance in a proposal. My method is to ask its author what banner headline he could write over his proposal. That either extracts the meat of the matter or reveals there is not much meat to begin with. I don't expect many big banner headlines to be written about the conference which produced this volume, but there is substance enough to justify some. And as far as rural development is concerned, I will give you my choice: Development Communication Must Be with, Not to, The People.

As Kearl's paper points out, the various models used so far are not quite up to the present task, no matter how well they may have served in the past. Development communication is not going to be the same again. Nevertheless, Kearl's paper and others in this volume have helped me to clarify my own observations as follows.

The examples of rural development we consider most successful seem to have taken place where there are no landlords. Conversely, places where development has backfired have all too often been where the landed have become richer and the landless have become poorer. Some of the areas where the Green Revolution has been considered most outstanding have been some of the places where the rich-poor gap has widened.

Is there a message for us here? Are we perhaps misguided in analyzing communication materials, and reviewing mass media versus interpersonal communication, without at the same time recognizing the land ownership problem?

If development communication must be *with* the people, are the people the landlords, the big landowners, the small landowners, or the tenants, or even the landless laborers and unemployed? I wonder what kind of headline I could write about a program born out of consultations with *all* those people!

What is needed is to include some land reform assumptions in any rural development model we create. Americans should remember that the land ownership problem exists in our own country, although on a rather grand scale. Kearl mentions research on Iowa farmers who did not adopt erosion control practices. A third of them were tenants and did not have the long-term security so essential for such long-term land improvements.

I agree with Kearl's comments about "not writing off the mass media." Too many assessments of the mass media in connection with rural development assume that the only target or audience is the lowly and barely literate peasant, and that the media should tell him precisely what he needs to do to farm better or live better. The truth is that in many developing countries a more important target of the mass media, particularly the printed media, should be people such as legislators, ministers, and top-level administrators. The media can reach these people, not with details on fertilizer doses but with perspectives on the larger aspects and issues of rural development.

Radio has received a great deal of comment in this volume, most of it favorable. However, one Latin American source cited by Kearl was particularly negative. Actually, in most developing areas, radio and television are in the hands of the government and hence are capable of serving usefully in development communication. I am confident that if the time comes when we have the kind of development communication this volume encourages, and if it merits the type of banner headline I have suggested, then the government that will endorse that kind of development will surely see to it that the electronic media are sufficiently supportive.

To some questions I do not see any clear answer. If development communication must be with, not to, the people, who is going to work with the people, who is going to consult, who is going to feed back the wishes of the people, especially if the people include the landlords, the landless, and the unemployed? Probably the numbers of people working in rural development are largely in place, but what kinds of people are they? Dr. Khan gave us some chilling revelations of the attitudes of his younger staff members in the Comilla program. He was able to mediate between them and the peasants, but there are not enough men like him to do this everywhere it is needed. Rao thinks training and education in Asian educational institutions may provide some needed supply. The greatest need among the thousands of fieldworkers in developing countries seems to me to be a change in attitude toward the people. But how is it going to take place? Perhaps rural development programs are going to need some development communication cadres such as Chu mentions in reviewing the China example.

Another observation has to do with the training needed by those who will communicate with, and not just to, the people. Perhaps we do not need skilled agricultural communication specialists at all levels. Maybe the answer will be para-agriculturists. Instead of barefoot doctors we may need barefoot county agents or village-level workers. They might not be much help to a specialized plantation operator, but to people who are on the ragged edge they might be decidedly useful. Whoever they are, they are going to have to be in sympathy with and accepted by the people with whom they work.

At the recent Integrated Communication Conference at the East-West Center, Heliodoro Diaz-Cisneros of the Puebla Project in Mexico gave us a striking example of this problem. Several young nursing graduates from Mexico City were brought into the Puebla project for some health care work. They knew nursing but they did not have the dialect used in the Puebla area, hence could not operate satisfactorily. Diaz reported that the project is now recruiting peasant women out of the villages and giving them sufficient training to serve the health needs of the moment. Probably they will be barefoot nurses. In any event, they will be understood by the villagers. To help in changing attitudes, it may be necessary to use mostly people who come from the soil. In too many past rural development programs, the agent is city-raised. He has a hard time being accepted by the villagers.

As chapter after chapter in this volume points out what has been wrong in the past, or cites the necessary ingredients of a successful rural development program, it becomes clear what a staggering job it would be to make operational the new models envisioned by Inayatullah. What is to keep developmental programs from following the same old paths? What will bring about communication with, and not to, the people? How are programs to be managed without making the rich richer and the poor poorer? I hope this volume will point the way.

Let me conclude with a suggestion aimed at steering future rural development programs in a better direction. This suggestion is that, following our ten-year reappraisal, development planners create a rural development version of what environmentalists call the environmental impact statement. This would be something like a model law, or perhaps guidelines for a rural development program. It might be undertaken by the Asian Center for Development Administration. With such guidelines, before a government or an international agency embarks on a rural development program, there would have to be a statement of the economic, social, cultural, and other impacts of the program. Such a statement would answer precise questions about who had been consulted and what sampling had been made of the wishes, needs, and thoughts of those for whom the program was being designed. It might be subject to review by a very high-level independent body, or perhaps preferably by a low-level body of the people for whom the program is intended. This general idea might fill the need to build something into the process of development planning that will almost automatically serve to expose weak points and head off some of the difficulties of the past.

D. RESEARCH ISSUES OF DEVELOPMENT COMMUNICATION

In this section we focus on "research issues" with clear implications for social change and the implementation of development strategies.

Dr. Gloria Feliciano, from her strategic position as dean of the Institute of Mass Communication in the Philippines, leads off with a review of the impressive growth of communication media and communication research in Southeast Asia (SEA) over the past decade. She concludes that increased communication does correlate with development; that more research using "qualitative measures of media well-being" is needed; that research serves development communication in three ways—as "initiator, facilitator, and legitimizer." Of these, looking toward the years of "development" still ahead for SEA, she gives communication research the priority role of "facilitator." This seems to us sound advice—if the powers that be, or are becoming, will truly be "initiators" in their development policies and "legitimizers" by their achievements rather than by the spurious use of controlled media to underwrite their "charisma."

Dr. Everett Rogers then gives us an evaluation of "where we are in understanding the diffusion of innovations." As a pioneer and mentor of diffusion research, Dr. Rogers aptly fills all the roles prescribed by Dr. Feliciano—initiator, facilitator, legitimizer. He shows how diffusion research has grown from a "bastard child" to legitimate maturity. But he is deeply concerned as well with the future of diffusion studies in terms of basic theory, research design, and pragmatic implementation. (See also his comment on the old paradigm in Section A above.)

Dr. Syed Rahim's penetrating comment on Rogers' paper states that "diffusion research has revitalized communication research in two ways." After elucidating these, Dr. Rahim goes on to raise three questions of major consequence for the future of communication research.

It is to the very question of the future of communication research that Dr. F. T. C. Yu addresses himself in the concluding paper of this section. As coeditor (with W. P. Davison) of the new *Mass Communication Research: Major Issues and Future Directions,* Dr. Yu is well placed to conclude this discussion of "research issues" that face development communication. His concise review of "where we stand" today, the many unsolved questions of the multinational corporation and of Mao's China, the theoretical issues of "change" and "fixity," the hovering wraiths of an "ethnicity" we thought defunct—all these remind us of the hard research tasks before us if, in the decade ahead, we are to grow wiser as well as older.

10. Communication and Development in Southeast Asia, 1964–1974

GLORIA D. FELICIANO

Introduction

The State of the Art

Modern media development in most Southeast Asian countries—while still highly inadequate to speed up national progress by Western standards—has accelerated during the last decade. This increased tempo of media growth has largely resulted from the strategic efforts of some governments to speed up their economic development. Thus, the second half of the 1960s saw the advent of modern printing facilities and techniques, the harnessing of electronic technology, and the transmission of audiovisual messages via satellite. The early 1970s witnessed the introduction of video tapes and audio-cassettes, and the use of multimedia for education and development programs, in some countries of Southeast Asia (SEA).[1]

Some indications of media growth are evident in recent reports. In the print media, the following data are reported in the 1974 *Asian Press and Media Directory*.[2] There are 6 copies of newspapers per 1,000 people in Laos; 22 per 1,000 in Cambodia; 7 per 1,000 in Indonesia; 9 in Burma; 24 in Thailand; 35 in the Philippines; 67 in South Vietnam; 74 in Malaysia—as contrasted to Singapore's 201 per 1,000, Hong Kong's 485, and Japan's 511.

Radio now covers a wider audience compared to the early 1960s, and has the farthest physical reach of any mass media, in SEA's villages. The transistorized battery-operated radio has further enlarged the size of radio audiences, especially in Southeast Asian countries where transistors come within the means of the rural population as a result of government support of local manufacture, assembly, or importation of transistor sets. This is reflected in the growth of the number of radio sets as compared to the situation ten years ago. South Vietnam has 120 radio receivers per 1,000 people, Indonesia 114, Burma 22, Malaysia 42, the Philippines 46, and Thailand 83.

Although television has increased in popularity since the mid-1960s, especially in the urban centers, it still reaches only a small proportion of SEA's rural population. Available statistics, however, show an increase in the number of sets during the last ten years, particularly for Malaysia, the Philippines, and Singapore. The 1973 figures show that Indonesia has 0.8 television sets for every 1,000 people, the Philippines 11, Thailand 7, Malaysia 25, and Singapore 95.

Like television, the potential of film for development has apparently not been fully recognized by the development planners of some countries in SEA. This can partly be gleaned from the slight increase in the number of cinema seats per 1,000 viewers from 1969 to 1973. The latest available data show that there are only 12 cinema seats for every 1,000 viewers in Thailand; 10 per 1,000 in Cambodia; 7 in South Vietnam; 6 in Indonesia; 11 in Burma; 29 in Singapore; and 35 in Malaysia.

UNESCO's media requirement (first stated in 1960), for a country to support normal growth, is 100 daily newspaper copies, 50 radio receivers, 20 television sets, and 20 cinema seats for every 1,000 people. Viewed against this requirement, it can readily be seen how inadequate the modern media (except perhaps radio) are to perform their development tasks in most Southeast Asian countries. This high level of media deficiency is all the more significant in the face of fast-growing populations that are widely dispersed over large, and very often inaccessible, geographic areas.

It is appropriate at this point to take a second look at the UNESCO media requirement for meeting development needs. Is it an appropriate and adequate measure? If not, does it perhaps need to be reconsidered in the light of the changed situation in the developing countries of SEA? Should not communication practices and behavior in these countries, particularly at the village level, be taken into account? What consideration should be given to other commonly used, if traditional, communication channels supportive of the modern media? How about patterns of the flow of information from these modern media to the rank and file of villagers?

Anyone who has traveled into the heart of Southeast Asia has probably observed that the two or three newspapers available in the village are shared by practically all the villagers via the community reading center; that a single newspaper copy is read by a literate villager to a sizable group of peers; that news is spread by each group member to his neighbors, relatives, and friends; that vernacular magazines can be rented from village corner stores at very nominal rates; that newspapers and magazines are borrowed from neighbors, relatives, or friends; that group listening to radio or group viewing of television programs is frequent.

Perhaps it is time to reexamine the existing UNESCO yardstick to make it more responsive to Southeast Asian communication needs and resources. In addition, it may be useful to look for other measures, perhaps qualitative rather than quantitative, that could serve as indicators, perhaps not so much of media development or growth as of a state of "health" or "well-being" of the media.[3] These might include such factors as : (1) the degree of acceptability of communication *vis-à-vis* other professions; (2) the extent of government support to information work; (3) the degree of participation of media professionals in decision-making bodies of government and private agencies; (4) the extent of use of communication media in support of development programs; (5) the degree to which communication graduates are employed in the media; (6) the enrollment ratio of communication students to those in the social sciences and the arts; (7) the media professional's social and occupational mobility; (8) the level of need in communication for visiting advisers or consultants; (9) the extent of involvement of women in the media; (10) the degree of communication within and between communication institutions; (11) the level of collaborative work in the media within and between countries; (12) the degree of support given by communication research to national development. These factors are interrelated, interdependent, and overlapping.

FACTORS OF MEDIA WELL-BEING

Acceptability of Communication as a Profession

A decade ago, journalism was ranked tenth in prestige among fifteen different professions by graduate students in one Southeast Asian country (Maslog 1969). Subsequent studies in 1968 and 1969 among students showed similar findings, anchored on the arguments that journalism is less challenging and concerned mainly with "story-telling," "developing gimmickry," "advertising-promotion work," and "manipulating public opinion" by indoctrination and propaganda. These students' perceptions appeared to be more or less shared by the various sectors of the society at large (Abesamis 1968; Crucillo 1969).

At the turn of the 1970s, however, the changing image of communication as a field of study and as a profession became evident. New journalism schools and communication institutes were established in some Southeast Asian countries.[4] The older, more established schools strengthened their curricular programs with the addition of more research, science-writing, and social science-oriented courses. At the same time, such Asian regional bodies as Asian Mass Communication Research and Information Center (AMIC), Press Foundation of Asia (PFA), and Association of Southeast Asian Nations (ASEAN) started holding communication media seminars, conferences, and workshops on a periodic basis to supplement those sponsored by local funding and by specialized U.N. agencies and international foundations. Empirical data on the subject may be gleaned from the proceedings of these meetings.

Government Support to Information Work

In Asian media seminars and conferences during the mid-1960s, it was not uncommon to hear media practitioners lament their economic plight—citing the low wage scales in their countries, the dearth of items in the information budget, and the low classification of information workers on the occupational ladder.

With the acceleration of development efforts from 1970 to 1975, the economic situation for media workers appears to have improved. This has been due partly to the creation, in some SEA countries, of information-education-communication (IEC) offices in government agencies dealing with such aspects of development as agricultural extension, population planning, health, nutrition, social work, community development, and labor relations. These IEC offices have a full complement of information personnel, for example, a director, communication planning officer, associate and assistant researchers, materials production specialists, and information writers or editors (Bautista 1970).[5]

Participation in Decision-making

Traditionally, the involvement of journalists and other information specialists in decision-making relating to national development has been made possible through their membership in, or affiliation with, existing information offices in the high echelons of government. These offices, which perform similar functions, are labeled departments or ministries of public information in some countries, offices of publicity or public relations in others. In still other SEA countries, they are known as ministries of culture (and broadcasting, in one case) and education (Roque 1974).

In recent years, however, media practitioners have had formal training in mass communication, a cross-disciplinary field that has a strong base in either the social sciences or the arts and humanities, or both. This kind of training has increased the communication specialists' ability to participate in the various spheres of developmental activity—in agriculture, science, industry, business, education, and cultural affairs. It is no longer uncommon to find communication specialists in interagency, multisectoral national development planning bodies, in both the governmental and private sectors, in countries of Southeast Asia.

Use of Communication in Development

One of the innovative concepts introduced in Asian development planning a decade ago was the use of mass communication in the service of education and development.[6] Heretofore, the media had been regarded in this continent primarily as vehicles of culture and leisure. In spite of the innovation, however, it was only a few years ago that the use of modern media in support of development programs received full attention in some Southeast Asian countries. The need for popular participation in achieving national development objectives led to the use of new knowledge, methods, and approaches via mass communication by governments and the private sector. This need led, in turn, to the emergence of new fields of study in communication training programs, designed to meet the skilled manpower requirements of development, for example, population, communication, nutrition communication, land reform communication. It has brought to life the population information specialist, the nutrition information officer, the agrarian information writer, to mention only a few.

The private sector has also made greater use of mass communication in recent years. Many firms and companies—in public relations, promotion, advertising, trade, business, banking—have utilized mass communication to plan, implement these plans, and then achieve their goals. They too have used communication specialists to activate their programs.

Communication Professionals in Media

Ten years ago, the great majority of working newspaper and radio personnel acquired their skills on the job. Many of them drifted to journalism from other careers. At that time, too, some of the more prominently placed self-made media practitioners were reluctant to admit college-educated journalists into their ranks. When given a choice between a high school graduate with native writing talent and a journalist with a degree and "acquired" writing abilities, the media employer, without any hesitation at all, chose the former.

In recent years, with more college-trained media people proving themselves on the job (after some period of adjustment to the "realities"), the prospects of job openings for this trained group in the media and allied fields have become brighter. This is particularly true for such categories of jobs as science writing, business reporting, sports writing, script writing, and media research.

Enrollment in Communication and Other Fields

The establishment of new communication schools, departments, or programs in about half of the SEA countries from 1970 to 1973 attests to the growing popularity of communication as a distinct area of specialization. Ten years ago, only one or two journalism courses were offered in most of these countries. Moreover, these courses formed part of the older, traditional disciplines, such as history, literature, or philosophy, and, in a few cases, business administration.

Three SEA countries report that enrollment in communication has been consistently increasing, whereas in other courses it has remained stable.[7] The accretion has been particularly high in broadcast communication and at the graduate level. What has accounted for the increasing enrollment in these fields? Surveys point to the following reasons: (a) placement of graduates in communication is easier than in the arts and humanities; (b) the magic of projection attracts imaginative young people, particularly females, to the course; (c) the novelty of the field *vis-à-vis* older courses also motivates adventurous young minds; and (d) the course requirements are perceived as "less demanding." Though not necessarily valid, this appeals to students who are not highly achievement-oriented (Roque 1974).

Mobility of Media Practitioners

It has been hypothesized that in the Asian scene, media practitioners tend to be more mobile—socially and occupationally—than their counterparts in the humanities or social sciences. While no hard data exist to support this hypothesis, there are indications that, if tested, the hypothesis might be supported. In several Southeast Asian countries, it is clear that many leaders occupying top positions in government were, at one time or another, practicing journalists, radio-TV commentators, or film celebrities.[8]

To what can this mobility be attributed? For the college graduates, could it be the cross-disciplinary character of the communication field? Is it due to the premium that Asians place on communication skills, both written and oral, but especially oral? The relatively more aggressive personality of the journalist? The magic of media projection? Or is it due to the influence wielded by media practitioners, especially in countries with great latitude for free expression?

Need for Visiting Communication Advisers

In the mid-1960s, the need for visiting communication advisers in schools, government agencies, and private business firms was urgent. At that time, communication education was the preserve of a handful of Asians trained in Western schools. Thus it was imperative to enlarge the corps of specialists in communication research, public relations, promotion and advertising, broadcast communication, and so forth. Those who came from the West contributed much to the development of the field—by their own work in the media, by training new leaders to take over after they had left, and by working with trained Asian counterparts to complement their expertise and experience.

Today this need for visiting communication advisers is not so strong, particularly in education. In most cases, the need is more for complementarity, for mutual assistance in a collegial kind of partnership. In very few cases, the advisers meet a particular short-term need for a level of expertise that is not yet available from the local staff. For some development projects, they accelerate the wheels of bureaucracy and the urgent tasks of national development are done at a faster pace.

Women in the Media

Studies have established that, in some Southeast Asian countries, rural women have functioned as primary sources of information as well as initiators, legitimizers, and decision-makers in introducing change to the village. Available studies have also shown that enlightened, modern, urban women do no less as communicators and assume even more prominent roles in modernizing the cities. The increasing participation of women in the communication media thus assumes great significance for development and should therefore be viewed with jubilation.

Communication among Institutions

Compared to ten years ago, there is now more openness, more dialogue among communication institutions and agencies within and between SEA countries. This has been a direct result of personal contacts among their representatives at conferences and workshops held locally and abroad. These contacts are needed to harmonize the direction of developmental programs, to optimize the use of resources, and to avoid wasteful duplication of efforts. Coordination among media institutions in different Southeast Asian countries will enable them, collectively, to seek solutions to their many common problems of mass communication and development.

Collaborative Work in Communication

Such coordination has actively been sought during the last three years. Compared to ten years ago, there is now more collaborative work in communication training, research, and exchange of materials. Mass media seminars and conferences, audiovisual projects, and other cultural presentations are now being jointly sponsored by the five member-nations of ASEAN—Singapore, Malaysia, Thailand, the Philippines, and Indonesia. Cooperative research projects among the various countries on information needs, media habits, and perception of symbols, coordinated by AMIC, were launched half a year ago.[9] AMIC has also encouraged exchange through its resource materials collection, based in Singapore, and its various bibliographic projects now underway.

Communication Research Support to Development

Last but not least among the factors contributing to the well-being of the Southeast Asian communication field is communication research. Available data show that this factor has been a positive influence in the qualitative growth of the media as well. Research has done this by systematically analyzing media weaknesses as well as the ways and means whereby their usefulness in development programs can be enhanced.

Communication research in SEA is still embryonic in development, journalism-oriented, school-based, Western-influenced, and multidirectional. Its present state reflects the media situation of which it is a part. However, while it tends to follow the mass media, it has not kept pace with them. Many factors have contributed to its slow growth, including the lack of professionally trained researchers, the dearth of resources and facilities to undertake research programs, weak support by related disciplines of the social sciences and humanities, and lack of appreciation of its value by some governments, the private sector, the mass media themselves, and the general public (Feliciano 1973).

In spite of these inhibiting factors, a number of studies started during the last five years are demonstrating their usefulness to development programs. These studies relate to agricultural innovations, agrarian reform, population and family planning, health, nutrition, and community development. Some of the more noteworthy findings and lessons may be discussed under four headings, namely: (1) Development communicators as change agents, (2) Message strategies for development programs, (3) Use of mass media in development programs, and (4) Audiences of development programs.

Development Communicators as Change Agents

Available studies show, in some SEA countries, empirical support for many findings on the diffusion of agricultural innovations in the more advanced countries, naturally with some qualifications and slight deviations. Asian counterparts to the main characters in the Western drama of technological change, including their persuasive attributes, have been identified.

Generally, the findings have established that personal channels are more effective than mass media in motivation and education campaigns relating to aspects of national development. This holds true for most Southeast Asian countries, particularly at the rural levels. The effectiveness of the personal agent rests on several factors, namely: (1) the highly personalistic character of developing societies; (2) the generally low levels of education among rural folk; (3) the equally low levels of motivation to seek new information from nonpersonal channels; (4) the generally low levels of rural competence to use the more formalized communication media; (5) the relative unavailability of mass media in the villages; and (6) the urban bias of the mass media (UP/IMC 1972–1975).

The primary conveyors of development information—whether it be agriculture, family planning, health, nutrition, or community development in general—are also the persuasive agents of change in Southeast Asian villages. These include relatives, neighbors, and friends, who usually overlap because of in-group marriages among villagers. Secondary communicators of development information, and equally persuasive conveyors of change, are the development workers: extension personnel in agriculture and forestry; the clinic staff in family planning; and the rural health, nutrition, and community development workers affiliated with either government or private agencies. A third source of development information is the influential opinion leaders, a group that includes elective officials, religious leaders, landowners, and professional communicators.

These three groups of development agents have been described, in studies on elites, as "authoritative," "reliable," and "trustworthy." Several broad characteristics of persuasiveness have been attributed to them by interviewees, namely: knowledgeability and expertise, sociability, experience, and positive physical, character, and mental traits (UP/IMC 1972–1975; Roque 1974). Recent studies show, however, that levels of knowledge among development communicators, on priority information areas in their respective fields, are still generally low. This is true even for those who had formal training in their fields prior to their field assignments. The same studies likewise show that they do not grow professionally at a rate commensurate with the development programs in which they participate (de Garnie 1972; Fugelsang 1971; Valdecañas 1975).

What these results seem to tell us, in terms of action that needs to be taken, is this: To accelerate development in SEA countries, we need to mobilize development agents and increase their efficacy by: (a) making provisions for upgrading their knowledge, skills, and competencies through periodic training programs; and (b) providing them with media materials designed particularly for them as change agents. These media materials should be specialized publications that are tailored to their needs, and not to the rural "mass," as has been the practice in several SEA countries in the past. Then these development agents would reach out to the rural mass via word-of-mouth, strengthened by periodic training and armed with specialized communication-support materials.

Message Strategies for Development Programs

Because of the urgency with which vast human resources must be mobilized for national development, one overriding goal of SEA countries has been to develop approaches capable of penetrating as large a segment of their populations as possible. Thus, outreach or quantitative audience coverage has been the primary concern. Such considerations as message strategies did not receive much attention until some time after the primary priorities had been satisfied. Moreover, communication research, when initiated in these countries, was focused principally on gathering audience data in which the media were interested.

Hence, it was not until the mid-1960s that some studies turned their attention to media messages. The initial efforts, made mostly in the universities, aimed at determining the development content of these messages. More recent findings have identified the deficiencies of our development messages (Idris and Noor 1972; Shanmugam, in Alfonso 1971). These show that: (1) print and broadcast media do not communicate development adequately, accurately, and fairly, particularly with respect to sensitive subjects such as national integration, agrarian reform, and, lately, family planning; (2) agricultural messages, in general, fail to make adequate use of: familiar words, phrases, settings, and characters; liberal illustrations with adequate explanations; rural dialects peculiar to various geographic areas; and attractive formats that make them more easily understandable to their intended users, that is, the farmers and homemakers; (3) the messages likewise fall short in the projection of deeply held rural values, such as respect for the aged and authority, filial ties, value of children, family solidarity, and others; (4) development handouts are usually deficient in the social, economic, cultural, and environmental aspects of projects, concentrating almost wholly on the technical aspects; (5) the thrust of the messages is often inconsistent with the prevailing needs of programs and with the low levels of knowledge of the intended audiences; (6) in general, the messages are seldom coordinated with other development service inputs.

These findings, coupled with first-hand experience in developing locally oriented and research-based communication materials, point up the need for pretesting messages to remedy many of the deficiencies just cited and thus to enhance their usefulness in development programs. The kind of pretests needed should not be too sophisticated in design; excessive demand for rigor and precision in data collection and analysis often retards rather than accelerates development. Experience has shown that scientific pretests take time—even when there is availability of funds, a trained staff with modern data-processing equipment, and reduced bureaucratic red tape in administering the tests. The need to localize development materials—due to wide differences in subcultures within and between geographic regions of a developing country—points to still another lesson in pretesting: that pretests need not cover wide and distant geographic areas so long as a representative sampling of the specific intended audiences of the material is ensured. It appears inappropriate to talk about communication materials for a national audience in Southeast Asian countries. Such an audience just does not yet exist.

Use of Mass Media in Development Programs

Communication research in SEA initially took two forms: (1) media "infrastructure" studies, that is, data and statistics on the role, number, audience, and profile of newspapers, other periodicals, and radio; (2) basic studies relating to specialized problems of the broadcasting industries, audiovisual education, and public relations. Initial preoccupation with such studies stemmed from the need to take stock of the historical situation, with a view toward understanding present problems and developing well-directed media strategies to solve them. These studies still serve the purpose of establishing a pool of benchmark data on which to measure development at future times. They also generate "hunches" or hypotheses that serve as springboards for other studies that have implications for development.

To a limited extent, the effectiveness of multiple media over any single medium in development projects has been shown in recent experimental studies. For example, radio messages supported by leaflets and further reinforced by personal follow-ups proved more effective than radio alone or radio-leaflet reinforcement without personal follow-ups. For instructional purposes, a film followed by group discussion was more effective than the use of film alone (SEAMEO 1974).

There is very meager knowledge in SEA on which media, and which of their characteristics, have been effective in "reaching" particular audiences, both physically and psychologically. In general, we have no answers to such questions as these: What type of radio program is effective for what purpose and for what audience? Nor can we yet answer such questions for any other folk media, mass media, or mixed media.

Audiences of Development Programs

A large number of the studies done during the past decade reflect the overemphasis of some areas and the neglect of others that may be just as important, or more so. For instance, the studies have focused heavily on one element of the communication process—audience characteristics, preferences, reactions to or attitudes toward, and use of media.

Some audience characteristics that may be used as indices of development have improved to some degree over the last ten years.

These include the following:

In general, audiences in Southeast Asia appear to have improved their levels of economy as shown by the increase in annual growth rate of per capita GNP (percentage). For instance, the following changes were reported for these countries from 1960–1972 to 1965–1972: Burma 0.8 to 1.0; Cambodia 0.9 to 3.8; Indonesia 2.1 to 4.3; Laos 2.1 to 3.1; Malaysia 3.1 to 2.9; Philippines 2.2 to 2.4; Singapore 7.1 to 10.3; and Thailand 4.6 to 4.2.

However, a high proportion of the people of these countries still can neither read nor write. Examples: illiteracy in Thailand is 67 percent, in the Philippines 28 percent. Also, population has continued to increase by more than a million each month. Many still suffer from hunger and malnutrition. Food supplies available today in rural sectors of some countries in Southeast Asia are inadequate for a healthy, active life, both in quantity and nutritional quality. Many people, particularly those in the rural areas, still generally follow traditional folkways and subscribe to age-old values and aspirations, which generally work against development. Some of these values held by rural folk in traditional villages are kinship orientation of traditional families, patriarchal character of the family with rigid and demanding role prescriptions for members, and the subservience of individuals to group norms, supernatural and superstitious beliefs, a fatalistic attitude toward life, and several others (Feliciano and Feliciano 1974).

Research data from three countries show rural audience preferences to include: (a) multicolored covers of leaflets, pamphlets, brochures, with realistic illustrations that are familiar to them; (b) generously illustrated formats with adequate accompanying textual explanations; (c) posters and flip-charts on white glossy paper; (d) texts that suggest or give straightforward solutions to village problems, written in the dialect of the province or district; (e) up-to-date information on innovations that detail the conditions under which these are adaptable; (f) mutually supportive text and illustrations; and (g) step-by-step accounts of how to use the innovations.

Audiences tend to value those media that are immediately available and useful to them. Thus, in general, urban audiences are inclined to place greater value on mass media—radio, television, newspapers—than on personal channels. The converse would be true in general for rural audiences. However, where both types are equally available and useful, audiences tend to place equal value on both types, regardless of whether they live in urban or rural areas (Roque 1974).

Concluding Remarks

In discussing the past ten years of communication and development in Southeast Asia, three conclusions may be advanced:

(1) Communication is correlated with development. Research data show that development in SEA today is proceeding at a faster pace compared to ten years ago. The development appears to be accompanied by a greater use of communication media by governments in SEA.

(2) Qualitative measures of media growth or media well-being may be more valid or appropriate to SEA than the existing numerical yardsticks. The regional communication situation, behavior, and practices appear to support this, although more adequate and conclusive data are called for.

(3) Communication research has started to demonstrate its usefulness to development programs by calling attention to what media can contribute to the process of change by serving as initiator, legitimizer, and facilitator. Of the three functions, that of facilitator appears to assume greater significance, considering the urgency of development in Southeast Asia today.

NOTES

1. Southeast Asia (SEA), for the purposes of this paper, comprises Burma, Cambodia, Indonesia, Laos, Malaysia, the Philippines, Singapore, Thailand, and Vietnam.

2. Other publications include *Statistical Yearbook, 1969* and unpublished country reports obtained from embassy publications and media seminar proceedings. Data that follow, on radio, television, and cinema, are all from the same sources.

3. The phrase and a few of the factors were inspired by Development Academy of the Philippines 1975.

4. Some of these schools were: *In Malaysia*—School of Mass Communication, Mara Institute of Technology (1972), Universiti Sains, Malaysia, School of Humanities Communication Program (1971), University of Malaya, Department of English, Media Research Group (1972); *in the Philippines*—Centro Escolar University, Department of Speech and Mass Communication (1971), Pamantasan ng Lunsod ng Maynila, Department of Communication (1974); *in Singapore*—Nanyang University, Department of Government and Public Administration (Journalism Course, 1970); *in Bangkok*—Chulalongkorn University Faculty of Communication Arts (1973).

5. The wage problems and prospects of media practitioners were discussed at length during the conference from which grew this volume.

6. This concept was diffused to Asian media specialists in a UNESCO seminar on "Broadcasting in the Service of Education and Development," Bangkok, Thailand, May 1966. This was, of course, preceded by our conference here at the East-West Communication Institute in August 1964.

7. The three countries are Malaysia, Philippines, and Thailand. See Roque 1974.

8. To cite a few examples: Indonesia's Foreign Minister Adam Malik, a journalist, was the founder of the Antara News Agency; Malaysia's Prince Tunku Abdul Rahman Putra was a playwright and film scriptwriter; Singapore's head of state Benjamin Henry Sheares published twenty articles in professional journals; Thailand's Foreign Affairs Minister Thanat Khoman published papers on Southeast Asian affairs; and the Philippines' Carlos P. Romulo, Francisco S. Tatad, Blas S. Ople, and Jose Aspiras, secretaries of Foreign Affairs, Public Information, Labor, and Tourism respectively, were former practicing newsmen.

9. The ASEAN countries are also participating in this AMIC cooperative research project.

11. Where Are We in Understanding the Diffusion of Innovations?

EVERETT M. ROGERS

> Research on mass communications and on the acceptance of new farm practices may be characterized as an interest in campaigns to gain acceptance of change. Despite their shared problems, these two fields have shown no interest in each other.
>
> Elihu Katz (1960:435)

> The studies of the diffusion of innovations, including the part played by mass communication, promise to provide an empirical and quantitative basis for developing more rigorous approaches to theories of social change.
>
> Melvin L. DeFleur (1966:138)

> Diffusion of innovations has the status of a bastard child with respect to the parent interests in social and cultural change: too big to ignore but unlikely to be given full recognition.
>
> Frederick C. Fliegel and Joseph E. Kivlin (1966:235)

> Diffusion research is thus emerging as a single, integrated body of concepts and generalizations, even though the investigations are conducted by researchers in several scientific disciplines.
>
> Everett M. Rogers with F. Floyd Shoemaker (1971:47)

The purposes of this chapter are (1) to summarize what we have learned from research on the diffusion of innovations that contributes to our understanding of the role of communication in change and development, (2) to discuss how the academic history and the intellectual structuring of this field have affected its contributions and its shortcomings, and (3) to indicate future research priorities on the diffusion of innovations, especially in light of the changing intellectual conceptions of development.

Our focus is especially on the last ten-year period, and on the diffusion research completed in the nations of Latin America, Africa, and Asia, but for comparative purposes we must also deal briefly with the origins and conduct of diffusion research in the United States.

The central theme of this paper is that diffusion research has played an important role in helping (1) put social structure back in the communication process, and (2) correct the essentially "timeless" nature of most other communication research.

THE RISE OF DIFFUSION RESEARCH AS AN INVISIBLE COLLEGE

From Revolutionary Paradigm to Classical Model

Although the origins of research on the diffusion of innovations trace (1) from the German-Austrian and the British schools of diffusionism in anthropology (whose members claimed that all changes in a society resulted from the introduction of innovations from other societies), and (2) from the French sociologist Gabriel Tarde (1903), who pioneered in proposing the S-shaped diffusion curve and the role of opinion leaders in the process of "imitation," the "revolutionary paradigm" for diffusion occurred in the early 1940s when two sociologists, Bryce Ryan and Neal Gross (1943), published their study of the diffusion of hybrid seed corn among Iowa farmers.

Any given field of scientific research begins with a major breakthrough or reconceptualization that provides a new way of looking at some phenomenon (Kuhn 1962). This revolutionary paradigm typically sets off a furious amount of intellectual effort as promising young scientists are attracted to the field, either to advance the new conceptualization with their research or to disprove certain of its aspects. Gradually, a scientific consensus about the field is developed, and, perhaps after several generations of academic scholars, the "invisible college" (composed of researchers on a common topic who are linked by communication ties) declines in scientific interest as fewer findings of an exciting nature are turned up. These are the usual stages in the normal growth of science, Kuhn (1962) claims.

Research on the diffusion of innovations has followed these rise-and-fall stages rather closely, although the final stage of demise has not yet begun (Crane 1972). The hybrid corn study set forth a new approach to the study of communication and change that was soon followed up by an increasing number of scholars. Within ten years (by 1952), over 100 diffusion researches were completed; during the next decade (by 1962), another 450; and by the end of 1974, another 1,200. So today there are over 2,600 publications about the diffusion of innovations, including about 1,750 empirical research reports and 850 other writings (Figure 1).[1] So, the amount of scientific activity in investigating the diffusion of innovations increased at an exponential rate

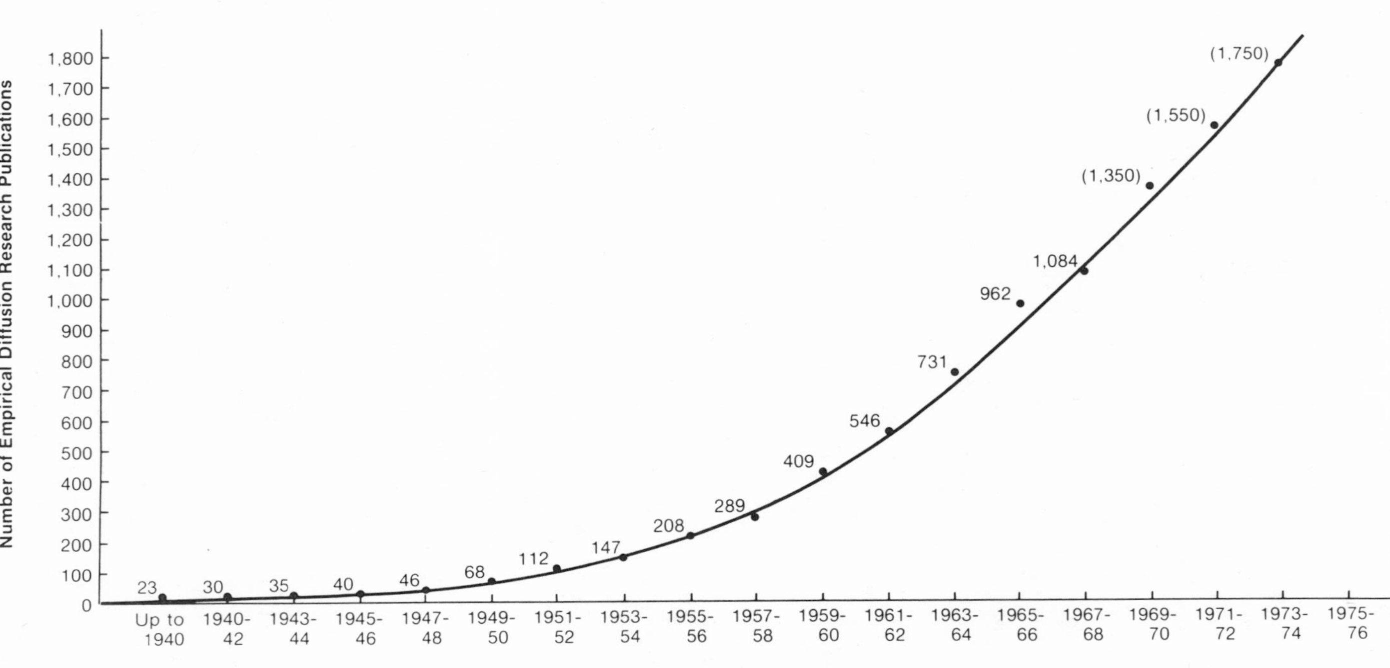

Figure 1. Cumulative Number of Empirical Diffusion Research Publications by Year

(doubling almost every two years) since the revolutionary paradigm appeared thirty-two years ago, as Kuhn's (1962) theory of the growth of science would predict.

The main elements in the "classical model" of the diffusion of new ideas that emerged are (1) the *innovation*, defined as an idea perceived as new by an individual, (2) which is *communicated* through certain *channels* (3) over *time* (4) among the members of a *social system*. The Ryan and Gross (1943) study focused on hybrid corn, one of the most important innovations in Midwestern agriculture. Data were gathered by personal interviews with all the Iowa farmers in two communities. The rate of adoption of the agricultural innovation followed an S-shaped, normal curve when plotted on a cumulative basis over time. The first farmers to adopt (the innovators) were more cosmopolite (indicated by traveling more frequently to Des Moines) and of higher socioeconomic status than later adopters. The typical Iowa farmer first heard about the innovation from a seed corn salesman, but interpersonal communication with peers was the most frequent channel leading to persuasion.[2] The innovation process from awareness-knowledge to final adoption averaged about nine years, indicating that considerable time was required for adoption to occur.

Diffusion research is a particular type of communication research, but it began outside of the academic field of communication. Mostly this was a matter of timing, as the Ryan and Gross (1943) study preceded the first university centers or departments of communication by a good dozen years. Research on persuasion and attitude change, on nonverbal communication, and on other important topics for communication research also began in psychology, anthropology, sociology, or other social sciences, and then came to flower in the hands of communication scholars. The diffusion research approach was taken up in a variety of fields: education, anthropology, medical sociology, marketing, geography, and, most of all, in rural sociology. Each of these disciplines pursued diffusion research in its specialized way, and, for some time, without much interchange with the other diffusion research traditions.

The Intellectual Watershed of 1960

The year 1960 was a turning point, in several respects, for research on the diffusion of innovations. For one thing, the old disciplinary boundaries began to break down, and diffusion research began to emerge as "a single, integrated body of concepts and generalizations" (Rogers with Shoemaker 1971:47).

Second, researchers in the academic field of mass communication began to engage in diffusion research, at first by investigating the diffusion of major news events carried by the mass media: Alaskan statehood, the launching of Sputnik, and President Kennedy's assassination. The most noted news-event diffusion study, itself representing a "mini-revolutionary paradigm," was by Deutschmann and Danielson (1960). Today, there are over 100 such news-event diffusion studies. Soon, communication scholars began to study many types of other innovations, including technological innovations in agriculture, health, and family planning, especially in the developing nations of Latin America, Africa, and Asia.[3]

The early 1960s marked the beginning of a sharp take-off in the number of diffusion studies in developing countries. Pioneering ventures in this direction by S. A. Rahim (1961) in Bangladesh and by Paul J. Deutschmann and Orlando Fals Borda (1962) in Colombia suggested that new ideas spread among peasants in villages in a generally similar pattern to their diffusion in more media-saturated settings like the United States and Europe. The diffusion process, and the concepts and models utilized to analyze it, seemed to be cross-culturally valid, at least in the sense that comparable results were found in the new settings.

There were compelling reasons for the fast growth of diffusion studies in developing countries after 1960. Technology was assumed to be at the heart of development, at least in the dominant paradigm of development popular until very recent years.[4] In fact, innovativeness was thought to be the best single indicant of the multifaceted dimension called "modernization," the individual-level equivalent of development at the societal or system level (Rogers with Svenning 1969). So microlevel investigations of the diffusion of technological innovations among villagers were of direct relevance to development planners and other government officials in developing nations. These research results, and the general framework of diffusion, provided both a kind of theoretical approach and an evaluation procedure for development agencies.

The number of diffusion researches in developing nations totaled only about 54 in 1960 (13 percent of all diffusion studies), but rose steeply to 331 in 1968 (30 percent of the total), and to over 800 or so by 1975, when over half of all diffusion studies were being conducted in Latin America, Africa, and Asia. The major developing country of study is India, which has over 450 of the 800 researches being conducted in developing countries.

An important boost to the internationalization of the diffusion field was the rise of "KAP surveys" in developing countries during the 1960s. KAP studies are sample surveys of knowledge (K), attitudes (A), and practice (P) (that is, adoption) of family planning innovations. K, A, and P are the logical dependent variables in evaluations of family planning communication campaigns, and as national family planning programs arose after 1960 in many developing nations (especially in Asia) to cope with the population problem, KAP-type diffusion researches blossomed on all sides. Over 500 such KAP surveys were conducted in seventy-two nations by 1973 (Rogers 1973:377); India alone was the locale for over half of these investigations.

With the exception of the Taichung experiment in Taiwan (Freedman and Takeshita 1969), the intellectual contribution of these KAP surveys "to scientific understanding of human behavior change has been dismal" (Rogers 1973:378). However, the KAP studies have provided a useful function by generally showing that most parents in developing countries want fewer children than they actually have, and that the majority desired a government family planning program. Even the harshest critic of KAP studies, Professor Philip H. Hauser (1967:405), stated that: "KAP survey results, erroneous or not, have helped to persuade prime ministers, parliaments, and the general population to move in a desirable direction and have provided family planning program administrators with 'justification' for budgets and programs."

Intellectually speaking, the family planning diffusion studies were generally disappointing, although several modifications in the classical diffusion model (such as the payment of incentives to promote diffusion, and the use of nonprofessional change agent aides to help overcome the taboo nature of family planning communication) did emerge when family planning programs found the model wanting (Rogers 1973). Also, the family planning diffusion studies gave a boost to field experimental research designs, as over a dozen such experiments in various nations followed the Taichung Study (Rogers and Agarwala-Rogers 1975).

The rise of these field experiments in diffusion research, in place of one-shot survey designs, helps to overcome three of its important conceptual/methodological biases (which also characterize other types of communication research):

1. Lack of a process orientation.
2. A pro-innovation bias (and an associated ignoring of causality).
3. A psychological orientation, leading to shortchanging structure.

Now we take up each of these three biases in order.

Lack of a Process Orientation

Every textbook definition of the concept of communication[5] either states or directly implies it is a process. Thus one might expect an overwhelming emphasis in research and theory on the conceptualization of communication as process. However, a recent analysis by Arundale (1971) shows that the research designs and measurements of communication almost never allow analysis of the over-time aspects of communication (that would be necessary to explore process adequately). Very few communication researches include data at more than one observation point, and almost none at more than two such points in time. So almost all communication research is unable to trace the change in a variable over time; it deals only with the present-tense of behavior. Communication thus becomes, in the actuality of communication research, an artificially halted snapshot.

Why has communication research not dealt more adequately with the change-over-time aspects of process?

1. We lack concepts and propositions that reflect a process-orientation.
2. Time-series data are expensive to gather, unless one depends on respondent recall, a procedure that is often less than satisfactory.
3. Repeated data-gathering over time leads to problems of respondent sensitization (unless one uses unobtrusive and nonreactive measurement methods), as communication research itself is a communication process.
4. Communication researchers are often pressured by research sponsors, doctoral requirements, and other logistic forces to produce immediate results; this is a strong discouragement to over-time research designs.

So, unfortunately, we define communication as process, but then proceed to treat communication as a one-shot affair in communication research.

Diffusion research is only slightly "less bad" in this respect than other types of communication research. Because *time* is one of the four essential elements in the diffusion process, and thus receives more explicit attention than in other types of communication research, it should be stressed in the research designs utilized in diffusion research.

Diffusion research designs consist mainly of correlational analyses of cross-sectional data gathered in one-shot surveys of the respondents, thus exactly following the method pioneered by Ryan and Gross (1943). By 1968 (the last time a tabulation was made of the methodologies used in diffusion studies), only 65 of the then 1,084 empirical diffusion publications (about 6 percent) reported results from field experiments, and most of these field experiments had been done since 1960 (our turning-point year in the diffusion field). Even allowing for the 67 diffusion publications (another 6 percent) that reported longitudinal panel studies at two or more points in time, the vast majority (about 88 percent) of all diffusion researches are one-shot surveys allowing only cross-sectional data analysis. Such research designs cannot tell us very much about the process of diffusion over time, other than what can be reconstructed from recall data.

Diffusion studies are particularly able to rely on "moving pictures" of behavior, rather than "snapshots," because of their unique capacity to trace the sequential flow of an innovation through a social system. However, diffusion researchers mainly have relied upon their respondents' ability to recall their date of awareness or adoption of a new idea. Essentially, the respondent is asked to look back over his shoulder and mentally reconstruct his past history of innovation experiences. This hindsight ability is much less than completely accurate and it undoubtedly varies on the basis of (1) the innovations' salience to the respondents, (2) the length of time over which recall is requested, and (3) individual differences in education, mental ability, and so forth.

Future diffusion research ought to develop improved methods for tracer studies, in which alternative sources of data are used to provide validity checks on recall data about time.[6] Much greater use should be made of field experiments and panel studies that, by their research designs, are able to take "moving pictures" of the diffusion process.

The Pro-Innovation Bias and Causality

Most diffusion research has an inherent pro-change bias in that it assumes the innovations studied are "good" and should be adopted by everyone. Undoubtedly hybrid corn was profitable for each of the Iowa farmers in the Ryan and Gross (1943) study, but most other innovations that have been studied do not have this high degree of relative advantage. Many individuals, for their own good, should not adopt them.

The pro-innovation bias, coupled with the unfortunate and overwhelming dependence on survey research designs, means that diffusion research has mostly studied "what is," rather than "what could be," about diffusion processes. So method has followed the assumption that innovation is good, that the present process of diffusion is satisfactory and needs only minor tune-up, rather than a major overhaul. Röling et al. (1974) have heavily scored diffusion research on this count, arguing that it has often led to increased inequity; field experimental designs are needed to test alternatives to current practice, rather than the replication of more surveys of "what is."[7]

The pro-innovation bias in diffusion research, and its overwhelming reliance on correlational analysis of survey data, often led in the past to avoiding or ignoring the issue of causality. We often speak of "independent" and "dependent" variables in diffusion research, having taken these terms from experimental designs and then used them rather loosely with correlational analysis. A dependent variable thus means little more than the main variable in which the investigator is interested. (In about 60 percent of all diffusion researches, the dependent variable is innovativeness, defined as the degree to which a responding unit is relatively earlier in adopting an innovation than other units in the system.) It is implied that the independent variables "lead to" innovativeness, although it is often unstated or uncertain whether this really means that an independent variable causes innovativeness.

In order for variable X to be the cause of variable Y, (1) X must precede Y in time-order, (2) they must be related, or co-vary, and (3) X must have a "forcing quality" on Y. Most diffusion researches have only determined that various independent variables co-vary with innovativeness; correlational analysis of one-shot survey data does not allow the determination of time-order. Such correlational studies face a particular problem of time-order that I call "yesterday's innovativeness": In most diffusion surveys, innovativeness is measured today with recall data about past adoption behavior, while the independent variables are measured in the present tense. It is obviously impossible for an individual's attitudes, formed and measured now, to cause his adoption of an innovation three years previously (this would amount to X following Y in time-order, and thus making it impossible for X to cause Y).

So again we see the importance of research designs that allow us to learn the over-time aspects of diffusion. Field experiments are ideally suited to the purpose of assessing the effect of various independent variables (the treatments) on the dependent variable of innovativeness.

In order for X to cause Y, they must co-vary. If such co-variance is very low, X is probably not a cause of Y. If their common variance is high, X may be a cause of Y. Diffusion researches have specialized in determining the correlates of innovativeness.

Forcing quality, the way in which X acts on Y, is a theoretical issue, rather than an empirical one. Much greater attention needs to be given in diffusion research to the theoretical reasoning as to why certain variables might have a forcing quality on others. Theoretical approaches from other fields of communication study may have application to conceptualizing the forcing quality of certain independent variables on innovativeness, and other dependent variables.

The Psychological Bias That Short-Changes Structure

The psychological bias in communication research stems (1) from its historical roots in academe, and (2) from the researchers' acceptance of how social problems are defined. Several early communication scholars come from psychological backgrounds, and it was only natural that their models of communication largely ignored social structural variables that affect communication. The transactional and relational nature of human communication tended to be overlooked, at least until fairly recently.

The Individual as the Unit of Analysis

The overwhelming focus on the individual as the unit of analysis in communication research (while largely ignoring the importance of communication relationships between sources and receivers) is often due to the assumption that if the individual is the unit of response, he must consequently be the unit of analysis (Coleman 1958). The monadic view of human behavior determined that "The kinds of substantive problems on which such research focuses tended to be problems of 'aggregate psychology,' that is, within-individual problems and never problems concerned with relations between people" (Coleman 1958: 28). The use of survey methods in communication research "de-structured" behavior:

> Using random sampling of individuals, the survey is a sociological meat-grinder, tearing the individual from his social context and guaranteeing that nobody in the study interacts with anyone else in it. It is a little like a biologist putting his experimental animals through a hamburger machine and looking

> at every hundredth cell through a microscope; anatomy and physiology get lost; structure and function disappear and one is left with cell biology. (Barton 1968:1)

Only recently has the main focus in communication research on the individual as the unit of analysis shifted to the dyad, clique, network, or system of individuals; to the communication relationships between individuals, rather than on the individuals themselves. Encouraging attempts to overcome the psychological bias in communication research are provided by the co-orientation model, by relational analysis,[8] by network analysis, and by the general systems approach.

These conceptual-methodological approaches suggest that even when the individual is the unit of response, the communication relationship (even thought it can't "speak") can be the unit of analysis via some type of sociometric measurement. Sampling and data-analysis procedures for relational analysis are being worked out, but we still lack relational concepts, and theories linking these concepts. Until communication scholars begin to think in relational terms, there will not be much relational analysis.

Person-Blame

The second reason for the artificially "de-structured" psychological bias in communication research is the acceptance of a person-blame causal-attribution definition of the social problems that we study: individual-blame is the tendency to hold an individual responsible for his problems. Obviously, what is done about a social problem, including research, depends upon how it is defined. Seldom do communication scientists participate in the identification and definition of social problems. So they borrow or accept these definitions from alarmists, government officials, and other scientists.[9]

Many illustrations of individual-blame can be cited in behavioral research. Caplan and Nelson find a high degree of individual-blame in psychological research on such social problems as highway safety and race relations. Person-blame assumptions affect communication research on poverty:

> Only very recently have some students of the poor come to see that it is the social structure, not the poor as individuals, that needs change. It is incomplete, for instance, to say that the poor lack knowledge where the system does not make information available to them. (1973:199)[10]

Person-blame rather than system-blame permeates most definitions of social problems; seldom are the definers able to change the system, so they accept it. Such acceptance encourages a focus on psychological variables in communication research. Often, the problem definer's individual-level cause becomes the researcher's main variable: television violence and aggressive behavior, the modernization of peasants, persuasion.

How can the person-blame bias be overcome? By keeping an open mind about the causes of a social problem, at least until exploratory data are gathered. By involving the participants and receivers in the definition of the problem, rather than just those persons who are seeking amelioration of the social problem. By considering structural variables, as well as intraindividual variables, in communication research.

Diffusion research was originally (and for many years) as guilty as other types of communication research in following an individual-blame approach:

> We note an assumption in diffusion writings that the rate of adoption should be speeded up, that the innovation should be adopted by receivers, etc. [This is a consequence of the pro-innovation bias of diffusion research.] Seldom is it implied in diffusion documents that the source or the channels may be at fault for not providing more adequate information, for promoting inadequate or inappropriate innovations, etc. (Rogers with Shoemaker 1971:79)

This psychological bias in diffusion research began with the hybrid seed corn study; strangely, Ryan and Gross (1943) did not gather sociometric data about the interpersonal diffusion of the innovation within their two Iowa communities of study even though (1) they found that interpersonal communication from neighbors was essential in clinching adoption decisions, and (2) their sampling design of a complete census of farmers in the two communities was ideal for gathering relational data for network analysis purposes.

Restoring Social Structure to Diffusion Research

The re-focusing of diffusion researches had to wait until later investigations, especially the drug study among medical doctors by Coleman et al. (1966). Then it became a common procedure for diffusion scholars to ask their respondents sociometric questions of the general form: "From whom in this system did you obtain information that led you to adopt this innovation?" The sociometric dyad represented by each answer to this question could consequently be punched on an IBM card (including data on the characteristics of the seeker and the sought), which then became the unit of analysis.

The relational data thus obtained was utilized to provide deeper insight into the role of opinion leaders in the two-step flow of communication, a conceptualization that was originated prior to most diffusion research by Lazarsfeld et al. (1944). The two-step flow hypothesis turned out mainly to be an oversimplification, later research showed (as the flow of communication may have any number of steps), but the concept of opinion leadership has much theoretical and practical utility. Diffusion researches were able to advance understandings of opinion leadership because of their unique capacity to focus on the flow of innovations, new messages (to the receiver) that seemed to leave deeper (and hence more recallable) scratches on men's minds. The tracer quality of an innovation's diffusion pathways aids the investigation of the flow of communication messages, and especially the role of certain individuals like opinion leaders in this flow. For instance, the complicated relationship of leadership and group norms, first raised theoretically by George Homans (1961:339), has received rather definite empirical elucidation by diffusion scholars, resulting in the proposition that: "When the system's norms favor change, opinion leaders are more innovative, but when the norms are traditional, opinion leaders are not especially innovative" (Rogers with Shoemaker 1971:219). For example, in relatively more modern Colombian villages, opinion leaders were much more innovative than their followers; but in traditional villages, the opinion leaders were only slightly more innovative than their followers, and the villages' innovators were perceived with suspicion and disrespect (Rogers with Svenning 1969:230–231).

Network Analysis of Diffusion

Most communication research has largely ignored the effect of social structure on communication behavior, as we pointed out previously, and diffusion research to date has only partly realized its full potential in this regard. Network analysis, defined as a type of research in which sociometric data about communication flows or patterns are analyzed by using interpersonal relationships as the units of analysis (Rogers et al. 1975), is the tool that promises to capitalize on the unique ability of diffusion inquiry to reconstruct specific message flows in a system, when combined with the capacity to overlay the social structure of the system on these flows. The innovation's diffusion brings life to the otherwise static nature of the structural variables; network analysis permits understanding the social structure as it channels the process of diffusion. About the only other place in communication research where network analysis has been used to restore social structure to the communication process is in a few recent investigations of organizational communication.[11]

The first, and very partial, attempts toward network analysis of the diffusion process simply identified opinion leaders in a system and determined their mass media and interpersonal communication behavior. This approach was only a slight extension of the usual monadic analysis toward a relation type of analysis.

Next, diffusion scholars began to plot sequential-over-time sociograms of the diffusion of an innovation among the members of a system. And tentative steps were taken toward using communication relationships (such as sociometric dyads) as the units of analysis. This advance allowed the data-analysis of a "who-to-whom" communication matrix, and facilitated inquiry into the identification (1) of cliques within the total system and how such structural subgroupings affected the diffusion of an innovation, and (2) of specialized communication roles such as liaisons,[12] bridges, and isolates (thus allowing communication research to proceed far beyond the relatively simpler issue of studying just opinion leadership). Further, the measurement of various structural indexes (such as communication integration, connectedness,[13] and system openness[14]) for individuals, cliques, or entire systems (like villages) now became possible, and could be related to the rate of diffusion occurring in these systems. General propositions began to emerge from such network analysis, for example, that system innovativeness is positively related to (1) connectedness, and (2) to system openness.[15]

These network analyses necessitated a new kind of sampling, as well as a shift to relational units of analysis. Instead of relying upon random samples of scattered individuals in a large population, the network studies depended on gathering data from all of the eligible respondents in a system (e.g., a village) or a sample of such systems (Table 1). Usually these sample designs meant less emphasis on the ability to generalize the research results, which was traded off for a greater focus on understanding the role of social structures on diffusion flows. If such research were to study social structure, it had to sample intact social structures, or at least the relevant parts of them.

The Strength of Weak Ties

Out of the network analyses of interpersonal diffusion grew a research issue that came to be called "the strength of weak ties" (Liu and Duff 1972; Granovetter 1973).[16] The proposition summarizing this research is that: The informational strength of dyadic communication relationships is inversely related to the degree of homophily (and the strength of the attraction) between the source and the receiver. Or, in other words, an innovation is diffused to a larger number of individuals, and traverses a greater social distance, when passed through weak ties rather than strong (Granovetter 1973).

Each individual operates in his/her particular communication environment for any given topic, consisting of a number of friends and acquaintances with whom the topic is discussed most frequently. These friends are usually highly homophilous (or similar) with the individual, and with each other, and most of the individual's friends are friends of each other, thus constituting an "interlocking network" (Rogers 1973). This homophily and close attraction facilitates effective communication, but it acts as a barrier to prevent new ideas from entering the network. So there is not much informational strength in the interlocking network; what is needed are some heterophilous ties into the network to give it more openness. These "weak ties" enable innovations to flow from clique to clique via liaisons and bridges. There is a cohesive power to the weak ties.

Network analysis of the diffusion of the intrauterine device (IUD) in the Philippines demonstrated this strength of weak ties: the innovation spread

Table 1. Comparison of Monadic and Relational Analysis in Research on the Diffusion of Innovations.

	Type of Diffusion Research Approach	
Characteristics of the Research Approach	*Monadic Analysis*	*Relational Analysis*
1. Unit of analysis	The individual	The communication relationship between two (or more) individuals
2. Most frequent sample design	Random samples of scattered individuals in a large sample (in order to maximize the generalizability of the research results)	Complete census of all eligible respondents in a system (e.g., a village), or a sample of such intact systems
3. Types of data utilized	Personal and social characteristics of individuals, and their communication behavior	Same as for monadic analysis, plus sociometric data about communication relationships
4. Main type of data-analysis methods	Correlational analysis of cross-sectional survey data	Various types of network analysis of cross-sectional survey data
5. Main purpose of the research	To determine the variables (usually characteristics of individuals) related to innovativeness	To determine how social structural variables affect diffusion flows in a system

most easily within interlocking cliques, among housewives of very similar social status (Liu and Duff 1972). But heterophilous flows were necessary to link these cliques; usually these "weak ties" connected two women who were not close friends, and allowed the IUD to travel from a higher-status to a somewhat lower-status housewife. So at least occasional heterophilous dyadic communication in a network was a structural prerequisite for effective diffusion.

One reason for the relatively slow rate of diffusion of family planning innovations in developing countries is that they are perceived as taboo.

Interpersonal communication about taboo topics is especially homophilous, and can occur only with a very restricted number of other individuals. Such ingrown and redundant networks for family planning ideas lead to a slow diffusion rate, thus illustrating "the weakness of strong ties."

The case of network analysis on the strength of weak ties illustrates an important recent trend in communication research: the concepts used in this analysis are relational constructs. Perhaps we are seeing the real beginning of relational thinking in communication research.

Diffusion Versus Social Revolution

The post-1960 rise of diffusion research in developing countries, which we documented earlier in this paper, gave a powerful impetus to focus on social structural factors. In Latin America, Africa, and Asia, the structure of a national society or of a local community was often in sharp contrast to Euro-America. Power, economic wealth, and information were usually more highly concentrated in a few hands, and this aspect of structure affected not only the nature of innovation diffusion but also the matter of who reaped the main advantages, and disadvantages, of such technological change. If innovations were diffused more rapidly, but if the basic socioeconomic inequities reflected in the social structure were unchanged, had development really occurred?

Third World scholars in the 1970s began to question whether the classical diffusion model, even if it were cross-culturally valid in its functioning, was contributing much to development. The issue was not simply one of putting structural variables into diffusion analyses (this was already well underway, as we have just shown), but of a needed bottom-up change in the social structure of society. In other words, a people's revolution. This point of view accompanied the paradigm shift in conceptions of development, especially the questioning of whether technology was indeed at the heart of development (Rogers 1975). The social problem of underdevelopment was being redefined, and along lines that seriously questioned its original Western orientation.

The classical diffusion model was conceived in sociocultural conditions substantially different from those in Latin America (and Africa and Asia), and hence, Diaz-Bordenave (1974: 215) argues, when the model is used uncritically, it does not touch the basic issues (such as the social structure) affecting rural development in these countries:

> If there is one thing we are learning in Latin America it is that in communication and [the] adoption of innovations, pure research that is ideologically free and politically neutral does not exist and cannot exist. The scientist who says that he wants to do research without committing himself to changing rural society is in fact as ideologically committed as the other who believes in research as a tool for human and social change. (1974:215)[17]

The social blindness of communication research in ignoring or overlooking the social structural context in which it is conducted is reflected in the subtitle of a paper on communication research in Latin America by Beltran (1974): "The Blindfolded Inquiry?"

American communication research, using its favorite tools of the audience survey and a content analysis of mass media messages, is mainly characterized by a preoccupation with the effects of mass media communication. The center of gravity in communication research is thus shifted away from mass media institutions, and who in society controls them, to how the receiver is affected by mass communication. Usually this focus on effects means that the goal of communication research is to determine the persuasiveness of messages in changing people's attitudes and overt behavior, for whatever purpose (Mattelart 1970).

So in escaping its predominantly "Made in the U.S." origins through its migration to developing nations, diffusion research came to be perceived in a wider perspective, and in a different light. An alternative to social revolution it is not. A helpful tool for human progress, when accompanied by a basic restructuring of society, it may be.

Conclusions

Our quick tour of the past thirty-two years of diffusion research provides many examples of Thorsten Veblen's concept of "trained incapacity": By being taught to "see" innovativeness, opinion leadership, and other aspects of the classical model of diffusion, we failed to "see" much else. Acceptance of a revolutionary paradigm by scholars in a field enables them to cope with uncertainty and information overload, through the simplification of reality that the paradigm represents. It also imposes and standardizes a set of assumptions and conceptual biases that, once begun, are difficult to recognize and overcome.

In my opinion the research designs, concepts, and measurement procedures of diffusion research have been very stereotyped. This similarity has facilitated the synthesis of diffusion findings, a task to which I have contributed; in fact all diffusion studies look a good deal alike. But such standardization of research approaches has also greatly limited the contribution of diffusion research (1) to more effective development programs, and (2) to furthering the scientific understanding of communication and human behavior change. Presumably this indictment is what one dean of a U.S. school of communication had in mind when he characterized the diffusion field as "a mile wide and an inch deep."

Nevertheless, I believe that research on the diffusion of innovations has played an important role in helping put social structure back in the communication process. Focus on structural variables has increasingly characterized diffusion research in the past decade, and the techniques of network analysis promise exciting further steps in this direction. Eventually, this trend may help communication research shed its psychological bias and person-blame orientation.

For network analysis to fulfill its potential, however, I feel we must improve the methods of data-gathering and measurement. Sociometric questions about communication behavior leave much to be desired; adequate evidence of their accuracy and stability over time are presently lacking. Needed are unobtrusive, nonreactive measures to provide validity checks on sociometry, leading to a multiple measurement approach. At present, I believe our data-analysis techniques for relational analysis of communication behavior have far outrun the quality of our measurement.

Longitudinal panel designs for network analysis of diffusion processes are also needed; along with field experiments, they help secure the necessary data (1) to illuminate the over-time process aspects of diffusion (and communication), and (2) to facilitate exploration of the causal relationships involved in communication behavior.

Past research on the diffusion of innovations has helped correct the shortcomings of the essentially "timeless" nature of most other communication research. Time is an explicit element in all diffusion researches. But the measurement of time is one of the most egregious methodological weaknesses of past diffusion inquiry through its overwhelming dependence on recall data.

Thus (1) network analysis of over-time data and (2) field experiments are robust tools offering promise for research on the diffusion of innovations in the years ahead.

The recent paradigm shift in conceptualizations of development (Rogers 1975) augurs important changes for future diffusion researches. As the definitions of development, and actual development programs, stress equality of distribution, popular participation in decentralized activities, self-development, and so forth, the concepts and methods of diffusion inquiry must change appropriately. Perhaps the diffusion of technological innovations will cease to be a central issue in the "new development."

Perhaps it should.

NOTES

1. All of these publications are held in the Diffusion Documents Center in the Department of Population Planning at the University of Michigan. A bibliography of the 2,600 items is currently in the process of publication, and will be available from the author (at no cost).

2. Most diffusion researches since, especially those in developing nations, and most particularly those studying relatively taboo innovations like family planning methods, have found interpersonal channels to be much more important than mass media channels. One reason, a recent study by Barghouti (1974 *b*) in Lebanon shows, is because the mass media contain very little content about agricultural innovations.

Only 9 percent of the villagers reported mass media channels for agricultural information, but 88 percent named these channels for political information (which a content analysis of the Jordanian media showed was featured in their messages, while agricultural content was not). The Barghouti study demonstrates the advantages, in diffusion research, of combining a content analysis of the media with a survey of the receivers.

3. Detail on the convergence of diffusion research with communication research is provided by Katz (1960) and Rogers (1967).

4. In addition to assuming that capital-intensive technology was the vital ingredient in development, the dominant paradigm assumed that a nation had to pass through an industrial revolution en route to development, that economic growth (guided by central planning agencies and quantified in aggregate terms like GNP) largely constituted the nature of development, and that the causes of underdevelopment lay mainly within the developing nation. After the paradigm shift, the newer conceptions of development stressed (1) the equality of distribution, (2) popular participation in decentralized development planning and execution, (3) self-reliance and independence in development, (4) integration of traditional with modern systems, (5) the quality of life, and (6) that the causes of underdevelopment lay both within and external to the developing nation (Rogers 1975). More detail on this paradigm shift is provided in my comment elsewhere in this volume.

5. A common definition of communication is the process by which an idea is transferred from a source to a receiver with the intent to change his behavior.

6. As was done, for example, in a study of the diffusion of a new drug among medical doctors: The physicians' recall data were checked against pharmacists' sales records for each doctor (Coleman et al. 1966).

7. In the newer conceptions of development, much greater attention is given to the equality of distribution of economic benefits, information, etc., rather than simply assuming that these advantages would eventually "trickle down" from the more advantaged sectors of a system.

8. Relational analysis is a research approach in which the unit of analysis is a relationship between two or more individuals (Rogers and Bhowmik 1971).

9. However, sometimes (probably rarely) an alarmist argues for redefining a social problem in system-blame terms. An illustration is the efforts by Ralph Nader in the mid-1960s, especially through his book *Unsafe at Any Speed,* to redefine the problem of highway safety in terms of safer automobiles and highways, rather than just reckless driving.

10. Similarly, Caplan and Nelson (1973:207) ask: "Why do we constantly study the poor rather than the nonpoor in order to understand the origins of poverty?"

11. Especially centered in the Department of Communication at Michigan State University. Network analysis of sociometric data about communication is a natural in organizational settings, which are highly structured environments. Strangely, however, there have been almost no studies of the diffusion of an innovation within an organization, although there are over 400 investigations of the organization-to-organization diffusion of innovations. In these latter studies, the methodology essentially destructures the organization into an individual-equivalent unit of analysis.

12. Defined as an individual who links two or more cliques in a system.

13. Defined as the degree to which the units in a system are interconnected through communication linkages.

14. Defined as the degree to which the units in a system exchange information across the system boundary with its environment.

15. Illustrative of such network analyses are Yadav (1967), Guimarães (1972), Shoemaker (1971), Allen (1970), and Rogers et al. (1975).

16. These two sets of authors independently discovered the diffusion strength of weak sociometric ties, and published articles with identical names within a few months of each other in 1972–1973, although approaching the issue in somewhat different ways. Although Professors Liu, Duff, and Granovetter were well read in the diffusion literature, they had not previously published on this topic, and their articles show a relatively fresh approach to analyzing diffusions networks. Perhaps this relative newness in working with the classical diffusion model was one requisite for the originality of their contribution.

17. This viewpoint, that communication research and communication researchers are themselves a part of the society they study, has been more fully recognized by non-U.S. scholars than by their North American counterparts. Halloran, a European, stated: "Research is a form of social control, although we often tend to rationalize our intention. . . . We should at least be prepared to look at the possibility that social science is just another unit in the service of the political-economic system, be it capitalist or socialist" (1974:12–13).

11a. Diffusion Research—Past, Present, and Future

SYED A. RAHIM

Diffusion research has taken communication research out of its narrow urban and media orientation. Most of it has dealt with problems in the rural areas, problems of rural and agricultural development. Researchers have actually gone into the rural areas, interviewed local people, and collected information on conditions in the villages. Diffusion research has taken communication out of its ivory tower and brought it to the common people, thus making it much more useful. I consider this a very great contribution, even if the quality of research has not always been satisfactory. Having said these few words in praise of diffusion research, let me now add a few critical comments on Dr. Rogers' paper.

One regret I feel about diffusion research is that the emphasis has been primarily on the diffusion of technological innovations, mostly material things like new fertilizers, seeds, or techniques. Very little attention has been paid to the diffusion of new ideas, of new ideologies, of new social relations, of new social institutions and values. During the last decades there has been a tremendous change in the world: political changes have diffused new ideas and institutions. For instance, many newly independent and developing countries have accepted socialism, essentially a Western idea, and adapted it to their local situations. The diffusion of the ideas of socialism in Africa, Asia, and Latin America is a very interesting phenomenon. But diffusion researchers have not studied such problems. Similarly, the diffusion of social innovations brought about by political or technological revolutions has not been adequately studied.

My second point is that diffusion research, in examining the communication relationship between initiators and adopters of innovations, has assumed a one-way dependency relationship. The source of innovation—the industrialized developed West—is superior to the receiver of innovation—the underdeveloped East. Not only between East and West, but also within each country, the source of innovation (innovator or early adopter) has a higher socioeconomic status than the receiver (late adopter). The receiver is dependent on the source. This unequal relationship has been reinforced by the paradigm and the findings of diffusion research. I think this is unfortunate, because it has in a way supported what has been referred to in this volume as the old paradigm of development. It also has tended to block the researcher from seeing the reverse flow of ideas and innovations from the poor to the rich, from the less developed to the more developed, from the peasants to the technicians, administrators, and scientists. I know from my own experience in Comilla that the Japanese rice experts who came to Comilla to help diffuse improved methods of rice cultivation picked up many "new" ideas from the best farmers of Comilla. These were ideas and techniques learned by Comilla farmers through long practice, but to the Japanese experts they were innovations. The second point, then, is that new ideas, techniques, and innovations often are transferred from the poor to the rich, from peasant farmers to commercial farmers and agricultural experts, from less to more developed countries, and from East to West. Such diffusion normally remains unrecognized and neglected, which I think is a serious weakness of diffusion research.

My third point is that the unit of analysis in diffusion research has almost always been the individual. But we know that individuals are members of a social system and are linked to each other by communication channels as well as by many other social relations. An apparently individual decision may in fact be the outcome of a complex process of group decision. The assumption of independent individual decisions made in the mathematical formulation of the diffusion process is inappropriate in a traditional village society, where the sanctions of authority and consensus are important determinants of individual decisions.

The paradigm of the diffusion and adoption process was modified and extended around 1967–1968 to take into account various kinds of decisions —individual, contingent, authority, and collective. However, in practice, very little attention has been paid to this, and very little research has been done on group or collective decisions in innovation adoption. This shows the extent of bias in diffusion research. The bias toward individual decision is primarily because the leadership in teaching and research in the diffusion of innovation is provided by U.S. scholars. I think that there is a definite cultural bias that persists in spite of the fact that Dr. Rogers and other scholars are aware of that bias.

In other papers in this volume, Dr. Chu has pointed out the importance of group pressure in China and Dr. Oshima has told us that group pressure also operates in Japan. We know that group pressure operates in every society, including the United States. The diffusion and adoption of innovations do not depend only on individual innovation decisions, but also on the groups, their attitudes, norms, and decisions. These group factors, I think, have been neglected in the analysis of innovation research.

Finally, I would like to make a brief comment on the importance of interpersonal communication in innovation diffusion. Researchers have consistently found that interpersonal communication plays a very important role in the diffusion and adoption of innovations. But they have not made much effort to explain and understand the crucial role of interpersonal communication. More intensive research in that line would probably help planners and practitioners in designing more effective programs of development and change.

12. Research Priorities in Development Communication

FREDERICK T. C. YU

Development communication research is a fast-growing but underdeveloped field of study with a promising but precarious future. That the convergence of political, economic, social, and technological trends will lead to still greater need for development communication research is obvious. But whether the field is prepared intellectually and institutionally for the needed job is by no means certain. The challenge, then, is to see if we can say something useful, or at least relevant, about the prospects and priorities of development communication research, without being merely trite and pompous.

Let me get into the subject with that familiar story about Alice and the Cheshire Cat.

> "Cheshire-Puss," she began, rather timidly . . . "would you tell me please, which way I ought to go from here?" "That depends a good deal on where you want to get to," said the Cat. "I don't much care where—" said Alice. "Then it does not matter which way you go," said the Cat.

We need, in short, a sense of direction—some thinking and rethinking about where we are going and what paths are open to us. Alice's problem is that no one would give her a map of Wonderland. Our problem is somewhat different—perhaps a bit more complicated. We have maps that do not seem to show the same Wonderland of Development. We have also differing maps of a "Preferred World" with even more confusing directions. The way for us to begin is to work out a map for our purpose, to find out where we stand and discover at least a few fixed points that will help us chart our course for at least part of the way.

WHERE DO WE STAND?

These are difficult days for students of development communication. In reviewing the so-called Decade of Development, we found that many of the emerging nations, as Alex Inkeles and David H. Smith put it, "developed very little, if at all, and some slid backward" (Inkeles and Smith 1974). As the world staggers from one economic disaster to another, relations between developed and developing countries are in shambles. "At stake," President Ford told us in his somber State-of-the-Union address in January, "is the future of the industrialized democracies, which have perceived their destiny in common and sustained it in common for thirty years." There is in the development communication community a deepening sense of disappointment, doubt, and disenchantment.

This is not something new that comes with the oil squeeze or the energy crunch. Even during the Decade of Development in the 1960s, Albert O. Hirschman already described a rather common experience of frustration shared by many students of development and communication when he wrote: ". . . it is not true to say that we have learned nothing from the experience of the past twenty years. It's just that what we have learned is not quite what we expected to learn" (1967:10).

Students of development communication were perhaps baffled by conditions in the so-called Less Developed Countries (LDC) during the 1960s. But they seemed to share some firm beliefs, if not clear ideas, about goals, strategies, and stages of development. They knew, more or less, what needed to be done in less developed countries and what role communication was to play. The problem was to get the LDC's to do all that was necessary to develop and to become modern.

Only eleven years ago, the study of international relations was described as "an unruly flock of activities" (C. McClelland 1963: 3–11). This was still considered the state of affairs four years ago when the American Academy of Political and Social Science met to discuss international relations research (Palmer 1970). The phrase may be still adequate to describe the current status of development communication research.

In a recent attempt to survey current knowledge and to identify some fruitful future directions, W. Phillips Davison and I commented about the field of communication research in general:

> . . . so much communication research does lack direction: it neither contributes to basic theory nor is it helpful in solving practical problems. On the one hand, researchers appear to be swimming in circles around small islands of theory established in the 1940's and 1950's; on the other, they are dashing off in all directions to describe widely disparate aspects of the communication process in varied contexts. (Davison and Yu 1974: 1)

There is perhaps a somewhat sharper focus on research needs in the study of development communication than in other divisions of communication research. That communication research should be, as Gloria Feliciano puts it, "fully harnessed to serve the ends of development" may have given many development communication researchers a sense of purpose (1973:15). But this assumption has also been a source of confusion in the field, simply because "the ends of development" mean different things to different people in different countries and at different times. Development communication research is going strong, and there is no sign of a slow-down in growth, but its need for intellectual nourishment has become increasingly evident.

Priorities for Future Research

I shall not attempt a catalog or shopping list of ideas or suggestions for future research. I will try to identify and anticipate a few critical problems, opportunities, and challenges with priority implications. My purpose is not to predict or persuade but to understand and, hopefully, to stimulate. Mine is an open-ended list.

1. The Role of the Multinational Corporations: New Engines of Development?

The giant global corporations represent a new power in the world. It is no exaggeration that they are producing an organization revolution as important in its implications for modern man as the Industrial Revolution. They are compelling us to rethink development. Richard Barnet and Ronald Muller state the case thus:

> Within the last ten years, global corporations have grown so fast that their combined total sales exceed the gross national product of every country except the United States and the Soviet Union. With more than two hundred billion dollars in physical assets under their control, the international corporations' average growth rate since 1950 has been two to three times greater than the growth rate of the most advanced industrial countries, including the United States. In 1971, General Motors, one of the giants of them all, had gross annual sales of twenty-eight billion dollars; Switzerland's gross national product was twenty-six billion. By making ordinary business decisions, the managers of firms like G.M., I.B.M., General Electric, and Exxon now have more power than most sovereign governments to determine where people will live; what work they will do, if any; what they will eat, drink and wear; what sorts of knowledge schools and universities will encourage; and what kind of society their children will inherit. Indeed, the most revolutionary aspect of the giant international corporations is not their size but their world view. Their managers are seeking to put into practice a theory of human organizations that will profoundly alter the nation-state system around which society has been organized for more than four hundred years. (Barnet and Muller 1974*a*:53)

To reemphasize, we are talking about a group of corporations whose combined total sales, as cited above, exceeds the gross national product of every country except the United States and the Soviet Union. During the last ten years, more and more of these American-controlled and American-based multinational companies have shifted their production overseas, principally to such low-wage areas as Hong Kong, Taiwan, Mexico, and most recently West Africa, where cooperative, trainable workers can be employed for under thirty cents an hour. "The essential strategy of the global corporation," to quote another article by Barnet and Muller, "is division of labor, and the drive to maximize global profits by combining the capital and technology of rich countries with the cheap labor of poor ones has been irresistible" (1974*b*:100).

These corporations raise a new question of the unit of development. Peter F. Drucker, who sees the multinational as "a response to the emergence of a genuine world economy," has this to say:

> This world economy is not an agglomeration of national economies as was the "international economy" of nineteenth-century international trade theory. It is fundamentally autonomous, has its own dynamics, its own demand patterns, its own institutions—and in the Special Drawing Rights (SDR) even its own money and credit system in embryonic form. For the first time in 400 years—since the end of the sixteenth century when the word "sovereignty" was first coined—the territorial political unit and the economic unit are no longer congruent. (Drucker 1974:133)

Some observers, like Yoshikazu Sakamoto, have serious doubts whether the nation-state is an adequate force to control the economic life of the citizens:

> In the past, economic foundations of authority rested in the fact that the unit of polity usually coincided with the economy, i.e., the "national economy." With the growth of multinational corporations, however, the integrity of "national economy" has been and continues to be eroded, revealing the inadequacy of the nation-state as a force to control the economic life of the citizens. (Sakamoto 1974:2)

There can be no doubt that these global corporations have enormous power to shape the societies of the less-developed world. The question is whether they are to be considered new engines of development or new barriers to development. Are they in the business of exploitation or of development?

They are revolutionizing the world economy through their control over four basic elements of economic life: technology, finance capital, labor markets, and market place ideology. The managers of these corporations, of course, insist that they are engines of development. Their argument is that these corporations are a source of needed capital for less-developed countries, that they employ—and also train—hundreds of thousands of workers, offering them higher than prevailing wages, that they bring new technology to developing countries, and that they stimulate the growth of these countries.

The president and chief executive of BankAmerica Corporation sees the multinational not only as an effective force for better cooperation in the business world, but also as a force for peace among nations. This is how he puts it:

> Conscientious executives involved in international business desire to find ways in which their firms can be not only valuable and therefore welcome in the nation-states in which they operate, but also forces for the general good and peaceful existence of the world community. Indeed, the idea that this kind of business enterprise can be a strong force toward world peace is not so farfetched. Beyond the human values involved, the multinational firm has a *direct, measurable, and potent interest in helping prevent wars and other serious upheavals that cut off its resources, interrupt its communications, and kill its employees and customers.* (Clausen 1972:21; italics added)

Barnet and Muller suggest an opposite view this way:

> When the global corporations proclaim themselves engines of development, we can judge their claims only if we know what policies they are pursuing. If a development model is to have any real meaning in a world in which most people are struggling just to stay alive, it must . . . provide solutions to the three great social problems of the late twentieth century: poverty, unemployment and inequality. . . . The evidence of the 1960's is now in. It is an unhappy fact that the development policies pursued by international corporations in those years contributed more to the exacerbation of world poverty, world unemployment, and world inequality than to their solution. (Barnet and Muller 1974*a*:79–80)

It is not the purpose of this paper to decide whether the multinationals are new engines for or new barriers to development. And it serves no useful purpose for us to try to toot the horn of either the alarmist or the apologist on the power of the multinationals. But we should, at least, take very seriously Drucker's conclusion that:

> The best hope for developing countries, both to attain political and cultural nationhood and to obtain the employment opportunities and export earnings they need, is through the integrative power of the world economy. And their tool, if only they are willing to use it, is, above all, the multinational company —precisely because it represents a global economy and cuts across national boundaries.
>
> The multinational, if it survives, will surely look different tomorrow, will have a different structure, and will be "transnational" rather than "multinational." But even the multinational of today is—or at least should be—a most effective means to constructive nationhood for the developing world. (1974:134)

What should be of special interest and concern to students of development is the power and potential of the multinationals to exercise significant influence over the mass media in developing countries. Barnet and Muller speak of the "globalization of the Madison Avenue agency," which accompanies the rise of the global corporation and the global bank. To them, one of the most important sources of power for the multinationals in developing countries is their control over communication—"their extraordinary competitive edge in using the technology of market manipulation to shape the tastes, goals, and values of the workers, suppliers, government officials and, of course, customers on whom their own economic success in that society depends" (Barnet and Muller 1974*a*:74).

Take television, for instance. Products of American television are already exercising an influence over television programming in many developing countries in much the same way that products of Hollywood did for movies a few decades ago. We are all familiar with the wide distribution abroad of such American TV products as "I Love Lucy" and "Perry Mason." "'Bonanza,'" observed Wilson Dizard, "has an estimated audience of 350 million viewers in fifty-nine countries" (1966:160). A CBS representative in Africa reports: "I think that most shows in the U.S.A. have been very successful in the African market. On 'Perry Mason,' one station has bought everything that we have available. They like 'Rawhide' very much" (Tyler 1966:68). Even nine years ago, ABC—via its Worldvision stations—already had widespread connections overseas. ABC International's networking service then required "each Worldvision station to make Class A time available within eight weeks for any program presold by ABC. For example, ABC can sell 'Batman' to an advertiser and then place 'Batman' along with designated commercials in any Worldvision country where the advertiser wants it to appear" (Tyler 1966:32).

This is not a frivolous matter, and it is easy to understand. Viewers in many developing countries get a substantial ration of American television products, which include many "late-late show" Hollywood films, simply because it is so much easier and cheaper for local producers to rely on these programs than to create new programs of their own.

Now what does all this mean to developing countries? And what research implications do we see?

2. The Case of China

Much has been said about China's impressive and intriguing experience in development communication and about its transferability (see chapter 7c). It is an important influence and a source of ideas because it challenges some very widely accepted beliefs about development and modernization and it jars us to some new thinking. One student of China explains it this way:

> Let us recall that man's intellectual history from 1776 to 1949 can only be understood against the backdrop of six great revolutions: the American, the French, the European revolution of 1848, the Paris Commune, the Russian, and the Nazi revolutions. Not all of these revolutions succeeded. But each was a bold attempt by revolutionaries to reshape the lives of their countrymen. The revolutionaries discovered new, dramatic ways to obtain political power,

> and they also raised profound questions about the nature and potentialities of man. As revolutionaries rather than reformers, they challenged the accepted order. This is why both the Meiji Restoration of Japan and Japan's postwar recovery, for all their success, have not had an intellectual impact upon the world. Japan's spectacular reforms pose no real threat to accepted values and institutions. (Oksenberg 1973:5–6)

It is important to keep in mind that China's development model is one of revolution and it challenges accepted order. This is perhaps too obvious to be mentioned, but it is often overlooked by those who insist on learning the Maoist way but not paying the Maoist price. It is hard for them to take seriously such Maoist teachings as "*Pu po, pu li*" or "No destruction, no construction."

We are dealing here with a formula for modernization that discourages urbanization, that encourages sideline and cottage industries in the countryside, that seeks to remove the difference between manual and mental labor, between industry and agriculture, and between city and countryside, and that does not pour hordes of peasants into big cities but teaches them about industry in the countryside. All these elements require a basic transformation of society that, as Mao teaches it, is based on the total transformation of man.

We hear a good deal these days about China's success in the revolution in public health. But this is the result of some very drastic changes. The system of medical education is now completely altered, and most students admitted to medical schools are supposed to be children of workers and peasants, often from adjacent districts. In other words, there is an admission policy on the basis of class origin. How many developing countries are prepared to have such a policy?

Mao's policy of reform of medical service means, first of all, lowering medical health standards in the country, at least for the time being (chap. 7c; Worth, in Lerner and Schramm 1972). This is probably unthinkable both to leaders in developing countries and students of development. The first steps that come to their minds when they think of medical education are to improve existing teaching facilities, to establish more hospitals in cities, and to send more students to medical schools in the United States and Europe.

To Mao, the key question in medical reform—indeed in every development policy—is: Who is to benefit from this aspect of development? In other words, the class consideration is foremost. To Mao, also, equalitarianism is far more important than economic efficiency and technocratic values. He attaches far greater value to economic efficiency through the use of all available human resources than economic efficiency based on modern instruments, narrow specialization, material incentive, or administrative techniques.

Mao's development plan is to build China on its most retarded elements—

the peasants—rather than its most advanced "elite" elements. Again, how many developing countries would want to do that?

A few weeks ago I had a chance to ask a distinguished student of China the question: Just how transferable is China's experience of development? He gave me this interesting answer:

> There is a sort of nasty way of answering a question like that. The answer is, you can do a good deal with China's developmental experience if you don't know very much about it. . . .
>
> The point . . . is that one can always extract a good deal from the Chinese experience but that we do not know the whole experience. Let me give you another illustration. [Mr. X] came back recently from a visit to China. He told me about one of his brothers who had finally "volunteered" to have a vasectomy after some weeks of meetings, of criticism, struggle and reform. To some family planning research scholars, this could be very much a success story. It is true, of course, that here is a man who finally volunteers to undergo this operation. But what do we know about what actually went through his mind when he was going through those months of severe criticism, reform and struggle? How are we to make use of this experience as a model for family planning? (personal communication)

3. The Element of Change

One theme of this volume is Communication and Change: Ten Years Later. Just how much of what we assume and study as change is really change? The answer is probably "not very much," if we see change as Nisbet does, as "a succession of differences in time in a persisting identity" (Nisbet 1972:1). The three key elements in the Nisbet model of change are: "differences," "in time," and "persisting identity." "Failure to note all three," Nisbet said, "and also their necessary union, is frequently responsible for confusion of change with forms of motion and interaction that are not change at all: merely motion and interaction" (1972:1). People always interact with one another and we are familiar with such common forms of interaction as "coercion, conformity, competition, exchange, and conflict." But, to Nisbet at least, none of these is change.

I am raising this question not because I think we should all accept Nisbet's notion of change. I am doing so because there are at least two kinds of changes: those Nisbet accepts as changes and those that he would consider merely motion or interaction. The type, nature, and amount of research needed to understand the two kinds of change are not necessarily the same, and we are complicating our own lives unnecessarily if we are determined to lump them together. One of Dr. Schramm's suggestions for research needs at the end of our summer conference at Stanford was to study the ways in which different cultures relate to change. What kind of change do we have in mind? This brings up the question of fixity.

4. The Problem of Fixity

We have interaction and motion all the time. They are constant. Change, again in the way Nisbet sees it, is not. There are good reasons to wonder whether the presumption that sociocultural development is a necessary condition of human existence is really tenable. If one reviews the history of China up to the nineteenth century, one could make a reasonably strong case that *continuity* and *conservation*, rather than *change*, have been the aspiration or desire in mankind, generally. There are good reasons to argue that change is not necessarily the rule in mankind generally. It may even be the exception.

Another important point made by Nisbet is this: "Social interaction is to be found in social fixity and persistence as well as social change" (1972:5). And finally, to quote Nisbet again: "The single greatest barrier, I believe, to our scientific understanding of change lies in our common refusal to recognize the sheer power of conservatism in social life: the power of custom, tradition, habit and mere inertia" (1972:6).

The conclusion is obvious. We need research to study these mechanisms. We need organic analyses of the chemistry of fixity, persistence, or lack of will to change. We need careful studies of the mechanism of social fixity.

5. Uses of the Past

There are good and important reasons for every country to make creative, selective, and skillful use of the past. We do not seem to have much research that would equip us to do so. Eisenstadt has told us that every country has a way of coping with its problems. To what extent and in what way are these old ways adequate? Modifiable?

There has been a good deal of controversy in China over this matter of the past. The debate is whether there should be preference for the past over the present (*po ku ho chin*) or preference for the present over the past (*ho ku po chin*). The "correct" answer is to make the past serve the present (*yi ku shih chin*).

Let me use China's medical delivery system again to illustrate the point. Victor and Ruth Sidel, in an excellent article on the subject (1974), cited three reasons for China's successes in this area. They are: decentralization, demystification, and continuity with the past.

Things like acupuncture come to mind. There are other effective practices in traditional medicine. The important point is that China has made a persistent effort to make her past serve her present creatively—and, in the political sense of the Chinese Communist party, "correctly."

A related point—and something of a problem in itself—is that not all development communication researchers know very much about the past of the countries they are working on. This applies not only to Western scholars but native researchers as well. Pearl Buck used to say very harsh things about modern Chinese—particularly Western-trained Chinese—who did not know very much about China. But this is by no means a problem monopolized by the Chinese.

6. The Problem of Ethnicity

The problem of ethnicity has not received as much attention in development research as it deserves. The problem has been with us and it could become worse as development goes along. Lucian Pye and I had a chance to talk about an apparently different question at our Communication and Change Conference ten years ago. The question was the role of communication in international negotiation. Following on that discussion, Pye made the following observation somewhat later:

> I think that in the early 50's I was perhaps a bit too optimistic that nationalism would very quickly reduce these ethnic problems. Now, you begin to see that these problems are just very deeply implanted and that even the more developed countries still seem to have them. I think ethnicity is something that is not that easy to get away from. You see this in the United States, in Europe, and I suspect Russia is going to have problems with their minority peoples, as they get more developed. I would assume that the very process of development in these countries is going to increase it. In a strange kind of way I think that is why in Burma it almost stopped development. . . . The process of development is going to change the basis of power among the different groups. It will favor one, hurt another, and there'll be more tensions. This is what Ne Win in a sense has accomplished, I don't think intentionally, because he has just . . . frozen things. So they are all . . . at the same level. (personal communication)

Daniel Patrick Moynihan, who is working on a book on ethnicity, has defined it (1974) as "ethnic loyalty emerging as the [leading] principle in the face of the Marxist assertion that it would be succeeded by class-bound loyalties."

Harold R. Isaacs, one of the most reflective writers on ethnic problems, has taught us a good deal about the need to track down what he calls the "snowman of ethnicity." In a recent article he wrote:

> By now, to be sure, a considerable volume of multidisciplinary literature has grown up about problems of multi-ethnic societies. Much of this has to do with the problems of politics, development, and pluralism in the "new" ex-colonial countries. The surfacing of the same set of issues and confusions in the "old" states of both Western and Eastern Europe and, even more turbulently, in the American society, has widened the field of awareness and scrutiny. In this very season, there must be dozens of American academic safaris tracking the snowman of "ethnicity," everyone sure now that it exists and is important, more important than most thought, but no one sure what it looks like, or whether it is abominable or not. The effort to get sharper about matters long left vague, to seek for some new terms of order among these old confusions, is at least underway. (1974: 15–41)

The footprints of this snowman of ethnicity, Isaacs tells us, have been around us for some time. The challenge is to track him down and to understand his role in development.

7. The Concept of Conflict and the Notion of Progress

Finally, a fundamental question:

Who
Makes What Development Plans?
For Whose Benefit?
Faces What Problems?
Gets What Results?
How?
And Why?

The question sounds political. But one shouldn't dismiss it as tiresome political talk. To do so is to push aside a wide range of critical and complex problems that no responsible student of development communication can afford to overlook.

Development is from something to something. It is done by some people and for some people. It may mean survival for one group, growth for another, and quality of life for still another.

Heilbroner states this view forcefully:

> . . . the central, inescapable, and indispensable precondition for "economic" development is political and social change on a wrenching and tearing scale. Economic development is not, alas, a mere matter of tactics to be decided among men of good will and then put into effect with all possible dispatch. It is, anterior to that, a contest among social classes. It is a process of institutional birth and institutional death. It is a time when power shifts, often violently and abruptly, a time when old regimes go under and new ones rise in their places. And these are not just the unpleasant side effects of development. They are part and parcel of the process, the very driving force of change itself. (1970:53–54)

But this is not a view of development that appeals to many Western-oriented students of development. They appear to be far more interested in a notion of progress than this concept of conflict. Ithiel de Sola Pool calls this notion of progress "a modern notion," or "the expectation that purposive action can bring progress." He explains it this way:

> In a world in which there is no progress, . . . the good fortune of one can be bought only by the bad fortune of another. If there are a limited number of good things in the world, then life's struggles are for their redistribution. . . . There can be no such thing as a true public policy if there is no such thing as a common interest towards which the general will can aspire. (1967:77)

We are not calling attention to the concept of conflict and the notion of progress to imply that one makes more sense than the other. We do so partly to raise some very basic problems but mainly to suggest that a serious student of development communication must find some way to tackle this fundamental question of "who makes what development plans for whose benefit" if he is to understand the uses of communication to guide or direct development or the role "the people" should or could play in all the so-called people-oriented development strategies.

Ideally, a paper on priorities for development communication research should include a tidy research plan and conclude with some specific recommendations. I cannot pretend to have such a plan to offer. I have tried, as indicated earlier, to identify and anticipate some critical problems, opportunities, and challenges with priority implications. As our continuing seminar on communication for development moves into its second decade, I offer these thoughts in the hope they may help us to grow wiser as we grow older.

E. CULTURAL CONTEXTS

Dr. Inayatullah opens this section with an important statement of the deep change in development thinking. His call for a "Non-Western Model" at our conference ten years ago is now set aside in favor of a larger context. Arguing that the classic "Western" model has not worked, he explains why an authentic "Asian" model failed to evolve historically and, given the current structure of the world arena, may never appear. These enlightening (and moving) pages lead Inayatullah to conclude that the great need today, East and West, is for a "global" model of development. Aware of the great difficulties this entails, he sets forth the conditions needed for its attainment. While some may dispute the validity of its exegesis or the viability of its conclusions, none will question the candor or courage of this paper.

Dr. Kato then takes up some of the communication issues raised by the global "context." It is true that we now have, for the first time in human history, a "world communication network" that is instantaneous, simultaneous, and continuous. But this has not yet produced a McLuhan "global village," perhaps something more like a Potemkin village that is mainly facade. "Global Instantaneousness," as Kato wryly reminds us, does not produce "Instant Globalism"—where it does, the results are no better than many other "instant" products of current design. Reinforcing these views in vigorous prose, Dr. Matson's comment includes one hopeful possibility—that the efforts to put "sophisticated" communication hardware and software on a "lowcost" basis may restore the "balance of imports" in intercultural exchange. May it be so!

The section concludes with a current statement of a unique project by Dr. Osgood. It is unique in many ways—here mainly because it brings together two "contexts," the internal "world" of living individuals everywhere and the external "world" in which they live. "Probing Subjective Culture" is the first effort to produce a worldwide "Atlas of Affective Meanings." It is surely a most valuable guide to all communication specialists who—sharing the "world" objectives of Inayatullah and wishing to avoid the "globaloney" pitfalls outlined by Kato and Matson—seek to learn our darkly mirrored future. The poet Marianne Moore counseled us to create "imaginary gardens with real toads in them." The psychologist Charles Osgood shows us a way to learn about "imaginative people in real worlds." We commend him to your attention.

13. Western, Asian, or Global Models of Development —The Effect of the Transference of Models on the Development of Asian Societies

INAYATULLAH

The Exchange of Development Models

Development of a society is a process of moving from what it is to what it aspires to be. Effective self-regulation of this process requires a high degree of awareness of existing constraints, and deployment of an effective strategy to remove constraints and realize potentialities. Such an awareness can be acquired through greater understanding of the experiences of one's own society and of others that have successfully removed similar constraints. Knowledge derived from the experience of other societies cannot be used effectively without putting it through a process of interpretation, inference, and experimentation.

When knowledge derived from different sources becomes systematized and generalized in such a way that it can be utilized to determine appropriate goals and means, then a society comes to acquire the necessary intellectual apparatus for accelerating its process of development. Through this apparatus, which is capable of experimenting and modifying development models, societies engage in a process of exchange. This produces beneficial effects when at least three conditions are met:

(a) The exchange of models does not occur within a structure of domination of one society by the other;

(b) There exists a body of knowledge that incorporates varied experiences and serves as a valid reference point for generalization;

(c) There is a high degree of empathy for what is unique to one society and not useful to another, a heightened mutual awareness that is indispensable to the growth of the body of knowledge mentioned in (b).

When all conditions are present, the exchange of development models is accentuated. Rarely, however, has exchange occurred in these ideal conditions; frequently one or more of the conditions are missing. In such cases, the exchange of development models tends to become a mere unilateral transfer from the dominant to the dominated society. This proves costly to both societies. The dominant society's contact with reality weakens. It distorts reality to rationalize its domination and deludes itself into believing in the universality of its own experiences. By imposing its own model, it alienates the dominated society and sets negative forces into motion. These produce either greater control of the dominated or withdrawal of the dominant from interaction.

The imposition of a development model on a dominated society also leads to a decline in its capacity to monitor its internal and external environments correctly and respond creatively to them. It loses internal coherence, self-steering capacity, and an authentic sense of values. There develops a serious internal division that leads to extreme irrational reactions of either total rejection or total acceptance of the imposed model.

Since the passing of colonialism, exchange between the West and Asia has passed through three stages:

(a) The first stage lasted to the end of the colonial period and was essentially a unilateral transfer of the Western model.

(b) The second stage began with the Second World War and ended with the 1960s, mainly a period of transition to independent nationhood.

(c) The third stage began with the occurrence of significant changes in the international power structure in the 1970s.

I will pass rapidly over the earlier two stages. Then I will assess the prospects for emergence of a genuine model of development in Asia, and finally will raise the question of whether the issue of a regional model has not lost its significance in view of the more important issue of development of a model for the international community.

Three Stages of Cultural Contact

The first stage of cultural contact between the West and the non-West developed in the seventeenth century. By effectively using new technology, the Western countries changed the balance of economic and military power *vis-à-vis* the non-Western world that had existed before the Industrial Revolution. Colonial expansion provided the first extensive contact. It generated among colonial officials, and subsequently scholars, an interest in the comparative analysis of societies. However, as this intellectual interest was shaped by the objective fact of Western economic and political domination, it was contaminated by it.

Emergence of the theory of evolution in the nineteenth century provided a new framework for ordering comparative data on societies. On the biological level, by treating *Homo sapiens* as a single species, it gave promise of universality. However, its sociological counterpart, Social Darwinism, by equating domination with cultural superiority itself—via such theories as the Protestant Ethic and Oriental Despotism—failed to keep this promise. Even classical economics, which built laws about the economy on the assumption of a rational economic man presumably living outside all cultures, was weakened by its own Western ethnocentric tendencies.

The messianic zeal that pervaded the actions of colonial administrators and Christian missionaries was blind to the value of any aspect of colonial cultures. The only restraint on colonial administration was the calculus of control. If the natives could be ruled through local chiefs who were pliant instruments, there was no need to transform the local power structure and earn local enmity. If changing any cherished aspect of local culture could lead to revolt and riots, it was more convenient to let the native remain undisturbed. To sum up, in the first phase, true exchange never developed. It was a unilateral transfer of a development model, pure and simple.[1]

The second phase of cultural contacts between the West and the non-Western world began after the Second World War, with widespread wars of national liberation that eventually led to the decolonization of the non-Western world. The Soviet Union emerged as a superpower possessing nuclear technology. The Communists took over mainland China. This shook the international power structure in which European nations were so preeminently hegemonous. However, the United States, which emerged from the war with enhanced technological superiority and economic prosperity, attempted to salvage the old power structure by a new "partnership" between the West, under its own leadership, and the non-Western world. By its very nature this partnership was unequal and devoid of ideological and economic foundations. The persistence of unequal relationships, and of the unilateral transfer of Western models, inhibited the emergence of a generalized theory of development. Though the empirical orientation of American scholarship did enrich its data base and raise its explanatory power, the political role continued to contaminate the scholarly role.

The evidence of this contamination lies in the type of questions about development they chose, or did not choose, to raise and investigate. They concentrated on clearly identifying the contours of the Western path to modernity, setting up Western institutions and values as an exclusive model of development. They focused on how the cultural heritage of non-Western societies was blocking their path to modernity and how "transfer of institutions" from the West could rescue them from their dilemma. They sought explanation of underdevelopment in the psychic domain, in the lack of "need achievement" or "psychic empathy," in "amoral familism," "traditionalism," or the concept of "limited good"—all factors closely related to the traditional culture of the less-developed countries. (These factors, indeed, are related to their backwardness but they did not fully explain the reasons for backwardness.) They did not inquire into the effects of the structure of international power, patterns of international trade, and distribution of international resources as factors blocking development. They ignored the impact of technical assistance policies on defining development, determining priorities, or sustaining and strengthening the existing power structure.

The modernizing role of military and civil bureaucracies, which had developed earlier contacts with the West and uncritically absorbed its culture, was eulogized and exaggerated, and their repressive antidevelopment role was deemphasized. This provided a much-needed legitimation to these regimes. It produced knowledge specifically to help this new elite in developing countries to face challenges to its shaky power. It suggested strategies of reform oriented to gradual, incremental, and peripheral changes in developing countries. It did not inquire what type of model would raise autonomy of action in developing countries; what type of political and economic system would free them from grinding poverty, social injustices, social stagnation, and ensure their continued development. The question posed invariably was in what way the Western model could be effectively transferred, and in what way the operation of free enterprise and liberal democracy could be ensured—regardless of the consequences to the developing society concerned. The elements of order and stability in political development were over-stressed; rising demands and radical movements were considered a threat producing political decay (Kesselman 1973: 139–154).

Since the end of the second phase, Western scholars are now increasingly realizing the inadequacy of the dominant development theory. There is a reluctant acceptance of the role of external factors in underdevelopment.[2] There is a greater appreciation of the role of tradition and its compatibility with modernization. Also the possibility of diverse routes to modernity is being accepted. There is a plea for abandoning the old paradigm (see chap. 3). But this plea apparently seems more concerned to rescue its basic framework, as it comes under increasing criticism, rather than to reorganize or abandon this framework.

The second phase of Western domination was differentiated from the first phase by a certain degree of reluctance to impose its ways on the non-Western societies.[3] There was a greater appreciation of the cultures and ways of the non-Western world that presumably need to be preserved for the sake of cultural pluralism and diversity. There was also a greater quest for understanding the mysteries of the Orient, though occasionally this quest was stimulated less by a need to appreciate and more by the need to develop effective strategy for its transformation. There was also a change in the style. The Western technical experts during this phase stressed the need for adaptation rather than adoption of the Western model. But all these changes did not change the essential core of the doctrine, which regarded modernity as a single package that the non-Western could accept or reject, but within which there was not much scope for selection. Real sympathy for the problems of the underdeveloped world was usually missing. Consequently Asian students, scholars, and bureaucrats continued to look at development through intellectual lenses that blurred and distorted the true image of their own societies. They were still fired with zeal to transform them into replicas of affluent and powerful Western societies, and saturated with bias for a development model that was not always relevant to their societal conditions.[4] A "captive mind" was born in Asia.[5] During the last decade, however, several significant changes have probably eroded the traditional structure of domination and unilateral transference of the Western model. These changes, hopefully, will facilitate the emergence of a critical-analytical orientation to an objective evaluation of Western and other models of development for their relevance to Asian problems. In this third phase, several factors are essential.

First, the traditional bipolar international power structure has been replaced by a multipolar power structure. As a result, interest in dividing the world into distinct ideological camps has considerably diminished. The technical assistance programs are now becoming less subservient to the confining shackles of superpower foreign policies. Consequently, the need to urge developing countries to accept development models as part of the technical assistance package has also declined. Moreover, with the availability of multiple (and not necessarily coordinated) sources of technical assistance, the opportunity for choice by Asian countries has increased.

Secondly, as a consequence, the attitude of the Western scholarly community, especially in the United States, toward the relevance of the Chinese model for developing countries has changed considerably. This has intellectual reverberations in Asia as well. Open discussion and comparison of the Chinese and Western models, and identification of some features of the Chinese model as more applicable to Asian problems, are no longer taboo in Asian countries. With the emergence of this new vigorous competitive model on the intellectual horizons of Asia, uncritical commitment to the Western model is likely to diminish further.

Thirdly, the emergence in Asia of regional cooperative associations (such as ASEAN) and of regional training and research organizations (such as the Asian Development and Planning Institute and the Asian Centre for Development Administration) has provided a new framework for the development of an intellectual posture likely to be more inventive, less imitative, and more appreciative of alternative models and strategies of development. The basic mandate of the Asian Centre for Development Administration, for instance, is to encourage a sense of self-reliance in Asian countries, to inculcate an attitude of learning from mutual experiences, and to stimulate inventiveness.

The concept of development itself has begun to change significantly in the Western intellectual community, though the new perspective continues to be a minority view. The new view is different from the old Western conception of development in three significant aspects: (1) The traditional objective of achieving levels of material affluence comparable to Western countries is no longer considered realistic or desirable. There is now greater concern with the elimination of poverty rather than the creation of affluence; greater stress on austerity to be exercised in both developing and developed countries to spare resources that can ensure moderate gains in development; and greater stress on distribution of the benefits of development (Seers, in Wilbur 1973: 6–13; Gaulet 1971; Dasgupta 1973). Other traditional goals so much stressed by developmentalists—national integration, homogenization of national and global culture, stabilization of the nation-state—have come to be questioned (Badgley 1971; W. Connors 1972). (2) There is a shift in the analysis of the causes of underdevelopment, from those purely internal to a society—the traditional concern of Western development literature—to external factors such as international power structure, patterns of international trade, and influence of multinational corporations (Hopkins 1970: 126–136). (3) There is a shift in emphasis on strategies of development. The new trend stresses self-reliance and indigenization,[6] which are direct frontal, rather than trickle-down, strategies of eliminating poverty (Haq, in Wilbur 1973:371–372).

These changes are likely to reduce communication barriers between the intellectuals of East and West, to lower ethnocentric biases in the perception of problems, and to favor the growth of empathy. It is with this in mind that I would now approach the question of whether there is an Asian model of development.

An Asian Model?

To the question of whether there is an Asian model of development, the answer is obviously no—for two reasons. First, Asia is basically a geographical rather than a cultural category. It has been an arena of conflict, as well as accommodation, between ancient cultural traditions and contemporary social and political movements. Moreover, different countries are endowed with different resources and have different types of economic systems and political requirements. Consequently, it would have required a great historic effort by Asian countries to develop a common model, bearing the imprints of a common Asian heritage, which would be relevant to contemporary Asian problems. Secondly, due to the foreign domination of Asian societies and the unilateral transference of foreign models of development, neither the necessary cultural contacts nor the political autonomy to develop such a model existed.

If the question were rephrased to inquire into the prospects for the future emergence of a genuine model of Asian development, the answer could be different. This would require four conditions: (1) that changes in the international power structure continue in the direction of greater diffusion of power and multipolarization; (2) that, with the emergence of regional institutions, the process of mutual learning in Asia be accelerated; (3) that Asian intellectuals develop a critical-analytical orientation that would enable them to establish a body of common knowledge relevant for Asian development; (4) that future Asian political elites make an autonomous and rational response to their common problems based on their body of common knowledge.

Asian societies have been, and continue to be, part of a larger international system and a global community. Strong cultural, economic, and political stimuli from this system have already penetrated into the fabric of their traditional culture, and have changed them considerably and probably irreversibly. These changes continue to be reinforced and reinvigorated by contemporary external contacts with the rest of the world through mass media, education and travel abroad, presence of foreigners in the country, circulation of books and magazines, and other means. Consequently, the option of reviving a total complex of traditional cultures, values, and institutions probably has been closed to the Asian elite. Only those values from the past could be revived that are compatible with modern needs. They could be traditional in form but would have to be modern in function.

On a more specific level, the traditional attitude of accepting deprivation, poverty, and sickness cannot be revived. The legitimacy of the traditional sacred order that supported this attitude has been irreversibly eroded. Not many poor and deprived would now accept their poverty as a supernaturally induced phenomenon. On the contrary, it is the ideologies that aim at removing poverty that appeal and secure votes. It is the ideology of "Islamic socialism" in Pakistan rather than Islamic revivalism that wins the political battle. It is the Gharibi Hatao (remove poverty) campaign that wins political support in India, while the struggle for revivalism of the ancient Indian culture is increasingly losing the battle.

Similarly, traditional legitimation of social and economic inequalities, which some Asian traditional cultural values supported, is increasingly weakening and cannot be repaired. Despite the resilience of the caste system and other social inequalities prevalent in Asian societies, these inequalities remain undefended. Even their protagonists consider them as transitory phenomena and defend them only in the name of order and stability, or development and growth, rather than in the name of moral or transcendental order.

The antiindustrial and antitechnology options of development are also closed and cannot be used to evolve a viable economy, society, and polity coexisting with the interdependent global community. There may be debates about the effective strategies of urbanization and industrialization. There may be room for evolving appropriate strategies to avoid the disruptions that modern technology creates in traditional social systems. But without technology, a certain degree of industrialization, and a concomitant social change, the huge Asian population cannot be freed from the poverty that Asians now find intolerable. Of course, by completely cutting off their society from external contacts, by complete regimentation of thought and extensive use of coercion, it might be possible to freeze Asian societies at a given historical moment, but it is unlikely that many Asian elites have the capacity or the will to opt for this.

If the future effect of tradition in defining the ultimate purpose of development in Asia will be minimal, so will the effect of the Western model. However, one needs to differentiate several of its components to assess their probable impact on future Asian development. First, there is the crucial cultural component of the Western model that stresses rational social action: an analytical-empirical approach for understanding nature, society, and self; a pervasive secular outlook; and a quest for continuous improvement and perfection of technology. Second, there is the institutional component embodied in liberal democracy: a capitalistic economic framework and a sovereign nation-state. The first component has been gradually detached from the second and has diffused throughout the world. The Asian intellectual and political elite have accepted it despite their ideological divisions. It provides the intellectual underpinning for development planners and implementers. This element of the Western model is unlikely to be abandoned by the Asians unless they also abandon their commitment to development itself.

It is the institutional components of the Western model whose future in Asia is uncertain. The Western countries set up liberal democracy as a model for themselves and generally sought to reproduce it in other aid-receiving countries (except where political and military conflict led them to support authoritarian regimes). The future of liberal democracy in Asia is probably bleak. For one reason, the effective detachment of the cultural from the institutional component, and the successful development of alternative forms by the Soviet Union and China, show that modernization is not a total Western package without scope for Asian choice. Asian elites have increasingly become aware of this option. Under certain conditions and constraints, they are likely to exercise it. For another reason, the Asian countries are in a race against time and demography. Their population is rapidly increasing, their resources are often meager, and their people are increasingly restive and demanding. They do not have the earlier option of developed countries, to expand into other lands to secure raw materials and captive markets. Nor do they have the option of squeezing their peasantries and working classes—first, because there is not much to squeeze, and second, because it requires high extractive and repressive capabilities which they do not possess.

The capitalistic approach leads, at least initially, to serious economic and social inequalities that generate social tensions and threaten social stability without ensuring that the era of affluence, after a period of sacrifices, is around the corner. These tensions can be controlled either through the integrative bonds of traditional family, kinship, and other social institutions, or through the effect of traditional ideologies sanctioning inequalities, or through widespread repression. With the increasing breakdown of traditional institutions, the first two mechanisms are not available to the Asian elite and the third is a negation of liberal democracy. Furthermore, to accelerate the pace of development, Asian countries need a high degree of consensus on developmental goals, a high mobilizational and administrative capacity. Liberal democracy in general has not proved capable of meeting this requirement.[7] On the other hand, the Chinese experience of development has demonstrated the efficacy of a different political framework incompatible with both the spirit and the form of liberal democracy.

The only successful Asian example of development combining Western cultural attitudes with capitalism and liberal democracy is Japan. But its lessons may not be considered applicable to other Asian countries, as the Japanese process of development, like the European, started much earlier, and its earlier phase occurred not under democracy but under an authoritarian regime. Asian elites may argue that they can afford the luxury of a liberal democracy only after they have achieved the level of economic development of pre-World War II Japan.

In contrast to the Japanese model, the Chinese model will in the future probably have greater appeal to Asian minds. If the present trend continues, the political and cultural relations of China with other countries of Asia are likely to increase, and with them a fuller assessment of Chinese achievements —especially their success in eliminating poverty, reducing inequalities, extending welfare services, and reaching an adequate level of agricultural growth—will become available to Asia. Special cultural features of this model (such as discipline, austerity, collectivity orientation) and some special institutional aspects (such as the decentralized structure of decision-making, and the self-sufficiency of ascending territorial units) are likely to win the attention of Asian elites struggling with overwhelming problems.

To sum up, the international quest for an appropriate new model of development is likely to intensify. This model is not likely to be a replica of either Western or Chinese or Japanese models, though it may have elements of all three. In choosing a model, the political elite in Asia has to take into account the effects of relative deprivation, of rising expectation, and of increasing frustration on the stability of their societies and regimes. They have to consider also the increasing impotence of the traditional social structure, as well as repressive political measures to contain the upsurge of aspirations for material welfare, equality of opportunity, and status. Consequently, they are not likely to seek the revival of traditional forms, at least not those that support the persistance of poverty and inequalities. But an acceptable model, to be realistic, would have to accommodate the use of modern science, technology, and industry to the still powerful effect of traditional values and social structure upon the behavior of the individual.

To the extent that all four assumptions mentioned earlier hold true in the future, the challenge of maintaining social order in the face of acute scarcity and rising social tensions is likely to constrain Asian elites to adopt similar goals and strategies of development; and, if it happens, this convergence could be characterized as an Asian model of development. However, this model is not a current reality, but a future possibility.

A Model for Mankind

The relevance of a development model is usually conceived in the context of the nation-state, that is, what model is appropriate for what country? In a certain sense this question has become increasingly irrelevant. It was born out of the traditional Western approach that the external environments of a nation did not play a crucial role and were generally beneficial for national development, except when the less-developed nations engaged in wars with neighbors or were threatened by exogenous ideological subversion. Within the context of this approach, the real issue was how to change the internal environment of a country to achieve its development by following a given model. Now that it is increasingly being accepted that external environments do play a crucial role in the development of countries, it must also be accepted that without creating beneficial external environments, development would not occur in less-developed countries. Within this new context, the crucial issue is no longer whether a given model of development is appropriate for a nation, but rather, what is an appropriate model for reconstituting the international political and economic relations to ensure a balanced development of the human community?

In considering a model for mankind, we have to make some similar assumptions and suggest similar goals and strategies to those now generally accepted for development within the national community. The first such assumption is that as all resources within a nation belong to the whole nation and should be utilized for the benefit of all its classes and regions so world resources belong to all humanity and should be used for the benefit of all humanity. This, however, is an assumption full of serious implications for the way the international community is organized at present. These implications should be faced in the same way as they are expected to be faced at the national level. For solving national developmental problems, we seek changes and adjustments in the national political order, social structure, and values, rather than giving up the goals of development. Similarly, to face the challenge of international development, we must seek similar changes in the current international order to accommodate the imperatives of international development.

As we are no longer willing to accept that the poverty of certain regions or classes in a country is caused purely by their own actions and therefore it is entirely their own responsibility to overcome it, so now it must also be accepted that the poverty of underdeveloped countries is not entirely of their own making and therefore they should not have to eradicate it on their own. The existence of foreign aid and technical assistance programs indicate that already this responsibility is accepted in principle. But technical assistance programs for various reasons have not met the challenge, in the true sense in which it was conceived they would. Full acceptance of this challenge would require greater austerity on the part of the whole human race, changes in the consumption patterns of the people in developed countries and the privileged classes in the developing countries, slowing down growth rates in developed countries, reducing inequalities in poor countries, as well as evolving new mechanisms for administering aid and redistributing world resources.[8]

Furthermore, a major lesson of political development in Western countries should be applied in order to develop effective political strategies for meeting the new challenge. This lesson is that the political and economic elite responded to the demands of the underprivileged only when organized political pressure was generated from below and was exercised to extract changes in the distribution of economic and political power. Application of this lesson for promoting international development will require a more effective organization of the poorer countries, a more activist international role, an understanding of the mechanics of the international economic system. Manipulation of economic levers can generate much more effective redistribution of economic resources than reliance on the goodwill, altruism, and generosity of the rich countries.

NOTES

1. Of course, during this phase certain types of cultural exchange also took place. For instance, colonial administrators learned the languages, customs, and mores of the colonial societies, and some eccentrics fell in love with these societies, married, and settled there. But in general, learning was more for the sake of control rather than appreciation. Also, although some of the colonial administrators undertook exhaustive studies of the local culture, enriching knowledge and to an extent modifying the zeal for transformation, these attempts were too marginal to affect the general character of the cultural exchange.
2. However, this realization is limited mostly to Leftist scholars in the West.

3. Occasionally this reluctance is based on the notion that primitive people in any case are incapable of operating Western institutions of democracy, free enterprise, and the nation-state.

4. Of course it is not implied here that the effect of local universities, or those in socialist countries, on Asian students and scholars was any better.

5. Professor Hussain Alatas, a distinguished Asian scholar commenting on the intellectual attitudes of Asian scholars, writes: "There is only a small minority among Asian social scientists who feel the need to develop an autonomous and creative social science tradition relevant to Asia as well as to the general development of the social sciences. The great majority of them are merely extending the use of social sciences current in Europe and the United States without the necessary adaptation which the very scientific process, if present, would tend to call forth. There is here not only a cultural lag in the domain of intellectual consciousness, but also an indication that in the world of learning, Asian scholars are still under intellectual domination." (Syed Hussain Alatas, "The Creative Mind in Development Studies," *International Social Science Journal* 24 [1]:9–10.)

6. Professor Ralph Braibanti stressed this in his keynote address to a Conference of Heads of Major Training Institutions organized by the Asian Centre for Development Administration (ACDA), Kuala Lumpur, February 27 to March 4, 1974; see his forthcoming "Conceptual Prerequisite for the Evolution of the Asian Bureaucratic System," to be published by ACDA.

7. For a similar assessment of the prospects of liberal democracy in Asia, though based on different arguments, by a scholar ideologically sympathetic to liberal democracy, see Edward Shils, "Fortunes of Constitutional Government in the Political Development of the New States," in *Development for What?*, edited by John H. Hallowell (Durham, N.C.: Duke University Press, 1964), pp. 102–143.

8. Maurice Strong, Secretary General of the U.N. Conference on the Human Environment, writes: "In effect, we just extend into international life the principles of distributive justice and minimum opportunities for all that are accepted as the basis for relations between rich and poor in most national societies today. This means a vast increase in the flow of resources between rich and poor countries, not merely on the basis of charity, but as a precondition to the kind of basic economic security which is essential to the health and stability of a functioning world system. And it will mean replacement of traditional development aid programs with more automatic and impersonal methods of transferring resources, such as use of special drawing rights and levies, tolls, or user charges on the use of the global commons of oceans and atmosphere and possibily on the utilization of non-renewable resources," *Saturday Review World*, Fiftieth Anniversary Year (December 14, 1974): 7–11.

14. Global Instantaneousness and Instant Globalism—The Significance of Popular Culture in Developing Countries

HIDETOSHI KATO

This is the age of coating. Medical tablets are sugar-coated. Book covers, wall paper, and other durable paper products are plastic-coated. Optical lenses are silicon-coated. Many of the things around us—furniture, automobiles, and appliances—are paint-coated. And even the planet on which we live is coated.

At the start of the last quarter of the twentieth century, the earth took on a unique coating of its own: an "electronic coating." The earth's surface is covered by innumerable electronic waves, intangible though they are. To ascertain the existence of such waves, turn on a radio at any spot on the earth. You will hear sounds originating from many parts of the world, twenty-four hours a day, without intermission. Radio waves are active all the time, covering every corner of the earth, and the transistor radio is the Geiger counter for such radio activity.

The coating started when Marconi first succeeded in his experimental trans-Atlantic wireless communication in 1901; this was followed by the invention of the vacuum tube, then by the inauguration of broadcasting in 1920 in Pittsburgh. In the initial stages, the coating was local, covering only a small geographical segment; but as the number of broadcasting stations increased, a wider coating known as the "network" evolved, first in the United States. By the beginning of the 1930s, most European countries and Japan had begun to have national radio broadcasting coverage. The coating, in other words, reached a national level, and the same coverage was achieved in most of the "developing" countries as well by the end of the 1950s. The invention of the transistor equipped millions of people in the world today with their own receivers.

The electronic coating, however, was found to have a unique characteristic in contrast to the older media of communication—such as the press, with its circulation primarily within national boundaries. If the power is strong enough, the territory that a broadcasting station can cover can be expanded considerably, to such a degree that the people of the neighboring countries also can listen to its programs.

Moreover, if a relay system is mobilized, broadcasting originating from a particular spot on the earth can be disseminated all over the world instantaneously. Such global broadcasting was experimented with as early as 1932, when the tenth Olympic Games were held in Los Angeles. Though the area covered by international broadcasting of the 1930s was limited, for the first time in the history of mankind, millions of people in different parts of the world came to be exposed to the same message simultaneously.

In particular, the combination of television and communication satellites made the reception of clear audiovisual messages possible in many areas. With the initiative of the BBC, in the summer of 1967 the first global television broadcasting was conducted with great success. Needless to say, we have now become accustomed to watching programs from various parts of the world via satellite. Incidents in Tokyo are seen in New York instantaneously and vice versa. What happens in Saigon has been watched by millions of families in Europe and vice versa.

With the widespread use of jet transportation, we have come to think that the world is small. The sense of distance, both psychological and physical, is now becoming weaker, if not disappearing. John McHale suggests that as a result of global networks of communication and transportation, "global shrinkage" has been taking place. Such global instantaneousness, generally speaking, has advantages, in the sense that the whole human population on the planet can be informed of major happenings of the world without delay. Global communication technology also has great potential for bettering understanding among peoples.

However, certain aspects of global communication are problematic, and in the field of popular culture, among other things, the emergence of "world popular culture" has negative effects as well as positive ones, especially in developing countries.

One of the striking effects of global communication in developing countries is that the popular culture materials to which the people of these countries are exposed are too "equal" to those that entertain the peoples of more developed societies. Take, for example, television programs. As a recent UNESCO survey pointed out, most of the television stations in developing countries in Asia, Africa, and South America broadcast a considerable number of programs produced in more developed countries. In an extreme case, imported programs in Guatemala occupy 84 percent of the total broadcasting time; in Zambia, the figure is 64 percent; Malaysia, 71 percent; Singapore,

78 percent; and Hong Kong, 40 percent, to mention a few others. The peoples of these countries are thus now watching programs for which the original target audience was the urban middle-class families of the exporting countries, mostly the United States and Japan. Middle-class values are presented on the screen, regardless of the type of program; the actors are surrounded by durable commodities, material conveniences, and many aspects of the "affluent society." Though there has not been any systematic research on the matter so far, the impact of programs produced in more industrial societies upon the minds of the peoples in developing countries must be grave and serious.

The contents of American and Japanese programs are, generally speaking, consumption-oriented, and it is not presumptuous to infer that the viewers in developing countries are influenced by this consumer philosophy. Indeed, one of my friends in the Philippines reports that the children there are extremely fond of television commercials. The danger is that the people of developing countries, not only children but also adults, may acquire more of a sense of consumership than producership. In the process of development, consumption must be accompanied by production. But what is happening in certain developing countries is that interest in consumption comes before interest in production. Does this trend suggest any possibility of a newer type of "development"? We do not know the answer yet.

An optimistic interpretation may be that the interest in consumption can motivate interest in production (a kind of philosophy that reasons "We want a refrigerator, let's make one"). But in view of the fact that the developed countries of the world are now suffering from overproduction of most industrial products, importing these products would be a more likely solution than encouraging industrialization. Or a compromise would be for more-developed countries to subsidize production in less-developed countries, where labor is less expensive, and to export such products to profitable markets.

According to the classic formula of development, the first stage is the accumulation of capital, followed by industrial production. After a few centuries, there comes the age of consumption. It seems that the developing countries today do not fit into this scheme. Instead, a consumer culture is approaching maturity while substantial production is still lacking. There is an irony in this trend, in the sense that the broadcasting system itself often has been a part of "foreign aid" programs that aimed at the promotion of development in developing countries.

In a broader context, there seems to be a contradiction between evenness in the flow of information and the unevenness of material wealth. Exposure to information, or popular culture materials in the context of this paper, is evenly distributed. The peoples of the world, regardless of their location, are exposed to the same values as transmitted by television, radio, and movies; yet the economic conditions of nations vary from the extremely rich to the extremely poor. Isn't it a tragedy that people can be watching the theme of affluence on a television screen while all around them their fellow countrymen are starving to death?

The area of popular culture presents us with a different kind of potential tragedy; with the diffusion of popular culture through mass media in developing countries, even the sense of national identities becomes endangered. In a recent study conducted in Thailand, it was discovered that the popular heroes are mostly Japanese television stars, rather than "local" figures. Thai children and teenagers can name foreign stars with whom they are familiar, but due to the relative lack of programs produced in Thai, they do not see or hear about their "national" popular heroes, other than those whose names appear in school textbooks. The sense of nationalism is, as many scholars have pointed out, essential for the social and economic development of developing countries. But what has been happening in the past several years discourages nationalism on the popular level. At the least, "foreign" popular culture does not serve to promote national identity and nationalism.

It is easy for us to talk about the "age of world popular culture," saying that the Beatles, Elvis Presley, James Bond, and many other popular heroes are universal heroes, liked and appreciated by millions of people across national boundaries. And this observation may be quite correct. However, the existence of these universal heroes implies that there may be a danger of "instant globalism" with the circumstance that less emphasis is given to national identity

At any rate, globalism today is only another name for internationalism, and internationalism presupposes solid national integrity and nationalism. The more-developed countries already have experienced the age of nationalism for a century or so, and have found that nationalism must be counterbalanced by internationalism. In the case of developing countries, however, the situation is very complicated. On the one hand, national unification and integrity are considered essential for development, but on the other hand, popular culture materials often present cosmopolitan values that are not necessarily compatible with the initial stage of nationalism. After all, James Bond may really be a secret agent whose mission is to confound the efforts toward nationalism and independence in developing countries that had been colonies of the West until only a few decades ago!

Another important aspect of popular culture in developing countries is the fact that the newer media of communication often have a profound impact upon the traditional media of communication. For instance, in some countries traveling story-tellers and singers are disappearing as the result of a wider diffusion of broadcasting. A historical example is the case of Japan in the early 1930s, when the radio and the phonograph were introduced.

Hundreds of street singers and traveling story-tellers were replaced by the electronic means of transmitting popular culture.

The same trend is now apparent in the developing countries of Asia on a much more drastic scale, since the electronic technologies of the 1970s, including television, are much more advanced than those of the 1930s. If the values particular to the culture are transferred to the contents of the newer media, then it won't cause too much of a problem; but usually, broadcasters prefer not to produce electronic versions of traditional communication. Instead, as we have seen in the preceding paragraphs, they are content to put imported programs on the air.

Even when conscious efforts are made to preserve traditional values, the newer technology places constraints on older modes of communication. A classic example, again in Japan, is the change that took place in the *sumo* wrestling game. Originally, *sumo* was part of the religious ritual to entertain deities performed in the yards of shrines, but as secularization increased, it became purely a spectator sport, as early as the eighteenth century.

Yet *sumo* as an entertainment retained some of the symbolic significance of its original form. For instance, the four corner pillars supporting the roof of the arena have symbolism based on the Chinese philosophy of the universe, and the *sumo* performers even kept the old ritualistic manners until broadcasters decided to transmit the game to the general public. In the first place, a time element became involved. In the ancient ritual of the game, two wrestlers were given ample time facing each other before a match started. The implication was to wait until the time became "mature." Sometimes two opponents would spend more than ten minutes before their match actually began. Radio broadcasters, however, did not like this ritual, for obvious reasons. They succeeded in limiting the "waiting time" to three minutes so that the day's series of matches could end at 6:30 P.M. This change in the form of the game took place in the late 1930s.

When the television camera came into the *sumo* stadium in the late 1950s, the producers of the sports program found the pillars in the way of the camera. Another negotiation took place and, finally, the *sumo* association agreed to take out the pillars to provide a better view of the arena for the television camera. In a word, the form of this traditional sport had to adapt to the newer communication technologies.

In the countries of Asia, the traditional arts are the oldest and richest in the world. And to establish continuities between traditional media and newer electronic media will be a great task for the people of these countries.

The basic problem in designing such continuities and promoting more "local" efforts is essentially economic. For example, the high ratio of imported programs in broadcasting in developing countries is simply a result of economic deliberation on the part of broadcasters. The importation of programs, especially television programs, is much less expensive than the local production of programs. Indeed, a series of thirteen one-hour programs can be purchased for several thousand U.S. dollars. Local production of one single thirty-minute program would cost U.S. $3,000 at least and it is doubtful if such locally produced programs can be competitive with the imported programs.

In short, the easiest way to attract a large audience for television in developing countries is to broadcast American or Japanese programs that can be imported for a nominal fee (which the producers of more-developed countries think of as an "initial investment"). China is probably the only country in Asia that avoided the danger by restricting the importation of popular culture from abroad, especially from the capitalist bloc. As a matter of fact, a UNESCO survey shows that there is very little importation of television programs into China, and the few imported are from Eastern Europe. In this way, China seems to have succeeded in preserving traditional culture and in constructing nationalism, although the arrangement had certain apparent shortcomings, such as the isolation of the people from much of the intercultural communications that other peoples enjoy.

Burma and some other countries are following this pattern of communication isolation. They prefer to establish solid nationalism rather than to become "instant globalists," and no one can criticize their decision at a time when this very sophisticated electronic coating is often found to obstruct national development.

I am not suggesting that developing countries must follow the Chinese pattern. Rather, I would like to suggest that there may be alternatives, where peoples of developing countries can take on a global coating and at the same time can be assured of their national identities and patriotism. For example, if more-developed countries can put more emphasis on the export of software techniques of program production rather than canned programs, then more independent "local" programs, which serve national development, can be produced. Moreover, if such local programs are to be successfully produced, they should be multicolor, multiparticipatory, and even multicoated. The danger we see now is that the coating is being applied by a few, all using the same color—a color that may not be enjoyed by all viewers.

14a. *The Global Village Revisited*

FLOYD W. MATSON

Professor Kato's provocative paper might equally well have been entitled "The Global Village Revisited," for not the least of its contributions is the critical qualification it lays upon the familiar romantic vision of Marshall McLuhan—that of a world community magically united through electronic enlightenment. Professor Kato makes us aware that, if present trends continue, the "instant globalism" made possible by mass communications technology may come to signify not the promise of cultural pluralism but the blight of cultural imperialism.

There are several ways in which global communication—for all its undeniable advantages in terms of the circulation of news and knowledge—threatens us with the homogenization of national cultures rather than their individuation and mutual enrichment. The most ominous portent has to do with the "passing of traditional society" (to use Daniel Lerner's famous phrase): the newer gesellschaft media of mass communication and plastic entertainment tend, on the order of Gresham's Law, to drive out the older gemeinschaft media of direct face-to-face encounter and interaction. As the traditional genres and rituals decline, in the face of the advancing tube, so do the binding myths and metaphors of archaic cultural history.

No doubt it would be excessive to speak of an "identity crisis" within the developing nations as a result of the invasion of technological media with their urban-industrial-bourgeois models of being and behavior; but it is plain from the evidence and argument of Professor Kato's paper that the diffusion of (popular) cultural materials and messages along the one-way conveyor belt of the massive media, running from West to East, threatens to undermine the traditional foundations of national identity as well as of cultural pride.

Apart from the threatened obsolescence of indigenous cultural heritages in the face of the "unfair competition" of imported media products, the trend toward instant globalism presages another kind of impoverishment: that which results from the quality and content (esthetic, ethical, and intellectual) of the packaged programs themselves. Like the "Disney version" of nature and society that has beguiled and misled movie audiences in Europe and Asia, as well as in America, for nearly half a century, the conventional television version of human nature and social conduct that is deemed most eligible for export is often that which has survived in the domestic marketplace through the triumph of mediocrity and the principle of the lowest common denominator. Accordingly it presents a scenario of social life shorn of its ambiguity and existential truth (let alone of wit and wisdom).

Audiences on the home front—in America and Japan—at least have the option of choosing among such bathetic fallacies, and even of choosing against them; but in the electronically less-favored nations, where the available channels are few and far between, and where the sheer novelty of television remains the primary reason for attending to it, these imported entertainments are likely to have a more immediate and less muted impact.

There is, of course, the possibility of a countervailing force against "instant globalism" within the less-developed nations—namely, the prospect that increasing technological development itself may alter the proportion of locally produced versus imported programs. The comparative statistics on television programming in developing countries cited by Professor Kato from a UNESCO survey tend to suggest that the greatest imbalance between imported and indigenous programs exists in areas with the lowest technological capability (e.g., Zambia, Malaysia, Guatemala) and that it is much less marked in more developed communities such as Hong Kong (where imported programs represent only 40 percent of total broadcasting time).

This restoration of the "balance of imports" on the cultural level, to the extent that it does occur, suggests the possibility that a developing technology may be accompanied by a developing "consciousness" with respect to the value of traditional customs, art forms, and other collective representations. In short, while some characteristics of mass communication encourage the evolution of a cosmopolitan "international style," other factors may be working to reinforce and reproduce distinctive local or regional expressions, entertainments, and institutions.

Whatever the facts may be on the import-export trade balance for popular cultural products, it seems clear from the experience of America and Japan that the establishment of mass entertainment media such as radio and television jeopardizes (where it does not immediately obliterate) the older, more parochial, and less "professional" modes of popular drama and recreation, such as street vaudevilles, chatauquas, story-tellers, carnivals, marionette shows, and the like.

Nostalgia aside, there would appear to be at least a few significant cultural losses entailed by this transformation of the public arts—notably the disengagement and distancing of audiences from the performance, the shift from active participation and involvement to passive observation, and the decline of spontaneity and amateurism in the face of commerical media demands for professional polish and "canned" production. This is not to romanticize the folk culture or the oral tradition as against the technological "tradition of the new," nor to deny the considerable advantages of professionalism and sophistication introduced by the mass media; but it is to reinforce the prudent warning voiced by Professor Kato to the effect that global communications technology may, like a powdered milk product, bring instant homogenization to all that it touches but is unlikely to convey instant enlightenment.

15. Probing Subjective Culture

CHARLES E. OSGOOD

Recent developments in technology—in transportation, communication and computerization, to say nothing of pollution and nuclear weaponry—are driving us willy-nilly into a state of global interdependence: either One World or No World. The same technology has made possible social science research on a global scale that would have been inconceivable only a couple of decades ago. Certainly our own research into human semantic systems, initiated about fifteen years ago, and involving now some thirty language-culture communities around the world, would have been inconceivable without parallel developments in the speed of communication and transportation and, particularly, in the computerized processing of masses of quantitative data.

There are many hypotheses about human nature that demand cross-cultural and cross-linguistic designs if what is common to the human species is to be disentangled from what is peculiar to certain segments of it. However, comparison across cultures is especially difficult when what anthropologists call immaterial traits are involved. It is one thing to compare skull shapes and count potsherds; it is quite another to compare values, feelings, and, most generally, meanings—what I have come to call "subjective culture." Elements of objective culture leave their traces on and in the earth, but elements of subjective culture are as fleeting as the living brains of those who think and believe them. Even more importantly, subjective culture is most naturally and directly assessed through the medium of language, and in cross-cultural comparisons this means that what has been called the "language barrier" must somehow be pierced.

This paper will take readers on an "exploration" of semantic space. I will begin with a very brief, but necessary, description of the Semantic Differential (SD) Technique for measuring meaning, as developed through the decade of the 1950s with a strictly ethnocentric (American English) focus. Then, shifting to a broader anthropocentric focus, I will trace the "toolmaking" and "tool-using" phases of our cross-cultural research. Toolmaking is the development of comparable SD's for our many languages; tool-using is the application of these SD's in the compilation of an "Atlas of Affective Meanings" for more than 600 concepts.

THE SEMANTIC DIFFERENTIAL TECHNIQUE

Let us imagine a hypothetical semantic space of some unknown number of dimensions. With the help of an analogy with the familiar color space we can at least conceive of a three-dimensional space and then, in theory, generalize to any number of dimensions.

Like all self-respecting spaces, this semantic one has a central origin—a locus of complete meaninglessness analogous to the neutral grey center of the color space. We can represent the meaning of any concept by a vector extending outward from this meaningless origin: the length of the vector would represent the degree of meaningfulness of the concept (*rage* having a longer vector than *annoyance*, for example), this being analogous to saturation in the color space; and the direction of the vector in the space, in analogy with both brightness and hue, would represent the nature or quality of meaning.

But to talk about "direction" in any space implies the existence of some reference coordinates or dimensions. What are the dimensions of the semantic space, and are they natural or arbitrary? This becomes an empirical measurement problem.

In ordinary natural languages, humans use substantives (nouns) to refer to entities, and qualifiers (adjectives) to differentiate among entities in the same conceptual classes. All natural languages also provide ways of quantifying—thus, "My Pierre is a very pretty *poodle*, but the one down the street is quite ugly." When I rate my poodle, *Pierre*, as a +3 on a seven-step pretty–ugly scale running from +3 through 0 to −3, I am creating a little sentence that says "Pierre is very pretty"—*Noun* (Be) *quantifier Qualifier*.

When a sample of people rate a sample of concepts against a sample of scales, the SD generates a cube of data as displayed schematically in Figure 1. The rows of the cube represent qualifier scales, the columns represent the substantive concepts, and the slices, front to back, represent the native speakers doing the rating. Each of the cells in the cube has a value that can vary from +3 to −3 through 0. There are many ways we can carve this semantic cube for analysis, and all of them presuppose—as do all linguistic

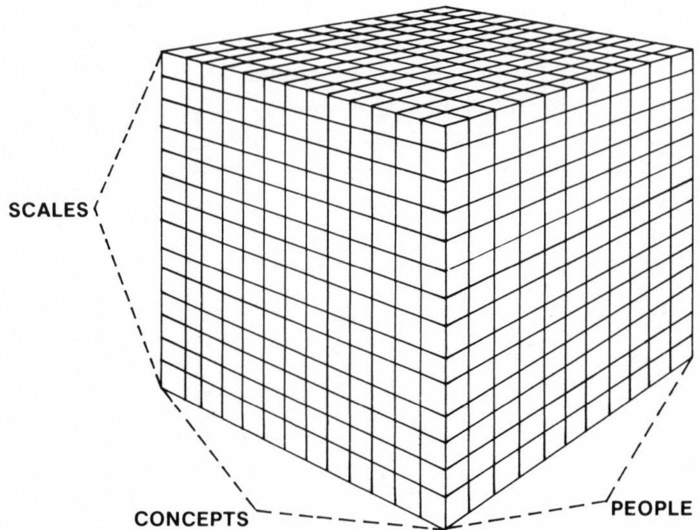

Figure 1. The Three-Mode Cube of Semantic Differential Data

and philosophical conceptions of meaning with which I am familiar—that semantic similarity is indexed by similarity in distribution of usage. Thus descriptive scales are similar to the extent that they are used the same way by subjects across concepts; concepts are similar to the extent that they produce the same kinds of "sentences" (e.g., *sympathy* [is] slightly hot and *devotion* [is] slightly hot); and we can even say that two speakers of a language possess similar semantic systems to the extent that the "sentences" they produce using the concepts and scales are similar.

During the 1950s we collected many such cubes of SD data and subjected them to factor analysis, with our main interest being in the scale factors (i.e., the semantic dimensions of qualifying). We varied the types of subjects (college students versus old people, differing IQ levels and political affiliations, and even normals versus schizophrenics), also the samplings of scales and of concepts, and even the methods of factoring—and we kept getting the same basic factor system shown in Figure 2. The vertical dimension clearly labels itself as Evaluation, or E, in terms of the scales loading high on it (good–bad, kind–cruel, honest–dishonest); the horizontal dimension labels itself as Potency, or P (strong–weak, hard–soft, heavy–light); and the back-to-front dimension (hot–cold, fast–slow, active–passive) seems to label itself as a kind of Activity, or A, factor.

This factor-analytic model provides a framework of underlying dimensions within which both concept and scale meanings, and their mode of interaction, can be displayed. Figure 3 provides an illustration. The solid black lines

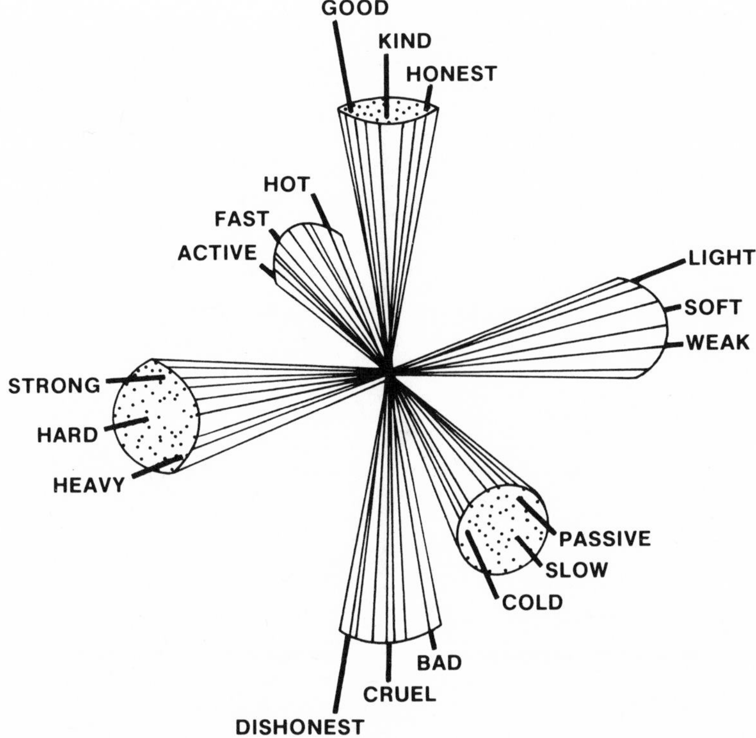

Figure 2. The Evaluation (E), Potency (P), and Activity (A) Structure of Affective Meaning

represent the E-P-A factors and the fine dashed lines represent the projections of a concept point (*coward*) and the termini of a scale (Kind and Cruel) on these three factors. All scales are assumed to be straight lines through the origin, here shown as a bamboo-type line, and we get the locations of the termini from the loadings of scales on the same factors. Thus Kind is very Good, quite Weak, and slightly Passive, and Cruel (reciprocally) is very Bad, quite Strong, and slightly Active. What happens when a subject rates *coward* on the Kind–Cruel scale? Geometrically, the answer is very simple: we just project the *coward* point at right angles onto the Kind–Cruel line (the arrow) and we find that this speaker said, "*Cowards* are slightly cruel!"

This E-P-A semantic subsystem can be described as affective meaning. It appeared to be based on the way humans universally attribute primitive emotional feelings to signs representing persons and things in their environment. However, up until 1960 our research had been focused on humans sharing a common (American) culture and speaking a common (English)

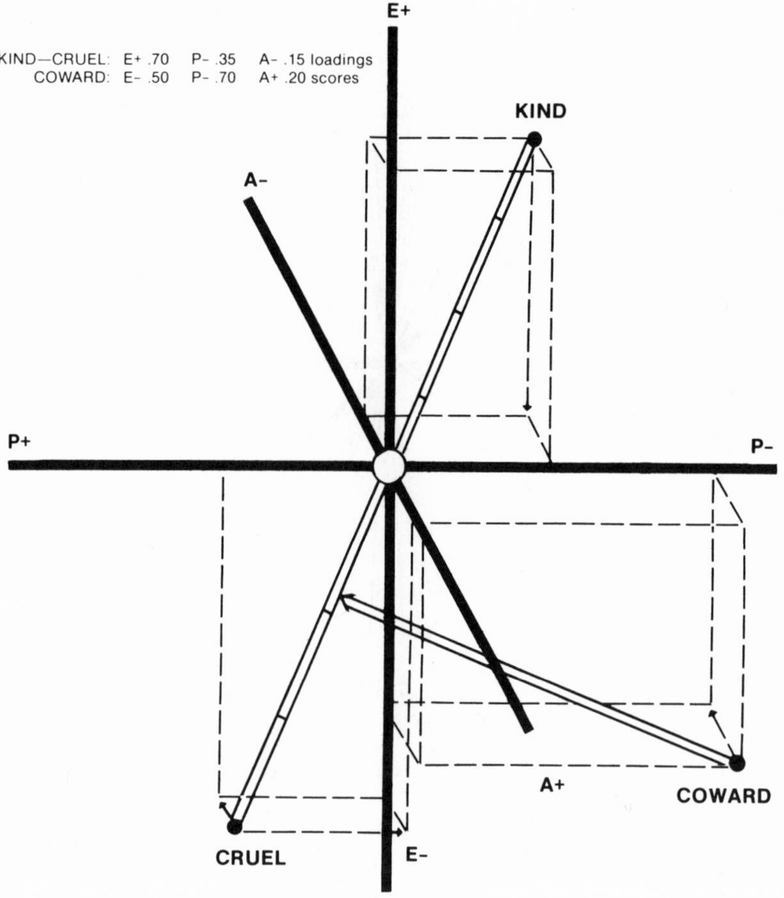

Figure 3. Geometric Representation of the Rating of a Concept on a Scale in the Semantic Differential Technique

language. It was at least conceivable that the dominance of Goodness, Strength, and Activity was attributable to something peculiar about American culture or the English language—or both. So now let us shift from ethnocentrics to anthropocentrics.

Cross-Linguistic Tool-Making

Cross-cultural research is about equally exhilarating and exhausting. Traveling in unfamiliar countries often entails failures to grasp cultural differences in time to avoid embarassing incidents, and I have had my fair share of these.

Our sampling among the world's communities began with six locations widely diversified in both language and culture: these were Finnish, Arabic (in Lebanon), Farsi (in Iran), Kannada (in Mysore), Chinese (in Hong Kong), and Japanese. During the near fifteen-year life of this project, we have gradually extended our research to thirty human communities (see Table 1). Since we were interested in gross differences in culture and language, we decided to maximize sociometric equivalences within communities—in all cases using teen-age male students in average high schools in urban settings.

The first step in "tool-making" was to obtain a sample of productive qualifiers in each community. A set of 100 nouns was used as stimuli in a modified word-association test to elicit 100 adjectives from each of 100 teen-age boys. The nouns were selected to be culture-common, being drawn mainly from lists developed by glottochronologists who study changes in word forms and meanings over long periods of time in families of related languages. Table 2 lists the 100 concepts that remained after careful translation checks. There are many abstract (*trust, choice, wealth*) as well as concrete (*house, cat, man*) concepts among the 100, and all are very familiar notions.

When the 10,000 qualifier tokens had been collected in each community (100 boys giving their responses to the 100 nouns), they were shipped to

Table 1. Community Symbols Identification

AD	Afghan Dari	IF	Iranian Farsi
AE	American English	(IH)	Israeli Hebrew
AP	Afghan Pashtu	IT	Italian Italian
BE	Black English	JP	Japanese Japanese
BF	Belgian Flemish	LA	Lebanese Arabic
(BP)	Brazilian Portuguese	MM	Malaysian Bahasa Kebangsaan
CB	Calcuttan Bengali	MK	Mysore Kannada
CS	Costa Rican Spanish	MS	Mexican Spanish
DH	Delhi Hindi	ND	Netherlands Dutch
FR	French French	(RR)	Romanian Romanian
FF	Finnish Finnish	SW	Swedish Swedish
GG	(West) German German	TH	Thailand Thai
GK	Greek Greek	TK	Turkish Turkish
HC	Hong Kong Chinese	YC	Yucatan (Mayan) Spanish
HM	Hungarian Magyar	YS	Yugoslav Serbo-Croatian

○ = "Atlas" collection still in progress

Table 2. The 100 Culture-Common Concepts Used in Qualifier Elicitations

1. House	21. Bird	41. Cat	61. Success	81. Man
2. Girl	22. Hope	42. Poison	62. Snake	82. Wednesday
3. Picture	23. Heat	43. Tree	63. Hand	83. Chair
4. Meat	24. Map	44. Hunger	64. Mother	84. Guilt
5. Trust	25. Husband	45. Choice	65. Knot	85. River
6. Tooth	26. Rain	46. Noise	66. Life	86. Peace
7. Defeat	27. Truth	47. Need	67. Head	87. Hair
8. Book	28. Stone	48. Doctor	68. Thunder	88. Food
9. Lake	29. Pain	49. Anger	69. Luck	89. Danger
10. Star	30. Ear	50. Tongue	70. Author	90. Policeman
11. Battle	31. Respect	51. Horse	71. Music	91. Father
12. Seed	32. Laughter	52. Marriage	72. Sleep	92. Fear
13. Sympathy	33. Moon	53. Game	73. Future	93. Root
14. Progress	34. Courage	54. Color	74. Egg	94. Purpose
15. Cup	35. Work	55. Heart	75. Crime	95. Fire
16. Wind	36. Story	56. Friend	76. Sun	96. Rope
17. Thief	37. Punishment	57. Death	77. Belief	97. Power
18. Bread	38. Wealth	58. Smoke	78. Money	98. Window
19. Love	39. Woman	59. Freedom	79. Knowledge	99. Pleasure
20. Fruit	40. Cloud	60. Dog	80. Fish	100. Water

Illinois and computer-analyzed in the native language (that is, blindly, untouched by Western minds!). The qualifier types were first ordered in terms of their overall frequencies and diversities of usage across the 100 nouns and then were pruned in terms of their correlations in usage with all higher-ordered types—this last to maximize diversity of the semantic dimensions tapped. The top-ranked 50 qualifiers resulting from this process were shipped back to the field, where their opposites were elicited, and they were thence transformed into seven-step bipolar scales.

The second step in "tool-making" was collection of data for concept-on-scale factorizations. Another group of teen-age male subjects in each community rated the same 100 culture-common concepts against the fifty bipolar scales. So imagine, if you will, thirty data cubes like that described earlier for American English (Figure 1). To determine the functional equivalence in usage (meaning) of scales in different languages independent of translation, we must put these thirty cubes into a single mathematical space for analysis, and this requires that at least one of the three sources of variance (subjects, scales, or concepts) be shared. Subjects are obviously different and the scales are quite varied, so that leaves us with concepts. Although we are sure that the 100 concepts did not mean exactly the same thing in all of the translations into more than twenty-five languages, they are carefully translation-equivalent and the data can be ordered in their terms.

The next step, then, was designing our monstrous pancultural factorization of the scale mode. I shall spare you the details of this operation, which I have reported elsewhere. The proof of this particular pudding, in any case, lies in the results of the factorization. If, despite some unknown variation in the meanings of the 100 concepts, our old friends E, P, and A come forth loud and clear and are represented by scales with reasonably high loadings for all communities, then we have demonstrated the universality of the E-P-A affective meaning system and can go ahead to construct comparable measuring instruments. In the next three tables, the results for E, P, and A, respectively, for twenty communities are displayed—but only for the "positive" terms of the four highest-loading scales. As was seen in Table 1, we use two-letter (usually Locus/Language) codes for our communities—thus AE for American English, AD for Afghan Dari, BF for Belgian Flemish, CB for Calcuttan Bengali, and DH for Delhi Hindi—but not where language and locus coincide, for example, FF for Finnish, FR for French, and GK for Greek. Of course, in order to communicate these results in Table 3, we have translated

Table 3. Pancultural Principal Component Factor Analysis
Factor 1: Evaluation

AE	AD	BF	CB	DH
.94 Nice	.88 Good	.91 Good	.93 Beautiful	.83 Glad
.92 Good	.85 Well	.89 Magnificent	.93 Lovely	.83 Good
.90 Sweet	.84 Safe	.88 Agreeable	.91 Kind	.81 Ambrosial
.89 Helpful	.82 Lovely	.88 Beautiful	.91 Finest	.80 Superior
FF	**FR**	**GK**	**HC**	**IF**
.88 Nice	.90 Pleasant	.93 Superb	.92 Lovable	.92 Good
.87 Pleasant	.89 Good	.91 Good	.92 Good (not bad)	.89 Worthwhile
.86 Good	.88 Nice	.88 Friendly	.91 Good (not poor)	.88 Best
.81 Light	.86 Magnificent	.85 Useful	.90 Respectable	.88 Auspicious
IT	**JP**	**LA**	**MK**	**MS**
.93 Valuable	.93 Good	.90 Sound	.78 Merciful	.93 Admirable
.92 Beautiful	.92 Pleasant	.90 Good	.76 Good	.93 Agreeable
.92 Desirable	.91 Comfortable	.90 Beautiful	.75 Delicate	.92 Good
.92 Good	.91 Happy	.89 Enlivening	.74 Calm	.92 Friendly
ND	**SW**	**TH**	**TK**	**YS**
.91 Pleasant	.86 Good	.88 Useful	.91 Beautiful	.93 Pleasant
.91 Happy	.84 Nice	.87 Comfortable	.90 Good	.92 Good
.90 Good	.82 Right	.87 Right	.90 Tasteful (art)	.91 Lovable
.87 Nice	.82 Kind	.87 Loving	.90 Pleasant	.89 Beautiful

all terms into English, but this had nothing to do with which scales appeared on which pancultural factors. A mere scanning of this table is convincing as to the universality of the Evaluative factor, and you will note that the loadings are nearly all in the .80s and .90s. Scales translating as Good, Beautiful, Pleasant, and Nice appear repeatedly.

While the scale loadings for the Potency factor, shown in Table 4, are somewhat lower (ranging from the .40s into the .70s), common strength and magnitude flavors are evident in scales translating as Big, Strong, Heavy, and Tall. But you will also note some generalizations of Potency into scales like Military, Difficult, and Brave. As is always the case, even for AE (American English), the Activity scales shown in Table 5 have somewhat lower loadings (ranging from the .30s into the low .70s), but, with the possible exceptions of DH (Delhi Hindi), LA (Lebanese Arabic), and MK (Mysore Kannada), the Activity flavor is clear and is evident in the most common scales: Fast, Quick, Alive (and Lively), and Active itself. Again you will note some common generalizations—to Young, to Noisy, and to Red and Bloody.

Table 4. Pancultural Principal Component Factor Analysis
Factor 2: Potency

AE	AD	BF	CB	DH
.68 Big	.55 Great	.57 Strong	.62 Huge	.47 Strong-of-its-kind
.68 Powerful	.45 Military	.57 Big	.60 Powerful	.47 Brave
.57 Strong	.40 Absolute	.54 Heavy	.55 Big	.46 Heavy
.57 Deep	.37 High, loud	.50 Deep	.54 Strong	.44 Difficult
FF	**FR**	**GK**	**HC**	**IF**
.60 Large	.68 Large	.60 Big	.76 Tall, big	.62 Heavy
.59 Sturdy	.59 Strong	.59 Strong	.75 Big	.50 Severe
.51 Heavy	.57 Huge	.46 Brave	.72 Strong	.47 Thick
.40 Rough	.52 Heavy	.39 Difficult	.68 Significant	.42 Stout
IT	**JP**	**LA**	**MK**	**MS**
.68 Big	.66 Heavy	.51 Large	.44 Wonderful	.60 Giant
.55 Strong	.63 Big	.42 Strong	.41 Huge	.58 Big
.54 Wide	.59 Difficult	.41 Long	.41 Big	.55 Major
.49 High, tall	.56 Brave	.38 Heavy	.34 Great	.54 Strong
ND	**SW**	**TH**	**TK**	**YS**
.57 Big	.50 Difficult	.50 Heavy	.67 Big	.72 Big
.55 Heavy	.50 High	.49 Deep	.58 Heavy	.67 Bulky
.54 Strong	.46 Strong	.43 Old	.53 Large	.67 Strong
.48 Special	.45 Long	.42 Big	.51 High	.55 High, tall

Table 5. Pancultural Principal Component Factor Analysis
Factor 3: Activity

AE	AD	BF	CB	DH
.61 Fast	.51 Fast, rapid	.69 Quick	.47 Alive	.47 Gay
.55 Alive	.41 Sharp	.65 Active	.43 Fast	.36 Thin (slim)
.44 Young	.40 Tender, soft	.42 Bloody	.43 Active	.34 Soft
.42 Noisy	.36 Narrow	.40 Impetuous	.38 Light	.30 Loquacious
FF	**FR**	**GK**	**HC**	**IF**
.67 Fast	.61 Lively	.55 Quick	.68 Agile	.53 Active
.66 Flexible	.57 Fast	.52 Young	.54 Fast	.52 Exciting
.64 Agile	.56 Living	.39 Active	.49 Alive	.41 Fast, sharp
.52 Lively	.42 Young	.39 Thin	.46 Red	.31 Warm
IT	**JP**	**LA**	**MK**	**MS**
.66 Fast	.48 Noisy	.35 Fast	.35 Loose	.56 Active
.47 Mortal	.45 Active	.31 Infirm	.34 Unstable	.46 Young
.47 Young	.44 Soft	.30 Thin	.33 Fast	.44 Fast
.40 Sensitive	.42 Fast	.29 Alive	.27 Few	.37 Soft
ND	**SW**	**TH**	**TK**	**YS**
.72 Active	.66 Bloody	.56 Agile	.50 Fast	.63 Lively
.71 Fast	.63 Swift	.44 Fast	.47 Living	.54 Fast
.51 Fascinating	.62 Lively	.39 Thin	.43 Soft (flexible)	.45 Young
.48 Warm	.54 Sensitive	.28 Naughty	.42 Young	.41 Soft

I think you will agree that this is rather convincing evidence for the universality of the E-P-A affective meaning system—and it must be kept in mind that, although procedures were standardized at all critical points, our young subjects were free to produce any kind of qualifiers and use them in any way in rating concepts to create any kind of semantic space.

But why E, P, and A? One reason is that—humans being a kind of animal (just scan any day's newspaper for ample evidence)—the most important questions about the sign of a thing, today as in the day of the Neanderthal, are: first, Is it good or is it bad for me? (Does it signify a cute Neanderthal female or a sabertooth tiger?); second, Is it strong or is it weak with respect to me? (Is it a sabertooth tiger or a rat?); third, Is it an active or a passive thing? (Is it a sabertooth tiger or merely a pool of quicksand that I can just walk around?). Survival of the species has depended upon answers to such questions. Another reason is that the SD technique forces subjects to rate all items—producing judgments like *Tornados* are very unfair, *Defeat* is quite cold, and *Power* is very hard (all "sentences" we would not ordinarily say in ordinary English). When faced with such items, people are forced to use scales metaphorically, and affect seems to be the common coin of metaphor. In the metaphor process, scales "rotate" in the semantic space toward alignment with their own dominant affective feature—Sweet-Sour toward E, Hard-Soft toward P, and Hot-Cold toward A. And, since in factor analysis the dimensions are run through the tightest clusters of scales, this means that massive E-P-A dimensions come booming forth, at the expense of finer, more denotative semantic features.

The final step in the tool-making phase of our cross-cultural research is the production of short-form semantic differentials based upon the pancultural factorization. From the "factor cones" for each community, we select those four indigenous scales that have the highest and purest loadings—hopefully ones that fall within the central region of intercommunity overlap. The pancultural semantic differentials thus consist of twelve scales, four representing each of the E-P-A factors. To the extent that we have identified truly universal dimensions of meaning, these pancultural SD's are reasonably comparable "yardsticks" for measuring the affective aspects of subjective culture, and we have thus succeeded in piercing at least one big hole in the language barrier.

Cross-Cultural Tool-Using

The major use of these pancultural semantic differentials so far has been in the compilation of what we rather grandiosely call an "Atlas of Affective Meanings." I say "grandiosely" because it only includes 620 concepts as sampled (to date) in only twenty-eight language-culture communities—but it is at least a beginning in the exploration of subjective culture. We need not detail here how we went about sampling conceptual domains, or how we labored to check the translations of the final 620 concepts, but our "Atlas" does run from A to Z, as any good Atlas should—from *accepting things as they are*, *accident*, *adolescence*, and so forth, through *marriage*, *masculinity*, and *master*, to *yesterday*, *youth*, and *zero*. Briefly, E, P, and A are the simple averages (with a +3 to —3 range) of the four scales representing each pancultural factor for each culture: E-Z, P-Z, and A-Z are the same scores standardized over the 620 concepts within each culture; F-Z are standardized scores on a familiar-unfamiliar scale; D-O is the concept's distance from the origin of the space, reflecting its affective intensity or meaningfulness; P-I and P-G are polarization measures—P-I averaged over individual subjects regardless of sign (no cancellation), and P-G according to sign (allowing cancellation or neutralization); CI, Cultural Instability, is simply the subtraction of P-G from P-I, and its standardized values, CI-Z, reflect within-culture, inter-subject agreement (minus values) or disagreement (plus values) in affect attribution to concepts. High positive values could represent multiple senses of the words, relative meaninglessness (amorphousness) of the concepts referred to, or—if these possibilities are eliminated—real intracultural conflict.

Just to illustrate these measures, we can compare American and Japanese meanings of *adolescence*: the standardized E-P-A scores indicate that while this period of life is slightly Bad and quite Weak, but very Active, for American teen-agers, it is felt to be very Good, Strong, and Active by the Japanese. Whereas *adolescence* has extremely high cultural instability (conflict) for Americans, it has a quite low CI-Z level for the Japanese—but our Japanese teen-agers do display extraordinarily high intracultural conflict (CI-Z = 2.5) about the notion of *accepting things as they are*.

The "Atlas" as a whole contains a tremendous amount of quantitative information. We estimate about 7,800,000 "bits" of raw data. Obviously this mass of numbers has to be organized into chunks and analyzed in revealing formats if it is to be comprehended by human minds. A way of chunking the data was to assign the 620 concepts, with considerable overlapping, to forty-seven categories of manageable size for analysis. Table 6 lists these categories organizing them under twelve "super-categories." Thus super-category Time includes The Age Continuum (from *birth* to *death* with stops in between), Months and Seasons, Time Units (from *moment* to *eternity*), and the trichotomous category Future-Present-Past (which includes contrasting sets of concepts like *tomorrow/today/yesterday*, and *progress/work/tradition*). Glancing through this table gives some idea of the variety of conceptual categories included in the "Atlas"—Male-Female, Emotions, See-Hear-Touch-Smell-Taste-(ables), Habitations, Body Parts, Modern-Transitional-Traditional Values, Intergroup Relations, Supernaturals, and just plain Stuffs.

The other way of making these data manageable was to devise a chain-linked series of computer programs for analyzing the categories: these were category analyses designed to highlight the most interesting aspects of the data. I will review these analysis formats and illustrate them with the small Color category (only eight concepts). But first a few words about how we are using these pancultural SD data in probing subjective culture.

Imagine 620 probes into the bared "brains" of our twenty-eight cultures —a vivid analogy, even if a bit disturbing. Given the pretty tight translation equivalences of these concepts, the probes should have roughly corresponding loci in the various cultural "brains." However, our probes are designed to give out only three kinds of signals, which can be called Evaluation "whistles," Potency "rumbles," and Activity "whirrings"—each signal being quantitatively variable in direction and intensity. We are looking for patterning in the signals arising from the various sets of probes.

If all or nearly all of the cultural "brains" give forth the same kinds of signals for a given set of probes—for example, $^{+}E^{-}P^{-}A$ for Domesticated as compared with Wild Animals—then we infer that relatively Good but Weak and Passive is a Universal way of feeling about domestication. If certain definable subgroups give out quite different signals from the others,

Table 6. Forty-seven Categories of "Atlas" Concepts (by 12 Super-categories)

1—Time
- A. Age continuum
- B. Months, seasons
- C. Time units
- D. Future-present-past

2—Ego identification
- A. Kinship
- B. Races, religions, continents, directions, -isms
- C. Male-female
- D. Ingroup, alters, outgroup
- E. Intimacy-remoteness

3—Abstract symbolisms
- A. Emotions
- B. Numbers
- C. Colors
- D. Geometricals
- E. Days

4—Concrete symbolisms
- A. Natural and potentially aesthetic
- B. See-hear-touch-smell-taste-(ables)
- C. Means-expressive-ends

5—Environmentals
- A. Food objects
- B. Animals
- C. Habitations

6—Carnalities
- A. Body parts
- B. Body characteristics, processes
- C. Sex and sensuality
- D. Health, sickness

7—Human activity
- A. Occupations
- B. Commercial, economic
- C. Work-play
- D. Success-failure

8—Interpersonal relations
- A. Private-public
- B. Social status
- C. Moral-immoral
- D. Intergroup relations
- E. Affiliative-achievement

9—Society
- A. Institutions
- B. Modern-transitional-traditional technology
- C. Modern-transitional-traditional values

10—Communications
- A. Literacy
- B. Language and literature
- C. Communications

11—Philosophy
- A. Philosophicals
- B. Supernaturals
- C. Idealism-realism
- D. Concrete-abstract
- E. Cognitive-gut

12—Things and stuffs
- A. Static, dynamic nature
- B. Static, dynamic artifacts
- C. Stuffs

then we infer a Subuniversal—for example, the Muslim communities' feelings about *Friday* versus *Sunday*. And if nearly all cultures groan and rumble for a concept (say, the color *black*), but one whistles and purrs (as the Mayans in Yucatán do), then we shall infer a Uniqueness for that culture—and try to find the reason for it from our informants. I will summarize the main data formats:

Format 1. Basic Measures. The first step is to pull from the "Atlas" the basic-measure data strips for all communities (twenty at the time most of our data was drawn up) for each concept in the category. Even in these unanalyzed basic measures we often pick up certain signals: we find, for instance, that while the concept *color* is much more positively evaluated than *black*, *black* is the more Potent by far. We note also some "sore thumbs" (unique deviations): the French have a "thing" about *black* (it is much more Passive than the mean for all cultures), and the Americans have a different "thing" about *black* (it is very much more "conflictual" than for others—and for readily discernible social reasons).

Format 2. Intercultural Correlations on Basic Measures. Next, each culture is correlated with every other culture on each of the basic measures across the concepts in the category. For colors, the average correlation is significantly positive across all cultures for E and nearly so for P and for A—so we can expect to find many universal trends here.

Format 3. Intracultural Ranks of Concepts on Basic Measures. In this step, we transform the measures of each type into ranks within each community. Thus we find that while American English, among others, ranks the concept *color* as highest and *black* as the lowest in Evaluation, our Yucatán Mayan friends rank *color* lowest, but *black* as 4 midway on the Evaluation scale. Using the criterion that no more than four of these twenty communities deviate from a universal trend (which one would expect to happen by chance only 1 percent of the time), we find that *color* and *blue* are universally $^{+}$E, and *black* and *grey* are universally $^{-}$E; the colors *black* and *red* are universally $^{+}$P, and *yellow* and *white* universally $^{-}$P. The Swedes and the Finns, our two most northern communities, display an interesting Subuniversal: for them, *yellow* (sunlight?) has unusually high Evaluation. And there are Uniquenesses beyond that of Yucatán Mayan on *color* and *black*: for example, the Hindi-speakers in Delhi find *grey* unusually Good (the term is used for the light skin color preferred in young girls) and *black* unusually Weak (it refers to the skin color of the Southern Indians).

Format 4. Componential Analyses of Ranks. After the fashion of cultural anthropologists, who have worked mainly in the domain of kinship terms, we have applied componential analyses to all of our categories. We try to intuit the possible cognitive bases for the differentiation of concept meanings and then see if they are predictive of how people attribute affect. In our componential analysis for Colors, to the three familiar physical components (Brightness, Hue, and Saturation), we add a Color/Noncolor distinction (for which *color* and the four hues are coded plus, and *black*, *grey*, and *white* are coded minus). Ideally, tests of the affective relevance of these components should be based on what linguists call minimal pairs—that is, pairs of concepts that have opposed signs on only the component being tested—but we often have to compromise.

The results of these componential tests for the Color category reveal a number of interesting universal tendencies. Across our little world, Brightness is more Valued and more Active then Darkness, but Darkness is more Potent; Brightness also is more familiar and has less conflict than Darkness. For an animal that depends dominantly on vision, these universal tendencies are not surprising. As to Hue, Reds are less Good than Blues, but more Active: Reds also tend to have more conflict about them. As to Saturation, Rich colors (*red, blue,* and we could include *black*) are more Potent than Pale colors (*yellow, green,* and we could add both *white* and *grey*). Colors (*red, yellow, green, blue,* and the word *color* itself) are more Good, more Active and less conflictual then Noncolors (*white, grey,* and *black*).

Format 5. Pancultural Distance Matrix. Segments of the total pancultural matrix are also extracted for analysis into an interconcept distance matrix for each community. If you could imagine models made up of eight little colored balls (representing our eight color concepts) distributed in a space defined by E, P, and A, one model for each community, you would have visual representations of the affective conceptual structures of colors in the minds of people of each culture. We can ask questions like these of such distance matrices: (1) What other color term is closest in feeling-tone to the generic term *color*? (It turns out to be *blue* for a majority of communities, but for Finland it is *red* and for Sweden it is *yellow*!); (2) How dispersed in the space are the various colors? (It turns out that our East Asians, the Thais, Hong Kong Chinese, and Japanese, show the greatest affective differentiation, and our West Asians and South Asians, the Afghans, Iranians, and all three cultures in India, the least differentiation among colors.)

We can also extract the diagonal of each square matrix to find the interculture distances for all pairs of cultures on all concepts. In this way we have found that Americans should get along fine about colors with the Iranians but never with the Swedes!

Some Universals and Uniquenesses in the Attribution of Affect

We are right now at the beginning of our attempt to interpret and report on the "Atlas" data. This involves relating our quantitative information to both the detailed commentary of our colleagues and other informants and a literature that, as you can see from the diversity of our concept categories, will extend out in all directions. This will be a very time-consuming task, and we anticipate that several volumes will be forthcoming. At this point I can only offer a sampling—a potpourri of bits and pieces that may bemuse or amuse—of some of the universal trends that are appearing, along with some interesting deviations. But first a caution: it is easy to slip into talking about cultures as wholes and in general—and it does save time and space—but we must try to keep in mind that our data come from teen-age boys, from particular urban sites within countries, and from only twenty-eight out of thousands of human cultures. So these data should be absorbed *cum grano salis*.

Our "Atlas" data are full of obvious differences in attribution of affect. Thus, we find that Emotions coded Pleasant have higher E everywhere than those coded Unpleasant, that Animals are more Active than Vegetables, that Liquids are more Active than Solids, that Solid geometricals are more Potent than Planes and these in turn more Potent than lines or points (and that a *pyramid* is one of the most Potent things on earth). Such findings may be obvious, but they are not trivial; with so much face validity where we know what to expect from our own Humanness, we can have much more faith that the Universals we did not expect are valid and that the Subuniversals and Uniquenesses reflect real cultural differences.

With apologies to the women for the biases of human nature, I must report that in both our Kinship and Male-Female categories, Male is regularly more Potent than Female. There is one intriguing exception to this dictum: the concept *widower* for nearly all communities (exceptions are Finland, Mexico, Turkey, Thailand, and Japan) is closer to female concepts in the Male-Female category (*female, femininity, woman, girl, and mother*) than to the matched male concepts—as if, in the minds of teen-age boys, a man loses his masculinity when he loses his wife! It might be noted that nothing like this happens to *widow*—she stays as feminine as ever. Interesting in this connection is the linguistic fact that, whereas most male concepts are unmarked (positive) with respect to their marked (negative) female counterparts (e.g., male-*fe*male, steward-steward*ess*), the case with widow*er* is just the reverse, the male word being marked by the addition of *-er*.

In connection with interpersonal relations, Figure 4 expresses some results from our Ego-Alter-Outgroup category. It displays the distances from the Ego (the concept *I, myself*) of *family, friend, relatives, most people, stranger,* and *enemy*. The heavy black line is the mean across all cultures, and you will note that although *friend* is a bit closer to *I, myself* than even *family*, the distance in feeling (E-P-A combined) increases steadily as we move outward from *friend* through various Alters toward the Outgroups *stranger* and *enemy*. Americans and Chinese are much closer to *friend* than to *family*, and the Hong Kong boys hold their *relatives* at an unusual distance as far as affective similarity to themselves is concerned. The Japanese see themselves as closer to everybody than the average, even *enemy*. But the teen-agers in Yugoslavia have the most unusual pattern; their feelings about themselves are closest to *stranger* and furthest from *family* (except for *enemy*)! Unless there is some translation problem here (and we have checked carefully), this is really something to work with.

Figure 5 gives the Evaluation ranks of the Days of the Week. Again looking

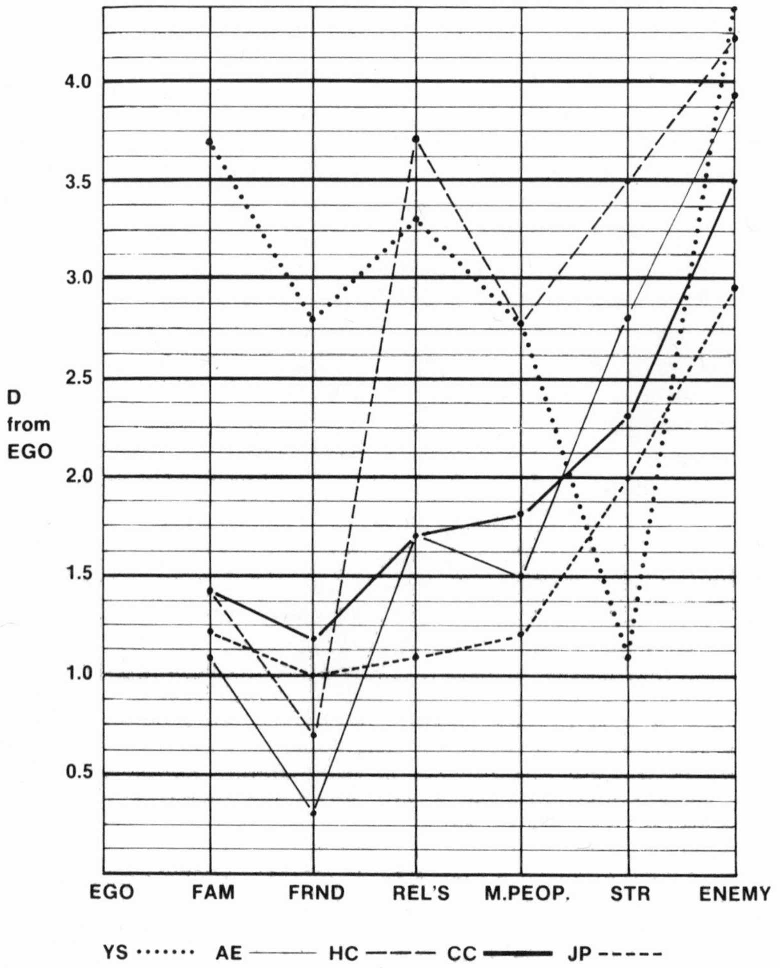

Figure 4. Distances from Ego (*I, myself*) of In-Group (*family, friend, relatives*) and Out-Group (*most people, stranger, enemy*)

first at the mean evaluation across all cultures (heavy solid line), you will note that *Monday* is the worst day of the week for most people and, with a slight negative dip for *Friday*, things keep looking up through the week until the best day, *Sunday* (the day of worship and rest for most of our cultures), is reached. Americans find *Tuesday* fairly good, get glummer through *Thursday*, but really pick up on *Friday*; unlike most—and I think for understandable cultural reasons—American teen-agers like *Saturday* (and even *Friday*) better than *Sunday*. Now compare the Iranians: their worst day is *Saturday*; they improve in mood pretty steadily through *Wednesday* and, after a dip for *Thursday*, reach their peak on *Friday*—which, for Moslems, of course, is their "Sunday." Now, if you mentally slide the IF curve forward just two days—so that the two days of worship are superimposed (their *Friday* on our *Sunday*)—you will find that the IF and AE curves match very closely except for the marked difference on "Saturday" (their *Thursday* being just another day of work and our *Saturday* being like a weekly holiday).

We have many categories in our "Atlas," in fact most, in which the correlations across cultures for E,P, and A are significantly positive (Colors, as we have seen; Animals; Natural Phenomena like *mountains, trees, jungles,* and the *moon*; See-Hear-Smell-Touch-Taste-ables like *sense of sight, ear, ice, perfume, and salt*; and even Philosophicals, Supernaturals, and just plain Stuffs), and these commonnesses, of course, are flatly contradictory to the thesis of "psycholinguistic relativity" espoused by Sapir and Whorf—that

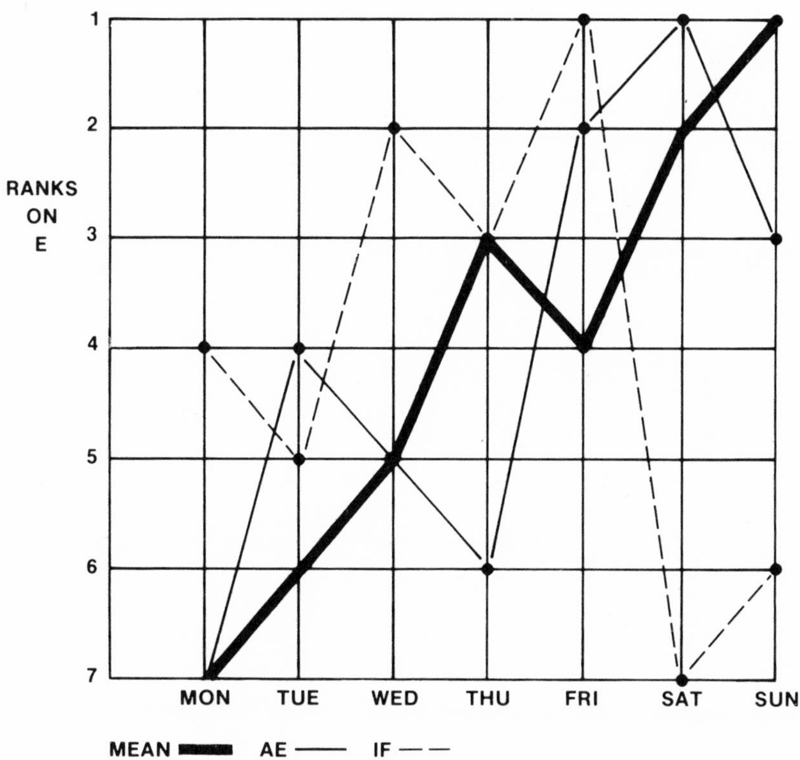

Figure 5. Evaluation Ranks of Days of the Week for all Communities (mean), Americans (AE), and Iranians (IF)

how we perceive, how we think, and even how we formulate our implicit philosophies depends upon the structures of the languages we speak. I can say with assurance that we have no clear evidence in all of our data of language determining thought, although there is much evidence for culture influencing thought.

We were interested in comparing our communities in terms of the relative weights they give to Age versus Sex in differentiating affect. So, as shown in Figure 6, we contrasted the distances between *boy* and *man* (age of males) and *girl* and *woman* (age of females) with those between *boy* and *girl* (sex of immatures) and *man* and *woman* (sex of matures). The diagram in the upper left gives the distance values for the means across all of our cultures at the time (N = 23). Note that the largest distances are in terms of the Sex of Matures (*man* vs. *woman*) and the *age* of Males (*man* vs. *boy*)—the Age of Females making relatively little difference (again, for teen-age boys). The American (AE) pattern is very much like the mean, except that Sex is equally important for both Immatures and Matures. The Dutch (ND) pattern exaggerates the American one—Sex of both Matures and Immatures having very

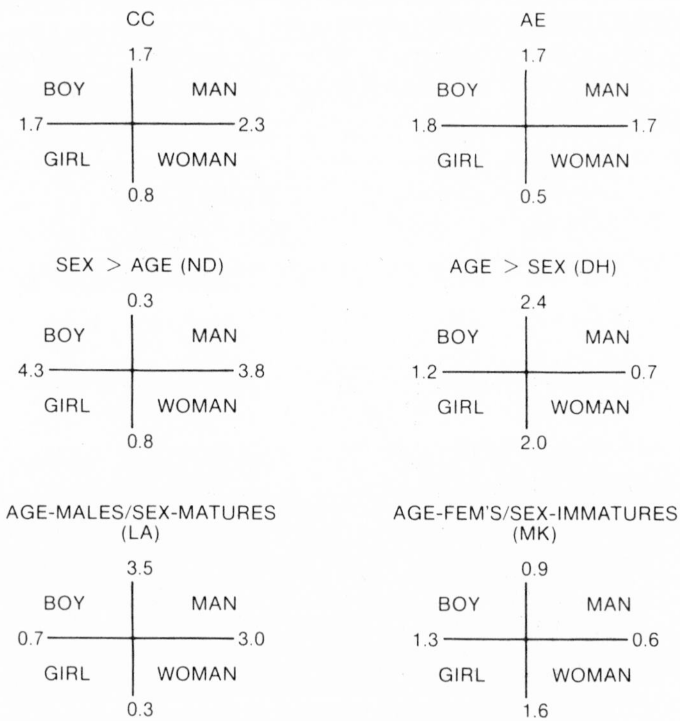

Figure 6. Age versus Sex as Differentiators of Affect

great weight and the Ages of either Sex having practically no weight. The Delhi Hindi-speakers (DH) show exactly the reverse emphasis, with the Age of both Males and Females having twice as much weight as Sex. Yet another community in India, Kannada speakers in Mysore and Bangalore (MK), completely reverse the usual pattern: for them it is the Age of Females and the Sex of Immatures that are important in determining differences in feeling. At the lower left is the pattern for Lebanese Arabic (LA); as you can see, the Lebanese exaggerate the typical pattern, with the Age of Males and the Sex of Matures making practically all the difference.

Figure 7 also illustrates cultural differences—in terms of three "scales" taken from three of our interpersonal relations categories. The "Supraordinateness Scale" (taken from our Social Status category) shows the average distances for each culture between the following pairs of concepts and the *ego*: *leader/follower*, *policeman/beggar*, *authority/illiterate*, *rich-people/poor-people*, and *master/servant*. The larger the value, in either direction from zero, the greater the differentiation being made between high and low status people, and if it is in the + direction the subjects are identifying more with high-status concepts. Note that our teen-age boys generally identify with higher status people, mostly so in the case of the Iranians, the Lebanese, and the Americans. Only the Thais, the Yugoslavs, and the Mysoreans identify more with the lower-status concepts.

The "Moral Polarization Scale" (drawn from our Moral-Immoral category) presents the mean distances between the concept pairs: *character/sin*, *charity/greed*, *devotion/adultery*, *discipline/cheating*, *duty/lying*, *forgiveness/guilt*, *honor/graft*, *justice/crime*, *kindness/murder*, and *missionary/prostitute* —surely a rendering of the Thou Shalt's versus the Thou Shalt Not's! On this scale the zero position represents the mean distance for all cultures combined. The highest polarizers, making gross "Puritanical" distinctions between the Shalt's and the Shalt Not's, are the Afghans and the Lebanese; the lowest polarizers, displaying either a tolerance of sin or a cynicism about the norms of the Establishment, or both, are the French (cynics?), the Thais (tolerators?), and the Finns (a bit of both?).

The last is our "Affiliative-Achievement Scale," drawn from our category of the same title. One might also call this a "Love-Power Scale." This gives the average affective distances between the pairs *respect/power*, *friend/leader*, *cooperation/competition*, *devotion/envy*, *sympathy/greed*, *accepting-things/taking-the-initiative*, *family/success*, *group/champion*, and *friendship/work*. Here the midpoint of the scale indicates the cross-cultural mean distance between these pairs. By all odds, and actually off the scale, the most achievement-oriented (or "power") group of teen-agers are the Japanese; also quite high in this respect are the Finns, the Dutch, the Hong Kong Chinese, and the Kannada speakers of Bangalore; the most affiliative- (or "love-") oriented teen-agers are the Mexicans, the Turks, the Afghans, the Yucatán Mayans,

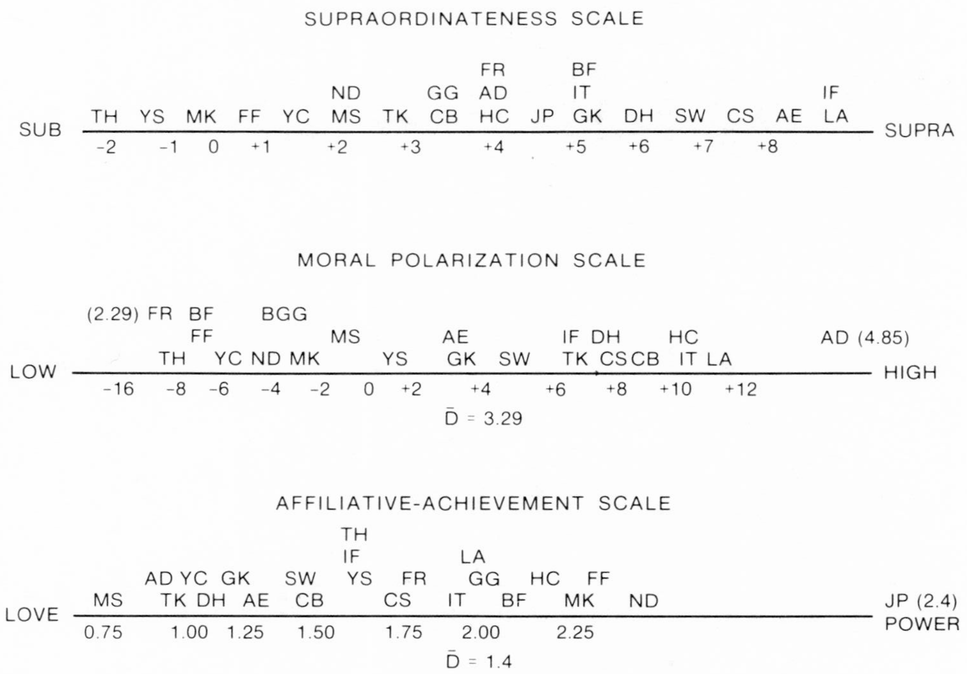

SUPRAORDINATENESS SCALE

FR BF
ND GG AD IT IF
SUB TH YS MK FF YC MS TK CB HC JP GK DH SW CS AE LA SUPRA
-2 -1 0 +1 +2 +3 +4 +5 +6 +7 +8

MORAL POLARIZATION SCALE

(2.29) FR BF BGG
FF MS AE IF DH HC AD (4.85)
LOW TH YC ND MK YS GK SW TK CS CB IT LA HIGH
-16 -8 -6 -4 -2 0 +2 +4 +6 +8 +10 +12
$\bar{D}$ = 3.29

AFFILIATIVE-ACHIEVEMENT SCALE

TH
IF LA
AD YC GK SW YS FR GG HC FF
LOVE MS TK DH AE CB CS IT BF MK ND JP (2.4) POWER
0.75 1.00 1.25 1.50 1.75 2.00 2.25
$\bar{D}$ = 1.4

Figure 7. Three Scales

and the Hindi speakers in Delhi. It is clear that many of the highlighted cultures on these scales make very good sense.

By Way of Conclusion

We are in mid-flight on our exploration of semantic space and subjective culture. The tool-making and tool-using (compilation of a modest atlas, at least) will soon have been completed for thirty human cultures, but we have just begun evaluating and reporting on the information in our hands. We feel that we have a potential gold mine here for the social sciences, but the problem is to trace the veins of the metal and separate the precious from the ordinary, a process that will take a long time and a lot of work.

Concern about the development, collection, and validation of social indicators has been growing rapidly over the past few years. However, to the best of my knowledge, this concern has been mainly with indicators of objective culture—GNP, number of telephones, automobiles, newspapers, et cetera, per capita, frequency of suicides and deadly conflicts, and so forth —not of subjective culture. Yet if there is anything we should have learned over the past couple of decades about the adoption of technological innovations, whether it be automation, crop rotation, or birth control, it is that people's attitudes, values, and customs are the prime determiners of social development. This concern has also been more with national than with international indicators—yet, as we have seen at the beginning of this paper, our technology is impelling us at an ever-increasing pace into one, interdependent world, where what happens "there" has as much relevance to our own future as what happens "here." And, although this concern with indicators often refers to social change, no formal analyses of the nature and measurement of change have been offered in connection with social indicators.

Although our "Atlas of Affective Meanings" is limited in scope at present, its technology is now developed to the point where it could be extended quickly and efficiently—not by us but by some national (or, better, international) agency. It does get at important dimensions of subjective culture in rigorous, quantitative ways; it is international in nature (although limited in the absolute number of world communities); and it does include the potential for assessing social change (we are planning a decade re-test of critical concepts during the next few years, and this could be done on a regular basis). If our progress toward One (Interdependent) World is to be anything but willy-nilly, then indicators of subjective culture and its changes are essential.

F. RETROSPECT AND PROSPECT

Dr. Lerner opens this section with a paper on the impact of new technology upon communication practice, social change, and therefore development. In explaining why aid programs by more-developed countries (MDC) have failed so often in less-developed countries (LDC), he brings to new life such concepts as "acceleration of history" and "mobilization of the periphery." His hopes for the future, like those of Dr. Matson in the preceding section, are that "low-cost" hardware and software may enable LDC to "leapfrog"—by transforming their Want: Get Ratios (WGR), with the help of production as well as distribution and communication technology, into some sort of "dynamic equilibrium."

Dr. Lasswell then outlines "alternative futures of world politics and society with special reference to the policies and processes of development." As creator of "the policy sciences," Lasswell is less concerned with "prophecy" than with "innovation;" he seeks not to predict the development future but to invent it. All of us concerned with shaping the future of the developing areas will find in this paper a rich source of guidance for future policies and programs.

Dr. Ramo projects a future in which technology can be focused more directly on meeting human and social needs. A pioneer in advanced aerospace and electronic technology, Ramo has written widely on the full use of science and technology to lighten human burdens and increase benefits in work, school, home, and leisure. His present paper on "Information Technology and Resources for Growth," adapted from his talk to the White House Conference on the World Ahead, projects some of the important roles our improved information technology can play in the manifold collective concerns of modern society, such as communication, transportation, pollution, urban and rural life. Addressed primarily to the producers of new technologies, Ramo's ideas could produce gifts beyond price to the less-developed countries.

Dr. Cleveland points out that the doomsayers may have been talking too loud too soon. He shows that the catastrophic projections of the "havoc-criers" have already proved wrong in some critical areas, for example, accepted forecasts that world population would reach 8 billion by the year 2000 have just been revised downward to 6 billion by the U.N. He illustrates the beneficent consequences thus: "Even with better diets, 6 billion people won't eat as much as 7 or 8 billion." His concise explanation is heartening for all of us: "What happened? Development and communications, that's what."

George Chaplin, editor of *The Honolulu Advertiser* and coeditor of the pioneering book *Hawaii 2000* (The University Press of Hawaii, 1973), gives us a brief glimpse of how a mixed group of concerned citizens was able to produce a collective work that defined Hawaii's problems in ways that are helping to shape its future. Their example has already stimulated parallel efforts among concerned citizens in many different places around the developing world.

Dr. Schramm and Dr. Lerner then conclude with a brief review of some important lessons for communication and development in the years ahead.

16. Technology, Communication, and Change

DANIEL LERNER

This paper will focus on new communication technology and its impact on development over the past decade—with a brief look at prospects for the next decade. Two major development patterns in the past quarter-century have been labeled: (1) "acceleration of history"; (2) "mobilization of the periphery." Since most of us are familiar with these two concepts, I need only review them briefly here.

Development Patterns: East and West

"Acceleration of history" is a concept that preoccupied European philosophers during much of the nineteenth century, as they sought explanations for the rapid transformations wrought in their own lifeways by the Industrial Revolution and its concomitants. If the Europeans were puzzled by their "acceleration," how much more of a "puzzlement" (as the King of Siam told Anna) is the much greater acceleration that has occurred throughout less-developed countries (LDC) in the past twenty-five years, and especially in the past ten years. Compared to our recent experience, the tempo of social change in the more-developed countries (MDC) of Western Europe and North America was leisurely indeed!

A great deal of the historical acceleration, both East and West, was initiated or reinforced by new technology. Communication technology played a major role and may be regarded as a Rostovian "leading sector" (Rostow 1960). Table 1 illustrates the acceleration of history by communication technology over the past five centuries.

Table 1. Five Communication Revolutions

Technology	*Media*	*Approximate Age in 1975*
Movable Type/Press	Print	+500 years
Camera/Film	Visual	100
Transmitter/Vacuum Tube	Audio	50
Transistor/Picture Tube	Audiovisual	20
Satellites/"Spinoffs"	First World Network	−10

You will note in the right-hand column above that the time interval between communication revolutions has been accelerated exponentially. For example, between the first revolution of print and the next, over four hundred years elapsed. People in LDC may well ask what the Europeans were doing during those four long centuries after movable type had been invented.

The fact is that all those centuries were needed to develop a new class of people who could use the technology. It was not until the nineteenth century that the "penny press"—the first important institutional product of print technology—came into being first in Britain, then elsewhere in Europe.[1] This was the Western "mobilization of the periphery," which we shall contrast with the Eastern process that is going on today.

Why did it take so long? Recall that, in the fifteenth century, the European population, like the LDC population today, was mainly rural, agricultural, illiterate, and poor. Needed was a new class of literate people who could read a daily newspaper. These new literates then needed to have an extra penny to spend for a newspaper. They also needed to be motivated to want to spend their penny on information rather than on cakes and ale. To accomplish all of this, at the historical tempo of Europe in that era, had to take about four centuries. The Western "mobilization of the periphery" thus evolved through the gradual transformation of stateways and lifeways over some twenty generations of people learning and adopting the new ways.

Contrast this with the LDC situation over the past quarter-century. Populations that were as rural, agricultural, illiterate, and poor as was Europe's five centuries ago suddenly were plunged into a world where print, film, radio, television—and now satellites—were already in operation. "Catching up" became their slogan. This required an instant "mobilization of the periphery" by the abrupt transformation of a single generation, an "acceleration of history" indeed!

A major communication effect of accelerating tempo was that the new electronic media made information readily available to people who could not read. Thereby it "mobilized" a periphery that only yesterday had not participated in the polity at all, indeed had hardly been touched by public affairs and public policy (what the French succinctly call *la chose publique*).

The populist spirit that accompanied the independence movements of most emerging nations demanded that these new technologies be put into immediate use.* This created, for the first time in history, major polities dominated by illiterate voters. Small wonder, then, that the Western model of modernization (what Eisenstadt's paper in this book calls the "old paradigm") had to undergo significant transformations.

The old paradigm depicted Western modernization as an evolutionary sequence in four phases: urbanization, literacy, media participation, political participation. This evolution, as we have seen, occurred over five centuries and is still in progress. Political participation—in the form of electoral democracy—came as a culminating phase in the long secular evolution of participant society. Many people do not realize that universal suffrage in the West was a very long time in the making. Western women began to receive the voting franchise only after World War I in some countries (1920 in the United States), after World War II in other countries. The voting age began to be reduced to eighteen in some MDC only in the last few years. Western "mobilization of the periphery," with over 500 years of evolution behind it, still continues today.

Contrast this, for example, with India, which, upon achieving independence in 1947, promptly conferred universal suffrage upon a population that was about 90 percent rural, agricultural, illiterate, and poor. Clearly, India could not follow the leisurely tempo of Western modernization. Acceleration of history was dictated by the quest for instant mobilization in India as in every other developing society-in-a-hurry. Contrast the Western evolution, in this sense, with the recent decision that all Filipinos over fifteen years old will vote in the upcoming referendum.

"Mobilization of the periphery" requires the acquisition of mobility by ever-increasing numbers of individuals. The Western sequence evolved from physical, through social, to psychic mobility. It began with the physical movement of individuals and families to cities. Urbanization was the first step toward social mobility because it was coupled with industrialization. In moving from farm to factory, the urban worker broke out of the traditional routines of subsistence farming in the extended-family work unit and entered into the monetized economy of modernity. As he acquired his extra pennies, he became upwardly mobile in social status. He went to school and learned to read; he bought a newspaper and learned about public affairs. In this way

*I use the term "populism" to denote recent LDC efforts to integrate the symbols and practices of nationalism and socialism. Some new nations are seeking to build simultaneously a democratic polity, a socialist economy, and a participant society.

he acquired the psychic mobility (what we have called empathy) that is an indispensable mechanism of modern lifeways. As David Riesman has noted, it was the urban worker who first came from the rural periphery to become the cash customer, the newspaper reader, the opinion giver, the voter (Riesman 1950). Western mobilization eventually produced an apparently seamless behavioral web conducive to self-sustaining growth.

This has not happened in LDC. Consider the process of urbanization, which was so critical in stimulating the modernization of the West. In the old paradigm it was determined that a "critical minimum" of urbanization was about 10 percent of the total population living in cities over 50,000. The impact on modernization was stated as follows:

> Only after a country reaches 10 percent of urbanization does its literacy rate begin to rise significantly. Thereafter, urbanization and literacy increase together in a direct monotonic relationship, until they reach 25 percent, which appears to be the "critical optimum" of urbanization. Beyond this, literacy continues to rise independently of the growth of cities. (Lerner 1964:59)

In the Western model the range of 10–25 percent urbanization was necessary to make "economical" the development of modernizing institutions —for example, the schools and print media that produced literacy, which in turn increased productivity. Beyond 25 percent, urbanization ceased to play a determining role because, at that point, enough people were relocated in cities to assure the "critical mass" of population requirements for modern production and consumption.

In many LDC during the past quarter-century, the Western sequence of development phases has been reversed. Along with the "population explosion" and the "media revolution" came an overwhelming rush to the cities. In South America, which is the most urbanized continent in the world, half or more of the total population live in the capital cities of many countries. In Southeast Asia, the "teeming millions" have largely relocated in cities over the past two decades. But this is not "urbanization" in the Western sense. Many of the LDC urban migrants do not enter into the productive life of the cities at all. They languish, unemployed or underemployed, on this new "periphery" and become what Herbert Gans has aptly designated "urban villagers."[2]

In this context, LDC urbanization cannot be expected to play the modernizing role that it did in the West. (Schramm and Ruggels, in Lerner and Schramm 1972). On the contrary, in many LDC the impact of urbanization has been counterproductive to development. Little benefit for development is obtained by the "tin can cities," *bidonvilles, ranchos, favellas, geçëkondü,* which blight urban landscapes throughout LDC. Let us look, then, at the consequences that have followed these significant alterations of the Western model.

The LDC Sequence: Three Phases

All of us at this conference appear to be agreed that development patterns vary considerably from one LDC to another and that these "culture-specific" variations are essential to a full understanding of any particular LDC. Yet, I believe that there are important "regularities" that are common to all of development experience over the past quarter-century. These "regularities" are manifested in a sequence of three phases: (1) rising expectations; (2) rising frustrations; (3) military takeover.

Phase 1: Rising Expectations

All of us are familiar with the "revolution of rising expectations," a phrase created by Harlan Cleveland and popularized by Eugene Staley, two members of our present conference (Staley 1954). At the start of the development decades, around 1950, "rising expectations" was almost universally regarded as a Good Thing—at least by Western and Westernizing development thinkers, planners, activists. It was believed that as people's expectations rose, their efforts to achieve (what David McClelland has called "need achievement") would increase accordingly (D.C. McClelland 1961). This was a direct extrapolation from the Western experience, in which rising expectations had indeed stimulated rising efforts, rising innovations, and rising productivity. Such sociological concepts as Max Weber's "Protestant ethic" were developed to account for the almost universal association of effort with reward in the Western mores.

Two decades later, most of us are aware that this Western association of reward with effort—of personal achievement to satisfy personal expectations—has not worked in LDC. None of us believes that this hiatus occurred because the peoples of Asia failed to accept the virtues of Protestantism. Indeed, most of us recall that the heroic Age of Exploration in the West (approximately 1400–1600) and the glorious Renaissance (approximately 1500–1700) preceded the Protestant Reformation. Hence, these first centuries of Western "progress" were activated mainly by certified Catholics from Portugal, Spain, Italy, Netherlands, and even Britain before Henry VIII.

Our interest in recalling this historical sequence is not antiquarian but analytical. If the Protestant Ethic does not adequately account for "progress" in the West, then elementary logic shows that its absence cannot adequately account for the failures of "development" in the East. What development analysts East and West, as represented in this conference, have converged upon to explain development setbacks is the failure to associate personal effort with personal reward. If this is so, it is a basic flaw in development theory, planning, and implementation. As such it is *a fortiori* a failure of development communication.

Some development analysts have blamed this on "consumerism." The use of this Americanism as an MDC epithet against the LDC poor seems to me unfair for policy thinkers—and, more important for development analysts, untrue. I believe that the desire for the material Good Things of life is natural and humane. Indeed, the "rising expectations" of LDC have gone far beyond material wants to embrace "quality of life" desires—information for self-betterment, education for one's children. I therefore prefer the more subtle proposition that the LDC failure to associate reward with effort derives from the fact that LDC were led—thanks to the counterproductive use of charisma and communication—to put the values of consumption before the values of production (especially productivity).

Just as LDC have reordered the Western sequence of modernization, so have they reordered the system of values that accompanied Western development. People who were granted the franchise upon independence, without being obliged to pass through the ordeals of a poll tax or a literacy test, naturally expected many of the good things of modernity to come their way without effort. LDC peoples have been more sharply oriented toward consumption than production by their experience of independence under charismatic leaders, who distorted their first exposure to the goodies of modernity. I consider this communication failure to rest as well upon charismatic LDC as upon cinematic MDC. Communication policy—and content—simply failed to convey that many centuries of rising productivity elapsed before the "idols of production" began to yield pride of place to the "idols of consumption."[3]

Phase 2: Rising Frustrations

Because their achievements—particularly in economic development—have lagged so far behind their expectations, many LDC peoples have moved from rising expectations into a second phase of rising frustrations. People simply have not been getting what they had been led to want by their charismatic leaders through a faulty "mass media" communication strategy. As a result, the "Want:Get Ratio" (WGR) has become seriously imbalanced and the LDC peoples have suffered continuing and deepening frustration.

Consider the emphasis placed upon radio by Egypt's charismatic leader Gamal Abdel Nasser:

> It is true that most of our people are still illiterate. But politically that counts far less than it did twenty years ago. . . . Radio has changed everything. . . . Today people in the most remote villages hear of what is happening everywhere and form their opinions. Leaders cannot govern as they once did. We live in a new world. (Lerner 1964:214)

Nasser put this thought into action on a very large scale. He allocated a significant portion of Egypt's resources to the expansion of Egyptian State Broadcasting (and its international channel "Voice of the Arabs"). He distributed free community receivers to villages throughout Egypt and other

Arab lands. By the use of radio and its associated change-agents (following the 1902 Leninist concept of "agitprop"), Nasser sought to build the Revolutionary People's Rally and transform the Egyptian polity on short notice (Lenin 1929).

But Nasser's high expectations suffered severe setbacks. In very many villages, the community receiver was attached to the mosque and its operation was controlled by the imam. A usual practice was to turn on the radio for the daily Koran readings and traditional Arab songs—and then to turn it off again when these programs were over. The political change-agents reported back that the radio was giving them little or no help in creating the new participant polity. The Revolutionary People's Rally promptly came under the influence of the local *oomdah*s, the traditional village autocrats. In his autobiography, Nasser acknowledged his many setbacks (Nasser 1955). In the last years of his short life, he avowed defeat of his political expectations. He died a frustrated man.

Another charismatic leader, Achmed Sukarno of Indonesia, explained rising frustrations, not in terms of the failure of his own communication policy, but rather by projecting the blame onto foreign communications. While in Hollywood, he accused the movie moguls of being "revolutionaries." Naturally, they were greatly surprised by this—since they were used to being called many bad names, but rarely revolutionaries. Sukarno explained that they were "unconscious revolutionaries" because, in nearly all of their films, somewhere or other there appeared a refrigerator. Indonesian moviegoers were naturally curious about these big white boxes and found out what purpose they served. They were delighted with the idea of a box that would keep foods cool and, following the consumer mentality, wanted one for themselves. Said Sukarno: "So you see that, in a hot country like mine, a refrigerator is a revolutionary symbol. In two hours any of your films can stimulate desires for more refrigerators than Indonesia can produce in 20 years."[4]

Phase 3: Military Takeover

The second phase of frustration thus led, as the Yale psychologists have never tired of telling us, to both regression and aggression. Both are highly counterproductive to development. Regression entails a great waste of scarce resources. An example is the continuous series of failed literacy campaigns that UNESCO politely calls "dysfunctional literacy."[5] In plain language, this means that people cannot read and the resources expended on bringing them literacy have been wasted.[6]

The other reaction to frustration, namely aggression, is an even more serious obstacle to development in recent LDC experience. Aggression not only wastes scarce resources but often willfully destroys them. I need hardly rehearse in detail the great eruption of aggressive action, in MDC as well as LDC, over the past decade. The aggressive reaction to frustration has been misguided because it displaces acceptable economic wants into the form of ineffectual political demands.

What people want usually must be produced by the economic sector of any society. The political sector is not itself a substantial producer of goods and services. At best, even where there is a large "public sector," government shapes production mainly by its control over the allocation of resources. However, most LDC governments have been too poor in resources to be able to exert very significant influence upon productive operations. LDC political regimes have been undermined because their economic sectors have failed to produce adequately.

What aggression, expressed in the "politics of the street," has led to is the third phase of recent LDC history, that is, military takeover. This is indeed a "regularity." As all of us are aware, most of Asia, like most of Africa and Latin America, is today under some form of military regime or martial law. A very rich literature attests to this regularity throughout LDC.[7]

Many of us decry and even despise military regimes. Yet, we need not despair. Historical experience, both East and West, indicates that military regimes are transitory. Coercion as a method of governance is inherently unstable. No coercive military regime has been able to repress the aspirations of its people over a very long period of time. Since the military are no better equipped than the politicos to boost production rapidly, they rely on repression rather than satisfaction of popular wants—on coercion rather than charisma. When the repression becomes unbearable, one military junta replaces another. As an instance, Syria had 27 such takeovers in its first decade of independence. There have been over 200 such takeovers since World War II.[8]

Eventually the population organizes and acts to get at least some of what it wants. This is the process that Gabriel Almond has referred to as "interest articulation" and "interest aggregation" (Almond and Coleman 1960). The process operates by the recognition and "articulation" of common group interests, by the cumulation and "aggregation" of these interest groups into instruments of political action, for example, a "movement" or a "party."

In recent LDC history, such political aggregations often have been organized and led by an innovative coalition of intellectuals (including journalists and students), junior officer cadres, and the new urban industrial workers (including the unemployed). In this process, communication has played an important role—a role that is certain to increase over the years ahead.[9]

Communication Technology and Future Social Change

We have seen that communication has played an important role in shaping and mis-shaping development patterns over the past quarter-century. Especially important, as illustrated by Nasser's reliance on radio for revolutionary "mobilization of the periphery," have been the mass media created by electronic technology. Dr. Schramm has put the matter in a nutshell in his earlier comments: "In the developing countries the last ten years have been the Decade of the Transistor."

Dr. Schramm further suggests that the next ten years may well become the Decade of the Satellite. Communication satellites are bound to produce a "multiplier effect" upon the world diffusion of mass media, telecommunications, and data transmission (e.g., computerized data management systems). It is therefore worthwhile to review briefly the present position with respect to communication satellites and their several "spinoff" low-cost technologies before we assess their probable increase in the next decade and project their impact upon social change around the world.

The Present Position: A Brief Review

During the past decade enormous strides were made, notably by the United States, in the development and utilization of "stationary communication satellites." These are satellites positioned 22,300 miles above the Equator. This "posture" enables them to maintain an orbital rate of speed that keeps them always beamed to the same area of the earth's surface—hence, in this sense, "stationary."

A major application of this satellite technology was undertaken by COMSAT (an acronym for Communication Satellite), which is an autonomous corporation in Washington, D. C., composed of public and private shareholders. In an effort to internationalize the American monopoly of communication satellites, COMSAT created INTELSAT (an acronym for International Telecommunications Satellite), which comprises over sixty nationalities as shareholders, both public and private, under the general management of COMSAT.

The INTELSAT system operates through three satellites "stationed" over the Pacific, Indian, and Atlantic oceans. By an ingenious system of "up-and-down" links INTELSAT makes possible a global system of electronic communication that is instantaneous, simultaneous, and continuous—the three main characteristics of any "mass media" system. INTELSAT thus created the First World Communication Network. This is a fine phrase that we have used for a long time. Even the American Delaration of Independence, two centuries ago, justified itself in terms of "a decent respect for the opinions of mankind." But it is only with INTELSAT, during the past decade, that communication technology has made the First World Communication Network into an operational reality.

A second American innovation of the past decade, with global consequences, has been the series of experimental communication satellites developed by the National Aeronautics and Space Agency (NASA). The first of these NASA products, the ATS-1 (Applications Technology Satellite), was placed in stationary orbit over Christmas Island in 1966. Used first for weather control experiments, it was authorized for other types of experiments in 1970. The first of these educational communications experiments was initiated by the University of Hawaii. This has produced the fascinating satellite complex known as PEACESAT, which links ten terminals throughout the South Pacific in a multilateral network,[10] that is, each terminal can receive and send signals to and from every other terminal in the network. The system operates in much the same way as a telephone "conference call," in which every party can speak and listen to every other party in the call.

The PEACESAT network possesses capabilities for telecommunications (telephone and telegraph), voice (radio), and data transmission (including facsimile). Last year I participated in a PEACESAT radio conference on how to educate the Micronesians to vote in their important plebiscite on self-government. I listened to the voices of people all around the South Pacific. I even engaged in a controversial exchange with another professor in Fiji. Altogether, I came away from this experience with a vivid sense of what communication satellites might do for the global diffusion of information and ideas leading to affirmative action.

This year my conviction was reinforced that PEACESAT is a communication technology that can significantly help LDC to "leapfrog" several centuries of Western development. During February and March 1975, I participated in the operation of six PEACESAT terminals, ranging as far east as Papua New Guinea and as far south as Wellington, New Zealand. The programs included a "correspondence course" of lectures on land tenure by a professor at the University of the South Pacific, which, via a "subsystem" of PEACESAT developed at Fiji, reaches ten remote Pacific islands without colleges of their own. Thanks to the "two-way" (multilateral) technology of PEACESAT, these correspondence courses could be handled as "seminars." For a professor who, over a period of thirty-five years, has found seminars more effective than lectures in "teaching," this was an impressive demonstration of the constructive use of new communication technology for LDC development.

Even more impressive, for people as well as professors, was the PEACESAT medical "conference"—which I caught at various stages in Suva, Noumea, Port Moresby, and Wellington—on the outbreak of dengue fever in various countries of the Pacific. Especially noteworthy was the message passed from the Saipan through the Wellington terminal that Tahiti (which, thanks to French intransigence, does not participate in the PEACESAT system) would like to borrow the equipment used for treating dengue fever, which was then located in Fiji. Other such satellite experiments with the ATS-1 have taken place in the past few years. The Alaskan experiment, for example, has focused on the challenging problem of rapid transmission of medical diagnosis and therapy between metropolitan centers and remote hinterlands.

The recent experiment in the Rocky Mountain states, which utilizes a sixth-generation NASA satellite (ATS-6), covers a wide range of educational activities. The effectiveness of this experiment in the American context, with its alleged "information overload," remains to be systematically evaluated. Whatever the verdict, this ATS-6 experiment on the American mainland leads us directly to a look at the prospects for satellite and related communication technologies over the years ahead.

Future Prospects: A Brief Preview

The ATS-6 developed by NASA leads directly into the next decade because this communication satellite was stationed over India in 1975 for a challenging series of educational experiments. For several years I was a consultant to the director of this Indian experiment—the late, great Dr. Vikram Sarabhai. Under his direction, unfortunately cut short by his premature death three years ago, the Indian experiment was a brilliant example of the "leapfrogging" process that communication technology makes possible. Given the constraints of India's own "acceleration of history" via its instant "mobilization of the periphery," successful leapfrogging over the long Western experience is what India needs most.

What is now scheduled to happen in India is also likely to occur in many other developing countries during the next decade. Brazil has already expressed great interest in acquiring a similar educational satellite for its own use. Every populous nation spread over a large land mass or archipelago is likely to want—and many are likely to get—such satellites. They are particularly valuable for "leapfrogging" in countries that have not yet made a large investment in the traditional modes of schooling that require costly buildings, equipment, supplies, and a large corps of highly trained professional personnel. In Southeast Asia, such countries as China, Thailand, Indonesia, and the Philippines are obvious candidates.

At the present time, American governmental activity in communication satellites appears to be decelerating. There is an ATS-7 on the drawing boards at NASA, but it is not clear when, or even whether, this latest model will be produced. However, American activity in the private sector is continuing, and some LDC countries-in-a-hurry have shown their readiness to spend their own money to acquire these "multipliers" of acceleration and mobilization. Indonesia has ordered a satellite system produced by the private conglomerate corporation owned by Howard Hughes. Iran is "shopping around," for other MDC are entering the satellite field more actively. Canada, Western Europe, the USSR, Japan, and others will doubtless be producing satellites during the next decade.

Beyond the satellites are the "spinoff" communication technologies that appear each year in ever-increasing profusion. While all MDC are deeply involved in electronic innovation, Japan probably has emerged as the most proficient producer of new communication equipment in the past decade. For example, Sony has produced a jeep-mounted, transistor-powered television receiver that can be used in the most remote villages without electrical power supply. This unit is capable of displaying live television, kinescopes, videotapes, cassettes—virtually the full range of audiovisual innovations that have become widely available in the last ten years.

This indicates that future developments will not be confined to education, important as that is. Our concern with rural development, reflected in several excellent papers at this conference, will surely be served by the Sony unit and similar innovations. There can be little doubt that the new technologies and techniques will be brought to bear upon the alleviation of rural poverty through the improvement of agricultural practices in the years ahead.

Another great area of innovation is arising through the linking of the satellite with the computer. Here in Hawaii, discussions have been going on about the creation of a "Library of the Pacific" by using the PEACESAT network in conjunction with the local ALOHA computer program or other data-management systems that have been developed elsewhere. We shall be examining such linkages in detail at a conference scheduled by the East-West Communication Institute in June 1976.

The satellite-computer linkage opens a vast field of innovation, which Simon Ramo, an active pioneer and forward thinker in this field, has called "intellectronics." Data mangement of this type can be applied to almost every sphere of activity in a society, rich or poor, and it can be used on a world-wide basis. Its effects are already becoming visible in such fields as transportation, government administration, banking and business administration, scientific research of all types. Its use will surely spread widely to include everything from hospital administration and medical care through high-rise construction and household chores. This is what we foresee in the technological developments of the next decade. What will these developments mean to us and the societies in which we live?

Retrospect and Prospect

We have seen that the communication developments of the past decade have not been an unqualified blessing. In some cases they have disrupted personal lives by creating expectations that could not be satisfied. Rising frustrations thus engendered have, in some cases, so severely imbalanced the Want:Get Ratio as to subvert political regimes and impede economic development.

We must be wary in appraising the popular impact of new technologies in the coming decade. While there is no reason for cynicism, there is every reason for informed realism—perhaps with a dash of skepticism. What this means is that we should not expect the technologies invented in the next ten years to be efficiently and equitably absorbed into our social system during the next ten years. The individual capacity to invent, in the contemporary world, always outruns the societal capacity to absorb—and the LDC capacity to absorb has proved especially erratic.[11]

There will doubtless continue to be disparities and frustrations, disequilibria and disruptions resulting from the accelerated tempo of technological innovations. However, if we keep our expectations relatively modest for the short run, and keep the longer run in perspective, then we may more reasonably be confident that the new technologies will eventually provide improvements in the quality of life. Such a perspective was revealed over the past quarter-century by the Israeli decision to postpone the installation of television for some fifteen years after the technology was readily available to the government. A similar perspective was shown in the past decade by the American decision to postpone production of supersonic transport (SST) for civil use, even though the technology was readily available. It is by such decisions that we are likely to bring rational policies to bear upon the heedless pace of technological innovation.

A similar perspective is greatly needed in LDC if they are to cope with the excessive "acceleration of history" and "mobilization of the periphery" into which they have already been thrust. Professor Harry Oshima's argument for a labor-intensive strategy is a good example of such a policy perspective. It would slow down the rural exodus and thereby help to contain the spreading unemployment and poverty in the urban areas. A focus on rural development would increase employment in agriculture and agroindustry, with the result that sorely needed food supplies in poor and populous countries would be raised. The general deceleration of technological change thus effected would greatly enhance social stability in the beleaguered LDC, and their capacities to absorb long-time innovations into durable institutions would gradually be improved.

Such thinking is needed to shape LDC communication policy as well. In recent years, communication scholars have begun to speak of "the end of the technological imperative." As one surveys the current mood expressed in journals and conferences, there appears to be a wide consensus that new communication technologies should be the servant, not the master, of communication policy. Clearly, LDC policy will seek to achieve "dynamic equilibrium"—economic growth and human betterment within a framework of societal stability. But the quest of every national policy, LDC or MDC, must in our time operate in a global context. We are, willy-nilly, becoming one world.

The great question, for the decade ahead, is whether the new world communication network will contribute significantly to world peace and cooperation. Here again, a realistic perspective will be tinged with some skepticism. We began to talk of a world communication network centuries before it came into being. Just so, we have been talking about world cooperation for decades without moving at all adequately toward it in our actual political life. Ten years ago Marshall McLuhan talked blithely about the "global village," but we know that it has not yet come into existence. Nor is it likely to do so over the next decade.

Consider the issue of direct satellite broadcasting. It was on this very issue that the United States was handed its most stunning defeat at both the United Nations and UNESCO. It is not appropriate here to discuss the pros and cons of the American position on this matter (although I will confess that I found more demerits than merits in its position). The relevant point here is that 101 nations lined up against the United States to express their distrust—and even their fear—of direct satellite broadcasting by any power with the technological capability of doing it. When anxiety is so widespread, it will take much more than technology to make world communication shape world cooperation. The "much more" that is needed must be produced by scholars as well as by those who make and operate public policy in our countries and regions.

Although we all have much to be modest about, there have been important "success stories" throughout LDC over the last ten years. Some of these are recounted in this book. In shaping the next ten years, communication specialists have a particularly important role in improving our societal capacity to absorb the new technologies. Let us hope that we shall play this role well.

NOTES

1. This is dated from 1830 in P. M. Sandeman, et al., *Media* (Englewood Cliffs, N.J.: Prentice-Hall, 1972), p. 39.
2. Herbert Gans, *The Urban Villagers* (New York: Free Press, 1965); this book laments the final disappearance of this phenomenon in America, which coincided with its spread through LDC.
3. Leo C. Lowenthal has used these terms to illustrate the importance of popular culture for development theory, a field ably represented in this book by Professors Kato and Yu.
4. Cited in Marshall McLuhan, *The Medium Is the Massage* (New York: Random House, 1967). Recall Kato's report on the Japanese audiences of American movies in the early 1950s who paid more attention to the dishwashers than to Frank Sinatra.
5. Compare S. C. Dube's reference to "functional deafness" (chap. 6).
6. Data ranging from "failed literacy campaigns" to "surplus college graduates" have been given in Lerner's publications since 1964.
7. See, for example, Leon Richards, "The Military and Trade Unions as Initiators of Political Stability and Instability in a Selected Number of West African Polities," Ph. D. dissertation, University of Hawaii, May 1974.
8. Data produced in Lerner's M.I.T. postgraduate seminar on "Research in International Communication."
9. See the three volumes produced by the joint CENIS-CENDES (USA-Venezuela) project, edited by Frank Bonilla and J.A. Silva-Michelena, and published by the M.I.T. Press (Cambridge, Mass.) in 1974.

10. The PEACESAT terminals are located at: University of Hawaii, Honolulu; Maui Community College, Hawaii; Hilo College, Hawaii; Office of the High Commissioner, Saipan; University of Technology, Lae, Papua New Guinea; National Broadcasting Commission, Port Moresby, Papua New Guinea; Department of Education, Pago Pago, American Samoa; Wellington Polytechnic, New Zealand; South Pacific Commission Headquarters, Noumea, New Caledonia; University of Guam, Guam.

11. This was foreseen two decades ago in M.F. Millikan and W.W. Rostow, *A Proposal* (New York: Harper and Row, 1957).

17. The Future of World Politics and Society

HAROLD D. LASSWELL

Introduction

The scope of this presentation is to outline alternative futures of world politics and society with special reference to the policies and processes of development. Separate treatment is given to economic changes elsewhere in this volume. However, some indication is provided here of the projected links among changes of all kinds.

Projections of the future are less relevant to prophecy than to innovation. In Martin Shubik's phrase, when the predicted future is undesirable, the policy analyst who makes the greatest contribution presents a "self-frustrating," not a "self-fulfilling," prophecy. We think in the present of the future as a means of acting now on behalf of a more desirable then. Alternative constructs are in varying degree "probable" and "preferable."

Preferred Goals: Quality of Life

If we were to complete a policy analysis of world politics it would be necessary to perform all the five intellectual tasks inseparable from problem-solving (namely, the clarification of goals; the description of trends; the analysis of conditions; the projection of developments; the invention, evaluation, and selection of policy alternatives).[1] Since our aim is more modest —limited to projections—we give minimum consideration to the other tasks. It is essential, however, to be explicit about our goals.

The authorized spokesmen of the world community have provisionally formulated a preferred world situation. The Universal Declaration of Human

Rights is a commitment to a quality of life in which individual human beings are progressively enabled to realize a fuller and more equitable existence. For example (Lasswell 1971:42–43):

Power. The declaration asserts the right "to take part in the government," "to be recognized as a person before the law," and the right "to effective remedy by competent national tribunals." Criteria of fair trial are enumerated together with a right of asylum. There is a right to "a social and international order."

Enlightenment. There is "freedom of opinion and expression" and a right "to seek, receive, and impart information and ideas through any media and regardless of frontiers."

Wealth. Recognition is given to the "right to own property" and to a "standard of living adequate for the well-being" of the individual and his family.

Well-being. The declaration recognizes the right to "life, liberty, and security of person" and condemns "torture" as well as "cruel" or "inhuman" treatment or punishment. There is a "right to rest and leisure" and a general right to "social security."

Skill. Recognized is the "right to work, to free choice of employment," and "to protection against unemployment." Also "everyone has a right to education" and "to participate freely in the cultural life of the community, to enjoy the arts and to share in scientific achievement and its benefits."

Affection. The declaration specifies the "right to marry and to found a family" and to engage in congenial association with others ("peaceful assembly and association"). And there is the right to be identified with a national community ("right to nationality").

Respect. The first article affirms that "all human beings are born free and equal in dignity and right. . . . Everyone is entitled to all rights and freedoms . . . without distinction of any kind." Obviously, there must be no "slavery or servitude," no arbitrary interference with "privacy, family, home, or correspondence," and freedom from attacks on "honor and reputation."

Rectitude affirms "freedom of thought, conscience, and religion. . . . Everyone has duties to the community," and there is no right to destroy the freedom of others.

Note that we distinguish between "values" ("preferred events") and the particular practices that comprise "institutions" specialized to the shaping and sharing of the values. Human cultures differ in the priorities assigned to values. They diverge to a much greater extent in institutional detail.

It is also worth noting that part of the Universal Declaration is intended to foster self-determination by individuals and groups. Self-determination includes a voice in the mutual accommodation of conflicting claims.

Our concern is with the development policies of the world community as a whole and of its component parts. The Universal Declaration indicates that the most comprehensive conception perceives development as movement toward a more perfect realization of human dignity. It is implied that policies are timed to realize a more satisfactory level of equal opportunity.

In an important sense, development policies are always "catch up policies." In the 1950s, development was intended to overcome opportunity lag on the part of countries that lacked a science-based technology. With more experience the conception of development has been broadened in two directions. It is coming to include the underdeveloped rural and urban areas of industrial economies, and the pursuit of a more differentiated social structure than the "standard" image of the "West."

The present outline utilizes the conceptual map of social process that some of us have evolved and extensively applied (Lasswell 1971:19). In general terms a social process is characterized by interactions among "participants" who are striving to optimalize "values" ("preferred outcomes") through "institutions" using "resources." The discussion begins with the "power" value and the institutions of government, law, and politics. As indicated above, we do not expand on "wealth" and "economic institutions." Our sequence does include "enlightenment," "well-being," "skill," "affection," "respect," and "rectitude," together with the relevant institutions.

Trends and Projections

As matters stand today we live in a divided, militant, and conflictual arena of world politics. A fundamental feature is the expectation of violence, the expectation that whether we like it or not many international controversies will lead to war, and many internal conflicts will precipitate revolutionary violence. The United Nations and other institutions of intergovernmental action are not able to elicit the support necessary to maintain a low level of violence or threat of violence in global affairs. When we examine the degree of equality among or within nations it is evident that opportunities for the control or the enjoyment of values are unequal.

Assuming that mankind will not destroy itself in the next generation or so, the future will be characterized by increasing interdependence. Even if travel, trade, and investment cease to expand at a rapid rate, it will be necessary for all participants in the world arena to take one another into account in forming and executing public or private policies. Symbolic interdependence, at least, does not diminish, even among garrison states.

Imagine a desirable construct of future developments. It would show the United States, the Soviet Union, China, and other powers evolving a structure of world public order in which coercive violence is at a minimum and institutions of government and law are strong. Furthermore, in every sector of the world community the direction of change would be toward balanced development and wide sharing of value outcomes. Balanced development implies sharing of science-based technology and scientific creativity at centers beyond the borders of the United States, Europe, and Japan. Widespread sharing means that besides wealth and power, all values are involved: enlightenment (knowledge), well-being (safety, health, comfort), skill (opportunity to cultivate occupational, professional, or artistic capabilities), affection (opportunities for love and loyalty), respect (freedom from discrimination), rectitude (opportunity to effect and apply norms of responsible conduct).

Imagine a counter-construct to the projected movement toward a preferred world. A divided, militant, and conflictual structure of world politics would continue save as it is mitigated by an effective integration of oligarchical elites who join forces to suppress the value demands of the less advantaged layers of society.

These alternative futures are presented for assessment and for the choice of policies intended to forestall or to accelerate eventual outcomes.

Institutions of Government, Law, and Politics (The Power Value)

A brief characterization of the power process is that power is the making of important decisions. Decision outcomes are the giving and receiving of support. The principal question about the future of decision is whether support will be directed toward or away from institutions of government, law, and politics, whose role is to reduce the expectation of violence while sustaining progress toward the preferred quality of life. Consider these constructs:

(1) It is unlikely that the basic expectation of violence will be diminished or that the divided and militant structure of a divided world will be superseded.

(2) The internal structure of power sharing or concentration will oscillate between oligarchy and more general participation; the expectation of violence will favor the spread of the oligarchical model in an incompletely integrated fusion of elites.

The United States did not attempt to "conquer" the world at the end of World War II despite the formidable military position that it enjoyed. The Marshall Plan fostered the recovery of Europe, which, it was hoped, would reduce the chances that misery would enable Moscow to "export communism" and enlarge its political domain. The Soviet Union sought to overcome its fear of eventual encirclement and strangulation by the capitalist states by the use of forced saving, industrial development, and a garrison-police strategy of internal management. By the 1950s the United States was concerned with economic assistance to underdeveloped countries outside Europe.

As the anticolonial revolution gained strength, successor states multiplied in place of empires—British, French, Belgian, and so on. Typically the first regimes were headed by figures whose charismatic aura was earned as specialized agitators, negotiators, party organizers, managers of underground violence. They marshalled the latent aspirations of the community for national identity, self-determination, and industrialization.

As Daniel Lerner has pointed out, the "revolutions of rising expectations" were superseded by "revolutions of rising frustrations." With disenchantment we have witnessed a succession of military, bureaucratic, and "one-party" or "no-party" systems of authority and control. Many of these have proved and will continue to prove inefficient, oppressive, and corrupt. The resulting changes, regardless of the ideological symbols in the name of which power will be exercised, typically substitute one unstable coalition for another (Lasswell and Lerner 1965).

During the next twenty years, political ideologies ("myths") can be expected to reflect the movement toward partial incorporation and restriction of the dominant symbol clusters of world politics. The past and future of the world political arena may be fruitfully conceived as a sequence of revolutionary movements that emerge in world eruptive centers and diffuse universality. They are, however, immediately restricted by the residual strength of established orders, and eventually by the gathering strength of new initiatives. The French Revolution (1789) spoke the language of "liberty, equality, fraternity," and championed the institutions of democracy versus aristocracy and monarchy. The world revolutionary vision of Paris was presently restricted to the service of the rising middle classes. In consequence of cumulative discontent, the Russian Revolution of 1917 spoke in the name of the proletariat against the capitalist class, thereby emphasizing the language of economics while partially incorporating the previous rhetoric of law and ethics. The social and political beneficaries of the new revolutionary wave were the administrative and technical classes of "socialist" or "communist" states.

The next revolutionary development of world significance (Nazism, 1933–1945) partially incorporated the economic symbols of "socialism" and the politico-legal ethics of "freedom," while elevating to prominence the symbolism of "race." Since in popular biology, "race" is identified with skin color, the appeal of any particular symbol is restricted to "black," "white," or "brown." Revivals of "religious" doctrines in competition with secular ideologies suffer from a corresponding disadvantage. The chances are that "radical" and "religious" myths will be invoked in many anticolonial countries to check the power of elite elements who work closely with foreign secular forces.

After the mid-1960s, a slow attrition of trust has been occurring in non-socialist states where multinational corporations were perfecting their strategies of operation. Contrary to the assumption that the developmental practices of the 1950s and 1960s were contributing to the emergence of stable, prosperous, and progressively democratic nation-states, many new and renewed states appeared to be unstable and nondemocratic, and to contain large population strata who were jobless and miserable.

The most challenging scientific and political interpretation of these trends is that they make manifest a structural characteristic of a large part, if not all, of world political economy. The reference is to an allegedly automatic slowdown and restriction of economic development. The middle-income skill groups, composed of white collar clerks, office help, technicians, subexecutive and professional groups, do not necessarily absorb the traditional shopkeepers, artisans, and farm workers; and local investors do not necessarily finance local enterprises.

Socialist states are not, and will not be, exempt from the tensions generated between center and periphery. Regions with tribal or national identities will continue to reassert themselves in various ways against the control of Moscow. The "national communism" of Yugoslavia was the precursor of parallel tendencies elsewhere. The most dramatic instance to date has, of course, been the reassertion of Chinese self-determination. On a more restrained scale are the policies of Eastern Europe (notably) those of East Germany, Poland, Czechoslovakia, Hungary, and Rumania).

The political instability of the next ten or twenty years will be nourished by the contrasts in timing that will characterize changes in political, economic, and social structure, including ideological myths and varying sentiments of identity. Elites that try to cut themselves off from foreign support will be endangered by the external balancing of power among socialist/nonsocialist states, and by the tendency of dissatisfied elements to form coalitions with outside forces. We have witnessed territorial splits (North and South Korea, North and South Vietnam, and in numerous African areas). It is not to be assumed that civil conflict will eventually terminate in reunion as happened in Cuba. When the principal divisions are in urban areas, as in Northern Ireland, Singapore, Buenos Aires, the techniques of violence (pro- or anti-regime) are adapted to the city environment.

Given changing levels of instability and in the size and equipment of modern armies, it is to be expected that paramilitary, small group, and individual acts of violence will multiply. The knowledge necessary to put together instruments of destruction will become commonplace. It is almost impossible to put an end to terror so long as elements in the population give aid and comfort to the perpetrators; and we have alluded to successive sources of tension in a world of "uneven development" (to revive Trotsky's famous phrase).

Terroristic acts provide provocation to counter violence and intimidation by established regimes, and to transform democratic into oligarchical structures of government. A sense of common "peril from below" drives regimes to work together, and to reduce the likelihood of major war among them. It is not unreasonable to anticipate that the perception of common interest will enable the principal powers to succeed in limiting the supply of available weapons (particularly nuclear), and evolve commitments that arouse confidence in their enforcibility.

It is pertinent to ask whether the rising tide of paramilitary acts will generate such fear and revulsion that a universal police force, presumably under U.N. auspices, will be provided with the moral and material support necessary to strengthen the instruments of public order. If such innovations are to be effective, the elite and mid-elite elements in the population of the globe must be willing to see a substantial transfer of the control of land and other assets to the rural and urban poor. In the light of past experience, massive transformations cannot be counted upon with much confidence.

(3) Within the framework of continuing instability, the structures specialized to the various functions of decision will continue to differentiate.

Our model of decision process includes seven categories of functions: intelligence, promotion, prescription, invocation, application, termination, appraisal. Though partly specialized in differentiated structures, these functions are always partially involved in every structure. It should be remembered that every policy process, private or public, exhibits a parallel differentiation of structure and function.

Intelligence. The intelligence function includes the gathering, processing, and dissemination of the information needed by participants in decision. Development decisions involve planning, and typically evolve specific commissions for the purpose. Information is required to assist the performance of the five intellectual tasks involved in all problem solving: goals, trends, conditions, projections, alternatives. The huge amount of detail generated in societies with a science-based technology can now be partially mastered with the aid of computers. Machines cannot, of course, choose the indicators or set the goals of a planning process. Among the indicators of a developing country are the multiplication of statisticians and computers. It is safe to forecast that this relationship will continue.

In coming years of insecurity, all established regimes will continue to rely on intelligence services to provide surveillance of the population. For this branch of the intelligence function, modern technology is devising sophisticated paraphernalia (e.g., telephone taps, radio-TV installations, pinhead microphones, ultra-red photography). Surveillance strengthens control by central authority over actual and potential opposition.

If official regimentation is to be at least partially prevented, it will be necessary for interest groups to use their influence to obtain and to retain enough access to information—official and private—to cultivate realistic policy programs and to direct informed criticism against official policies. As modern technology is adopted in a body politic, the division of labor is complicated by the emergence of new technical and managerial tasks, and new commodities and services. Interest groups come into being to fill the gap between central decision structures and the new component elements in society.

Not all national governments are able to command the information or to mobilize the power required to regulate foreign governments or foreign private activities that penetrate their borders. This is the well-known plight of colonies and of neocolonial governments. It is also the predicament in which the government of the United States, and of other industrial powers, find themselves in relation to multinational corporations. Recently they are becoming aware of how their access is frustrated to the basic information required for taxing and regulatory purposes. Not only are factories shifted from one country to another, but transfer of assets within the transnational corporate network destroys the significance of traditional import-export records. We learn of separate bookkeeping arrangements for each tax authority, as well as for the stockholders and for genuine planning. Accountants have demonstrated their skill in obfuscation for the benefit of clients. In coming years the tug of war will continue between public and "private" government, and a major battleground will be the intelligence activities.

Promotion. The promotional function is the mobilizing of support for or against the goals, objectives, and strategies of public policy. In the nineteenth century, the countries with a large-scale popular base developed the two-party and multiple party systems, which engaged in promotional operations at every level of jurisdiction. The Soviet, Fascist, and Nazi challenges to liberal regimes relied on the "one-party" (or, more properly, the "single political order") system. In India and in some other ex-colonial powers that were indoctrinated with the party system, the struggle will continue to guide promotional activities toward action rather than checkmate. Successive waves of insecurity and of institutional change are to be expected before the variable passions of the many will be modified into a steadier stream of influence. The "overpromises" of early development will be succeeded by reluctant and intermittent realism.

Prescription. The prescribing or legislating function articulates official norms and sanctions. By no means are all prescriptions published in the form of statutes, treaties, regulations, proclamations, and the like. Laws are often accepted and applied in traditional fashion without benefit of other than an oral text. Even where legislatures and assemblies exercise little authority, they have educational consequences for public knowledge of the common interest.

Probably there will be a varied record of institutional change as developing countries seek stability by obtaining more public understanding and support. Small executive councils will expand by the use of traditional assemblies, conventions, or legislatures. Any executive authority that feels rebuffed will be tempted to stop the process of enlargement and revert to a more peremptory system. Many African states will cope erratically with newer problems, since the social fabric includes active tribal differences.

Invocation. The provisional characterization of a concrete set of circumstances in terms of a prescription is invocation. The initial phase of administration is to explore how and when a statute, or any other prescription, is to be put into effect. It includes the establishment of structures and the allocation of resources. Invocation also includes complaints, since a complaint characterizes a concrete situation as violating an established policy. The recent spread of the ombudsman role has demonstrated a wide latent demand for such a functionary, and the probability is that demands in the name of human rights will be coupled with demands for a responsive official of this kind.

Many traditional societies have complaint procedures embedded in the system of obligations that tie authority to kinsman or tribesman. The transfer of the function to an ombudsman may be smooth.

Application. The postinitiation phases of an act that conforms to a prescription are applications. If arrest, indictment, and trial are examples of invocation, appeals acted on by a higher court are application. If obtaining the funds and personnel for a bridge are part of the initiation phase, the building and operation of the bridge are application.

Most of the administrative activities of a government are applications. In former colonial countries where local persons have been incorporated into the middle and upper ranks of the public service, a typical problem is the tension between career officials and political leaders who prefer more amenable personnel. Transition problems arise where traditional practices that may not have been perceived as corrupt are stigmatized as corruption. These difficulties occur in a body politic that attempts to install impersonal norms of conduct and to supersede obligations to protect and enrich the family, or to appoint and promote on the basis of merit (not according to tribal or religious affiliation).

The image of central government in colonial powers and in revived monarchies or empires has been largely negative. They are presented as rapacious for taxes and soldiers, and as indifferent to the weak. A continuing source of instability is the resentment against the "system" that is bred in the weaker levels of the body politic. Transition governments frequently fuse the negative features of old and new.

Termination. Termination is the cancellation of a prescription and the arrangement of compensation, if any, for legitimate expectations established during the life of a prescription. Social change almost invariably implies that some established rights are terminated. Peaceable acceptance of a new order may be accelerated if, for instance, expropriated land is compensated. But the terms of compensation are crucial. Compensation may be too heavy for the body politic to meet without tying its hands; or terms may be so nominal that they confirm grievances and generate disloyalty to the public order. Many countries will expropriate land and private enterprises in the immediate future as they have in the past. It is safe to foretell that successive waves of insecurity will accompany all but the most adroit and fortunate policies of termination.

Appraisal. Appraisal summarizes policy operations in terms of effectiveness and efficiency, and identifies the factors that account for success or failure. Planning looks ahead. By contrast appraisal looks to the recent or more remote past, even though the results exert an immediate impact on the regime.

The most spectacular acts of appraisal are the investigations conducted by a new set of leaders to stigmatize their predecessors. Often these exercises are so biased or incompetent that it is inappropriate to regard them as appraisals. Rather, they are part of promotional campaigns designed to consolidate support for the new regime.

Insofar as public policy is realistic it relies on appraisal to provide the facts for judging past and present policies. Unless the leadership is willing to encourage competent and candid appraisal (financial, legal, and so on), public policy will proceed blindly, and depend to a disproportionate degree on intimidation and favoritism.

Professionally, competent appraisal depends on opportunities to utilize the analytic skills of the political, social, legal, medical, and engineering disciplines. Probably there will be continuing expansion of nationally based schools, and gradual upgrading of the professional level of governmental and private operations.

Note particularly the potential role of nongovernmental scholars and scientists. If universities can achieve de facto independence of gross political pressure, they may be able to supplement the rhetoric adulation or protest by informative studies of government and society. At first these will be limited to technical matters. The competence, comprehensiveness, and openness with which appraisal functions are conducted by officials and unofficial agencies is an indicator of the self-confidence and capability of the body politic.

Institutions of Inquiry, Research, and Dissemination (Enlightenment Value)

The references to intelligence and appraisal in connection with the power process indicated how knowledge is drawn upon and affected by political purposes. The present discussion adopts a related but separable frame of reference for the examination of a changing society. The outcome at the focus of interest is, not the giving and receiving of support in the political process, but the giving and receiving of knowledge.

It is true that knowledge is used for many purposes besides the advancement of knowledge itself. But it is important to recognize that in a complex world the pursuit of scientific and technical knowledge generates distinctive institutions and careers that focus on knowledge as a principal value. Up to the present, the centers of "Western" civilization have monopolized the cultivation of astronomy, physics, chemistry, biology, and the social sciences. It is notorious that developing countries rarely participate in the growth of fundamental science. A question for the next decade or so is whether new subcenters of top creativity will emerge. No one item—computer banks, laboratories, libraries, observatories—is enough to initate or sustain a center that contributes to world enlightenment in the sciences. Existing centers will probably continue to dominate.

Exceptions may occur if oil rich elites decide to pour vast sums into capitalizing great university and research facilities, and provide a total community setting after the model of cities specialized to advanced military technology elsewhere in the world (the Soviet Union and the United States, for example).

High quality specialists can be induced to stay in scientifically underdeveloped countries if they are provided with regular opportunities to study and conduct research at major centers. The world university movement is taking many forms (the U.N. University in Japan is the most recent). Some scientists are already accustomed to visit certain laboratories in Europe for a few weeks every year for the purpose of maintaining professional visibility and prowess. Traveling seminars will become more frequent and world interuniversity networks will reduce the isolation of investigators.

It is also possible to extend joint projects that bring local knowledge and locally based specialists into regular communication with each other. Despite continuing instability it may be feasible, subject to interruption, to extend the network of cooperating scholars who are interested in following world trends in every area—linguistics, child development, basic health care, and so forth. These reports will include analyses of how programs of "intervention" have affected change in predisposing circumstances.

The future of worldwide development depends on whether science and technology are able to meet the energy requirements of mankind. It is generally agreed that fossil fuel reserves will be rapidly located and exploited in the next few years, notably from the continental shelves off Scotland, Alaska, Southeast Asia, Antarctica, and California.

In most of the Western world the only alternative that is likely to produce substantial amounts of energy in the near future is nuclear fission. Safe storage of nuclear waste has not been satisfactorily solved, and the assignment of a great priority to resolving this matter is probable.

Fossil fuel will eventually be exhausted. Moreover, its use generates abundant waste. Within the next twenty years it is probable that rapid steps will be taken toward tapping clean, universal, and inexhaustible sources of energy. Geothermal, solar, bioconversion, hydrogen, and nuclear fusion energy resources are promising options. Nuclear fusion is an unlimited source of energy dependent on the control of nuclear fusion reaction in light atoms, which is the source of energy of our sun. Several decades are probably necessary to solve the technical problems involved. Hydrogen has suddenly become a feasible energy source and promises to produce revolutionary results in from ten to twenty years.[2]

Scientific discovery and reporting are at one end of the continuum of patterns constituting enlightenment. The gathering, processing, and transmission of news is at the other. In coming years the conflict between interests favoring and opposing media freedom will fluctuate continually. Technology has already put satellites in the skies and cheap transistors in our hands, and we can expect personal equipment to become smaller and cheaper. There are, of course, well-known techniques by which a territorial elite can protect its population from access to unwelcome news. The simplest is jamming. But jamming is perpetually provocative of efforts to discover why the elite is so worried. More effective is defense by distraction, trivialization, and overabundance. The focus of attention is overwhelmed with music and culture (classical, popular), and with news and commentary that dilutes and parochializes.

Specialists recognize that communication technology is almost at a stage where it can be used, if desired, to popularize any findings, no matter how complex, at the focus of attention of all elite, mid-elite, and rank-and-file members of any territorial or functional group. What is implied is a synthesis of skills among those whose specialities include the arousal of interest, the gathering and analysis of realistic information, and the managing of equipment. During the next years we will witness a continuing struggle—with successive successes and failures—waged by public interest specialists to reach the focus of world attention with a shared image of reality equivalent to the common map communicated as the myth in primitive societies. There will be continuing tension with both the parochial interest of local elites and the parochial tradition of local population.

Representative of the devices that will be used to organize an enlightened response among large and small groups are the "social planetarium" and "decision seminars." The planetarium device was evolved in the last century as a means of popularizing astronomy. Audiovisual presentations depict alternative versions of past trends and conditions, and outline possible versions of the future. The scale can be as small as classrooms or as large as the consolidated museums or zoological and botanical gardens of a city or a region. Initiatives may be taken by schools, libraries, museums, civic associations, or governments. The plan may also be to elicit participation on the part of both experts and amateurs, old and young. (A step toward community planning and participation was taken by the Governor's Conference on the Year 2000, sponsored by the State of Hawaii. See chap. 19a.)

Institutions of Wealth (Wealth Value)

See the paper by Oshima, chapter 2.

Institutions of Safety, Health, and Comfort (Well-being Value)

Population estimates for the next twenty years usually assume that direct or indirect measures of control will have modest results. Under favorable circumstances of economic growth, population might arrive at the replacement rate by the end of the century. It is believed to be almost unavoidable that the total population will expand to between 6.5 billion and 8.5 billion in the next seventy-five years, with nearly all the growth in the underdeveloped countries.

These figures project a model of change in the food supply, postulating that institutions will be perfected to anticipate and cut off local shortages, and to readjust supplies, by such substitutions as soybeans and fish as protein sources (accompanied by declining grain and beef crops).

Political insecurity will continue to sacrifice lives in civil conflict and war; and from time to time great losses of life are to be expected in accidents generated by modern technology (e.g., nuclear radiation, stray nuclear bombs, etc.). Accidents may occur with sufficient frequency to stimulate promotional activities designed to improve the regulatory procedures of governments at every level.

Medical technique will continue to proliferate in every field. Increased life expectancy, deferred aging, and limited rejuvenation are probable. Drugs with no adverse side effects will be devised, but drugs will continue to be dangerous unless we can overcome the alienation that often accompanies modernization and development. Appetite and weight control will be more certain. Technical means will be improved of coping with the neurochemical factors in mental illness, including senility. Limited "hibernation" will be available for deep relaxation. Transplantation will be widely extended, and genetic knowledge will make it possible to supervise conception and development.

Although the level of medical care will rise throughout the developing world, the elite elements (families included) will continue to have access to the top facilities, including those at the principal world centers.

Institutions for Education, Standard-Setting, and Expression in Occupations, Professions, and the Arts (Skill Value)

Policies of "selective development" will become more frequent in developing countries (Oshima, in Lerner and Schramm 1972). The term refers to policies that moderate the timing of different components of change in order to avoid large-scale displacement of rural population to urban slums, and to encourage the integration (rather than the abandonment) of traditional ways of life and modes of artistic expression with the universalizing culture pioneered by earlier industrial countries (Lerner, Montgomery, and Lasswell, forthcoming).

Selective development directly influences the timing of opportunities provided for the acquisition and exercise of skills appropriate to change technology. Older skills and relationships are left relatively undisturbed until investments are made in village clusters, while building an infrastructure for further growth (i.e., in the areas of transportation, irrigation, communication, energy sources, schools). Selective development does not imply that heavy industry is permanently excluded from national or regional plans. The aim is to minimalize the costs of large-scale cultural change.

Selective development will continue to evolve as a result of disappointing experiences with early programs. "Universities" were sometimes multiplied in helter-skelter fashion. The principal consequence of this action was widespread disenchantment resulting from illusory expectations that on graduation a suitable opportunity would be available for the exercise of novel skills (Lerner 1964).

Whether the interpretation is true or false, the Chinese revolution is widely believed to provide an ideology and a program for the use of education as an instrument of public policy rather than as a tool of individual ambition. Intermediate students are expected to carry literacy and record-keeping skills to the countryside. Advanced students are responsible for adapting their medical, engineering, biological, or other skills to the needs of the local community. Periods of participation in the countryside at different stages of a career are expected to mitigate tendencies toward bureaucratic rigidity and isolation. Regular occasions for communication—including explanation and criticism—are supposed to keep the administrators modest and honest.

With these currents loose in the world, it is likely that the comfort-serving tendencies of the skilled—who feel that they have made some sacrifice of immediate pleasure to acquire skill—will be subject to more frequent challenge than in the past.

Institutions of Family, Friendship, and Loyalty (Affection Value)

Policies of selective development will probably retard change in such potent institutions as family and tribe, and modify the consolidation of national and world identity. To an important extent the "family is the enemy of the state," meaning that the interests of an institution specialized to power are often in flagrant conflict with family claims (notably the claims for military service and taxes). Once crystallized around an ideological core, an established system of family organization is self-perpetuating. The division of labor in a society that adopts modern technology is highly individualized, since women as well as men receive independent income. If the state also provides social security, one of the principal value expectations that maintains the family is undermined. Extended families tend to break into nuclear units, and new patterns of cooperation and cohabitation emerge. These tendencies, though slowed, will doubtless continue.

Institutions of Social Recognition and Discrimination (Respect Value)

Social change in which disrespected races, tribes, or classes improve their position will be accompanied by the usual demand to humiliate the traditional humiliator. The Nazi measures against Jews, gypsies, and other stigmatized targets constitute a relatively full list of the policies to be anticipated.

Another demand—which is closely linked with the one mentioned—is the thirst for ego inflation. In new nations great stress is typically laid on emblems of the collective self and on ceremonies that exalt the past, present, and future. The national myth is elaborated. Parallel phenomena are exhibited by upwardly mobile families or groups of any kind. Acute sensitivity characterizes the dealings of the *parvenu* with others, and it is to be anticipated that many "trivial" incidents will be exaggerated in an effort to overcome lingering sentiments of inferiority.

Selective development is a policy orientation that will be easier to pursue in the future than in the 1950s and 1960s, when national self-esteem was so often perceived as dependent on achieving a carbon copy of the "West." Selective development will be made acceptable, where it is adopted, as a demonstration of national greatness. The timing of investment in ways that forestall disorganization will often be integrated with art programs designed to integrate new and old designs, materials, and procedures. Networks of exhibits and awards will contribute to the process.

The public order of developing as well as relatively developed countries will remain unstable in the degree that a satisfactory place is not found for every individual member of the body politic. To be jobless or to be engaged in a meaningless task is to suffer a more acute deprivation than loss of income. The individual person is rejected by a society that has no place for him. This is the supreme disrespect that a social environment can impose. In preindustrial societies, the network of family and tribal activities and obligations typically provided a role for everyone. When industrial development is managed in such a way that it isolates the individual from a sustaining environment, the cumulative indignation of the rejected produces "the respect revolutions" that seize on symbols of religion, race, economics, law, or what not to justify drastic change. The social transformations of coming years will witness successive waves of change until more enduring respect relationships are stabilized.

Scientific technology can be expected to continue to devise "gadgets" that can be used to confer distinction on individuals. The "robot slave" is not far away, and individual flying platforms will combine ego-gratification with transportation. Communication equipment will be micromodeled until every person is a mobile sending and receiving station. Skin color can be changed and other cosmetological changes afford means of reducing some unwanted differences among human beings.

More pertinent to the self-respect of human beings are improvements that can be made in their potentialities. Genetic knowledge constitutes the sharpest challenge to the demand to respect equality of opportunity. It is to be assumed that elites will seek to consolidate their respect and power positions by using knowledge to perpetuate inequality.

Institutions Specialized to the Norms of Responsible Conduct (Rectitude Value)

The countries in control of the most advanced chemical and biological knowledge will face the most acute problems of defining and applying norms of responsible conduct. For analytic purposes, responsible conduct is understood as the clarification and application of norms defining the role of the community toward all members of the human species. For the purposes of the present inquiry we have postulated the conception of human dignity as a word norm.

Technology is already sufficiently advanced to pose the question of limits, if any, on chemical control of character. We are already facing the problems connected with "lie detection" and the use of medical examinations to determine the political reliability of an officer, an official, or indeed any citizen. Paradoxically, a key issue can be whether these methods should be used on behalf of freedom, seeking to determine whether the candidate for office or an official is privately committed to the use of such methods for partisan purposes.

The new wave of antiscientific sentiment in countries of advanced technology is clearing the way for waves of mysticism and religion. Efforts to overcome a sense of alienation are producing "communal" experiments intended to provide a setting where a "new morality" can flourish. Countries that have only recently modified their traditional cultures will evolve leaders who seek to revive the older systems of faith and to counteract the unsettling effects of change. A major question will be whether moral and religious leaders fuse with political elites on behalf of oligarchy or democracy.

We do not overlook the place that space exploration can play in the pursuit of an all-inclusive conception of man's past and future. It is not to be forgotten that artificial and moon satellites are more than knowledge platforms. They may be precursors of extended habitats for a species that finds it more congenial to grow than to achieve population zero. The morals of growth are typically justified in the name of transempirical imperatives. An ideological struggle will continue between those who want parochial results now and those who identify themselves with the universalizing potential of man.

The tension may, of course, be resolved by self-induced disaster at any moment.

NOTES

1. The five tasks are successfully used to organize the volume by Garry D. Brewer and Ronald D. Brunner, eds., *Political Development and Change: A Policy Approach* (New York: The Free Press, 1975). Note especially the literature on "Projection" and the critical analysis of specific contributions in part 4.

2. For concise discussions of science and policy, see: *Public Policy toward Environment 1973: A Review and Appraisal,* Annals of the New York Academy of Sciences 216 (1973), and a pamphlet, "Environment and Society in Transition: World Priorities," World Academy of Art and Science (Suite 1009, 50 Rockefeller Plaza, New York, New York, 10020).

18. Information Technology and Resources for Growth

SIMON RAMO

The world between now and the end of the century will have its fill of technology and resource issues—problems, opportunities, developments, breakthroughs, controversies. Some of the problems will include a growing gap between developed and underdeveloped nations in per capita consumption of critical materials that are even now in increasingly short supply, growing pollution, and failure to adjust social systems to rapid technological change. Alongside these negatives, there are the positive potentials of vastly improved communication and transportation, plentiful energy made available by nuclear techniques, and abundant freshwater obtained by de-salting the seas, weather control, new means for tapping the earth's hidden resources, superior birth control techniques, and even, perhaps, control of aging.

The pessimists are convinced civilization is doomed already by the rate at which we consume the earth's limited resources and the attendant impact on the environment. The optimists are picturing a fantastically better world that future technological developments will bring us. But neither projection necessarily leads us to useful anticipations. In this conference we are interested in prediction presumably in order to prepare for change, to anticipate and plan for the inevitable, to recognize and select alternatives early where the developments are not inevitable but rather subject to our discretionary actions. To be successful anticipators of the use and development of technology and resources, it is important to recognize, of course, that nothing will happen that is not permitted by the laws of the physical universe. But not everything that can happen will happen. Social-economic-political aspects, not technological ones, will determine what actually does occur.

Politically, our goals and priorities will select (even if often in a most complex and hidden manner) how we allocate our resources. Economically, the matching of production and distribution with demand will have powerful votes also, certainly ahead of mere technological feasibility.

So if we want to arrive at useful anticipations we are forced to consider the interface problem of technology with society. We shall look toward the future through a series of specific examples. At the outset, however, let us disclose part of what these examples are going to suggest:

1) For real future progress toward the best use of our resources and technology, a systems approach will be needed, emphasizing interactions amongst numerous technological and nontechnological or socioeconomic parameters.

2) Great economic and social return will result from intelligent investment in advanced technology, with increased productivity alone more than compensating for the cost.

3) Intensive political pressure resulting from public demand to solve "social-engineering" problems—urban development, pollution control, improved health care, better education, superior transportation—will exert a powerful, selective effect in the coming decades on the allocation of resources and the application of technology.

4) Our hybrid economy, part free enterprise and part governmentally controlled, will take on a new form constituting a virtual Social-Industrial Complex. This developing team of government and business would be greatly influenced by resource and technology matters.

5) In contrast with the present apparent (recessionary) surplus of engineers and scientists, a severe shortage will emerge with a need particularly for new interdisciplinary professionals, "sociotechnologists."

Information Technology

Let us turn now to examples that will bring out these key sociotechnological issues. Consider first the new technology many see as the most important of all because it amounts to the creation of synthetic brainpower. Developments in electronics are making it certain that in the coming decades man will have far greater ability to handle the information basic to all of his pursuits—production, distribution, education, accounting, banking, medicine, law, government. Equipped with these technological aids, he will be able to sense, acquire, store, process,communicate, display, categorize, deliberate, perform logical operations upon and utilize information with vastly greater capacity, speed, versatility, interconnection, and geographical spread than is possible for the unaided human mind and senses.

Applied to business and industry, the coming information technology will enable the human managers to operate closer to total awareness and control of the surrounding situation with optimum scheduling and on-line measurement of deviations from plan. The incoming orders would be virtually instantaneously processed to schedule labor, materials, cash flow, product distribution, and inventories. A logical eventual step is the interconnection of information flow among industrial entities whose interlocked schedules would act in response to market actions and production operations in real time. Payment for services and materials would flow through the network, the banks dealing with money transfers on an electronic basis and even the government taking its tax cut automatically.

At that stage, the development of new man-machine partnerships to make possible the superior handling of the information with which man is engaged would be a step eagerly anticipated. Is not such an advance the greatest boon that science and technology could give to society? With its enormously increased overall brainpower, the machine partner could take on the more mundane tasks, the high-capacity handling of needed information with the geographical span and speeds appropriate to our busy, complex life. The human partner would then be free to rise to higher plateaus of judgment, creativity, decision-making, and social and cultural attainments. Greater productivity could ensue. U.S. attainments could be exported, helping to provide our needed satisfactory balance of payments.

But, to achieve these benefits, there are some corollary difficulties to be faced and handled. For one thing, the modifications of the structures of all activities needed to exploit the new information technology will involve massive start-up costs. Almost everyone involved would have at least a small console to tie him into the information network and, indeed, most of these electronic information systems become economical only when there are millions of terminals (even as with telephony or television). Billions of dollars, properly reckoned as operating losses, will be required, with many more billions at risk for years before turnaround into a profit period can be achieved. The pioneering capital needed is in excess of what even the largest private corporations are likely to consider sensible. Despite the potential economic and social gain inherent in the productivity increase and greater flexibility the technology would provide, the speed with which this kind of technology can come into being is greatly contingent on new organizational teaming of corporations and government. The government may need to sponsor large-scale experiments to develop the basic ideas, perhaps seeking improved information flow in government operations as the first proving ground, and it must be willing to allow, even encourage, the setting up of private industry teams to share risk.

The Robot Society versus Instant Democracy

But there is more to consider, particularly on the nontechnical side of the matter, before we can assess the probabilities of our seeing soon the development of information technology to the degree of which we have been speaking. For instance, the average citizen is already concerned that we are moving inexorably into an increasingly technological society not of his asking. The specific advance that extends the human intellect—the handling and control of information—is to him a leading symbol of the technological threat. Here he sees the human participant losing out as the electronic machinery moves into partnership with him. Not only is he frightened of a computer-controlled robot society, but he is also afraid of the "planned economy"—an automated socialism with no free decision-making, individual initiative, or personal incentives.

Yet the availability of advanced information technology does not have to lead us to a state-controlled economy. Instead, we can use it to reach a higher form of free enterprise. In a "computerized" society, to oversimplify a little, all of the information needed for control—from airplane schedules to pickle distribution—is made available at the right place at the right time. Many millions of interconnected electronic devices would be everywhere, picking up, processing, and disseminating information. Would each citizen then be associated with a "super telephone-TV set" telling him where to be and what to do? The answer can and should be "No," because the same system—a national network of computers, communications gear, electronic memory, and information input and output consoles—that can order millions of people about as though they were robots, can just as well ask them to choose a preference from a group of well-presented alternatives. The public could tune in on the issues and take part by expressing their reactions electronically in two-way communication—"instant democracy." Information technology could be used to achieve a more informed citizenry with an extent of participation in decision-making never imagined in all the previous "pretechnological" history of man.

Freer Enterprise

As to the feared planned economy, we must recall that the foundation of true free enterprise is the free market. The closer people can be to a free choice of how to spend their money and the greater the possibility that all goods can be offered for sale in a free market, then the closer we come to realizing full free enterprise. Thus, if a nation attains a high flow of information reaching every nook and cranny of its economy, the ingredients are present for a free market in which everyone could quickly know what is available. A proposal to produce something by a manufacturer could be immediately considered by potential purchasers. We could respond electronically in our homes to a "commercial" that describes contemplated future automobile models with a substantial discount for orders placed immediately. We could step to our consoles and push the right buttons to make our commitment, automatically depleting our bank accounts electronically in the process. Applied nationally to cars, air conditioners, furniture, refrigerators, clothes, frozen foods, vacations, and educational courses, such direct communications could be used by the network's clients to schedule manufacturing and distribution in advance, making highly efficient every industrial activity from the ordering of basic raw materials to the setting up and manning of plants and transportation facilities. The profit-to-risk ratio would rise dramatically as the entrepreneur and the consumer would be involved together in an "on-line" market exchange.

A natural role for government would exist in such an electronicized free-enterprise economy, and it would not be as a rival to the private sector. The government should set the rules, referee, license, and ensure objectivity and fair opportunity in the workings of the information service.

Advancing technology, in this instance as in every other, merely offers us choices. It does not determine the direction in which our society must go.

Environmental Technology

This audience scarcely needs to be reminded that control of pollution now enjoys determined citizen backing. Despite all the controversy that exists, I submit that if, worldwide, all scientific knowledge and technological developments were used to the fullest in an optimum match with social and economic factors, the problem of pollution could be solved. Granted, disturbance to the air, land, and waterways would not be zero in that optimum situation. However, the effect on the environment would be of a nature and amount calculated and designated not only as tolerable but as providing economic and social payoff on the investment.

But such an all-out, wise use of technology simultaneously by all nations in harmony with agreed-upon social criteria is an absurdly unrealistic ideal for attainment by 1990 or 2000. What we can hope for is our endeavoring earnestly to approach such a condition and winning the contest between such efforts and the continuation of the present chaotic actions and demands concerning our environment.

Consider, for example, a rather typical situation, a concentration of a million or so in population around a bay, the waterway already very badly polluted. One alternative for the future would be to freeze the population and industry at its present size and then go about duplicating facilities and the organization of specialized skilled personnel elsewhere to provide for the necessary expansion of population and industry. At the new location we could then presumably go on to pollute the nearby waters to arrive at the same bad density point, at which time the whole exercise could be repeated.

Another possibility is superior economically. It is to accept the penalty of the added costs of reducing pollution and then allow the area to grow in a controlled manner rather than to be arbitrarily limited by a pollution situation that arose without anyone's planning for it. With technology put to work fully, it is very probable that with only a slight percentage increase in present costs—for manufacturing plants, public sewage facilities, transportation operations, utilities—a successful depollution program could be carried out. By "successful" we mean here, as an example, that the community might be able to double its present one million population with environmental degradation held constant or perhaps even improved somewhat.

Urban Rapid Transit

Allocation of resources and technological development efforts on projects pertaining to urban problems will probably receive and will certainly deserve a high priority in the next decade. Let us illustrate this area by a look at urban rapid transportation. With this example we can highlight the importance of applying advanced technology well—and equally important, the difficulty of arranging that such application take place.

An employee in a large city may live ten miles from his work with no real option, in view of the city's "design," of living closer. He drives this ten-mile stretch in one hour polluting the air as he goes and using up a great deal of his energy and patience in the miserable traffic. He leaves his investment to stand all day in the parking lot. There is no rapid transit system that he might use to get to work. Tired before he even starts, he accomplishes the equivalent of thirty hours work in forty, but it takes him fifty hours portal to portal. The same thing applies to the rest of his and his family's life, whether the transportation needs are concerned with education, medical care, shopping, or recreation.

Look at the productivity waste, or better, the productivity improvement potential! We have a 50:30 ratio, a 5:3 gain to shoot for, not the 2 or 3 percent usually mentioned for annual productivity increase ambitions. The potential economic payoff of a soundly designed rapid transit system is sinful to ignore and it is unlikely that we shall go on indefinitely giving it inadequate attention.

Electric Power Generation

On the technological horizon few possibilities for the future are more exciting than the availability of virtually limitless, clean electric power generation by controlled thermonuclear fusion. A primary fusion fuel, deuterium, occurs naturally, can be separated from seawater and is, therefore, virtually inexhaustible. Thus, successful development of fusion power technology would solve the problem of depletion of fossil fuels. As a power source, thermonuclear fusion presents no radioactive waste products and could never explode, only collapse.

Substantial experimental work has been carried on to learn the principles of controlled thermonuclear fusion power generation, with promising results. However, to complete the research and arrive at practical designs will require many more years with the greatest of efforts. The combination of increasing power demand, shortage of conventional materials, and the pollution problem (to resolve which would require more rather than less energy consumption) suggests that such new thermonuclear approaches gradually will be recognized as meriting more support, and in a decade or two successful techniques may emerge. Of course, as was the case with another nuclear energy approach, the nuclear reactor, this cannot happen without large government-sponsored programs. Practically speaking, the return-to-risk ratio and the enormous start-up costs would be beyond exclusively private investment.

The Pervasive Importance of Wise Use of Technology

Even a half-hearted attack on our top-priority, technology-related problems will require the strongest effort of which we are capable in the productive allocation of resources and in technological development backed by scientific research. It is hard to predict the specific resource and technological developments that will emerge in the next decade or two. It is not difficult to anticipate that between now and then we shall be engaged in a contest, on the one hand, to use science and technology to the fullest, and, on the other, to control the nature and speed of technological development. By another ten years it may become crystal clear—the evidence is available today—that these two sides of the contest are not and should not be placed in opposition. We cannot attack problems soundly without full use of science and technology, even as we can no longer tolerate misuse of these tools.

If time permitted we could add numerous other examples to information technology, environmental control, urban problems, and electric power generation. New educational technology, for example, has the potential of increasing the effectiveness of the educator and making possible systems of education that will provide high returns on the investment of funds. Or take health care, where present procedures, simply extended, will utterly fail to provide for the increased expectancy of care. Clearly we need—and science and technology can provide part of the means to—new approaches, such as a trained paramedical personnel force, improved preventive medicine, better testing and categorizing procedures, and creative hospital designs based on superior information handling, instrumentation, scheduling, and patient monitoring. The same kind of comments can be made about crime control, housing technology, use of ocean resources, and other high-priority fields.

But more examples would merely strengthen the conclusion that almost every priority need of society involves issues of resources and technology. Sometimes the problem is adjustment to technological change. Or it may be the difficulty of achieving prudent use of resources and technology. The intelligent application of technological tools is vital in arriving at solutions to the problems, and most often we are in a position to do something effective. Applying our means at hand and our creativity will yield economic returns and social benefits. However, we possess great organizational inadequacies: lack of established means to set goals and compare alternatives, and inability to put together the private and governmental entities necessary to get on with what we want to, and can, accomplish.

Thus it is the organizational problem that must be licked if technological advance is to yield social advance. To create the new pattern of private and public sector cooperation, some of us must get over the hangup that insists that government is already too involved in the planning of change and that it should leave the making of advances and the removing of ills wholly to the private sector. Many of the rest of us must abandon the line of thought that says private action is the exercise of "selfish interest" and therefore bad, and that consequently we must become a totally government-directed nation. Almost everyone knows we are actually operating a hybrid society, part free enterprise and part government-controlled, but this knowledge doesn't prevent a large number of us from espousing one simplistic view or the other and avoiding in this way adequate discussion of innovative, cooperative organizational schemes. Consider that for most of the coming decades, large-scale advances involving private enterprise resources (even with considerable government participation) would require that private corporations engage in cooperative efforts that are precluded by existing antitrust law interpretations. Our organizational concepts defining the role of business and government were based upon an earlier nontechnological and noninternational society. They must be modified soon to meet the problems of the coming years.

The Missing Profession

The 1970s opened with an apparent surplus of scientists and engineers, many of whom are now unemployed. This oversupply hardly jibes with the picture we have painted of social and economic forces driving us to apply the most direct, forceful, mass effort with all of the natural and human resources and creativity that we command. Urban development, controlling the environment, the changeover in the way we operate business, government, and the professions in response to the availability of electronic information systems—each one of these fields, if directed properly in its development, would appear to be able to absorb quickly all the trained, intellectually qualified individuals we could conceivably produce.

Granted, the problem is one of organization—clarifying goals, arriving at decisions, setting up teams, working out the national bookkeeping so that we can apply funds where they are needed to get on with the projects that we need and can afford. But the existence of these great organizational and administrative difficulties, which must somehow be surmounted, should not confuse us into believing we have a surplus of capable, educated people. The appearance of such a surplus should be, in fact, a sign to us that we are poor organizers and planners. How absurd it is, for example, to say, as some do, that we cannot afford to tackle the problem of learning how, with least cost and best results, to depollute our waterways, while engineers and scientists who could make progress on such efforts are drawing unemployment relief funds.

Soon it will become apparent that we have a shortage of properly trained people, particularly the practical intellectual with a multidisciplinary background. We cannot suddenly turn a large fraction of our engineers into experts on the social side of the problems or opportunities. Because it will be the only way to get the job started, we shall, for a decade or more, create "social technologists" (perhaps we should say "polysocio-econo-politico-technologists") in the school of hard knocks. These will be key performers in applying science and technology fully to the needs of our society. They will become expert at doing so by the pragmatic, day-to-day synthesizing of arts and disciplines and experiences and motivations and human ingenuity.

In another decade our universities will be turning out graduates who have specialized in these social-engineering problems. It may take until then before this interdisciplinary "technology-society" field is properly understood and categorized, with enough general principles tied to it that it can be taught as an intellectual discipline. For one thing, the "people" problem is vastly more difficult to resolve than the problems of physical science and technology. Large and powerful industrial organizations make products and distribute them, but their products are physical. When it comes to filling our needs, we are strong on "things" and not so strong on "man," and this imbalance will handicap us. The disciplines that make up our professions today will split, merge, expand, and readjust themselves in the academic institutions and in the world at large, where the new professions now missing will take root partly in the old professions and partly in the new needs and opportunities.

Penalties and Benefits

From the examples we have discussed it is possible to draw some final conclusions. Particularly, we can summarize now the penalties that will be evident for all to see in the future if we do things mostly wrong. Equally we can note the benefits that will emerge if we apply our resources and technology in the right way.

Doing it wrong means to continue to countenance an antitechnology wave, confusing this tool of man, technology, with its misuse by man himself. It means going on without setting goals, without planning, without study of alternatives, with selection by crisis, using up all of the materials we can lay our hands on and feverishly building our technological systems, our energy consumption, and our production as though it were our contemplated, determined goal to do so at the highest rate. If such action, and our per capita consumption of materials and energy, are emulated to the maximum extent by the rest of the world, then we shall surely create even greater world instability. We shall inadvertently promote contests of increasing severity among nations for acquisition and control of resources. Under such circumstances, it is difficult to see how the world can survive in any state except one of increasing waste and pollution, increasing xenophobia among nations, and decreasing moral and ethical values.

Further, doing it right means to recognize that we are going to have shortages of materials, and so we had better apply technology to the fullest to avoid waste of materials, discover new materials, use them most effectively, and invent and create substitutes. It means to recognize that the whole world will suffer from pollution unless there is world cooperation on goals and controls, and that pollution will be minimized by wise technological developments and ample energy supply.

Doing it right means, in short, using technology to the fullest to preserve and increase our resources, whether it be more brainpower or more electric power. It means recognizing that to use technology fully, and not misuse it or fail to use it, to get the most of our resources, to influence the other nations of the world to cooperate toward these ends, we shall often have to invent new roles for government and new patterns for government-industry-science cooperation. Doing it right means to get rid once and for all of inhibitions about accepting the teaming of government and industry and science and deliberate goal-setting activities. It means serious study of social-technological-economic interfaces, much planning, and considerable control. We must abandon the idea that to articulate objectives and study alternative plans is to embark on a one-way road to a complete state control of the economy and the life pattern. Instead it may be that to have freedom where it counts will require planning for freedom. Neither a state-controlled life nor one of unrestricted free enterprise will suffice or satisfy us. Instead, new and developing organizational hybrids of varying kinds, depending upon the projects to be performed, need to be accepted as the pattern for the future.

Because of the potential of social and economic payoff, and because citizen appreciation of this potential is increasing, political pressure will predominantly grow in the direction of action and soundness. Thus, I believe that we can look forward to a time when the resource and technology situation of the world might improve substantially. As we stand in 1990 looking at the year 2000 and beyond, we might have more hope then than we have today for the long-term stability of our highly technological society.

The Less-Developed Countries

Many countries of the world where resources—natural, technological, fiscal, and human—are relatively scarce will not be able to innovate so rapidly and across so wide a front of social problems. But, by applying the principles

The section entitled "The Less-Developed Countries" has been added by Daniel Lerner.

outline above, they can surely put themselves in a better position in a decade to turn innovations made anywhere in the world to their own use.

Like the more-developed countries, they would have to begin by improving their information technology. This would bring the less-developed countries into the worldwide information network and give them early access to innovations that are being discussed and debated anywhere. Early access would mean that they need not inevitably be "left behind," as they have been in the past, when innovations occur. As they equip themselves with the technological resources and human skills needed to "listen in" on the discussions, they will learn how to "talk back" in the debates by raising questions, offering criticisms, making suggestions.

Thereby the less-developed countries would become participants in the process of innovation. This is a very different concept from the outdated notion of a simple "transfer of technology" from more- to less-developed countries—a notion that has proved to be anything but simple and, in very many cases, rather unworkable.

By acquiring early access to the worldwide information network, less-developed countries would participate in the working out of innovations before they even reach the planning and executing phases. They would thus be in the hitherto unattainable position of being able to decide, in the context of their own needs and resources, whether they wish to adopt or adapt or even improve any innovation being proposed anywhere in the world.

This would have great positive effects on relations between the more- and less-developed countries. Among these effects would be the prevention of misunderstandings and even conflicts that can readily be avoided when all parties concerned in an innovation can discuss it freely while it is still in the "talking stage." In the times preceding an accessible worldwide information network, nations often fell into dispute and even went to war over such matters as the use of resources. By sharing the available information technology, on a global basis, many of these disputes can be avoided. Where any issue remains in dispute, even after thorough discussion, it need not be settled by war. We now have a widespread understanding that some of the earth's resources, such as the air and the seas, are to be shared by all of the world's peoples. We even have the beginnings of world institutions that can adjudicate disputes over such issues. If ever there was a resource that could eliminate the causes, or at least reduce the occasions, of war, it is the technology that gives us all access to a worldwide information network.

The sharing of information enables us to move from a "transfer" toward a "transformation" of technological innovations that pass between more- and less-developed countries. A case in point is the Satellite Instructional Television Experiment (SITE) in India. India "adopted" a single piece of technology from the United States—that is, an ATS-6 communication satellite. It "adapted" the accessory hardware needed to operate this satellite by making its own technological innovations—that is, a dish antenna for receiving satellite signals on the ground that is made of chicken mesh rather than high-cost metals. It "improved" the use of the satellite system, in the Indian context, by applying it in new and different ways.

We expect this example to be multiplied many times around the less-developed countries before we reach the year 2000. If this expectation is correct, then we shall by 2000 have learned what is perhaps the most important lesson of development and growth: namely, that growth is poorly served by conflict over larger shares of the existing pie and is better served by cooperation in learning to make bigger pies with bigger shares for all.

19. "Human Needs" and "Outer Limits"—Toward a New Planetary Bargain

HARLAN CLEVELAND

Barring some cataclysm, the centerpiece of world politics in the next few years will be the development and distribution of resources to serve human needs. What human beings need is of course extremely relative—to culture, to expectations, to time of life. Yet the gross facts about world poverty, the failure of trickle-down, the raw gap between those who have enough and those who don't are each year more and more disturbing to the rich and more and more outrageous to the poor.

The notion that the world community should so arrange its internal affairs so that every man, woman, and child at least has life, and perhaps even a chance at liberty and happiness, is consonant with the declared values of most modern societies. It is reflected in the U. S., Meiji, and Russian constitutions, in the thoughts of Plato and Aquinas and Santayana and Mao Tse-Tung, in declarations of independence by Indonesians and Africans, not to mention French and Americans, in the United Nations Charter and the Universal Declaration of Human Rights, and in the Charter of Economic Rights and Duties of States. Americans will shortly be inundated with Bicentennial reminders of the comparable truths we hold—within practical limits, anyway—to be self-evident.

Every industrial nation has a government-guaranteed standard of "enough," expressed as guaranteed income, a minimum wage, a poverty line, job tenure, unemployment compensation, and the like. But despite the exhortations of great religious and political leaders through the centuries, equality of access to the necessities of life has never been operational for the world community as a whole. It quite suddenly is today. A new bargain of planetary scope is in the making—and the bargaining about needs and resources will probe deeply into the distribution of wealth and income inside both the "developing" and the "developed" polities.

If the more affluent peoples are asked to modify their living standards and rearrange their priorities, which for most of them may require important changes in life-styles and workways, they—and especially their political leaders—will want to know that the changes are worthwhile, that they give promise of meeting the basic needs of the needy—rather than of speculators, brokers, feudal chieftains, and military governors. At the same time, in the poorer countries, the political courage and administrative drive to be self-reliant (get population growth under control, maximize food production, extend education, assure employment) will also depend on the larger bargain—on assurance that the "advanced" economies don't advance past the limits of environmental prudence, and on large and unpatronizing transfers of resources and technology.

Can it be done? Can our burdened biosphere absorb the shock of taking seriously the incandescent idea that "all Men are created equal"? (Jefferson wasn't sure he meant women too, but we are.) The predicament of exploding population and dwindling resources raises a question. But it is no experts' mystery; in the United States in 1975, the "problematique" is a topic for living room conversations, and has edged its way into prime-time television.

Recently, a brave and skillful writer managed to combine birth control and the ozone shield in a short episode of "All in the Family." Mike didn't want to bring a baby into a world in which hair spray threatened to destroy the ozone and give everybody skin cancer. "All right," says Gloria at last, "Let's compromise. You let me have a baby and I'll let you have my hair-spray. . . . Michael, you just can't go on being afraid of life."

In academic meetings, corporate board rooms, and government bureaus, the Michaels have had the floor. The projections of population, the imminence of starvation, the congestion of cities, the resentment of cartels, the politics of petrodollars, the fouling of air and water, and the proliferation of weapons can be readily spliced together to make the case for catastrophe. Often in history catastrophe has been a best seller.

Cassandra was always right, but the gods arranged for her to be always ineffective. Her modern disciples—the early Club of Rome for one—may have a more upbeat destiny: they will be proved wrong, partly because they were effective. In crying havoc they taught that our natural environment is finite and fragile. They were not very clear what to do about it; the prescription seemed to be some variant of "Don't just do something—stand there." Yet the lesson was taken to heart; environmental caution is already policy for dozens of governments and millions of individuals.

Notwithstanding the deceptively quantitative projections to which we are all exposed these days, none of us really knows the outer limits of the only biosphere we inhabit together. They are inherently unknowable, because they depend mostly on what we the people do in moving toward them. The "outer limits" of any resource are essentially determined by our definition of the resource, our perception of how much of it exists (only God knows for sure), our decisions about how much we really need, how much it's worthwhile to get at, how much we can re-use, and what other resources we can use instead.

The havoc-criers, watching their exponential curves climb up and up, predicted catastrophe if we didn't rethink "growth" as the central principle of economic planning and political action. But even as they pointed with alarm, the curves of some key indicators were going limp.

• The United Nations has just come out with a forecast (the median of several possible curves) that points toward a world population of around 6 billion in the year 2000. We are passing the four-billion mark this month or next. Previously the accepted forecasts had ranged between 7 and 8 billion. Even with better diets, 6 billion people won't eat as much as 7 or 8 billion.

What happened? Development and communications, that's what. It turns out that as people clamber up the income ladder and move into the towns and cities, the status of women changes, the reasons for having large families subtly mutate, the technologies of family planning become available, modern media get the word around—and the fertility rate skids off its exponential trajectory.

• In the most affluent societies, people who can afford "more" are spending not on quantity but on quality, and beyond that on "symbolic consumption." The first automobile may be a Cadillac, but the second is a small car—and the next increment may be a bicycle or a magazine about auto racing. Once there is enough food, interest turns to better cuisine, even if that means less nourishment. The struggle against obesity produces soft drinks with one calorie; drinking such a beverage is an almost wholly symbolic act. Beyond "enough," it seems, is satiation; and beyond satiation are many choices and possibilities that may be less harmful to the environment than we had previously thought.

• Our success in miniaturizing electric circuitry and other industrial functions means that growing cost-effectiveness can be less resource-hungry too. Compared with only a decade ago, computers have become 10 times smaller, 100 times faster, and 1,000 times cheaper to operate.

• Once upon a time, people were expendable and things were regarded as unique: chinaware, real estate, even clothing were handed down from generation to generation. In postindustrial society, it is people that are unique, and things—the paper plates, the transitory apartment, the fashion-dated clothing—that are thrown away (and increasingly recycled). This shift the futurists call "ephemeralization"—the trend that leads from impersonal tangible wampum to credit cards with unique-to-you electronic pulses—has to presage a shift away from resource-intensive economics. Indeed, the ultimate resource will increasingly be information, which is not even subject to the law of conservation of energy. If I give you a lump of coal, you have it and I don't. If I give you a piece of information, we both have it, and can multiply its owners at will.

• Young people in the affluent societies, and planners in the developing countries, are beginning to opt for styles of life and patterns of growth that move away from energy-intensive, materials-wasteful, nature-polluting ways we had come to think of as the regrettable but necessary cost of "industrial civilization."

• Young or old, a growing proportion of our personal "consumption" is shared with others. Not everybody can have a lawn but anybody can use a public park—and even those who don't use it are happier because they could. Personal transportation constipates the cities, so more people use mass transit more often. The consequence: more people are better served with a smaller per capita drawdown on resources.

Last year Maurice Strong, the creative Canadian businessman who heads the United National Environmental Program, began asking: Can we meet the minimum human needs of all the world's people without transgressing the outer limits of the biosphere? A study by John and Magda McHale for the Aspen Institute project on The Planetary Bargain—which points to the trends just cited—has already suggested that the answer to this question may be too easy. On one important condition, we the people of the biosphere can probably lay our hands on more than enough of the relevant resources to enable all members of a growing world population to maintain a minimum standard of life (some of them will even have a crack at liberty and happiness), without threatening the "outer limits" of an astonishingly rich and adaptable environment. If . . .

The "if" is a question about our collective will to get on with it, to use our imagination to invent the institutions of interdependence, to develop the capacity to manage complexity and finance great leaps forward. It would be foolish to treat this condition as anything but an enormous uncertainty. But it helps to know that the primary obstacle to making good on our 200-year-old pretensions about "all Men" may not be the fragility of nature after all, but merely the familiar and correctable orneriness of man.

19a. The Hawaii 2000 Experience

GEORGE CHAPLIN

In writing this paper, I wear two hats. The first is that of a unique and rather old profession. I hasten to add that it is not the oldest profession, although there are some so unkind or so unperceptive as to fail to make the distinction.

A great many people have rather fixed and negative notions about newspaper editors. It's been said that an editor is a man who separates the wheat from the chaff—and then prints the chaff. I will only observe that if editors have aberrations, they also have a lot of company. When Ann Landers, the columnist, spoke in Honolulu most recently, she made the statement that every fourth person in America is a mental case. She said: "Think of the three friends closest to you. Ask yourself: Are they really sane? Are they truly sound? Is their behavior fully acceptable? If the answer is 'Yes,' then it's you!"

The second hat I'm wearing today is that of the amateur futurist, and in that connection let me quote the alleged Chinese proverb that prophecy is always extremely difficult—especially regarding the future. As an example, there was the task force named by President Hoover to study national trends and foretell the results. The task force worked diligently and predicted accurately much that followed, overlooking only The Great Depression.

Well, I suppose we have to try harder. But really the matter of delving into the future is not to predict it, not to forecast it, but to see what can be done about designing it, shaping it, even trying to invent it, for we can take it as certain that if we do not try to determine our destiny, someone else will do it for us.

My paper will discuss Hawaii's modest efforts in the field of future study, but first let me convey a few general observations.

Arthur Clarke, the scientist and writer, likes to say that the future ain't what it used to be. And Alvin Toffler of *Future Shock* believes that the future has prematurely arrived, that it's already here. A sign in a New York bakery proclaims, "Revolutionary new, old-fashioned doughnuts." And that great Chicago scholar, Mayor Daley, is quoted as saying, "Today, the real problem *is* the future"—adding, by way of comfort—"I don't see any more serious divisions in [America now] than we had in the Civil War and on other occasions." Marshall McLuhan says that we shape our tools and thereafter our tools shape us. And a newspaper reader, looking up from his front page, exclaims, "What in the world is going on?"

What is going on appears to be the beginning of the greatest transformation since the Creation—or at least since Adam turned to the first lady and said, "You know, Eve, we're in a time of transition." The rapid rate of change has us all spinning. Everything is compressed. Everything happens faster.

Even in the ancient pre-Sputnik days of 1954, the late Dr. Robert Oppenheimer was telling a Columbia University audience that "one thing that is new is the prevalence of newness, the changing scale and scope of change itself, so that the world alters as we walk in it; so that the years of a man's life measure not some small growth or rearrangement or moderation of what we learned in childhood, but a great upheaval."

The result is that we live in our small world, our "global village," precariously balanced between survival and catastrophe. We are caught up in multiple revolutions against values and institutions. We seek affirmation of our identity and we are hungry for fulfillment. We are, each in his own way, trying to puzzle out the answer to the question put by Sir Julian Huxley: "What are people for?"

We are also asking ourselves about interdependence, about how decisions in one place affect every other place. A few sheikhs in the Middle East have done far more than the Club of Rome and the M.I.T. study by Dennis Meadows to stimulate discussions about the limits to growth. They also reminded us, by the reactions of people in long lines to buy gasoline—even in this Aloha State—how much latent hostility there is in most of us.

So, how do we begin to address ourselves seriously to all these problems of swift and enormous change? How do we take charge of change and direct it into beneficial channels? We don't pretend to have the answers in Hawaii but at least we are off and jogging in pursuit of them.

A couple of years ago, it seemed evident to some of us in these Islands that while there had been some conferences and activities around the world dealing with the long-range future, these primarily involved specialists, mostly in the academic world. There had been no large-scale engagement of laymen in trying to design the kind of alternative futures in which they would like to live—and have their children and grandchildren live. There was suggested a Governor's Conference on the Year 2000 (which is not all that far away)—and in August 1970 it came about, funded with $65,000 from the Hawaii legislature.

The first act of the conference leadership was to name thirteen task forces pretty well covering the whole spectrum of the state's activity. One task force dealt with education, another with the economy, still another with housing and transportation, a fourth with the political process, a fifth with the arts, and a sixth with life styles—with others covering the natural environment, science and technology, Hawaii and the Pacific community, and the quality of personal life.

Each task force had twenty-five to thirty-five members, representing a cross-section of the community, but with a heavy accent on youth. There were some 350 people in all. Each task force was given this assignment: (1) to give a picture of present conditions in its field; (2) to project the most desirable, apparently attainable, future in its field; and (3) to discuss what is currently needed in policy and decision-making to move the society in the preferred direction.

While the task forces were working for six months preceding the conference, a series of interim programs was held in an effort to "turn on" Hawaii about the project. These consisted of lectures, panels, discussion sessions, ETV programs, and a mini-conference addressed by Robert Theobald, the socioeconomist. Finally the task forces turned in their reports (which form a substantial part of the book, *Hawaii 2000: Continuing Experiment in Anticipatory Democracy* [The University Press of Hawaii, 1973]), and these served as the focal point of workshops at the conference. The 350 task force members were delegates and another 350 persons also were invited and attended.

For the general sessions, we featured some of the world's leading futurists: Arthur Clarke from Ceylon; Robert Jungk, a great humanist from Germany; Charles Williams, the staff director of the National Goals Research Project in the While House; Saburo Okita, Japan's leading economist; Yehezkel Dror, the distinguished Israeli futurist. And to do critiques we had such outstanding figures as John McHale, Hidetoshi Kato, Hahn-Been Lee, and Raymond Studer.

Alvin Toffler opened the sessions with a filmed message from New York. He said: "I view [this] as a pioneer experiment with anticipatory democracy that will be watched closely by other people in London, in Tokyo, in Stockholm, and in other centers of the United States. . . . "

In retrospect, the major benefit of the conference and related activity has been the sensitizing of some hundreds of people, including some of our political leaders, to the notion that they can have a hand in formulating their future.

Out of that 1970 conference came a permanent nine-member State Commission on the Year 2000. The commission views itself more as an educator than a planner. Our efforts to date range from cosponsorship of various future-oriented conferences (for example, on health, communications, the administration of justice), to establishment of a speakers' bureau, to operation of a pilot program in community planning in four high schools, to stimulation of a large private-sector project termed "Alternative Economic Futures for Hawaii."

This last undertaking, cochaired by Herbert Cornuelle, president of Dillingham Corporation, and by myself, is focusing on economic options presently and potentially open to our island state. Sponsorship and half of the $60,000 funding is by the Chamber of Commerce of Hawaii, which is playing no part, however, in policy decisions as to structure, guidelines, and operations. Matching funds are from individual businesses and labor unions.

Task forces are operating in the fields of agriculture, commerce, tourism, manufacturing, government services, military, social services, education, new technologies; and for the islands of Maui, Hawaii, and Kauai. As a beginning, the task forces produced reports on what maximum, moderate, and minimum development in their respective fields would bring over the next eleven years—to 1985.

That first stage was primarily fact-finding, analysis, and projection, without regard for what may be desirable or undesirable in a larger social context. The intent was to postpone value judgments until a later time, so that we would not be diverted initially from the economic focus. The task force reports then went to a preliminary scenario committee, for discussion of tradeoffs and compromises indicated in terms of what is "desirable," "acceptable," "undesirable" from the viewpoints of lands and tax structure; of Neighbor Island concerns; and of impact on human and environmental resources.

The most crucial phase, now in process, is an attempt to construct a final comprehensive scenario that will relate purely economic values to humanistic values in a realistic manner. Then, through a major conference or other mechanism, we will seek to evolve action recommendations for the public and private sectors, designed to head us in what appears to be a desired direction.

Beyond our efforts locally, there has been a rippling-out effect that we find gratifying. The Hawaii experience has been largely responsible for a similar project now underway in the State of Iowa. Our experience has contributed to a Washington 2000 project based in Seattle, to planning for a Minnesota state project, to the North Carolina Commission on Policies and Goals, to a recent futures conference in Puerto Rico, and to a Malaysia 2001 project being considered for all of that nation. Additionally, Hawaii has played a part in the establishment of a futures commission by the United Nations.

There is no guarantee of success when one gets involved in considering alternative futures. It has been observed that "planning for the future is a complex, frustrating, and exciting task." The philosopher Whitehead put it nicely when he said, "It is the business of the future to be dangerous."

One danger, as noted (by Maryjane Dunstan and Patricia Garlan in their book *Worlds in the Making,* 1970) is that "We are driving rapidly into a new and unexplored terrain with our eyes firmly fixed on the rear-view mirror. Instead of looking where we are or where we are going, we focus on where we have been. Our perceptions, conceptions, values, systems of mental, emotional, personal, and social organization, our very consciousness—all have been developed in interaction with past environments, and these do not prepare us to see a different road ahead."

But with imagination and determination we can make ourselves indulge in mind-stretching. We can design alternative futures and then work to make what we think is the best of them come true. We have often heard the phrase, "self-fulfilling prophecy." This is just another way of saying that having a dream of what one wants can be the first step toward making it a reality.

If people learn to take charge of rapid change and guide it well, all of humanity is the beneficiary. If we fail, we invite disaster. What an exciting and wonderful challenge to our intelligence and our compassion, and to our dedication to the proposition that betterment of the individual is the noblest of all dreams!

20. Looking Forward

DANIEL LERNER AND WILBUR SCHRAMM

The chapters of this book illustrate vividly that we have come a long way in the study of development communication over the last ten years. The 1964 conference was bright with hope and promise; the meeting in 1975 was more somber. But it was also more realistic, and vastly better supplied with research data and experience. Consequently it was possible for the participants to talk about communication, not anecdotally as had been a common pattern in 1964, but rather in terms of documented evidence of what it had accomplished in development programs; and to examine those programs themselves against the backdrop of ten years of intensive effort in the less-developed countries, supported by economic and technical assistance that between 1962 and 1972 increased from less than $8 billion to more than $19 billion annually.

So viewed, some areas of the landscape, such as the growth of relevant research in Asia and the development of radio as a universal channel in LDC, are bright. Others, such as the assessment of economic growth of LDC in per capita terms, are rather dark. The critical area of our concern in this book—the process and effects of public communication in LDC—appears in varying shades of gray.

Perhaps any realistic landscaping of complex terrains is bound to produce bright, dark, and shaded tones. Such was the ancient analectical Confucian wisdom of Yin and Yang. Such was the Marxist wisdom of modern Europe, which relied upon the dialectical interaction of thesis and antithesis to produce synthesis. Such as well is the contemporary wisdom of "mixed economies," which, in the homely terms of Fisher Ames, suggest that "Democracy is like a life raft: you never sink, but your feet are always wet."

If we have lost our early and excessive optimism about the immediate future of LDC, this is all to the good for our thinking about the proximate future. If we do not succumb to an antithetical spasm of pessimism—for example, that only military regimes and martial laws can maintain stability in LDC that also need per capita growth—then we are in a far better position than we were ten years ago to think and plan for a better future.

We, as editors, are not going to undertake the task of summing up. There is no way we could literally summarize this book; its parts speak for themselves and make a whole. Nor shall we presume to speak for the participants, for we did not seek to establish a "consensus" at the conference. Instead, we shall speak only of some of the conclusions that we as conference conveners and book editors took away from the conference. And since the brightest and darkest areas are conspicuously visible in the separate chapters, we shall focus on the shaded gray.

Ten Years of Development

The factor that darkens even many of the bright areas in LDC over the past decade is the swift growth of population. This has made it difficult, if not impossible, for some LDC to register significant economic gains. In India, for example, the decade has shown very substantial growth on most indicators of economic development. However, these gains are virtually wiped out when they are stated in per capita terms. The lesson is that "real" development cannot occur so long as population growth exceeds economic growth.

Related to the "per capita lesson," in a field that bears directly on communication rather than economic growth, is the literacy lesson. As they gained independence, most of the new nations undertook literacy programs. In many cases they were aided by UNESCO and other international bodies. During much of the 1960s, the world was increasing its literate population by a quarter of a million each year. Yet, although the number of literates in the world has increased during the 1960s, their proportion in the population actually decreased. Here again the lesson is that world literacy cannot increase so long as its growth is outrun by population growth.

Throughout the less-developed regions, people have been led to want more than they can get. This can be attributed in part to the spread of the mass media, which inevitably show and tell people about the good things of life that are available elsewhere. It is only natural that people should learn to want these things, which range from material commodities such as a motor bike to more "spiritual" matters such as higher education for their children. In part, the chronically unbalanced "Want:Get Ratio" in LDC must be attributed to the "charismatic" leaders of the new nations. In one LDC after another, leaders have conveyed to their people the impression that, with independence, life would get much better much faster. Thereby they raised hopes that could not be met, wants that could not be satisfied.

As people in the poor countries were being shown and told about the "goodies" available in developed countries, they were also being taught about their own inferiority—at least in terms of wealth and well-being. Recognition of the disparities between the rich and poor countries produced among some a sense of hopelessness, among others a sense of aggressiveness. Both apathy and aggression usually are counterproductive to genuine development efforts.

Just as comparison of rich with poor countries produced a destabilizing effect on popular perspectives, so did comparison of rich and poor within each LDC. The growth of cheap public transportation contributed as much to this phenomenon as did the mass media. During the decade, millions of villagers were able to ride a bus to the Big City. There, for the first time, they saw for themselves "how the other half lives." This, along with high population growth and rural underemployment, produced the excessive urbanization that marked the past decade in LDC. The lesson, as Professor Oshima has pointed out, is the need to decelerate both population growth and urbanization—to turn, rather, to a labor-intensive strategy of rural development.

This is not to say that there has not been a significant number of "success stories" in LDC during the decade. Successes are possible and, with planning and dedicated effort, can be made to happen. The Comilla project in Bangladesh reviewed in this volume, the Green Revolution in such areas as the Punjab, the accomplishments of the Amul Dairy Cooperative project in Gujerat are examples all taken from one part of one continent. But the overall results of the Development Decade, and in particular the circumstances we have mentioned, help to explain why we expect to hear during the next ten years less about economic growth, more about quality of life; less about industrialization, more about rural development; less about a single model of development, more about the conditions of development; less about "transfer" of technology, more about transformation of technology; less about competing interests, more about interdependence.

Development Communication Ten Years After

What have we learned in ten years about the use of communication for development? That as it grows, development accelerates, as one of the ablest communication researchers in Asia testifies in this volume. Evidence of that is in the summary papers in preceding pages, but even more encouraging is the evidence from the field that planned communication has come to be considered an essential part of most development programs, especially in family planning, health, and agriculture, that more nearly adequate budgets are being allocated to it, and that staff members in increasing numbers are being sent for the necessary professional training. Furthermore, communication research has started to demonstrate its direct usefulness to development programs, and it too is being called upon, far more widely than was the case ten years ago, to guide planning and operations.

We have learned also that most media, well used, can contribute to development—not only television from the ATS-6 satellite to India or from ground towers to El Salvador and the Ivory Coast, but also the humbler, less costly, less complex media like slides and posters at village meetings, traditional media like the dances and puppet shows of Southeast Asia, and above all the medium of interpersonal, face-to-face talk. Dollar for dollar, the smaller, less expensive media may often be more efficient in a development program than the larger, more expensive ones. And any medium is likely to be more effective when combined with two-way communication of one kind or other.

In 1975, far more than 1964, development communication tends to be discussed in terms of a total program of social change. And perhaps the most significant difference observable "ten years after" is a shift in the center of gravity of such programs from the center toward local theaters of activity. "Trickle down" communication received a bad report card in 1975. Kearl talked about a shift in communication policies away from "a relatively narrow focus on transmission of messages from authoritative central or national sources to a broader view that encompasses communication at and among all levels in a developing agricultural country." Feliciano emphasized the importance of local and interpersonal communication as compared to mass channels, in Southeast Asia, for motivation and education campaigns. Rogers concluded that one of the most important legacies of diffusion research was that it put "social structure back into communication research."

The China papers by Chu and others made clear that a chief goal of communication in that country is to unlock local energies for local development. That was also the goal of the remarkable Mother's Club in Oryu Li, Korea, described in this volume by Kincaid and Yum, and of the rural development project that was installed by the efforts of Akhter Hameed Khan in one thana of Bangladesh and is now being adopted throughout the country. Unlocking local energies, a need specified in our earlier book, is parallel to the change in priorities toward rural development, and we expect to find the same sort of goal and the related communication programs bulking larger and larger in the development activities of the next ten years.

But such a program aimed at catalyzing local activity, local planning, local communication cannot be done with conventional mass media thinking that emphasizes one-way communication and generalized messages. It must include a strong component of social organization and interpersonal communication. It requires persons in charge of planning communication to understand the social structure and how change can take place in it—not merely how messages go out. We have now gone far beyond the level of communication skill that prescribes, as one article did in the middle 1960s, that a development campaign must have five radio announcements a week! Given this situation, one of the most encouraging signs emerging from the conference was evidence of the growth of more broadly trained development communication and planning staffs, and a notable increase in number of institutions within the LDC conducting research and training in communication.

Although the mood of the conferees was more somber than ten years before, they were by no means discouraged. The feeling was rather that development had proved more difficult and the necessary strategies of communication more complex than had been anticipated ten years earlier. But on the other hand, more is known, more experience is in hand, more resources of skill and understanding are available.

"Projections of the future are less relevant to prophecy than to innovation," Lasswell says in his brilliant paper in this volume. In terms of prophecy, the participants in the conference seemed to expect a difficult decade ahead—demanding, violent, uncertain, unstable, tense—in which, as Lasswell says wryly, "the tension may, of course, be resolved, by self-induced disaster at any moment." But the challenge of this conference, as its members looked ahead, was to innovation—to use what we now know of communication and development in ways equal to the challenge of the times.

The Contributors

George Chaplin has been editor of the *Honolulu Advertiser* since 1959. Before that he was editor of the *New Orleans Item,* and served on the staff of several other newspapers. He held a Nieman Fellowship at Harvard, has won the Overseas Press Club, the Headliners, and the John Hancock awards, and is now president-elect of the American Society of Newspaper Editors. He is cochairman of the Hawaii Commission on the Year 2000, and is coeditor of the book *Hawaii 2000*.

Godwin C. Chu came to the East-West Communication Institute as a research associate after serving as director of Research and professor in the School of Journalism, University of Southern Illinois. Born in Peking, educated on the Chinese mainland and in Taiwan, he earned a doctorate in communication from Stanford; he has taught at the National Chengchi University, Stanford, and the University of Victoria.

Harlan Cleveland was president of the University of Hawaii from 1969 to 1974 and is now director of the Aspen Institute's Program in International Affairs, with headquarters in Princeton, New Jersey. In the 1940s he served as a foreign-aid executive, in the 1950s as a magazine publisher and graduate school dean, and in the 1960s as assistant secretary of state and U.S. ambassador to NATO.

S. C. Dube is director of the Indian Institute of Advanced Study, in Simla. He was formerly professor of Anthropology at the University of Saugar, and director of the Indian National Institute for Community Development. He is the author of several books, and contributed two articles on Indian development to *Communication and Change in the Developing Countries.*

F. Tillman Durdin has reported the news from China for thirty-five years, first as editor of a Shanghai newspaper, and since 1937 as a correspondent, later bureau chief, for the *New York Times.* He has been a Nieman Fellow and has won numerous awards for his reporting. At the time of our conference, he was a senior fellow at the East-West Communication Institute.

S. N. Eisenstadt is currently professor of Sociology at the Hebrew University in Jerusalem. He received his doctorate from the same university, and pursued postgraduate studies at the London School of Economics and Political Science. He has been a visiting professor at Oslo, Chicago, Harvard, and the Massachusetts Institute of Technology, and is the author of a number of books, of which the most recent is *Tradition, Change, and Modernity.*

Gloria D. Feliciano is professor of Communication and dean of the Institute of Mass Communication, at the University of the Philippines. Her undergraduate degree and her M.A. in agricultural information are from the University of the Philippines. Her doctorate in mass communication is from the University of Wisconsin. She is the author of numerous articles and books.

Chaudry Inayatullah is Development Administration expert at the Asian Centre for Development Administration in Kuala Lumpur. His doctorate in political science is from the University of Indiana. A native of Pakistan, he has served on the staff of the Pakistan Academy for Rural Development, the University of Islamabad, the United Nations, and the U.N. Research Institute for Social Development in Geneva. In his writings, he uses only the name "Inayatullah."

Hidetoshi Kato divides his time between the Communications Design Institute in Kyoto and the East-West Communication Institute, where he is a research associate and specializes in the area of Popular Culture. He graduated from Hitotsubashi University in Tokyo, and took advanced work at Harvard and Chicago. He was recently appointed to the faculty of the Gakushuin University in Tokyo.

Bryant E. Kearl returned in 1974 to his professorship in agricultural journalism at the University of Wisconsin, after several years as executive director of the Asia office, Agricultural Development Council, in Bangkok and Singapore. He holds a doctorate in political science from the University of Minnesota, and has served the University of Wisconsin as vice-chancellor and associate dean of the Graduate School.

Akhter Hameed Khan began his career in the Indian Civil Service in 1936, but resigned in 1944 to become a teacher. Ten years later he became director of

East Pakistan's Community Program, and then director of the famous Comilla Academy of Rural Development. He is now working as an adviser to the Rural Development Academy in Peshawar, Pakistan.

D. Lawrence Kincaid received his doctorate in communication at Michigan State University, and immediately joined the East-West Communication Institute as a researcher. His research has been in the area of modernization and development, and the diffusion of innovations.

Harold D. Lasswell is professor emeritus at Yale University and director of the Policy Sciences Center. He is probably America's leading political scientist and was formerly president of the American Political Science Association. He is the author of many classic works, from his early *Propaganda Technique in World War I* to his recent *A Pre-View of Policy Sciences.*

Daniel Lerner is Ford Professor of Sociology and International Communication at the Massachusetts Institute of Technology, and divides his time equally between M.I.T. and the East-West Communication Institute. He took his doctorate at New York University, and later taught at the University of Paris, Columbia, and Stanford. He is the author of many books and papers on development and communication, including the classic, *The Passing of Traditional Society.*

Floyd W. Matson is professor of American Studies at the University of Hawaii. His doctorate in political science is from the University of California at Berkeley. A former journalist in the United States and a media analyst in Japan, he has published a number of books including *Prejudice, War and the Constitution,* which won the Woodrow Wilson Award of the American Political Science Association.

Charles E. Osgood is professor of Psychology and Communication at the University of Illinois, where he has also headed the Institute of Communication Research and the Center for Comparative Linguistics. He has been president of the American Psychological Association (A.P.A.), and has received numerous honors and awards including the Distinguished Scientific Contribution Award of the A.P.A., and the Kurt Lewin Award of the Society for the Study of Social Issues. He earned his doctorate at Yale. He is the author of many books and papers, including the influential volume, *The Measurement of Meaning,* in 1957.

Harry T. Oshima is professor emeritus, University of Hawaii, and visiting professor at the University of the Philippines. His doctorate in economics is from Princeton. His long experience in international economics includes teaching at American University, Stanford, Washington, and Hitotsubashi in Tokyo; consultation to the Economic Research Center at the University of Singapore; and numerous projects in research and analysis.

Syed A. Rahim was chief of the Rural Institutions Sector of the Bangladesh Planning Commission until he joined the East-West Communication Institute as a research associate in 1974. Before he went to the Planning Commission he had been fourteen years with the Academy for Rural Development, in Comilla, where he became director of Research. He was educated in Bangladesh and at Michigan State University where he received his doctorate in communication.

Simon Ramo is vice-chairman of the Board and chairman of the Executive Committee of TRW Inc. An outstanding engineer and executive, he holds doctorates from several universities and serves as trustee and research associate at the California Institute of Technology. He was scientific director of the Intercontinental Ballistics Missile program and is a member of the State Department's Committee on Science and Foreign Affairs.

Everett M. Rogers, after teaching at Michigan State for a number of years, became professor of Journalism and Population Planning at the University of Michigan, and in 1975 joined the faculty of Stanford as professor of Communication. His doctorate, in sociology, is from Iowa State University. He is the author of numerous articles and books including *The Communication of Innovations.*

Eugene Sathre is a doctoral candidate in political science at the University of Minnesota, and currently holds a doctoral internship at the East-West Communication Institute.

Wilbur Schramm came to the East-West Communication Institute in 1973 as director, after eighteen years as professor of International Communication and director of the Institute for Communication Research at Stanford. Before that he had been a professor, director, and dean at the Universities of Iowa and Illinois. He is the author of twenty-two books and about one hundred papers. In October 1975, he relinquished the Institute directorship and was named the first Distinguished Center Researcher.

R. Lyle Webster was the first director, from 1970 to 1972, of the East-West Communication Institute. He took an M.A. at the Columbia Graduate School of Journalism and a Ph.D. at American University, joined the information staff of the U.S. Department of Agriculture and ultimately became director of Information for the department. For six years in India he served as consultant to the Ford Foundation in connection with the information aspects of the "Package Program" for agricultural development. Among many other foreign assignments he headed a team in 1960 that studied the agricultural communication system of the Soviet Union.

Frederick T. C. Yu, coauthor with W. Phillips Davison of the recent volume *Research in Mass Communication,* is professor and associate dean of the

Graduate School of Journalism at Columbia University. He was born in China, came to this country to study at the University of Iowa, from which he received his doctorate, and later held a postdoctoral fellowship at the Massachusetts Institute of Technology and at Harvard. He also worked on the *Washington Post*, and has taught at Iowa, the University of Southern California, and the Chinese University of Hong Kong.

June Ock Yum was a graduate student in communication at the University of Hawaii, on a grant from the East-West Communication Institute, and is now a candidate for the doctorate at the Annenberg School, University of Southern California. Her undergraduate study was at Seoul National University.

Literature Cited

Abegglen, James C. 1973. Management and Worker: The Japanese Solution. Tokyo: Sophia University.

Abesamis, Maria Elena. 1968. "Attitudes of High School Seniors toward Journalism as a Career." Undergraduate thesis, Institute of Mass Communication, University of the Philippines.

Abramovitz, Moses, and David, Paul. 1973. "Reinterpreting Economic Growth." *American Economic Review* 63:428–439.

Alfonso, Herminia M., ed. 1971. *Philippine Journal of Communication Studies* 1(1):97–106.

Allen, Richard K. 1970. "A Comparison of Communication Behaviors in Innovative and Non-Innovative Secondary Schools." Ph.D. dissertation, Michigan State University.

Almond, Gabriel, and Coleman, James S. 1960. *The Politics of the Developing Areas.* Princeton, N.J.: Princeton University Press.

Almond, Gabriel, and Verba, Sidney. 1963. *Civic Culture: Political Attitudes and Democracy in Five Nations.* Princeton, N.J.: Princeton University Press.

Apter, David E. 1968. *Some Conceptual Approaches to the Study of Modernization.* Englewood Cliffs, N.J.: Prentice-Hall.

Arundale, Robert B. 1971. "The Concept of Process in Human Communication Research." Ph.D. dissertation, Michigan State University.

Aziz, Sartaz. 1973. "The Chinese Approach of Rural Development." *International Development Review* 4:2–7.

Badgley, John H. 1971. *Asian Development: Problem and Prognosis.* New York: The Free Press.

Barghouti, Shawki M. 1974*a*. "Integrated Functional Education in Machakos District." FAO PBFL Report No. 13.

———. 1974*b*. "The Role of Communication in Jordan's Rural Development." *Journalism Quarterly* 51:418–424.

Barnet, Richard, and Muller, Ronald. 1974. "Global Reach." *New Yorker* (Dec. 2) 53–128; (Dec. 9) 100–159.

Barton, Allen. 1968. "Bringing Society Back In: Survey Research and Macro-Methodology." *American Behavioral Scientist* 12:1–9.

Bautista, Pauline F., ed. 1970. *Proceedings of the International Seminar on Development*. Diliman, Quezon City, Philippines: Institute of Mass Communication, University of the Philippines.

Beal, George M., Rogers, Everett M. and Bohlen, Joe M. 1957. "Validity of the Concept of Stages in the Adoption Process." *Rural Sociology* 22:166–168.

Beisenhertz, P. C. November 1972. *What Instructional Research Says to the Researcher*. ERIC ED 073 134.

Beltran, Luis Ramiro. March 17–22, 1974. "Rural Development and Social Communication: Relationships and Strategies," in Crawford, Robert H., and Ward, William B., eds., *Communication Strategies for Rural Development: Proceedings of the Cornell-CIAT International Symposium* (Ithaca, N.Y.: New York State College of Agriculture and Life Sciences, 1974), pp. 11–27.

———. September 1974. "Communication Research in Latin America: The Blindfolded Inquiry?" Paper submitted to International Scientific Conference on Mass Communication and Social Consciousness in a Changing World, at Leipzig.

Benda, Harry J. 1960. "Non-Western Intelligentsia as Political Elites." *Australian Journal of Politics and History* 6:205–208.

Bendix, Reinhard. 1967. "Tradition and Modernity Reconsidered." *Comparative Studies in Society and History* 9:292–346.

Blackmer, Donald, and Milliken, Max, eds. 1961. *The Emerging Nations: Their Growth and United States Policy*. Boston: Little, Brown.

Bodenheimer, Suzanne J. 1968. "The Ideologies of Developmentalism: American Political Science Paradigm—Surrogate for Latin American Studies." *Berkeley Journal of Sociology* 35:130–159.

Bohlen, Joe M. 1967, 1971. "Research Needed on Adoption Models." First published in *Sociologia Ruralis* 7(1967):113–129. Reprinted (1971) in Schramm, Wilbur, and Roberts, Donald, eds., *The Process and Effects of Mass Communication*. Urbana: University of Illinois Press.

Bostian, Lloyd. 1966. "Mass Media Communication in Brazilian Agricultural Development." Paper presented at Association for Education in Journalism meetings, at Iowa City, Iowa.

———. 1970. "The Two-Step Flow Theory: Cross-Cultural Implications." *Journalism Quarterly* 47(1):109–117.

Brown, Lester R. 1974. *In the Human Interest*. New York: W. W. Norton.

Brown, M. R., and Kearl, Bryant. 1967. "Mass Communication Development: The Problem of Local and Functional Relevance." University of Wisconsin Land Tenure Center Paper No. 38.

Brumberg, Stephen F. 1972. "Nonformal Education for Rural Development: Case Study No. 1: Acción Cultural Popular." Mimeographed. Essex, Conn.: International Council for Educational Development.

Buber, Martin. 1947. *Between Man and Man*. Boston: Beacon Press.

Cano, Jairo, and Winklemann, Don. 1972. "Plan Puebla: Análisis de Beneficios y Costos." *El Trimestre Económico* (October-December): 783–796.

Caplan, Nathan, and Nelson, Stephen D. 1973. "On Being Useful: The Nature and Consequences of Psychological Research on Social Problems." *American Psychologist* 28:199–211.

Carlisle, R. D. B. 1974. *College Credit through TV: Old Idea, New Dimensions*. Lincoln, Nebr.: Great Plains National Instructional Television Library.

Clausen, A. W. 1972. "The International Corporation: An Executive's View." *The Annals of The American Academy of Political Science and Social Science* (September): 12–21.

Coleman, James S. 1958. "Relational Analysis: A Study of Social Organization with Survey Methods." *Human Organization* 17:28–36.

Coleman, James S.; Katz, Elihu; and Menzel, Herbert. 1966. *Medical Innovation: A Diffusion Study*. New York: Bobbs-Merrill.

Connors, Mary M. 1974. "Tanzanian Political Organization—Its Relation to the People and the Goals of Development." Paper presented in a seminar on communication and development, Institute for Communication Research, at Stanford, Calif.

Connors, Walker. 1972. "Nation Building or Nation Destroying." *World Politics* 24: 319–355.

Cook, A. 1974. "What TV is Doing to America." *U.S. News and World Report* (September 30):47.

Cowlan, B.; Jamison, D.; Polcyn, K.; Singh, J.; Smith, D.; and Wolff, L. 1973. *Broadcast Satellites for Educational Development: The Experiments in Brazil, India, and the United States*. Report No. 5. Academy for Educational Development under Contract No. AID/csd-2829, Office of Education and Human Resources, Bureau for Technical Assistance, Agency for International Development.

Crane, Diana. 1972. *Invisible Colleges: Diffusion of Knowledge in Scientific Communities*. Chicago: University of Chicago Press.

Crawford, Robert H. 1974. "Developing a Communication Support Program," in Crawford, Robert H., and Ward, William B., eds., *Communication Strategies for Rural Development: Proceedings of the Cornell-CIAT International Symposium* (Ithaca, N.Y.: New York State College of Agriculture and Life Sciences), pp. 60–68.

Crawford, Robert, and Adhikarya, Ronny. August 1972. "The Use of Traditional Media in Family Planning Programs in Rural Java." Paper prepared for annual meeting of International Association for Education in Journalism, at Carbondale, Ill.

Crucillo, Florida A. 1969. "Attitudes toward Journalism of Education, Music, and Engineering Students of the University of the Philippines." Undergraduate thesis, Institute of Mass Communication, University of the Philippines.

Dandekar, V. M. 1972. "Effectiveness in Agricultural Planning." Singapore: Agricultural Development Council Teaching Forum, No. 19.

Dasgupta, Sugata. 1973. "Towards a No-Poverty Society." In *Effective Anti-Poverty Strategies*. Bangkok: Union Publishing.

Davison, W. Phillips, and Yu, Frederick T. C., eds. 1974. *Mass Communication Research: Major Issues and Future Directions*. New York: Praeger.

DeFleur, Melvin L. 1966. *Theories of Mass Communication*. New York: David McKay.

de Garnie, I. January-March 1972. "The Social and Cultural Background of Food Habits in Developing Countries." *Nutrition Newsletter* 8 (1): 58–61.

Dervin, Brenda. 1971. "Communication Behaviors as Related to Information Control Behaviors of Black Low-Income Adults." Ph.D. dissertation, Michigan State University.

Desai, A. R., ed. 1971. *Essays on Modernization of Underdeveloped Societies*. Bombay: Thacker and Co.

de Sola Pool, Ithiel. 1967. "The Communications Revolution as a Strategy of Modernization." Mimeographed. Berlin: Deutsches Institut fur Entwicklungspolitik.

Deutsch, Karl. 1961. "Social Mobilization and Political Development." *American Political Science Revue* 55: 463–515.

Deutschmann, Paul J., and Borda, Orlando Fals. 1962*a*. *La Comunicación de las Ideas entre los Campesinos Colombianos*. Monografías Sociológicas 14. Bogotá: Universidad Nacional de Colombia.

———. 1962*b*. "Communication and Adoption Patterns in an Andean Village." Mimeographed. San José, Costa Rica: Programa Interamericano de Información Popular.

Deutschmann, Paul J., and Danielson, Wayne A. 1960. "Diffusion of Knowledge of the Major News Story." *Journalism Quarterly* 37:345–355.

Development Academy of the Philippines. January 1975. *Measuring the Quality of Life: Philippines Social Indicators*. Tagaytay City, Philippines: Development Academy of the Philippines.

Diaz-Bordenave, Juan. 1974. "Communication and Adoption of Agricultural Innovations in Latin America," in Crawford, Robert H., and Ward, William B., eds., *Communication Strategies for Rural Development:*

Proceedings of the Cornell-CIAT International Symposium (Ithaca, N.Y.: New York State College of Agriculture and Life Sciences, 1974), pp. 212–218.

Diaz-Cisneros, Heliodoro. 1974. "An Institutional Analysis of a Rural Development Project: The Case of the Puebla Project in Mexico." Ph.D. dissertation, University of Wisconsin.

Dittmer, Lowell. 1973. "Mass Line and Mass Criticism in China—An Analysis of the Fall of Liu Shao-Ch'i." *Asian Survey* 13(8): 772–792.

Dizard, Wilson P. 1966. *Television, A World View*. Syracuse, N.Y.: Syracuse University Press.

Dorner, Peter. August 1973. "Institutions as Aids to Development." Mimeographed. Paper presented at 15th International Conference of Agricultural Economists, at Sao Paulo, Brazil.

Drilon, J.D. Jr. 1974. "Spreading New Rice Varieties—Then and Now," in Crawford, Robert H., and Ward, William B., eds., *Communication Strategies for Rural Development: Proceedings of the Cornell-CIAT International Symposium* (Ithaca, N.Y.: New York State College of Agriculture and Life Sciences, 1974), pp. 117–126.

Drucker, Peter F. 1974. "Multinationals and Developing Countries, Myths and Realities." *Foreign Affairs* (53): 121–134.

Dube, S. C. 1958. *India's Changing Villages*. London: Routledge and Kegan Paul, Ltd.

Dunstan, Maryjane, and Garlan, Patricia. *Worlds in the Making*. Englewood Cliffs, N.J.: Prentice-Hall, 1970.

Eisenstadt, Shmuel N. 1964. "Breakdowns of Modernization." *Economic Development and Cultural Change* 12:345–367.

———. 1966. *Modernization: Protest and Change*. Englewood Cliffs, N.J.: Prentice-Hall.

———. 1971. *Political Sociology*. New York: Basic Books.

———. 1973. *Tradition, Change and Modernity*. New York: John Wiley & Sons.

———. 1974. *Traditional Patrimonialism and Modern Neo-Patrimonialism*. Beverly Hills: Sage.

Esman, Milton J. 1974. "Popular Participation and Feedback Systems in Rural Development," in Crawford, Robert H., and Ward, William B., eds., *Communication Strategies for Rural Development: Proceedings of the Cornell-CIAT International Symposium* (Ithaca, N.Y.: New York State College of Agriculture and Life Sciences, 1974), pp. 70–78.

Falcon, Walter P. 1962. "Farmer Response to Price in an Underdeveloped Area: A Case Study of West Pakistan." Ph.D. dissertation, Harvard University.

Feiner, A. 1974. "Health Care and Education on the Threshold of Space." *Science* 186 (December 27):1178–1186.

Feliciano, Gloria D. 1973. "An Overview of Communication Research in Asia." Paper No. 6. Honolulu: East-West Communication Institute.

Feliciano, Gloria D., and Feliciano, Rogelio D. June 10–19, 1974. "The Social-Psychological Variables of Family Planning Recruitment Programmes." Background paper prepared for the Experts' Meeting on "Social-Psychological Aspects of Family Planning Programmes," ECAFE, at Bangkok.

Felstehausen, Herman. 1973. "Conceptual Limits of Development Communication Theory." *Sociología Ruralis* 13(1):39–54.

Fett, John. 1974*a*. "Gatekeepers in Agricultural Information Dissemination," in Crawford, Robert H., and Ward, William B., eds., *Communication Strategies for Rural Development: Proceedings of the Cornell-CIAT International Symposium* (Ithaca, N.Y.: New York State College of Agriculture and Life Sciences, 1974), pp. 186–194.

———. 1974*b*. Personal correspondence with Bryant Kearl.

"First International Seminar on Communication and Change in Southeast Asian Countries." *Proceedings.* 1968. Manila: University of the Philippines.

Fliegel, Frederick C., and Kivlin, Joseph E. 1966. "Attributes of Innovations as Factors in Diffusion." *American Journal of Sociology* 72:235–248.

Frank, Andrew Gunder. 1967. *Capitalism and Underdevelopment in Latin America: Historical Studies of Chile and Brazil.* New York: Monthly Review Press.

Freedman, Ronald, and Takeshita, John Y. 1969. *Family Planning in Taiwan: Tradition and Change.* Princeton, N.J.: Princeton University Press.

Frey, John C. October 1952. *Some Obstacles to Soil Erosion Control in Western Iowa.* Res. Bull. 391, Iowa Agricultural Experiment Station.

Fugelsang, Andreas. 1971. *Outlook in a National Nutrition Education Campaign: National Food and Nutrition Commission.* Luseka, Zambia: Associated Printers.

Furtado, Celso. 1970. *Obstacles to Development in Latin America.* Translated by Charles Ekker. New York: Anchor Books.

Gallaher, A., Jr. 1968. *Perspectives in Developmental Change.* Lexington, Ky.: University of Kentucky.

Gaulet, Denis. 1971. *The Cruel Choice.* New York: Atheneum.

Goldthorpe, John H. 1971. "Theories of Industrial Society: Relections on the Recrudescence of Historicism and the Future of Futurology." *European Journal of Sociology* 12:263–288.

Gould, S. 1973. *Diversity by Design: Commission on Non-Traditional Study.* San Francisco: Jossey-Bass.

Goussault, Yves. 1968. "Rural Animation and Rural Participation in French Speaking Africa." *International Labor Review* 97:525–550.

Granovetter, Mark S. 1973. "The Strength of Weak Ties." *American Journal of Sociology* 78:1360–1380.

Grunig, James. 1974. "Commission in a Community Development Agency." *Journal of Communication* (Autumn): 40–41.

Guimaraes, Lytton. 1972. "Communication Integration in Modern and Traditional Social Systems: A Comparative Analysis across Twenty Communities of Minas Gerais." Ph.D. dissertation, Michigan State University.

Gunn, H. N., Jr. 1974. "Inside the Program Cooperative." *Public Telecommunications Review* 2 (4): 16–27.

Halloran, James Dermot. *Mass Media and Society: The Challenge of Research.* Leicester, England: Leicester University Press, 1974.

Harper, Francis, ed. 1964. *Out of China—A Collection of Interviews with Refugees from China.* Hong Kong: Dragonfly Books.

Hatch, John K. 1974. "The Corn Farmers of Motupe: A Study of Traditional Farming Practices in Northern Coastal Peru." Ph.D. dissertation, University of Wisconsin.

Hauser, Philip H. 1967. "Family Planning and Population Programs: A Book Review Article." *Demography* 4:397–414.

Havelock, R. G., and Havelock, Mary C. 1973. *Training for Change Agents.* Ann Arbor, Mich.: Institute for Social Research.

Hayami, Yujiro, and Ruttan, V. W. 1971. *Agricultural Development: An International Perspective.* Baltimore: Johns Hopkins Press.

Heady, Earl O. 1965. "Priorities in Adoption of Technology." Ames, Iowa: Iowa State University Center for Agricultural and Economic Development report on Economic Development of Agriculture.

Heilbroner, Robert L. 1970. *Between Capitalism and Socialism.* New York: Vintage Books.

Hirschman, Albert O. Winter 1967. "The Principle of the Hiding Hand." *The Public Interest* 6: 10–23.

Homans, George C. 1961. *Social Behavior: Its Elementary Forms.* New York: Harcourt, Brace and World.

Hopkins, Terence K. November 1969. "Third World Modernization in International Perspective." *Annals of the American Academy of Political and Social Science* 386:126–136.

Hopper, W. David. 1957. "The Economic Organization of a Village in North Central India." Ph.D. dissertation, Cornell University.

Hornik, R. C., McAnany, Emile; Mayo, John; and Schramm, Wilbur. August 1973. "Television and Educational Reform in El Salvador." Final Report to the Agency for International Development. Mimeographed. Stanford, Calif.: Institute for Communication Research.

Hoselitz, B. F. 1961. *Sociological Aspects of Economic Growth.* New York: The Free Press.

Hunsberger, Warren S., ed. 1957. *New Era in the Non-Western World.* Ithaca, N.Y.: Cornell University Press.

Huntington, S. 1965. "Political Development and Political Decay." *World Politics* (April): 386–430.

Idris, A., and Noor, I. B. N. June-July 1972. "Action, Involvement, Development and Approaches of Communication in Malaysia." Paper prepared for the Asian and Far East Academic Communication Seminar, sponsored by the East-West Communication Institute, Honolulu.

Inkeles, Alex, and Smith, David H. 1974. *Becoming Modern.* Cambridge, Mass.: Harvard University Press.

Institute for Social Education. 1973. *The Electric Company, In-School Utilization Study: The 1971–1972 School and Teacher Surveys, Center for the Study of Education.* Tallahassee, Florida: Florida State University.

Isaacs, Harold R. 1974. "Basic Group Identity: The Idols of the Tribe." *Ethnicity* 1:15–41.

Johnson, Sherman E. 1965. "Combining Knowledge, Incentives, and Means to Accelerate Agricultural Development." Ames, Iowa: Iowa State University Center for Agriculture and Economic Development report on Economic Development of Agriculture.

Katz, Elihu. 1960. "Communication Research and the Image of Society: Convergence of Two Traditions." *American Journal of Sociology* 65: 435–440.

Katz, S., and McGowan, Frank. 1963. *Selected List of U.S. Readings on Development.* Prepared for the U.N. Conference on the Application of Science and Technology for the Benefit of the Less Developed Regions. Washington, D. C.: USGPO.

Kearl, Bryant. 1965. "Communications in Economic Development." Res. Paper No. 7. Mimeographed. Madison, Wis.: Land Tenure Center.

Kerr, Clark. 1969. *Marshall, Marx and Modern Times: The Multidimensional Society.* Cambridge: Cambridge University Press.

Kerr, Clark, et al. 1964. *Industrialism and Industrial Man.* Oxford: Oxford University Press.

Kesselman, Mark. October 1973. "Order of Movement?: The Literature of Political Development as Ideology." *World Politics* 26(1): 139–154.

Kincaid, D. L.; Park, H. J.; Chung, K. K.; and Lee C. C. 1974. *Mothers' Clubs and Family Planning in Rural Korea: The Case of Oryu Li.* Case Study 2. Honolulu: East-West Communication Institute.

Klausner, S. Z., ed. 1967. *The Study of Total Societies.* New York: Praeger.

Korten, David C. July 1974. Background paper for 1974 Annual Conference of International Committee on Management of Population Programmes (COMP). Mimeographed.

Krishna, Raj. 1961. "Farm Supply Response in the Punjab (India-Pakistan): A Case Study of Cotton." Ph.D. dissertation, University of Chicago.

Kuhn, Thomas K. 1962. *The Structure of Scientific Revolutions*. Chicago: University of Chicago Press.

Kumar, N., and Chandiram, S. 1967. *Educational TV in India*. New Delhi: Arya Book Depot.

Kuznets, Simon. 1966. *Modern Economic Growth*. New Haven, Conn.: Yale University Press.

Kyratonis, D., and Vonhoff, R., eds. 1972. *Multi-Media Systems in Adult Education: Twelve Project Descriptions in Nine Countries*. Munich: International Central Institute for Youth and Educational Television.

Land, H. W. 1971–1972. "The Children's Television Workshop: How and Why It Works." Summary and overview of the final report prepared pursuant to grant #OEG–0–71–1279(725) from the National Center for Educational Technology, United States Office of Education, Department of Health, Education and Welfare, under EPDA part D. New York: Nassau Board of Cooperative Educational Services.

Lasswell, Harold D. 1971. *A Pre-View of Policy Sciences*. New York: American Elsevier.

Lasswell, Harold D., and Lerner, Daniel, eds. 1965. *World Revolutionary Elites: Studies in Coercive Ideological Movements*. Cambridge, Mass.: The M. I. T. Press.

Lazarsfeld, Paul F.; Berelson, B.; and Gaudet, H. 1944. *The People's Choice*. New York: Duell, Sloan, and Pearce.

Lenin, V. I. 1929. *What Is To Be Done*? New York: International Publishers.

Lerner, Daniel. 1959. *The Human Meaning of the Social Sciences*. Cleveland and New York: World.

———. 1964. *The Passing of Traditional Society*. New York: The Free Press.

———. 1968. "Modernization: Social Aspects." *International Encyclopedia of the Social Sciences*. Vol 10, pp. 386–395. New York: Macmillan and The Free Press.

———. November 1971. "Is International Persuasion Sociologically Feasible?" *Annals of the American Academy of Political and Social Science* 398:44–49.

Lerner, D., and Lasswell, H. D. 1951. *The Policy Sciences*. Stanford, Calif.: Stanford University Press.

Lerner, Daniel; Montgomery, John D.; and Lasswell, Harold D. 1976. *Values and Development*. Cambridge, Mass.: M. I. T. Press.

Lerner, Daniel, and Schramm, Wilbur. 1972. *Communication and Change in the Developing Countries*. Honolulu: University Press of Hawaii.

Levy, Marion J., Jr. 1965. "Patterns (Structures) of Modernization and Political Development of Political Science." *The Annals of the American Academy of Political and Social Science* 358: 29–40.

Lewis, John W., ed. 1970. *Party Leadership and Revolutionary Power in China*. London: Cambridge University Press.

Ling, S. Spring 1973. "Alaskan Satellite Seminar: A Case History of Providing Teachers In-Service Training in Remote Rural Areas via New Telecommunications Technology." "A Prototype: Research for Better Schools Symposium for Improving Productivity of School Systems through Educational Technology." Mimeographed. Washington, D.C.: Teleconsult, Inc.

Liu, Alan P. L. 1971. *Communication and National Integration in Communist China*. Berkeley: University of California Press.

Liu, William T., and Duff, Robert W. 1972. "The Strength in Weak Ties." *Public Opinion Quarterly* 36:361–366.

McAnany, Emile. 1973. *Radio's Role in Development: Five Strategies of Use*. Stanford, Calif.: Institute of Communication Research.

McAnany, E.; Hornik, R.; and Mayo, J. December 1973. *Studying Instructional Television: What Should be Evaluated*. Report to UNESCO. Mimeographed. Stanford, California: Institute for Communication Research.

McClelland, Charles A. May 1963. "An Unruly Flock of Activities: Comments on the State of Activities." *Background* 7(1): 3–11.

McClelland, D. C. 1961. *The Achieving Society*, Princeton, N.J.: Van Nostrand.

MacDonald-Ross, M. 1969. "Programmed Learning–A Decade of Development." *International Journal Man-Machine Studies* 1:73–100.

McKim, R. 1973. *Experiences in Visual Thinking*. Belmont, Calif.: Brooks-Cole.

McNamara, Robert S. September 24, 1973. Address to Board of Governors, International Bank for Reconstruction and Development, at Nairobi, Kenya.

Mager, R. F. 1968. *Developing Attitude toward Learning*. Palo Alto, Calif.: Fearon Publishers.

Mahar, J. M.; Zamora, M. D.; Owenstein, H. 1971. *Themes in Culture and Other Essays*. Quezon City, P.I.: Kayumanggi Press.

Maisel, R. 1973. "The Decline of Mass Media." *Public Opinion Quarterly* (Summer) 159–170.

Mao Tse-tung. 1967. *Quotations from Mao Tse-tung*. New York: Bantam Books.

Maslog, Crispin. 1969. "Journalism Ranks 10th among 15 Professions." *Press Forum* January: 3–4.

Merton, Robert K., ed. 1950. *Continuities in Social Research: Studies in the Scope and Method of "The American Soldier."* New York: The Free Press.

Montgomery, John D., and Siffin, William J., eds. 1966. *Approaches to Development: Politics, Administration and Change*. New York: McGraw Hill.

Mosher, A. T. 1966. *Getting Agriculture Moving*. New York: Agriculture Development Council.

Moynihan, Daniel Patrick. December 15, 1974. *New York Times*, p. 1.

Nader, Ralph. 1965. Unsafe at Any Speed. New York: Grossman.

Nakane, Chie. 1970. The Japanese Society. Berkeley, Calif. University of California Press.

Nasser, Gamal Abdel. 1955. *Egypt's Liberation*. Washington, D. C.: Public Affairs Press.

Nisbet, Robert, ed. 1972. *Social Change*. New York: Harper Torchbooks.

Oksenberg, Michael, ed. 1973. *China's Developmental Experience*. New York: Praeger.

Oshima, Harry T. June 1973. "A Labor Intensive Strategy for Southeast Asia." *Kajian Ekonomi Malaysia* 10(1):66–94.

———. December 1971. "New Directions in Development Economic Research." *Kajian Ekonomi Malaysia* 8(2):18–38.

Palmer, Norman D., ed. 1970. *A Design for International Relations Research: Scope, Theory, Method and Relevance*. Monograph 10. Philadelphia: American Academy of Political and Social Science.

Polsky, R. M. 1974. *Getting to Sesame Street: Origins of the Children's Television Workshop*. Praeger Publishers Special Studies in U.S. Economic, Social, and Political Issues. Sponsored by the Aspen Program on Communications and Society, United States. New York: Praeger.

Population Council. January 1974. *World Population: Status Report 1974, A Guide for the Concerned Citizen*. Reports on Population/Family Planning, No. 15. New York: The Population Council.

Pye, Lucian. 1962. *Politics, Personality and Nation Building: Burma's Search for Identity*. New Haven, Conn. Yale University Press.

Rahim, S. A. 1961. *The Diffusion and Adoption of Agricultural Practices: A Study in a Village in East Pakistan*. Research and Survey Bulletin 12. Comilla, Pakistan: Academy for Rural Development.

Rao, Hadha. December 1972. "Communications Linkages in Transfer of Agricultural Technology." *Economic and Political Weekly* 7(53): A-157–A-170.

Riesman, David. 1950. *The Lonely Crowd*. New Haven, Conn. Yale University Press.

Riggs, Fred W. 1964. *Administration in Developing Countries: The Theory of Prismatic Society*. Boston: Houghton Mifflin.

———. 1966. *Thailand: The Modernization of a Bureaucratic Polity*. Honolulu: East-West Center Press.

Rivkin, Arnold, ed. 1968. *Nations by Design*. New York: Anchor Books.

Rogers, Everett M. 1967. "Mass Communication and the Diffusion of Innovations: Conceptual Convergence of Two Research Traditions." Paper presented at Association for Education in Journalism, at Boulder, Col.

———. 1973. *Communication Strategies for Family Planning*. New York: The Free Press.

———. 1975. "The Anthropology of Modernization and the Modernization of Anthropology." *Reviews in Anthropology* 2(3):345–358.

Rogers, Everett M., and Agarwala-Rogers, Rekha, eds. 1975. *Evaluation Research on Family Planning Communication*. Paris: UNESCO Technical Report.

Rogers, Everett M., and Bhowmik, Dilip K. 1971. "Homophily-Heterophily: Relational Concepts for Communication Research." *Public Opinion Quarterly* 34:523–538.

Rogers, Everett M.; Park, H. J.; Chung, K. K.; and Lee, S. B. 1975. "Mothers' Clubs in the Diffusion of Family Planning Ideas in Korean Villages: An Illustration of Network Analysis." Paper presented at the American Association for the Advancement of Science, at New York.

Rogers, Everett M., with Shoemaker, F. Floyd. 1971. *Communication of Innovations: A Cross-Cultural Approach*. New York: The Free Press.

Rogers, Everett M., with Svenning, Lynne. 1969. *Modernization among Peasants: The Impact of Communication*. New York: Holt, Rinehart and Winston.

Röling, Niels; Ascroft, Joseph; and Chege, Fred Wu. August 1974. "Innovation and Equity in Rural Development." Paper presented at the World Congress of Sociology, at Toronto.

Roque, Francisco H., ed. 1974. *First Training Program in Mass Communication for ASEAN Nationals*. Diliman, Quezon City, Philippines: Institute of Mass Communication, University of the Philippines.

Rostow, W. W. 1960. *The Stages of Economic Growth*. Cambridge, England: Cambridge University Press, 1960.

Roth, Guenther. January 1968. "Personal Rulership, Patrimonialism and Empire Building in the New States." *World Politics* 20: 194–206.

Ruskin, R. S. 1974. *The Personalized System of Instruction: An Educational Alternative*. Washington, D.C.: ERIC Clearinghouse on Higher Education.

Ruttan, V. W., and Hayami, Yujiro. 1972. "Strategies for Agricultural Development." *Food Research Institute Studies* 11(2): 129–148.

Ryan, Bryce, and Gross, Neal. 1943. "The Diffusion of Hybrid Seed Corn in Two Iowa Communities." *Rural Sociology* 8:15–24.

———. 1950. *Acceptance and Diffusion of Hybrid Corn Seed in Two Iowa Communities*. Res. Bull. 372. Iowa Agricultural Experiment Station.

Sakamoto, Yoshikazu. Summer 1974. "The Future of the United Nations." *Unitar News* 6(3):2.

Schramm, Wilbur; McAnany, Emile; and Mayo, John. March 1971. *Television and Educational Reform in El Salvador. Complete Report on the Second Year of Research*. Report No. ICR-RR-7. Stanford, Calif.: Stanford University Institute for Communication Research.

Schultz, T. W. 1964. *Transforming Traditional Agriculture*. New Haven, Conn.: Yale University Press.

Shils, Edward. 1962. *Political Development in the New States*. The Hague: Mouton.

Shoemaker, F. Floyd. 1971. "System Variables and Educational Innovativeness in Thai Government Secondary Schools." Ph.D. dissertation, Michigan State University.

Sicat, Gerald P. 1974. *New Economic Directions in the Philippines*. Manila: National Economic and Development Authority.

Sidel, Victor, and Sidel, Ruth. April 1974. "The delivery of medical care in China." *Scientific American* 230:19–27.

Sigmund, Paul E., ed. 1972. *The Ideologies of Developing Countries*. New York: Praeger.

Singh, Jai P., and Jamison, Dean T. 1973. *The Satellite Instructional Television Experiment in India: A Case History*. St. Louis: Washington University Center for Development Technology.

Smith, P. J. 1972. "Britain's Open University: Everyman's Classroom." *Saturday Review* (April 29):40–50.

Southeast Asian Ministers of Education Organization (SEAMEO). 1974. *Proceedings of Seminar-Workshop for Information Officers of SEAMEO*. Los Banos, Laguna, Philippines: University of the Philippines Press.

Spiro, Melford E. 1968. "Culture and Personality." *International Encyclopedia of the Social Sciences*. Vol. 3, pp. 558–563. New York: Macmillan and The Free Press.

Staley, E. 1954. *The Future of Underdeveloped Countries*. New York: Harper.

Strong, Maurice. December 14, 1974. "The Case for Optimism." *Saturday Review World* 2(7):7–11.

[No author listed.] 1972. *Tachai: Standard Bearer in China's Agriculture*. Peking: Foreign Languages Press.

Tarde, Gabriel. 1903. *The Laws of Imitation*. Translated by Elsie Clews Parsons. New York: Holt.

Taylor, Carl; Ensminger, Douglas; Johnson, Helen W.; Joyce, Jean. 1965. *India's Roots of Democracy*. Bombay: Orient Longmans.

Tyler, Ralph. October 1966. "Television around the World." *Television Magazine* 32–35, 58–61.

Umali, D. J. September 1974. (quoted in) "*The Searca Diary*" (newsletter of the Southeast Asia Center for Graduate Study and Research in Agriculture). Los Baños, Philippines.

UNESCO Executive Board. October-November 1967. *Resolution and Decisions Adopted*. Item 4.4.1. Paris, 77th Session.

UP/IMC/UNESCO/UNFPA. 1972–1975. *Project on Research, Development of Materials, and Training in Family Planning Communication*. Progress

Reports 1–12 and Terminal Report. Diliman, Quezon City, Philippines: Institute of Mass Communication, University of the Philippines.

Valdecañas, Ofelia C. 1975. "A Study of the Communication Profile of Community Nutrition Workers in Camarines Sur." Master's thesis, University of the Philippines.

Velazquez, Gabriel. 1974. "The State of Rural Development—Time for Action," in Crawford, Robert H., and Ward, William B., eds., *Communication Strategies for Rural Development: Proceedings of the Cornell-CIAT International Symposium* (Ithaca, N.Y.: New York State College of Agriculture and Life Sciences, 1974), pp. 2–10.

Walton, J. Spring 1972. "Political Development and Economic Development." *Comparative International Development* 7:39–63.

Ward, Robert, and Rustow, Dankwart A., eds. 1963. *Studies in Political Development*. Princeton, N.J.: Princeton University Press.

Weber, Max. 1947. *The Theory of Social and Economic Organization*. New York: The Free Press.

Wilbur, Charles K., ed. 1973. *The Political Economy of Development and Underdevelopment*. New York: Random House.

Wilkening, Eugene A. 1949. "The Acceptance of Certain Improved Agricultural Programs and Practices in a Piedmont Community of North Carolina." Dept. of Rural Soc. Prog. Report No. 8. Raleigh, N.C.: North Carolina Agricultural Experiment Station.

Witherspoon, J. P. August 1974. *State of the Art: A Study of Current Practices and Trends in Educational Uses of Public Radio and Television*. Washington, D.C.: Advisory Council of National Organizations and the Corporation for Public Broadcasting.

Yadav, Dharam P. 1967. "Communication Structure and Innovation Diffusion in Two Indian Villages." Ph.D. dissertation, Michigan State University.

Yang, Martin C. 1945. *A Chinese Village*. New York: Columbia University Press.

Zolberg, Aristide R. 1966. *Creating Political Order: The Party States of West Africa*. Chicago: Rand-McNally.

Index

About the Editors

WILBUR SCHRAMM is Distinguished Center Researcher at the Communication Institute of the East-West Center. Before joining the Center in 1973, he had been for eighteen years Janet M. Peck Professor of Communication, and Director of the Institute for Communication Research, at Stanford. He has done research on four continents and is the author of twenty-five books and more than 100 articles.

DANIEL LERNER is Ford Professor of International Communication and Sociology at the Massachusetts Institute of Technology, and has also taught at Stanford, Columbia, and the University of Paris. For the last several years, he has divided his time between M.I.T. and the East-West Center. He is the author of many books and papers, including the classic *Passing of Traditional Society* (1958).

2 11 45